Europe's Uncertain Path 1814–1914

Blackwell History of Europe

General Editor: John Stevenson

The series provides a new interpretative history of Europe from the Roman Empire to the end of the twentieth century. Written by acknowledged experts in their fields, and reflecting the range of recent scholarship, the books combine insights from social and cultural history with coverage of political, diplomatic and economic developments. Eastern Europe assumes its rightful place in the history of the continent, and the boundary of Europe is considered flexibly, including the Islamic, Slav and Orthodox perspectives wherever appropriate. Together, the volumes offer a lively and authoritative history of Europe for a new generation of teachers, students and general readers.

Published

Europe between Dictatorship and Democracy: 1900–1945
Conan Fischer

Europe's Troubled Peace: 1945–2000
Tom Buchanan

Europe in the Sixteenth Century
Andrew Pettegree

Fractured Europe: 1600–1721
David J. Sturdy

In preparation

Europe: 300–800
Peter Heather

Europe in Ferment: 950–1100
Jonathan Shepard

The Advance of Medieval Europe: 1099–1270
Jonathan Phillips

Europe: 1409–1523
Bruce Gordon

Europe from Absolutism to Revolution: 1715–1815
Michael Broers

Europe's Uncertain Path

1814–1914

State Formation and Civil Society

R. S. Alexander

WILEY-BLACKWELL

A John Wiley & Sons, Ltd., Publication

This edition first published 2012
© 2012 R. S. Alexander

Blackwell Publishing was acquired by John Wiley & Sons in February 2007. Blackwell's publishing program has been merged with Wiley's global Scientific, Technical, and Medical business to form Wiley-Blackwell.

Registered Office
John Wiley & Sons Ltd, The Atrium, Southern Gate, Chichester, West Sussex, PO19 8SQ, UK

Editorial Offices
350 Main Street, Malden, MA 02148-5020, USA
9600 Garsington Road, Oxford, OX4 2DQ, UK
The Atrium, Southern Gate, Chichester, West Sussex, PO19 8SQ, UK

For details of our global editorial offices, for customer services, and for information about how to apply for permission to reuse the copyright material in this book please see our website at www.wiley.com/wiley-blackwell.

The right of R. S. Alexander to be identified as the author of this work has been asserted in accordance with the UK Copyright, Designs and Patents Act 1988.

Library of Congress Cataloging-in-Publication Data

Alexander, R. S., 1954–
  Europe's uncertain path, 1814–1914 : state formation and civil society / R.S. Alexander.
    p. cm.
  Includes bibliographical references and index.
    ISBN 978-1-4051-0052-6 (hbk.) – ISBN 978-1-4051-0053-3 (pbk.)   1. Europe–Politics and government–1815–1871.   2. Europe–Politics and government–1871–1918.   3. Political culture–Europe–History–19th century.   4. Political culture–Europe–History–20th century.   5. Civil society–Europe–History–19th century.   6. Civil society–Europe–History–20th century.   7. Nationalism–Europe–History–19th century.   8. Nationalism–Europe–History–20th century.   9. Social change–Europe–History.   10. Europe–Social conditions.   I. Title.
    D363.A587 2012
    940.2′8–dc23

                                        2011031981

A catalogue record for this book is available from the British Library.

This book is published in the following electronic formats: ePDFs 978-1-4443-4739-5; Mobi 978-1-4443-4741-8; ePub 978-1-4443-4740-1

Set in 11/13pt Dante by SPi Publisher Services, Pondicherry, India
Printed in Singapore by Ho Printing Singapore Pte Ltd
1 2012

Contents

Maps

Figures

Preface

The book that follows is a political narrative. Why focus on political history rather than the other subdisciplines? In governing, rulers and politicians have to take military, diplomatic, economic, social, and cultural developments into account. For this reason, political history constitutes a nexus; all the other subdisciplines are connected by, and related to, it. Knowledge of political history thus provides a starting point for more advanced study of the other subdisciplines and, better yet, underlines the limitations of viewing any of them in isolation. Why should a student care about politics? Even if you do not take much interest in those who govern you, you can be certain that they take interest in you and that their decisions affect you from the cradle to the grave. Study of nineteenth-century Europe helps to explain why states have become so influential, for better and worse, in the lives of all citizens.

Europe's Uncertain Path is divided into ten chapters and a conclusion. Two thematic chapters are dedicated specifically to discussion of demographic, economic, social, and cultural trends. Their function is to supplement the other chapters through consideration of how major trends affected government. International (including military) and domestic political developments are analysed in eight narrative chapters organized along chronological lines so that the reader can trace how they evolved. By carefully situating decision-making within its long- and short-term contexts, we can better understand the motivation of leading political figures and assess the consequences of what they did. Politics is a product of ideology (a more or less coherent system of ideals or values) and pursuit of material interest through the acquisition of power. Thus to comprehend politics we need to know the leading ideologies of the period. In assessing our own contemporary politicians, few of us would however be content to look solely at the ideals they express in campaign speeches, public addresses, or legislative debates. Rhetoric tells us something; yet there is much to be said for the adage that action speaks louder than words. What did political figures actually do? We cannot cover everything of consequence, but a major objective of this book is to provide the reader with sufficiently broad knowledge of principal developments that he or she will be prepared to undertake more specialized reading in the future.

In discussing politics, I have tried to give due consideration to both inter-state relations and domestic developments. The period 1815–1914 was framed by vast international wars; nevertheless, with several important exceptions, it was primarily one of peace. The foundations for the states system were put in place at the start of our period and came to be known as the Concert of Europe. In formal terms, the Concert consisted of meetings of representatives of the great powers to discuss crises wherein their interests might come into potentially dangerous conflict. More important than formal conventions however were a number of informal practices derived from prior experience during the Revolutionary-Napoleonic Wars. Foremost among the latter were recognition that war among the powers might bring the destruction of participating regimes, and that peaceful diplomacy required genuine consideration of the vital interests of other powers. Despite moments of stress, the Concert system largely succeeded until the Crimean War of 1854–56 commenced an intense period of wars that ended in 1871. Thereafter the powers avoided war among themselves until 1914, although the states system and the character of diplomacy had dramatically changed.

A key to this transformation of the states system was recognition by several leading statesmen that nationalism could be put to the purpose of buttressing the regimes they served. Foreign war was the means by which Count Cavour and Otto von Bismarck (respectively) unified Italy and Germany. Unification enhanced the power of the monarchs of Piedmont-Sardinia and Prussia and enabled Cavour and Bismarck to establish Italian and German states that denied the aspirations of democratic nationalists. Equally important was the way Cavour, Bismarck, and the French Emperor Louis-Napoleon Bonaparte based their diplomacy on *real politic*. The latter gave short shrift to belief that peace among the powers was necessarily conducive to the stability or interests of a particular state. Worse still, each of these statesmen employed deceit to achieve their objectives, undermining trust. Peace after 1871 rested far more heavily on calculations of military force in the formation of alliances. The leaders of nationalist movements seldom exercised direct influence over governments; yet the temptation remained for states to act aggressively in foreign relations to secure the support of the growing number of nationalists. For a time, overseas imperialism was something of a safety valve for rivalry among the powers in that the rest of the globe provided plenty of opportunity for expansion with limited risk of direct conflict in Europe. By the turn of the century, however, the number of potential "prizes" had diminished, and thereafter rivalry came to be focused closer to home – in North Africa and the Balkans. As tensions rose, resort to great power conferences was renewed; unfortunately the informal understandings that had made the Concert of Europe successful prior to the Crimean War no longer existed.

Few phenomena have as much impact on the lives of citizens as modern wars and hence examination of how and why the Concert system was gradually eroded presents itself as a principal concern for this study. Diplomacy was not however conducted in isolation; domestic and foreign policies often were closely intertwined. Thus tracing the connections between foreign and domestic policy constitutes a second theme for detailed analysis. Victory in war could lend prestige to a regime and thereby fortify it, but defeat could open the door to dramatic change by means of revolution or reform.

Partly due to the way in which I have conceived of this work, hard decisions have had to be made as to which states will be given consideration in terms of domestic politics. One of my objectives is to provide sustained discussion throughout the entire period. Touching upon individual states incidentally, and only in so much as to demonstrate overarching themes, is inadequate for tracing how they progressed from one point to another and can leave the reader wondering about the period between the two points of discussion. Sustained discussion comes at a cost and while I have tried to be as comprehensive as possible, there are regrettable omissions. In selecting Britain, France, Spain, Italy, and the German, Austro-Hungarian, and Russian Empires for sustained analysis, I have included the leading states and sought to give adequate representation to west, central, and east Europe. Other states do come up for discussion, but only in relation to particular topics.

Europe is the subject of this book; yet the period was characterized by the emergence of the nation state. Partly due to overseas imperialism, belief in a European identity, based largely on cultural characteristics such as religion, language, and ethnicity, gained ground. Nevertheless, conception of European boundaries was fluid and frequently ambiguous. Whereas the orient could be defined as "other" with relative ease, where to place the Slavs of central and eastern Europe remained problematic and the Balkans region was viewed as a bridge or crossroad between Europe and the Islamic world. Moreover, Europe as a source of identity was utterly overshadowed by the growth of nationalism and the century was dominated by boundary setting within Europe. Similarly, while cultural organizations such as the Roman Catholic Church or political movements such as socialism and feminism had an international character, it was the institutions of the nation state that increasingly imposed themselves upon the consciousness of the average citizen or subject. Still, the objective here is not to write a fragmented account of separate nations. To avoid the latter outcome, continuous comparison will be made of the ways in which the various regimes developed. Toward this end, I have grouped the states on the basis of rough constitutional similarities.

At least as difficult as the selection of states for consideration is the task of identifying the main themes of domestic politics. The nineteenth century was prolific in the formulation of new ideologies and discussion of the leading "isms" is obviously essential. While these ideologies will be largely familiar to many readers, they may not be entirely so. Liberalism, for example, arose in a certain historical context and thereafter evolved as context changed. Moreover, the character of liberalism varied according to where one looks. Although simplistic working definitions have a purpose, study of history provides opportunity for deeper understanding. People change, as do the "isms" they espouse, and rigid formulations often obscure the complexity of real life.

All the same, generalization is necessary, if only for the sake of brevity. In reflecting on how the nineteenth century constituted a transition from earlier times to the twentieth century, I have identified a number of principal themes that will be traced through the entirety of this book.

The first consists of state formation. What did governments do? Over the course of the period the size, power, and scope of the state expanded significantly, partly due to the wealth generated by industrialization and commercial expansion, and partly because states spent relatively less of their revenues on the military. Initially states expanded in a traditional field of activity – provision of law and order; underlining this development was, however, a shift toward preventing disorder rather than simply reacting to it once it had occurred. Especially after the revolutions of 1848, states became increasingly involved in the provision of education systems, development of transportation and communications infrastructure, and urban renewal. Thereafter regulation of economic (particularly industrial) relations and rudimentary provision of social welfare came to the fore. In sum, the influence the state exercised over the lives of Europeans increased dramatically, although it did not reach the levels attained in the twentieth century.

Why did such vast change occur? In analyzing state expansion, we can trace the development of several related general causes. Running throughout the nineteenth century like an electric current was preoccupation with social order. Often inflated accounts of mob violence and the brutality of the Terror during the French Revolution exacerbated fear of what might happen if control over the masses were lost. Traditional sources of authority such as the society of orders had been weakened during previous centuries, and they were badly damaged, or even destroyed, during the Revolutionary-Napoleonic era. Slowly but surely the state filled this vacuum and the process was sustained by anxieties over what contemporaries viewed as bewilderingly rapid economic, social, and cultural change.

From the 1820s onwards, scholars, writers, and journalists were preoccupied by what became known as the "social question." Rural poverty, exacerbated by rapid demographic growth, was in fact endemic; yet it was the swelling ranks of urban poor who drew most attention. Frequently composed of recent migrants from the countryside and sometimes identified as alien, "dangerous classes," the urban poor sparked a mixture of fear and sympathy. Concern that the urban poor had become detached from traditional sources of morality contributed to growing conviction that the state must do more to prevent social conflict. In consequence governments increased their efforts to promote economic expansion, built mass education systems, and reshaped the urban landscape.

Perhaps the most powerful inducement for increased intervention on behalf of the poor was the argument that all of society would benefit by it. The novelist Charles Dickens was just one of many authors who believed that disease and corruption born of physical or moral squalor could not be confined and would inevitably spread throughout society. Following the opinions of contemporary experts, the public saw moral and physical hygiene as closely linked, and state attempts to promote public health through increased regulation grew. Along similar lines, arguments that an educated, healthy workforce would be more disciplined and productive could be deployed in favour of state regulation of economic relations and provision of at least minimal levels of social welfare. Finally, towards the turn of the century, the spread of nationalism and imperialism also fostered arguments that in a world in which only the fittest survive the state must promote a healthy and robust populace.

A second grand theme is the gradual emergence of mass politics through the establishment of political rights and institutions. A starting point in this process was the creation of elective bodies which possessed powers independent of the state executive. A second stage consisted of extension of the franchise so that greater numbers could participate formally in the political system, strengthening the legitimacy of claims to represent the nation. At the start of our period regimes were either autocratic (with no sharing of powers by the monarchy with a representative body) or plutocratic (wherein the members of a representative body were chosen by a small, male, elite). By 1914 most states had representative institutions of one sort or another, although the powers held by these bodies, especially the ability to hold governments accountable, varied considerably. None of the states was fully democratic; women were still excluded and the proportion of enfranchised adult males also varied from state to state. But even when these limitations are taken into account, the process of democratization remains striking.

Mass politics does not consist simply of enfranchisement; rights of expression, assembly, and association are also fundamental. In recent times historians have paid growing attention to the emergence of what is termed "civil society" – in essence, the establishment of nongovernmental organizations and institutions that contribute to the formation of public opinion. Here we find a progression that ran roughly parallel to the process of democratization. Until the revolutions of 1848, and then again in the 1850s, rights of expression were narrowly restricted in most states. In consequence, opposition often took the path of clandestine publication or indirect allusion. Nevertheless, several long-term developments corroded the ability of regimes to repress criticism or control opinion. Expanding literacy spread political consciousness. Technological and marketing innovations reduced the costs of publication and improvements in transportation and communications facilitated dissemination. Economic growth increased the number of individuals or families who possessed sufficient wealth and leisure time to become better informed, and who believed themselves qualified to have some say in matters of government. The impact of such developments was gradual and more pronounced in some states than in others; all the same, the ability of states to control opinion through censorship or restrictions on publishing rights had dramatically declined by the Great War.

Equally consequential was expansion in the number and size of voluntary associations. Although most states initially sought to repress political organization, allegedly cultural associations often served as a cover for political discussion and ambition. Formation of economic and professional organizations also could have significant political consequences. Attempts by the state to control such formations slowly declined, partly due to sheer force of numbers, and partly because elite elements often joined voluntary associations. By the 1870s much of Europe had contracted what came to be termed an "association mania" and the trend accelerated thereafter. Some theorists have posited that voluntary associations are inherently liberal in that they provide a counterpoint, and hence limit, to state authority. Not all such associations were necessarily tolerant of the right of others to organize however, and some lobbied for increase in state power. One way or another, increased freedom of expression and association made politics more complex by adding to the number of voices making at times conflicting demands upon governments.

Early in the century advocates of reform often saw in representative government the means to correct unjust government and rectify social problems. Much of the politics of the century thus consisted of battle to establish parliaments, to strengthen parliaments in relation to state executives, and to extend franchises. To establish a representative system of government was one thing, however; to make such a system effective in the provision of good government was another. It took time and experience to find an effective balance between the claims of the state and of representative bodies, and to develop parties capable of representing the masses in a disciplined fashion. Already by the 1880s anti-parliamentary mass movements had entered the scene. They would remain on the fringes of power until 1914; nevertheless they were an ominous portent that mass politics might not necessarily lead to democracy and representative government.

How did elites respond to the emergence of mass politics? The first point to note is that members of the socioeconomic elite were divided in their attitudes toward political regimes and ideological systems. While some individuals embraced, or accepted a need for, extension of political rights, others sought to resist. Among the latter, repression was initially the primary recourse, but especially after 1848 conservatives increasingly sought to accommodate demand for change by adopting systems that gave an appearance of representative government while denying its substance. Elections could be vitiated if the state managed to control them. Even where elections were free of state control, their import would be limited if representative institutions possessed little independent power. The Napoleonic formula of government allegedly for the people, but not by the people, remained much in evidence in 1914.

If the challenge of how best to adjust to mass politics remained unresolved, much had nevertheless changed. How did change come about? Alteration of political systems was achieved by two principal means – gradually by reform or rapidly by revolution. The paths of reform and revolution were not entirely separate and their relationship was complex. The cause of reform could be strengthened or weakened by the threat of revolution, and the possibility of revolution might be increased or diminished by reform. Whichever the means, the chances of success were greatest when a combination of elite and non-elite elements challenged unpopular regimes. Yet even when the latter scenario existed, the position taken by the military, or the militaries of the great powers, could still prove determinant. Ultimately there was no single formula for change and much depended on specific context. It thus makes sense to start by considering the context in which the long nineteenth century began.

Acknowledgements

During the writing of this book my colleagues Penny Bryden, Simon Devereaux, Andrea McKenzie, Tom Saunders, and David Zimmerman offered helpful advice at various points, and Dr. Bryden also read the manuscript, seeking to reduce the number of errors and infelicities I had committed. I would also like to thank the three anonymous readers and general editor John Stevenson for their insightful and constructive criticism and suggestions. None of the above individuals are, of course, in any way responsible for any remaining imperfections, which are attributable solely to me. The work was much longer in the making than I had initially proposed and so I am especially grateful for the patience and forbearance shown me by Tessa Harvey, commissioning editor, and Gillian Kane, editorial assistant, and all of the people at Wiley-Blackwell with whom I have worked. Tenured faculty are fortunate creatures and I also very much appreciate the periods of sabbatical leave granted to me by the University of Victoria for the undertaking of this project. Above all, I wish to thank Penny and Lizzie, to whom this work is dedicated.

1

A World Half Restored
The Vienna Settlement and the Restoration Regimes

After the Revolutionary and Napoleonic eras, the treaties that constituted the Vienna Settlement redefined the borders of most European states, and in many cases determined the regimes that would rule those states. Consideration of the Settlement thus provides an opportunity to introduce nineteenth-century European politics. Domestic and foreign policies were intricately linked, and decision-making was restricted to narrow elites. Much as they might have liked to, statesmen could not, however, simply reverse all of the change that had occurred since the outbreak of the Revolution of 1789. Certain elements of the pre-1789 social and political order were so badly damaged or decayed that they could not be restored, and in some cases it was in the interests of the powers to maintain legacies of the Revolutionary-Napoleonic era. The powers thus created a new order that combined traditional elements of the *ancien régime* (old order) with institutions, laws, conventions and practices of more recent vintage.

When they gathered at Vienna in September 1814, delegates of the smaller states held great expectations. An article of the First Peace of Paris, signed on May 30, 1814, had called on the powers previously engaged in the Napoleonic Wars to convene for a congress that would reorganize Europe after the collapse of the French Empire. Many delegates thought they were summoned to a constituent assembly in which they could exercise influence. Although the four great powers (Britain, Russia, Prussia, and Austria) did want ratification by the other states, they had already agreed that they alone would make decisions as to territorial distribution. Emperor Francis I of Austria attempted to divert the delegates, sovereigns, princely families, and lobby groups of the lesser states with lavish entertainment organized by a festivals committee. Between 40 and 50 tables were set at the Hofburg Palace

Europe's Uncertain Path 1814–1914: State Formation and Civil Society, First Edition. R. S. Alexander.
© 2012 R. S. Alexander. Published 2012 by Blackwell Publishing Ltd.

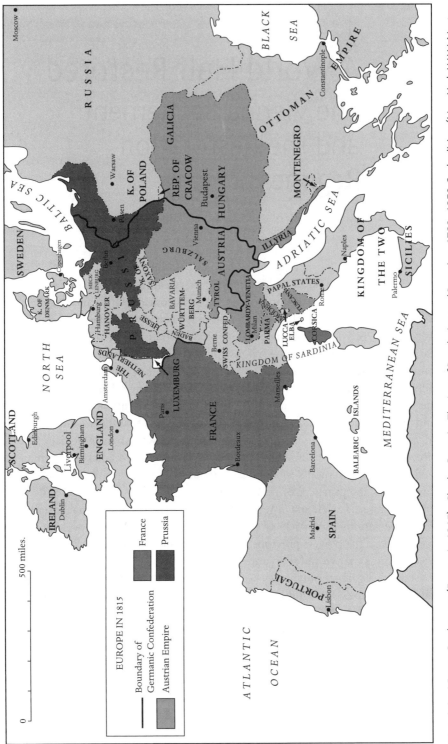

Map 1.1 Vienna Settlement (Europe in 1815). Charles Breunig, *The Age of Revolution and Reaction, 1789–1850*, 2nd edition (New York: W.W. Norton & Co., 1970), p. 132.

Figure 1.1 The Congress of Vienna. Hardenberg is seated on the far left. Metternich is standing, pointing at Castlereagh, who is seated with his legs crossed. Talleyrand is seated on the right, with his forearm on the table. © Bettmann/Corbis.

for banquets at which diners could plow their way through eight courses each evening. Nevertheless, frustrated dignitaries often wasted time quarreling over minor matters of precedence; given that they felt they had been invited under false pretences, endemic bickering was to be expected. They did have input in certain issues. Delegates from the minor powers participated in constitutional committees for Switzerland and a new German Confederation, and in a committee that developed new guidelines for diplomatic protocol. All the same, the great powers reserved the most vital considerations for themselves. Viewed from this perspective, the Congress of Vienna can be seen as a harbinger of a century in which regimes sought approval without accepting genuine accountability (Figure 1.1).

Initially there were four principal power brokers: Lord Castlereagh, the British foreign minister, Tsar Alexander I of Russia, Prince Metternich, the Austrian foreign minister, and Prince von Hardenberg, Prussian chancellor and foreign minister. Although Alexander's mercurial temperament caused conflict, he was determined to maintain his prestige as the "liberator" of Europe and would compromise at crucial moments so as to avoid isolation. Due to the distance between Vienna and London, Castlereagh could act with considerable independence, but he adhered to broad policy outlines established well before the Congress. Given that Britain had no continental territorial ambitions, Castlereagh was well placed to play the role of "honest broker"; nevertheless his self-righteousness was irritating – Alexander disliked being told that his policies were not in the interests of the Russian people. Metternich believed that his diplomatic cunning had brought the fall of Napoleon and was convinced that "error never had access to my mind."[1] Despite the machinations of rivals at the Austrian court, he had solid backing from his sovereign during confrontations with the Tsar. Having to contend with the devotion of King Frederick William III to Alexander, Hardenberg was more constrained in pursuing Prussian objectives. Prussia's position as the weakest of the powers meant that while it was the most avid for gain, it was the least able to stand against the others. By January 1815 Prince Charles Maurice de Talleyrand-Périgord, the French foreign minister, had wormed his way into the decision-making of the great powers. Initially Talleyrand set himself up as the spokesman of the smaller states. While the other powers politely listened to his arguments, they were not swayed; it was a squabble among the four that gained Talleyrand a say. Once the directing council of four had become a council of five, Talleyrand happily dropped the guise of representing the smaller states.

In the Final Act, the ultimate statement of the Congress signed on June 9, 1815, the principle of "legitimacy" was strongly emphasized as a foundational principle. Espoused particularly by Talleyrand, an aristocratic former clergyman who had advocated state sequestration of Church lands during the Revolution and served Napoleon in typically treacherous fashion as foreign minister, "legitimacy" loosely implied that the regimes overthrown from 1789 onward should be reconstituted. However, while statement of the principle served rhetorically to repudiate all that had been created by the Revolution and Napoleon, "legitimacy" was set aside whenever it conflicted with more fundamental objectives. Three main priorities guided the Settlement: reduction of French power, rewards for the four great powers for their part in dethroning Bonaparte, and establishment of a rough equilibrium of power.

Reduction of French power occurred in two stages. The First Peace of Paris was lenient. The French would give up claims to lands beyond their 1792 borders, but they would retain certain acquisitions made after 1789 – Avignon, the Venaisson, and parts of Savoy, the Palatinate, and Belgium. Captured French colonies would be returned, although Britain would retain Tobago and Santa Lucia in the West Indies, and Mauritius, Rodriguez, and the Seychelles in the Indian Ocean. In granting generous terms, the powers had several considerations in mind. Having reinstalled the Bourbon dynasty, they wanted to enhance the regime's prospects for maintaining rule in France. They also wanted to reconcile the French public to the new European order they envisaged; hence King Louis XVIII was obliged to grant a constitution that included provisions for a parliament. Finally, they also wanted to maintain a French state sufficiently strong that it could play a part in maintaining equilibrium of power on the Continent. Such calculations had to be adjusted after Napoleon re-established his rule at Paris on March 20, 1815. The statesmen gathered at Vienna carried on with their deliberations, refused to deal with Bonaparte, and marshaled their forces for a second onslaught on the "usurper." By June 18 the French army had been defeated at Waterloo, and on June 22 Napoleon was again forced to abdicate.

What to do with the French? The Second Peace of Paris, signed on November 20, 1815, fell somewhere between the leniency of the first treaty and the demands of the Prussians, who pressed for dismemberment. French borders would recede to those of 1790 and several fortresses on the northern and eastern frontiers would be yielded. The French must pay an indemnity of 700 million *francs* within three to five years, support an army of occupation of 150 000 men until final payment, and return previously looted art treasures. Subsequent French desire to revise the Vienna Settlement sprang partly from wounded pride, and partly from the fact that while forcing France to disgorge her acquisitions, the other powers consolidated or extended their own.

Before assessing territorial redistribution, it is instructive to note what was not on the table. The British had already ensured that there would be no discussion of their navy's "right" to stop and search neutral shipping in times of war, and over-seas colonies seized by the British would be considered only in so much as the British wished them to be. Similarly, Russian acquisition of Finland and Bessarabia were accepted as a *fait accompli*.

The main battles occurred over Poland and Saxony. Alexander wanted to reconstitute Napoleon's Grand Duchy of Warsaw with himself as ruler. He did not intend to include the lands Russia had seized during the eighteenth-century partitions of Poland, although he pressed Prussia and Austria to yield the provinces they had taken. Given Russian presence in the Duchy, Alexander was strongly positioned, though he overstated the matter when he alleged "there can be no argu-ment with six hundred thousand troops."[2] The Prussians were willing to agree, provided they were compensated in Saxony, which had made the mistake of rea-ligning with Napoleon in mid-1813. Neither Russian expansion in Poland nor Prussian expansion in Saxony appealed, however, to Metternich, and Castlereagh wanted Prussia to be compensated in the Rhineland. Clashes between former allies turned ferocious and at one point Alexander gave Metternich a dressing down that, according to Talleyrand, "would have been thought extraordinary even toward one of one's own servants."[3] It was this dangerous rift that enabled Talleyrand to gain France an alliance with Britain and Austria in early January 1815. Whether the alli-ance was more than a bluff is questionable; yet news of it soon convinced Alexander to compromise, mostly by sacrificing the demands of Prussia.

The powers would create a new "Congress" Poland with Alexander as monarch. Austria would retain the province of Galicia, with Cracow constituted as a free city. Prussia would retain Danzig and the province of Posen, but yield the rest of her Polish acquisitions. Ultimately, Congress Poland amounted to about three-quarters the size of Napoleon's Grand Duchy, itself a pale reflection of the former Polish state. The Prussians had to settle for taking roughly two-fifths of Saxony; the rest remained an independent state. Fortuitous Prussian acquisition of the former

Duchy of Westphalia and of lands on the left bank of the Rhine would, however, provide the base for subsequent industrial power.

Austria made gains principally in the Italian peninsula. Austria reacquired the province of Lombardy and annexed Venetia, including a strip of territory along the Dalmatian coast. Elsewhere highly dependent regimes were established, often with Habsburgs as rulers. Marie Louise, wife of Napoleon, but more importantly daughter of Austrian Emperor Francis I, became the ruler of Parma. Archduke Ferdinand, brother of Francis, was reinstated as Grand Duke of Tuscany, and Grand Duke Francis IV, a cousin of the Austrian Emperor, was re-established as ruler of Modena. Ferdinand IV of the Kingdom of the Two Sicilies, a Spanish Bourbon, was tied to the Habsburgs through marriage and owed his acquisition of Naples partly to a promise to Metternich that he would not grant the Neapolitans a constitution. Moreover Ferdinand rescinded a parliament previously gained, due to British influence, by Sicilian landowners. Austria also played the principal role in the Papacy's recovery of most of its former possessions; Metternich would have to negotiate traditional Papal antipathy to Austrian domination of Italy, but he could hope that support from the Church would help secure conservative rule throughout Austria's sphere of influence.

British policy reflected shrewd calculation of global interests. British gains consisted partly of securing recognition of far-flung maritime acquisitions that secured naval supremacy. Bases at Heligoland in the North Sea, Malta in the Mediterranean, the Cape Colony in the southern tip of Africa, Ceylon in the Indian Ocean, and Santa Lucia, Tobago, and Trinidad in the Caribbean provided opportunities to control trade routes. British interests were also pursued by Castlereagh's efforts to ensure that no power could dominate the continent. Re-establishment of Spanish, Portuguese, and Dutch independence worked to Britain's advantage. Conversely, Castlereagh's advocacy of abolition of the slave trade sprang from a humanitarian impulse. Lobbying at Vienna yielded a declaration condemning the practice, and various inducements led Holland and Sweden to join Britain and Denmark in decreeing total abolition in 1815. In pursuit of liberal support, Napoleon had decreed abolition in French colonies during his brief return, and thereafter Louis XVIII felt obliged to follow suit. Although Spain and Portugal proved harder nuts to crack, cash payments, beginning in 1817, induced them to sign agreements to suppress the trade, initially north of the equator, and then totally.

For a long time historians have argued that above all the great powers sought a balance of power, but this interpretation has been challenged by Paul W. Schroeder.[4] The term "balance of power" has a liability in that it implies a system wherein the leading states have roughly the same amount of power. Such was not the case in 1815; Britain and Russia were significantly stronger than the other powers. What in fact was achieved was an equilibrium wherein none of the powers could unilaterally dominate the continent. Such equilibrium was fostered partly by creation of intermediary states whose independence was guaranteed in law by the great powers. Intermediary states could act as buffers between the powers, and their mere existence would make any drive for hegemony more difficult. The notion of "equilibrium" is not, however, entirely novel; earlier historians tended to use the terms "balance" and "equilibrium" interchangeably, without clearly distinguishing between the two. Given this scenario, rather than eliminate use of the term "balance of power," it seems more appropriate to employ Schroeder's notion of equilibrium as a more precise definition of what balance of power actually meant.

Equilibrium was achieved partly by surrounding France with states better able to defend themselves. Prussian expansion in the Rhineland was directed toward this end; so too was Dutch acquisition of the southern Netherlands (Belgium), Luxembourg, and a small parcel of land along the left bank of the Rhine. Piedmont-Sardinia gained through annexation of the former Republic of Genoa. Switzerland added three cantons (Geneva, Valais and Neufchatel), and by adopting a constitution negotiated at Vienna acquired an international guarantee of her neutrality.

Arrangements in central Europe were guided by desire to provide security for the German states. There was no attempt to restore the three hundred or so states that had comprised the Holy Roman Empire; internal divisions had made the latter far too vulnerable to French expansion. Thus much of the concentration instigated by Napoleon, including significant enlargement of Baden, Württemberg, and Bavaria, was retained. The remaining 38 states, including Prussia and Austria, would combine in a German Confederation headed by the Austrian Emperor. The Confederation was in essence an organization for mutual defense rather than a step toward creation of a unified German state.

The Nature of the Restored Regimes

Legitimacy thus played little part in territorial distribution. Nor did re-established regimes constitute a full-blooded reversion to the *ancien régime*. The latter point becomes obvious if we consider several legacies of the Revolutionary-Napoleonic era.

Although the Revolution began in France in 1789 as an attack on royal despotism, it soon extended into the realm of social relations. In their attempt to create a regime which could be held accountable, the revolutionaries started with the principle of national sovereignty. To delimit the function of the state, revolutionaries drew up a constitution that proclaimed certain "natural" rights, and divided power between the government and a legislature of elected representatives of the nation. Among these rights were freedom from arbitrary arrest, freedom of opinion and expression, and freedom of association. Simultaneously, the revolutionaries also attacked social privilege. One set of laws would apply to all social groups, entry into state office would be based on merit, all would be subject to taxation, and any remaining seigniorial obligations would be abolished. Pursuit of equality often entailed a drive for uniformity and hence the Revolution brought destruction to a broad array of corporate privileges, ranging from guild monopolies to regional exemptions from taxes. It also inspired a secularizing trend that eroded the status of the Catholic Church. The ideal of equality had limited impact on gender relations; women did make gains in family law, but they were excluded from the political sphere. All the same, the Revolution enunciated a template of ideals that inspired advocates of change throughout the nineteenth century.

The Revolution also fostered increased expectations of what the state should do. Especially during the period of radical Jacobin ascendancy, governments began state provision of social services that included mass education and aid for the impoverished. Such programs collapsed under the strains of war, but their short-term existence provided examples for the future. More immediately consequential was a conservative backlash against the chaos that ensued from too much rapid change. As much of France (and a good deal of the rest of Europe) fell into virtual anarchy, desire rose for a state capable of maintaining order. Bonaparte exploited such desire to develop a state in which power was highly centralized. The Napoleonic model of government was by no means as intrusive as twentieth-century totalitarian regimes; nevertheless, a major part of Napoleonic rule lay in enhancing the repressive capacity of the state. Like his Revolutionary predecessors, Bonaparte spread French institutions and laws to conquered lands. The Revolution thus had extensive impact outside France, but in the long run political liberty advanced more as a shared ideal than as a practical reality.

Napoleon knew that prosperity served as an antidote to opposition and hence his administrators busied themselves with compiling information about society and the economy. The Imperial penchant for economic planning was far from the command economies of the twentieth century, and its inspiration can be located in the reforming impulse of enlightened despotism. All the same, the Napoleonic state was significantly more developed than its *ancien régime* predecessors, and its impulse to render the public docile through provision of material needs was stronger.[5]

Using these three broad, and at times contradictory, Revolutionary-Napoleonic legacies – creation of liberal, if not democratic, rule, fostering of civil equality, and enhancement of state power, we now can turn to the Restoration regimes, asking to what extent they constituted a return to the pre-Revolutionary era.

Constitutional Monarchies

With the exception of Switzerland, European states were organized as dynastic monarchies. Among the latter there was a rough division between autocracies and constitutional monarchies wherein rulers shared power with parliaments. The leading constitutional monarchies were Britain and France.

Of all the European states, the one least in need of "restoration" was Britain. The French Revolution had actually impeded political change, although the Act of

Union of 1801 was a noteworthy exception. By the terms of the Union, the Dublin parliament was abolished; henceforth Ireland would elect 100 members to the House of Commons at Westminster, and 28 peers and four Church of Ireland bishops would enter the House of Lords. Despite promises made at the time, no Act of Emancipation, which would have enabled Catholics to sit in the new United Kingdom parliament, followed.

A feature of the state was its limited nature. Many Britons associated government with elite patronage and wanted to keep it as cheap as possible. Radicals were alarmed that the number of government offices had increased from 16 000 in 1797 to almost 25 000 by 1815. Policy-making state departments were however small; in the early 1820s the Home Office had a staff of 17, the Colonial Office 14, and the Foreign Office fewer than 36. Most of the state's attention was directed toward foreign relations and the departments in charge of supply for the armed services were relatively large, maintaining some 4000 employees. In the domestic sphere, taxation was a chief preoccupation. Customs, Excise, and Stamps and Taxes agencies employed close to 20 000 officials. Provision of law and order was also a major concern; yet here one is struck by how little the central government provided. There was no national police force; in the event of mass disorder, officials must turn to their own constables, local militias, and the regular army. Because the role of the home army was crucial, it was essential to ensure that the "right" sort of fellow commanded the troops. In a notorious state paper the Duke of Wellington justified the purchase of officer commissions as follows: "it is promotion by purchase which brings into the service men of fortune and education; men who have some connection with the interests and fortunes of the country."[6]

Most responsibility fell to local authorities. In the counties, lords lieutenant and justices of the peace played the key roles in quelling disorder. While the lords took the lead in organizing response to crisis, it was the justices of the peace who performed the bulk of day-to-day work – in addition to justice they handled tasks ranging from monitoring upkeep of roads to supervision of workhouses. Local magistrates were neither trained nor paid and their services were voluntary; hence they were drawn from the local elite and enjoyed a great deal of autonomy. There was little uniformity in the organization of government in corporate towns, and the functions of mayors, aldermen, bailiffs, and municipal councils varied according to town charters. Complicating matters further was the existence of agencies (for policing, street repair, water and light provision, market supervision and the like) that owed their existence to private acts of parliament and were independent of the town corporations. The net effect was a great deal of overlapping jurisdiction. All too often, limited government brought what it was supposed to avoid – inefficiency.

In theory, the political system rested on a balance of the interests of the Crown, the aristocracy (in the House of Lords), and the common people (in the House of Commons). Yet the relative power of the three components was shifting. The monarchy had been tarnished by defeat in the American War of Independence, and during the Revolutionary-Napoleonic era royal influence over the cabinet had diminished as King George III lapsed into insanity. Since the 1780s parliament had cut back on the number of state sinecures (appointments that were designed solely to secure loyalty) by which the Crown had been able to influence members of parliament (MPs). With the decline of sinecures, the Crown turned to appointment of the lords as a means of enhancing influence. Conversely, an increasingly independent Commons, composed largely of country gentry, could pose challenges for the government. Initiative in the lower house often rested with individual MPs who could push for select commissions to investigate whatever issues they might wish to pursue, and bills proposed by the cabinet were by no means certain of passing.

Adding to the complexity of passing legislation was the absence of a disciplined party system. Among the 658 MPs there were three main *blocs* formed partly on personal or patronage ties, and partly on ideological lines. The Tories were suspicious of constitutional reform and defenders of landed interests, royal prerogative, and the central place of the Anglican Church in the regime. The Whigs were more inclined to take an adversarial position with the Crown, more attached to commercial, manufacturing, and financial interests, skeptical about close ties between Church and State, and at times open to reform. The leading advocates of change were the Radicals, who were especially eager to enhance the power and independence of the Commons so that it could keep "Old Corruption" (the use of the state to further elite, particularly Tory, interests) in check. While the Tories were in effect the governing party, and the equally aristocratic Whigs had similar numbers in the Commons, Radical MPs were few in number. In combination, these features placed independent (unaligned) MPs in an often-decisive swing position. Moreover, members generally voted according to their own lights. The parties did not elect an official leader; instead they had several prominent figures. Pursuit of power often dictated whether these factions cooperated, and there were significant divisions within all three *blocs*.

The right to choose MPs was held by a small minority. Prior to 1832 there were roughly 478 000 voters. The extent of the franchise varied dramatically among the electoral units (boroughs and counties), and many "rotten boroughs" were secured by patronage or corruption of a handful of voters rather than genuine contestation. Little effort had been made to adjust to demographic change; while certain sparsely populated villages elected MPs, many cities did not. Nevertheless, partisan divisions, often between Anglicans and the non-Anglican (Dissenting) Protestant sects, were hardening and many seats were fiercely contested.

Although Britain was a plutocracy, the import of public opinion was rising. Figures such as the Tory George Canning or the Whig Henry Brougham derived their influence from ability to mobilize public support. They were not necessarily typical of MPs, but even among the Tories there were factions well aware of a need to serve more than just the landed interest. A broader sense of obligation was encouraged by relatively high literacy rates, a flourishing press over which the government exercised little control, and relatively widespread political association. Ultimately what distinguished Britain was the growing weight of public opinion in the calculations of elite politicians. These points become more obvious if we turn to the Continent.

To recover the French throne, the Bourbon pretender Louis XVIII found it necessary to submit to pressure from the allied powers to accept a constitution known as the Charter. Even so, there was uncertainty over the mixed nature of the regime because the preamble to the Charter stated that the King had granted the constitution "voluntarily and by the free exercise of our will."[7] Politics would thereafter revolve around the issue of whether the Charter constituted a contract by which the monarch was bound. Lurking here was a fundamental issue – did sovereignty rest solely with the monarchy or with the nation? Or could it be divided? If the monarch alone was sovereign, could he not abolish parliament?

Such issues hung like dark clouds; yet institutions proved enduring. A Chamber of Peers initially consisted of a mix of former Imperial senators and men appointed by the King; in the future the Crown would make all appointments. The lower house, the Chamber of Deputies, was elective. Based on tax payment, the franchise was highly restrictive; roughly 90 000 male property owners were entitled to vote. Nevertheless the lower house could claim to represent the nation, however imperfectly, and did exercise significant power. Legislative initiative technically rested solely with the government, but deputies circumvented this restriction by forwarding public or private petitions to parliamentary committees which then sent recommendations to the government. Better yet, state budgets required annual parliamentary approval, creating opportunities to exert influence. Perhaps more significant than such structural considerations, were more elusive aspects of political culture. From very early on, political factions confronted governments and such groups soon saw in parliament a place where they could seek to influence policy.

While the regime thus bore certain affinities to the British system, it differed in fundamental regards as Louis XVIII adopted the legal and fiscal reforms of the Revolutionary era, including the Napoleonic government model. Key components of the model were chain of command and government appointment, rather than election, of local officials. Just as he retained parliament while turning it into a rubber stamp for the executive, so too did Bonaparte maintain local and regional councils which could do little more than advise state officials. Such bodies provided opportunities for consultation with the "notables" (elite elements of the public), but real power rested with institutions such as the Council of State, a body of appointed experts who drafted legislation and trained officials such as the prefects. The chief administrative units in France were called departments and each one had a prefect. The prefects wielded extensive power and were responsible for a range of tasks similar to the administrative functions of British magistrates. In the Napoleonic system, however, officials were hired, paid, and dismissed by the central government. They were trained in an ethos that was hostile to notions of representative government, and the fact that they administered elections would produce all sorts of problems for parliamentary independence.

Thus the position of parliament in France was insecure, and similar uncertainties surrounded the constitutions established in the lesser German states between 1814 and 1820. Of the 36 states that, in combination with Prussia and Austria, composed the German Confederation, only a couple possessed roughly the same territories they had held in 1789, and better than half the population had new rulers. Thus the smaller states faced challenges of integration and some rulers saw in constitutions a means by which internal unity could be promoted.

States such as Saxony, Hanover, Mecklenburg, Nassau, and Saxe-Weimar retained or slightly modified the old system of estates, whereas several rulers modeled constitutions loosely on the French Charter. Like Louis XVIII, the latter rulers disavowed national sovereignty, viewing constitutions as gifts they granted to their subjects. Most adopted a bicameral system, finding in upper houses a means to placate former imperial knights and counts. Only Baden followed the French example of a lower house elected by individuals in regional districts rather than corporate bodies. Baden thus became the first German regime with a modern representative system; more typical was the lower house in Bavaria, where unelected nobles and churchmen occupied a quarter of the seats. Franchises were narrow and elections were managed by the state. Nevertheless, in the south German states of Wurttemberg, Bavaria, Baden, and Hesse-Darmstadt constitutions provided for freedom of the press and association, religious toleration, and legal equality. Lower houses used their right to approve legislation and became the centers of political attention, although they could not initiate legislation, had limited budgetary control, and often found their efforts weakened by conservative upper houses.

Despotism in Italy and Spain

Constitutional regimes were exceptional. More typical were states wherein representative government had no place and the Napoleonic administrative model had put down roots. Even so, the Revolution had triggered liberal aspirations that would challenge despotic regimes in Italy and Spain.

The concept of "restoration" does appear, upon first glance, to apply to Italy. Whereas Napoleon had reduced the peninsula to three states, after the Vienna Settlement there were eight and the Italian map looked much as it had done in the eighteenth century. Except in the Papal States, Italians were ruled by dynastic regimes, and all eight states were authoritarian. Much, however, depended on the character of individual rulers. In the immediate aftermath of liberation, most rulers wanted to give an impression of rejecting all things French. Victor-Emmanuel I made a determined effort to return to the *ancien régime*, abolishing all Napoleonic legislation in Piedmont, though he found retention of the *gendarmerie* (a semi-military rural police force) useful. The papacy reversed the Napoleonic Codes. In Tuscany the Habsburg Grand Duke also rejected Napoleon's reforms, but he developed the similar traditions of Austrian enlightened despotism and here was the rub: most rulers could see how Napoleonic institutions elevated the powers of the central government. Even the Austrian Emperor retained most of the

Napoleonic Kingdom of Italy's administrative institutions in Lombardy; Marie-Louise did the same in Parma and also kept the Napoleonic Codes. Napoleonic administrative and judicial structures and laws suited Ferdinand I so well at Naples that in 1816 he extended them to Sicily.

The greatest immediate problem for Italian rulers lay in the demands of reactionary elements who expected restitution of their former privileges. Influenced by the Catholic revival of the period, many rulers turned control of education over to the Church, though few followed the Piedmontese example of reconstituting the ecclesiastical courts. There could, however, be no question of restoring Church lands previously expropriated and sold to private individuals, even in the Papal States. Similarly, rulers had to cope with nobles demanding reconstitution of corporate privilege and administrative decentralization. Rulers soon re-established the nobility as a distinct social group; yet they drew a line at returning old privileges and jurisdictional powers.

Napoleon had achieved much of what enlightened despots had sought by consolidating the Revolution's destruction of restrictions placed on the state by the *ancien régime* society of orders. While they may or may not have been enlightened, Restoration rulers were sufficiently despotic to appreciate his methods. Even in Piedmont, provincial councils of local notables nominated by the King in newly acquired Genoa were established due to conditions set by the great powers at Vienna. Although they could block imposition of new taxes, otherwise the councils were simply advisors to royal officials. In the Papal States, reform in July 1816 contained both reactionary and modernizing elements. The state was divided into 17 provinces. Five beyond the Apennines were placed under the authority of legates (and hence were called the Legations); papal delegates governed the 12 closer to Rome. While the provinces gained advisory bodies called congregations that possessed a lay element, the legates and delegates were all cardinals or priests and they possessed powers roughly equivalent to those of French prefects. Baronial jurisdiction was abolished in the Legations and Marches and although this feudal relict remained in the other provinces the dues previously paid to the barons were terminated. Thus while the regime regained its distinctly clerical nature, a more modern system was introduced.

Spain provides a similar example of the limits to restoration. When Ferdinand VII returned from captivity in April 1814, liberals who had led resistance to the French expected him to accept the constitution they had given Spain in 1812. A constitution that established basic civil and political liberties and created a parliamentary system, however, held little appeal for a Bourbon king. Nor was the constitution's onslaught on corporate privilege appreciated by reactionary nobles or Catholic clergymen. They too had fought against the French and enjoyed more popular support than liberals due to the latter's anti-clericalism, desire to remove regional privilege in the name of national unity, and inclination to convert common land into private property. When right-wing elements called on Ferdinand to reject the liberal constitution, he happily did so, unleashing brutal repression of the liberals.

Spanish reactionaries were not bent simply on undoing the work of liberals; they wanted reversal of all the efforts of early-modern Spanish enlightened despots to reduce corporate power and privilege. In a manifesto presented to the king, it was claimed that "to exclude the nobility destroys the juridical order and strips society of its splendour, whilst depriving it of the generous spirits needed for its defence."[8] Ferdinand balked at the latter demands and, after a period of reflection, could see that there was much in the liberal revolution that he might wish to preserve.

Because he could count on the loyalty of the army, and turn from the reactionaries to the reforming ministers and bureaucrats of his father's reign, Ferdinand had a measure of choice as to what he wished to retain from the past. Nobles gained the restoration of their seigniorial territorial and economic privileges, but there was to be no return of their former judicial attributes. Royal decrees enabled the Catholic Church to retrieve some of its old advantages: previously dissolved religious communities were allowed to re-occupy their old houses, the Jesuits were permitted to return, the Inquisition and Index of prohibited books were re-established, and an evangelization campaign was launched to extirpate the effects of what the Bishop of Pamplona described as "an era of confusion, disorder, and crimes."[9] But Ferdinand refused to order the return of Church lands that had been seized and sold off, and effectively reasserted Crown control through his powers of appointment, naming some sixty new bishops. Moreover, the desperate state of Crown finances inclined Ferdinand to attack fiscal privilege. Thus in 1817 the elites of Castile and Aragon found themselves subjected to a universal income tax, and municipal indirect taxes were unified throughout the kingdom, eliminating regional inequalities. While Navarre and the Basque provinces retained the right to determine their own levels of taxation, they soon lost their exemption from conscription. They could avoid this military obligation through financial payments, but their fiscal privileges had thereby been undermined.

The Eastern Autocracies

Although the eastern autocracies of Prussia, Austria, and Russia had been less directly affected by French revolution, they all had been threatened by French expansion. They responded in differing ways in seeking to mobilize resources for defense, and what was most notable was the extent to which the Prussian state undermined the old society of orders.

Restoration Prussia was partly a product of reforms undertaken to combat Napoleon, and partly the result of older traditions. Prussia's expansion under the Hohenzollern dynasty in the seventeenth and eighteenth centuries was directly attributable to a remarkably efficient bureaucracy. It was the superior ability of the administration to extract economic and human resources that enabled Prussia to hold its own in battle against significantly larger states. Prussian expansion also fostered centralization of power, as rulers used the army to chip away at the rights of provincial estates to approve state taxation. Although the estates acted as vehicles for noble interests, noble opposition was weakened by creation of a "service nobility" that manned the bureaucracy and monopolized the officer corps of the army.

A school of thought known as cameralism imbued the Prussian state with a strong inclination to intervene in society and the economy. Cameralist writers argued that rulers should create a large and productive population that would yield more by way of tax revenue, and under Frederick the Great Prussia became a model of "enlightened despotism" as the state fostered canal building, industry, overseas commerce, and immigration. Frederick even broached social reform by reducing the feudal obligations of peasants on Crown lands; however, he took no measures to emancipate serfs on private lands. He could not afford to antagonize the *Junkers* (noble landowners) who were the backbone of the army.

It took the shock of defeat by Napoleon in 1807 to jolt the monarchy into reforms that further undermined the old social order. In October 1807 serfdom was abolished on royal lands, and as of 1810 it would be abolished everywhere. Serfs would be free to leave the domains of their lords, no longer required permission to marry, and could take up a trade. Commoners could purchase land formerly restricted to noble ownership, and nobles gained the right to enter trade. Desire to modernize could also be seen in expansion of the education system as the state took on a primary role in the training and appointment of teachers and supervision of schools at all levels. Moreover, in 1807 Prussian Church administration was unified under state control, a process which would be continued in 1817 after acquisition of the predominantly Catholic Rhineland.

While the state thus reduced corporate privilege, the principle of national sovereignty made little headway as the plans of reformers for creation of representative institutions were set aside after the wars of liberation. Far from honoring past promises, in 1823 King Frederick William reconstituted provincial estates that possessed only limited advisory powers and were dominated by the nobility. Hopes raised by the ambiguous edict of May 22, 1815 promising "representation of the people" by an "assembly of representatives of the land"[10] thus were dashed, creating resentment, particularly in the Rhineland provinces. Nevertheless, in terms of legal equality, weakening of the regulatory powers of guilds, and subordination of the Church to the state, Prussia had taken a major step away from the old society of orders.

Given that Joseph II had been the most enlightened of the despots, it was ironic that the Austrian Empire underwent no such transformation in the Revolutionary-Napoleonic era. In the 1740s Joseph's mother Maria Theresa had begun state rationalization by dividing Habsburg lands in Austria and Bohemia into ten administrative districts run by Crown-appointed War Commissars who took over taxation and conscription responsibilities previously exercised by the local Estates. Along with centralization of power came economic and social reform: guild monopolies were limited, internal customs were suppressed, laws were passed to prevent lords from abusing peasants, and seigniorial obligations were reduced. From 1765 to 1780 Maria Theresa ruled jointly with Joseph. Although both were devout Catholics, they removed the clergy's exemption from taxation and made Crown permission mandatory for publication of papal bulls. Subsequently Joseph closed hundreds of monasteries, used the property thus acquired for state charity institutions, asserted state control over seminaries, and established civil marriage. With Joseph as sole ruler, reform accelerated in the 1780s. Judicial procedures were rationalized, peasants were emancipated from serfdom, noble patrimonial justice and tax exemptions were abolished, and German became the sole language of state administration. To watch over the entire edifice, Joseph created a secret police.

The need to create a network of spies derived from growing noble, Catholic, and particularistic backlash. By the time Joseph died in 1790 there were revolts in Hungary and the Austrian Netherlands, and resentment smoldered in Bohemia. Leopold II soon found it necessary to grant concessions to the clergy and nobility, and when he died in 1792 his son Francis[11] reversed most of Joseph's reforms.

Thereafter the Revolution strengthened reaction by associating reform with Jacobinism. Plans to abolish feudal obligations were shelved and compulsory labor service began to increase. In 1793 French publications were banned, newspapers were prohibited from reporting on events in France, reading rooms, libraries, Masonic lodges, and learned societies were closed, and a censorship commission began to re-examine works published since 1780, banning some 2500 of them. Not even repeated defeats, loss of territory, and destruction of the Holy Roman Empire could shake Francis's determination to avoid structural change. The privileges of the Church and nobility remained unscathed, guilds continued, and the Hungarian Diet reasserted its autonomy. Despite rapidly growing debt, the fiscal system was left untouched and administration remained chaotic. Failure to remove the limitations placed on state power by the society of orders would gravely affect Austria's ability to retain great power status in the future.

There were reasons why Tsar Alexander's adoption of a liberal pose at the Congress of Vienna drew skepticism. Russian government was despotic and monarchs claimed to rule by divine right. Ever since Peter the Great had replaced the office of patriarch with a Holy Synod, Russian rulers had possessed extensive control over the Russian Orthodox Church. The nature of the relationship could be heard in the oath sworn by members of the Synod: "I swear by Almighty God that I resolve, and am in duty bound, to be a faithful, good, and obedient slave and subject to my natural and true Tsar and Sovereign."[12] Such close ties between Church and State were anathema to liberalism, as was serfdom. The latter remained widespread in parts of Europe, but it varied in degree of bondage. Where serfdom remained in the west, a noble generally controlled only the property of the peasant. In Prussia, prior to reform in 1807, bondage extended to the person: nobles determined peasant marriage, the practice of a trade, and the right to leave the land. In Russia bondage was complete; a peasant was tied to the soil, could not leave the village without consent, could not own property, and could be bought or sold.

During the reign of Catherine the Great noble power had been entrenched. Noble ownership of peasants had been recognized in law, and the former right of peasants to appeal to the state against abuse had been abolished. Local government had been parceled out between state appointees and officials elected by the nobility, who had also gained provincial assemblies wherein they could determine their corporate affairs. Noble monopoly of the officer corps of the army and the civil administration had been confirmed, as had noble exemption from taxation. After the death of Catherine in 1796 Paul I had sought to rein in the nobility, but he was assassinated by a court faction in 1801. Clearly, there were limits as to what a monarch could do, even if he or she wanted to undermine the society of orders.

Nevertheless Russia was not a playground for nobles, partly because they were far from united. The tsar possessed vast tracts of land that could be distributed to loyal servants who thereby gained gentry status. Moreover, early in her reign Catherine had promoted western culture and Enlightenment ideals had affected a part of the nobility. Thus a strong ruler could play divide and rule among conservative and liberal factions, and draw on the inclination of the bureaucracy to enhance the power of the state. The remit of the Tsarist regime lay primarily in territorial expansion, and noble dominance was secure only as long as it complemented expansionist objectives.

Tsar Alexander I started out with benevolent intentions. Although he confirmed the Charter of Nobility, he also announced that he would grant a constitution and abolish serfdom. In the event his reforms proved less far reaching. During the period of 1801–1805 several changes were made. The Senate was restored and became the supreme judicial and administrative body of the state; the government was organized on a western model with clearly defined ministries and ministers directly responsible to the Tsar, new universities were founded, and secondary education was increased. None of this constituted representative government, however; the Tsar still ruled by decree. Similarly, there was no attempt to impose emancipation of the peasantry, although a decree in 1803 encouraged voluntary liberation and about 50 000 peasants (perhaps 1% of the total) were freed. Subsequently Mikhail Speranski directed a second phase of reform from 1807 to 1812. Speranski established the Council of State, a body of senior officials who advised the Tsar as to legislative projects. When Speranski proposed, however, to change the fiscal system, noble opposition to removal of their tax exemptions led Alexander to dispatch him into exile.

Thereafter Alexander's illiberal tendencies came to the fore. Education was put under the control of Church conservatives who expelled liberal professors, and writing on political issues was forbidden. The most unpopular of all Alexander's measures was creation of military colonies in 1810. The purposes of the colonies were to supply troops for service abroad, aid in border policing, spread new agricultural techniques, and colonize new lands. Alexander hoped to turn all state peasants (about half the total rural population) into military colonists; unfortunately the soldiers resented having to labor in the fields and peasants disliked the interference in their private lives that went with imposition of military discipline. A British observer commented that the military colony was "held in utter abhorrence by the peasantry [and] detested by the regular army"[13] and, indeed, massive revolts in 1817 and 1819 testified to his observations. There were perhaps 750 000 people in the military colonies and therein lay the seeds of a long tradition of revolution.

Perhaps to impress other rulers, the Tsar's liberal side remained evident in his treatment of Finland and Poland. Exemption from serfdom, conscription, and taxation granted in 1809 kept the Finns quiescent for the following decades. In November 1815 Alexander granted Congress Poland a constitution that to a surprising degree retained the institutions and laws of the former Duchy of Warsaw. The constitution provided for a bicameral parliament (the *Sejm*) that would meet every second year; although members of the Senate would be nominated by the state, the lower house would be elected on a relatively broad franchise. The constitution also guaranteed religious freedom and *habeas corpus*, and provided for freedom of the press. Government would be conducted in Polish and separately from that of Russia, and Poland would have its own army, although Alexander's brother Constantine would command it. All the same, royal power remained great: the Tsar would control appointment of all state officials, could initiate or amend legislation, could bypass parliament on budgetary matters, and would determine foreign policy. Moreover there was a threat in the challenge Alexander threw down at the opening of the parliamentary session of 1818: "The results of your labours will show me whether I will be able to abide by my intention of expanding the concessions I have already made to you."[14]

The Ottoman Empire

Although the Ottoman Empire will not be given sustained discussion in this volume, it played an important role in the states system and hence we need to note certain characteristics of the regime. The sultan's European territories were extensive and included roughly nine million people. What distinguished the Ottomans, in the eyes of most Europeans, was that they were Islamic. Yet the Ottomans were relatively tolerant. Far from seeking to force conversion, they organized state administration in terms of religious affiliation and the Church, especially the Greek Orthodox Church, played a major role in local government. The various communities developed separately, linked only by an Ottoman ruler who allowed a good deal of self-government, but inspired little loyalty.

Once greatly feared, the Empire was notoriously weak by 1815. State revenues were much reduced by employment of tax farmers – private contractors mostly concerned with lining their own pockets. Worse still, the state was increasingly unable to maintain public order as repeated defeat in warfare corroded Ottoman prestige. Although local Muslim leaders known as *ayans* had risen to prominence as agents of the central government, in the performance of their duties they had assembled their own armies. Such forces could be turned against the central government, or used to exploit peasants. Christian notables developed similar forces.

Often stretched thin by foreign war, the Porte frequently compromised with the *ayans*, appointing them to official posts and using their forces to supplement the regular army. A succession of former *ayans*, nominated as *pashas* (provincial governors) then sought to establish autonomous principalities. Whereas in the west noble possession of private armies had been overcome by the growth of royal standing armies, in the Ottoman Empire military organizations such as the *janissaries* were as apt to rebel against as to obey the sultan. Sultans such as Selim III did recognize the need for reform; Selim sought to build a new infantry that would be given western-style training and subdue the *janissaries*. Attempted change then triggered revolt among the elements that possessed an interest in keeping the Ottomans weak. Although the rebellion of 1807 was overcome, Selim lost his life and ultimately was succeeded by Mahmud II.

The problems that Mahmud and subsequent sultans would repeatedly encounter could be seen in Serbian revolt. In the war of 1788–91, Austrian forces occupied Serbia, and many Serbs fought in the Habsburg Free Corps, gaining military skills and organization. Habsburg government was, however, accompanied by a Catholic Church bent on converting Orthodox Serbs; this experience, in combination with Slavic ties, would incline Serb leaders to look for Russian aid after the Ottomans regained control in 1792. While the sultan was willing to grant concessions, *janissaries* and rebel *ayans* then began to pillage Christian and Muslim villages. With the Ottoman government unable to provide much by way of aid, Serbs organized their own defense. Thereafter Serb fortunes rose and fell in tandem with Russian support. Initial success inclined the Serbs to shift their objectives from increased autonomy to independence, but internal divisions and inconsistent Russian backing ultimately led to compromise in 1815. The Serbs received favorable tariff and trading agreements, and they would occupy leading positions in the administration and judiciary.

The revolt of Serbia was a harbinger for the remainder of the century: drives for independence, a central authority weakened by fractious internal elements, and foreign intervention would characterize the "sick man of Europe." Repeated Russian involvement in Balkans wars of independence resulted partly from geostrategic considerations (the status of the Turkish Straits and defence of the Black Sea) and a strong current of support for Slavs and Orthodox Christians manifest in belief that Russia had a historical mission in the region. The latter sentiment would at times render Russian statesmen dangerously blind to the interests of the other powers.

Ultimately, all European states had to pay attention to public demand, if only to monitor or repress dissent. Few states, however, possessed political institutions designed to ensure responsible government, and even where such institutions existed, they were weak. Only Britain possessed a regime wherein the place of an independent parliament was well established. In France the security of parliament was shadowed by royal rejection of the principle of national sovereignty and, implicitly, division of power. The basic hostility of Austria and Prussia raised doubts about the prospects of constitutional regimes in the German Confederation, and the rulers of Spain and the Italian states had little sympathy for notions of representative government. Russia remained firmly autocratic, although the constitution granted Congress Poland was a striking experiment.

Even where regimes contained an element of representative government, franchises were designed to exclude the vast majority. Politics does not of course consist solely of parliaments and voting; yet even if we take a broader view of what constitutes political culture, restriction is more striking than participation. Freedom of expression, particularly in the press, was reasonably well established in Britain, and recognized as a constitutional right in France and several of the German states. Nevertheless, freedom of the political press was anything but secure outside of Britain, and virtually nonexistent in the eastern autocracies. Even the British placed restrictions on freedom of association and assembly, and continental governments were inclined to repress these liberties.

If liberal or democratic ideals found little place in contemporary systems, this did not mean that Europe had returned to the pre-Revolutionary status quo. The principle of "legitimacy" played only a minor role in the Vienna Settlement. Priority had been given to establishing a rough equilibrium among the powers and in their desire to secure stability the powers had greatly altered the boundaries and populations of many states. The powers had involved themselves in constituting political regimes, and while they set a valuable precedent for cooperating to resolve inter-state disputes, they also set a less positive precedent for intervention in the domestic affairs of less powerful states.

The restored regimes frequently differed from those that had existed prior to 1789. Already weakened by eighteenth-century enlightened despotism, the *ancien régime* society of orders was further undermined during the Revolutionary-Napoleonic era. Many Restoration rulers were besieged by requests for the return of corporative privileges; yet it was not in the interest of rulers to renew privileges that limited state power. No ruler dared to reverse the massive redistribution of wealth that French or French-inspired governments had conducted through expropriation and selling off of lands, generally at the expense of the Catholic Church. Similarly, certain Napoleonic institutions were retained by rulers who saw in them a means to enhance their power. Even Prussia had dealt a major blow to the old society of orders through abolition of serfdom. Though noble privilege was not completely eradicated, Prussia had taken a modernizing step that distanced her from Russia and Austria.

Thus most Restoration rulers chose, or were obliged, to consolidate at least some of the changes first undertaken during the Revolutionary-Napoleonic era. In seeking to strengthen state power, they hoped to restrict, or entirely eliminate, the political liberties associated with 1789. The inclination of rulers to set up consultative bodies, which gave an illusion of self-government, or to turn parliamentary bodies into puppets for the governing executive, however indicated recognition that the public could not simply be ignored. Despite such stratagems, memories of, and longings for, more liberal regimes were going to be difficult to eradicate.

2

Political Contestation from the Vienna Settlement to the 1830 Revolutions, 1814–1832

Dissatisfaction grew throughout the period of 1814–32. Calls for change resulted partly from the spread of liberalism, which in turn was tied to concerns about the relation between society and politics. Government was a means by which privilege was conferred and opposition to social or cultural (essentially religious) privilege could rapidly transform into demand for expansion of political rights or calls for reduction in the size of the state. Reformers frequently exaggerated the benefits that would result from alteration of a regime, and conservatives just as often overstated the harm that would occur. In consequence political change became fiercely contested. Prior to its arrival change generated excessive fear and after its establishment it produced disappointment when it failed to fulfill expectations.

In his study of the period the historian Michael Broers has identified five main political groups – reactionaries, conservatives, liberals, radicals, and nationalists. Such categories are necessarily based on broad generalization and they seldom perfectly describe any individual. Individuals change and at a given time they often combine elements of differing belief systems. Nevertheless the categories do provide a useful means to begin discussion of the emerging ideologies.[15]

In addition to wanting to erase the impact of the Revolution and Napoleon, reactionaries wanted to reverse the changes made to the *ancien régime* by the enlightened despots of the eighteenth century. Writers such as Louis de Bonald, a political and socialist theorist who had emigrated from France during the Revolution, rejected liberal emphasis on individual rights and argued that the society of orders was divinely inspired. Thus reactionaries rejected the concepts of

Europe's Uncertain Path 1814–1914: State Formation and Civil Society, First Edition. R. S. Alexander.
© 2012 R. S. Alexander. Published 2012 by Blackwell Publishing Ltd.

national sovereignty and social equality, and often advocated close ties between Church and State, seeing both as bulwarks of social hierarchy. The complement to the latter was patriarchy and hence French reactionaries pushed for, and secured, abolition of divorce in 1816, a measure designed to restore "order" in the family and a rejection of Revolutionary secularism. Reactionaries frequently championed Church control over education so that the young would not be "infected" by liberal or democratic beliefs, and they fought tooth and nail against secular education systems. In their idealized vision of the *ancien régime*, the two privileged orders (the nobility and clergy) and monarchs had cooperated in governing society. Such cooperation depended on state respect for elite privilege, and elite recognition of the legitimate prerogatives of royal sovereignty. Like conservatives, they placed a premium on social order, but in their desire to turn back the clock they threatened the very order they prized.

Conservatives were the heirs of enlightened despotism. Unlike liberals, they were not compromised by collaboration with the Revolution and Napoleon, and they would dominate Restoration government. Conservatives generally delineated their politics through policy rather than philosophy, and their pragmatism makes them difficult to define in ideological terms. Consideration of Edmund Burke, frequently described as the founder of modern political conservatism, provides a warning of the complexity of applying British examples to the Continent. Due to his attacks on the Enlightenment's penchant for social and political engineering, Burke could easily be misread as a reactionary. The British state that he wished to preserve was, however, far more liberal than those of the continental regimes. Continental conservatives such as Metternich were suspicious of institutions or groups that might challenge the central government. They were advocates of reform in so much as it rationalized government, strengthened administration, and provided stability. Given circumstances wherein it contributed to social order conservatives could compromise with demands for representative institutions, provided the Crown retained ultimate sovereignty. Like liberals, they tended to advocate removal of privileges that limited trade or hampered state unification. Indeed in certain circumstances the line between conservatism and liberalism can be very difficult to draw. German historians frequently point to what they term bureaucratic liberalism, by which they refer to the efforts of civil servants to bring about social and economic reform. If, however, we apply advocacy of representative government as a litmus test of liberalism, even the reforming civil servants of Baden fail the test – their primary goal was to strengthen the state and they were, in essence, conservative.[16]

Liberals remained champions of the early ideals of the Revolution. They still advocated the sanctity of private property, social equality, freedom of expression and conscience, and constitutional government. They had, however, concluded that too much emphasis on individual liberty had given rise to anarchy in the 1790s and then to tyranny under Napoleon. Most were constitutional monarchists; they wanted a royal executive capable of maintaining order. Continental liberals were less opposed than their British counterparts to state intervention to advance prosperity, but like British liberals they wanted regimes wherein ministers would be responsible to elected officials. The right to choose elected officials should be restricted to those who demonstrated capacity through possession of property or formal education. According to the Rhineland liberal David Hansemann, the vote should be confined to a "true [as opposed to a numerical] majority" because "its broader education gave it greater insight, and its wealth gave it a greater interest in the existence of a solid, strong and good state government."[17]

An ideological line between liberalism and radicalism is also difficult to draw. Both groups held that eventually all males should possess the vote, although liberals were more inclined to postpone broadening the franchise. Even so, in their debates over suffrage reform, liberals were divided over whether inclusion should be based on social class or individual capacity. The latter position drew liberals closer to radicals. Radicals shared liberal belief in national sovereignty and representative government; they were, however, more democratic in believing either that all (males) should hold the vote as a right, or that a large proportion of the (male) masses possessed sufficient capacity to take a direct role in politics. Despite frustration with conservative monarchies, only a small number of radicals advocated creation of republics. More central were battles to secure representative government where it did not exist, and parliamentary government where it did, to combat government suppression of freedom of expression, assembly, association, and petition, and to overcome or prevent social privilege and religious intolerance.

Nationalism had already begun to reveal its unsettling complexity. In France nationalism was associated with the Left. Among the Revolutionary watchwords, nationalism was tied to fraternity – a belief in unity based on mutual responsibility. Although marked by chauvinism, French nationalism also had a cosmopolitan element derived from belief in popular self-determination. All peoples should be free of the tyranny of despotic monarchs and national sovereignty should be the foundation of all political systems. Elsewhere nationalism had developed partly as a reaction against the imposition of French institutions. National liberation could mean freedom from French liberalism for Spanish conservatives or from Napoleonic tyranny for Spanish liberals. Often it meant unification of what Benedict Anderson has termed an "imagined community" – a culturally driven force increasingly based on language and tradition rather than choice.[18] Such communities were not, of course, wholly a product of imagination and nationalist movements were strongest when they built on historical, linguistic, or social realities. During the Restoration scholars busied themselves with identifying what they considered the definitive characteristics of nations and their ideas gradually spread, especially among students.

How extensive was political participation? Even where representative systems existed, participation was restricted to small numbers of male property owners who qualified to vote or hold office. Yet the battles fought by elite groups had significant consequences for all of society and at moments of crisis mass elements did enter the political forum, either through demonstrations and petition campaigns, or through riot or revolt. Especially after the Revolutionary era, governments knew that they could not afford simply to ignore the masses. Conversely, opposition groups were torn between desire for support and fear of the possible consequences of mass entry into the political realm.

How did political beliefs spread? A crucial characteristic of the nineteenth century was that the means of transmission expanded and diversified, making control more difficult. Among the literate, opportunity to read books was increasingly complemented by publication of journals and newspapers. Many of the latter publications were ephemeral, lasting only a short time before collapsing. Even the more successful newspapers depended on a relatively small number of subscribers, although subscription figures were a poor indicator of readership because copies of newspapers or journals frequently were read by upwards of ten individuals. The importance of newspapers did, however, steadily rise and much of the material presented focused on politics, especially where parliaments (and speeches) could be reported on. At least as important were small-scale pamphlets and brochures that were cheap to produce and more easily distributed.

Meanwhile the number of places where information could be gathered also grew. During the eighteenth century literary salons had served as vectors for the transmission of the ideas of Enlightenment *philosophes* to the elite. Salons continued to spread in the nineteenth century and politics increasingly determined membership; so much so that some salons were the nuclei for political parties or *blocs*. At less exalted levels, cafés, tea houses, and taverns also provided places where individuals could gather to discuss issues that concerned them, and many subscribed to journals. Many urban centers also possessed reading rooms or clubs where members could read publications and talk. Such institutions required licenses which might or might not ban political literature; however, even ostensibly literary publications could be full of political allusion, and banned publications could be circulated clandestinely.

Despite expanding literacy, mass culture was essentially oral and visual. Political contestation thus entailed battle over what was said or seen in public. Freedom of assembly frightened unpopular regimes partly because assemblies provided opportunities for orators to influence large numbers. Even rural market places were subjected to police surveillance and authorities were especially concerned to prevent political demands from merging with economic grievance. Theaters had to be carefully monitored. Despite the best efforts of censors, even the slightest inflection of certain lines could produce charged reactions from audiences and theaters often became battle zones wherein allegiance was declared through applause, hissing, whistling, and occasional brawls.

States possessed a wide array of means by which they could seek to influence the public. State ceremonial and military processions, holiday festivals, commemoration of past events, public architecture, and patronage of the arts could all be deployed to deliver a message. Where relations between church and state were close, the pulpit could be used to disperse propaganda. Against such an arsenal, opposition groups developed ingenious ways to express dissent. Simple refusal to participate in ceremonial or a festivity could be taken as an expression of discontent. More overtly challenging was the cultivation of the signs, symbols, or rituals of alternative ideological systems. Under a repressive regime, subtler means could be adopted. States could ban the emblems of former regimes; yet how much could its agents do if large numbers of students decided to dress themselves in the colors of a banned flag? Too much repression could prove counter-productive.

A problem with symbols and images is that it is difficult to control what people see in them. Similarly, while historians can point to the means of transmission, it is virtually impossible to measure their impact with precision. Nevertheless, it is obvious that governments and their opponents engaged in propaganda wars that intensified throughout the century, drawing increasing numbers into the political fray.

Failed Revolutions

Having installed rulers throughout the continent, the powers had an interest in their fate. The Vienna Settlement called on the powers to meet periodically and they did so in the Concert of Europe, a series of congresses held regularly until 1821, and thereafter on an ad hoc basis. However, a faultline opened over whether the Concert should serve as a vehicle by which the powers could regulate the affairs of other states. While at first the idea was simply to form a Quadruple Alliance to ensure that France honored treaty obligations, Tsar Alexander, then under the influence of a religious mystic, wanted also to create a "Holy Alliance" to protect religion, peace, and justice. The British politely refused what Castlereagh described as mystical nonsense and although Prussia and Austria were more inclined to appease the Tsar, they did not take the proposal seriously. Nevertheless the issue would soon return and prove highly contentious for two basic reasons: foreign intervention was a repudiation of the principle of national self-determination, and it was not necessarily the case that all the powers had an interest in preserving reactionary regimes.

Initially all eyes were on France, where the monarchy needed to overcome suspicion that the King would favor the former privileged orders. Tensions were exacerbated by the return of exiles who in 1814 gained the appellation "ultraroyalists" because they were more intransigent than Louis XVIIII. The fact that these reactionaries clustered round the King's brother Artois, heir to the throne, made matters worse. Although there was no dramatic purge of former Napoleonic officials from the state, the government committed errors that heightened public alarm. In initiating legislation to restore unsold lands expropriated during the Revolution, an official praised émigrés who had refused to compromise with

Revolutionary or Napoleonic France. Meanwhile expiatory ceremonies for victims of the Revolution implied that the Revolution was one great sin from top to bottom. While Allied demands and fiscal retrenchment necessitated reduction of the army, simultaneously handing out plumb positions to émigrés rubbed salt into the wounds of officers who found themselves decommissioned or put on half pay.

Royalists had thus cleared the path for Napoleon's "Flight of the Eagle" in March 1815. After escaping from exile on the island of Elba, Napoleon landed on the Mediterranean coast with perhaps 1100 soldiers and marched toward Paris. Threatening to hang priests and nobles from the lampposts, he took on the guise of champion of the Revolution and crowds and soldiers flocked to his banner. Thereafter he granted freedom of the press to (nonroyalist) journals, allowed freedom of association to semipolitical organizations called federations, and called on the liberal Benjamin Constant to cowrite a revision of the Imperial constitution. Only weeks before Constant had described Bonaparte as a modern day Attila the Hun and so his rallying to Napoleon struck many as shamelessly opportunistic. Constant's conversion was, however, emblematic of a major transformation; too many reminders of the *ancien régime* had reforged links based on shared opposition to reaction among radicals, liberals, and Bonapartists.

Royalist resistance was unimpressive and it was Allied arms that again drove Bonaparte from the throne in July. Revenge upon individuals who had rallied to the "usurper" duly followed the battle of Waterloo. The "White Terror" of 1815–16 consisted partly of laws that allowed officials to set aside due process of law in repression of dissidents, and partly of murder and pillage orchestrated by ultraroyalists in the south. While it strengthened the grip of the central government in the short term by placing positions of influence in the hands of devoted royalists, it also ran the risk of triggering further revolt. Louis XVIII did not look like much of a king and his nickname among the people was "the Fat Pig," but he did have considerable political acumen and he did not want his life further unsettled by another flight into exile. The King therefore signaled a break from reaction by dismissing the ultraroyalist-dominated Chamber of Deputies. The latter had been a product of the peculiar conditions (defeat, occupation, and White Terror) of August 1815, and in the fall of 1816 the electorate heeded the King's call by delivering a lower house composed largely of moderate royalists.

The Duke de Richelieu, head of the cabinet, could then turn to the path of reconciliation. As an aristocratic army officer, Richelieu had emigrated from France in 1792 and later served Tsar Alexander as governor of Odessa. He thus was well placed to represent France in relations with the occupying powers. Napoleon had left behind little by way of national debt, enabling the finance minister to float loans at low rates to pay off reparations, and occupation was over by the end of 1818. France was then invited to join the other powers in a Quintuple Alliance, although the Quadruple Alliance was maintained.

Between 1817 and 1820 governments tried to gain acceptance by the moderate Left. In February 1817 a law replaced a two-tier voting system with direct elections.

In March 1818 the Saint-Cyr Law provided for annual funding of 40 000 army conscripts who would serve a minimum of six years. Promotion would be based on service rather than social standing. What was critical, however, was to rally the army to the regime through recognition of accomplishments during the Revolutionary-Napoleonic era. Ultraroyalists opposed both laws and even Richelieu considered them too liberal. After Richelieu resigned in December 1818, Duke Elie Decazes, a personal favorite of the King, went further in wooing liberals with abolition of preliminary press censorship in May 1819.

Prior to the departure of Allied troops, French ultraroyalists had asked that the occupation be extended because the Left was recovering its influence. The character of a recently formed Liberal Opposition was determined partly by reaction against government efforts to control parliament. During elections the administration organized campaigns for "official" candidates favored by the government, used patronage to woo the electorate, and mobilized voter turnout. To counter such tactics, Liberals formed electoral committees during campaigns and used the press to express opposition when no elections were in the offing. Liberals believed that the Chamber of Deputies represented the nation; hence their determination to fight government control of elections. Equally pronounced, however, was Liberal opposition toward any form of corporate privilege, be it for the nobility, clergy, or guilds.

Because many Liberals were former Jacobins or Bonapartists, some royalists assumed that the Opposition must be bent on a revolution and alarm heightened as Liberals gained ground in partial elections from 1817 to 1819. Assassination of the Duke de Berry, nephew of the King, then provided ultraroyalists with a pretext in February 1820 to attack both the Liberals (although they had no ties with the assassin) and the government for having compromised with the Left. Louis XVIII was subjected to intense emotional pressure by the royal family, a hotbed of ultraroyalism, and had to give way by dismissing Decazes.

The result was a second Richelieu ministry that passed several repressive laws in the late spring. To block Liberal progress, the wealthiest quarter of the electorate, among whom noble landowners formed a high proportion, would elect 178 deputies. They would also continue to vote for the 258 deputies chosen on the basis of the old electoral system. Preliminary press censorship was temporarily re-instated and anti-sedition laws provided the state with means to attack opponents, leading to the collapse of most Liberal journals. Although all of these measures were passed in parliament, Liberals concluded that the Charter had been violated. They had a point in that government manipulation of the electoral system did challenge the principle of representative government. Whether subsequent resort to revolt was wise was another question. Evidence of conspiracy would not, however, be uncovered until August 1820, by which time revolution had already erupted elsewhere.

Deeply suspicious of any potential rival, Ferdinand VII was above all determined to rule Spain as an absolute monarch. To do so he needed to restore state finances so that he could rebuild the central government. Previously the colonies had provided an important source of revenue; however, by 1814 Argentina, Uruguay, and Paraguay had achieved independence, and Venezuela, Columbia, and Bolivia were in revolt. A force of some 10 000 men dispatched in February 1815 failed to deliver a knockout blow to resistance forces, and while the government could assemble a larger force, it lacked the transport and naval shipping necessary to carry it across the Atlantic. Instead an expeditionary force concentrated close to Cadiz was left to cool its heels.

Due to appointment of a ludicrous number of officers, the army of 184 000 men was far too costly, and the reactionary prejudices of a war minister made problems of reduction worse. Civilians who had joined the army in 1808 were dismissed while senior appointments went to officers who had contributed little to the liberation of Spain. When in 1817 Cadiz merchants established relations with the expeditionary force, liberalism began to mix with the grievances of officers. It did not hurt that Lieutenant-Colonel Rafael del Riego could distribute funds provided by a merchant to half-starved soldiers; still, Riego's revolt of January 1820 would have achieved little had it not sparked widespread rebellion led by disaffected officers. Riego demanded in a *pronunciamiento* (a political pronouncement by a military official) that the King restore the constitution of 1812. Whether the initial revolt was truly liberal in inspiration is, however, questionable. Military commanders were motivated mostly by personal grievance and popular participation in revolts had more to do with resistance to conscription than ideology.

Whereas an earlier tendency among historians to attribute revolution in Spain to freemasonry has come under question,[19] there is little doubt that revolt in Italy was stirred by secret societies such as the Carbonari (literally the coal burners) which used masonry as a cover for political organization. Having originally joined to liberate Italy from Napoleonic rule, some members aspired to the unification of Italy. Many had democratic tendencies, and they found in the Spanish constitution of 1812 an attractive model. Largely middle-class in character, the Carbonari numbered perhaps 300 000 small-scale businessmen and property owners, minor officials, military officers, and members of militias. Although the restored regimes were not especially formidable, they did have Austrian backing. Thus the Carbonari needed allies, and to some extent they shared common ground with liberal notables (Figure 2.1).

Revolt began in July 1820 in the Kingdom of Two Sicilies, where it quickly gained the support of much of the Neapolitan army. Many state officials had been retained from the previous regime headed by the Napoleonic Marshal Murat and they also viewed the revolt favorably; they disliked Austrian influence and wanted a constitution, although they did not share the Carbonari's democratic tendencies. When King Ferdinand I was forced to accept the Spanish 1812 constitution at Naples, Muratists dominated a newly formed government. Thereafter tensions between Muratist and Carbonari parliamentary deputies grew, and the revolutionary regime was further weakened by a revolt of Sicilians who wanted autonomy from Naples.

Figure 2.1 A secret meeting of Italian *carbonari*, c. 1815–1830. © Bettmann/Corbis.

In the north, Carbonari and liberal elements developed plans to establish constitutional regimes. Despite the reactionary character of King Victor Emmanuel, conspirators hoped that revolt against the Austrians in Lombardy and Venetia would entice the House of Savoy and the Piedmontese army to join them. Thus they contacted Charles Albert, second in line to the throne and considered more liberal than his brother Charles Felix. Unfortunately for the conspirators, intensified repression intimidated opponents of the Habsburg regime and prevented revolt. Nevertheless Piedmontese conspirators went ahead in March 1821 and seized Alessandria, forming a provisional government in the name of an Italian Federation that would remain independent until Victor Emmanuel proclaimed himself "King of Italy." Victor Emmanuel favored resistance to the revolt until mutiny broke out among his army at Turin; he then abdicated. Charles Albert became regent in the absence of his brother, and as rebellion spread he proclaimed the Spanish constitution.

In reaction to the revolts in Spain and Italy Metternich called for solidarity among monarchs and claimed that the rebellions were orchestrated by an international revolutionary network centered at Paris. Along these lines he warned Tsar Alexander that secret societies were "a real power, all the more dangerous as it works in the dark, undermining all parts of the social body, and depositing everywhere a moral gangrene which is not slow to develop and increase."[20] There was a grain of truth in Metternich's assertions. There were conspiratorial societies operating in many countries; yet their ties did not go much beyond mutual sympathy. In truth his rhetoric sprang from desire to frighten conservatives into support for repression, and he could point to developments in Britain and the German states as further evidence for his allegations.

Britain had entered a difficult postwar transition. With national debt close to three times the size of gross national income, and parliamentary abolition of income tax, fiscal retrenchment became the cornerstone of policy. Reduction in the armed forces saw some 180 000 men demobilized, adding to high levels of unemployment. Radicals such as William Cobbett, a formidable pamphleteer and journalist, attributed economic dislocation to political corruption and the Tory government of Lord Liverpool made matters worse by passing the Corn Laws. The Corn Laws taxed wheat imports whenever domestic prices fell below a relatively high level, thus benefiting the landed elite to the detriment of consumers. Hardship gave rise to a dramatic increase in the frequency of food and wage-reduction riots, and episodes of Luddism (machine smashing).

For the governing elite, the merging of political and economic grievance was worrisome. Radicals demanded that reform be the reward for wartime sacrifice; in 1817 some 700 petitions were presented by 350 towns to parliament. Most Whigs were, however, reluctant to endorse reform when it was associated with a threat to propertied interests, and even the Radicals fought among themselves over proposals for franchise extension. After a rally in December 1816 at Spa Fields, an angry crowd marched on the tower of London, looting along the way. In the summer of

1819 at St Peter's Fields in Manchester, a gathering of perhaps 60 000 attended a reform meeting. When the authorities sought to arrest the speaker, soldiers charged the crowd, leaving six dead and hundreds injured. The soldiers were both regulars and yeomanry. Shortly thereafter police informants uncovered an alleged plot to assassinate the cabinet. In each instance Liverpool's government responded with repression. After the Spa Fields riots parliament passed the Coercion Acts, temporarily suspending *habeas corpus* and extending a law against seditious meetings. After the Peterloo "Massacre," the Six Acts prevented delays in trials for misdemeanors, authorized seizure of arms, increased penalties for libel and sedition, forced newspapers to pay a stamp duty, prevented meetings for arms training, and banned unauthorized political gatherings of more than 50 people. Of the 18 arrested Cato Street conspirators, six were hanged and five were transported overseas. Meanwhile the prime minister made clear his view that no attempt should be made to use the state as an instrument to ameliorate the suffering of the poor: "on enquiry, it would be found that by far the greatest part of the miseries of which human nature complained were in all times and in all countries beyond the control of human legislation."[21]

Repression also became the order of the day in the German states, where discontent resulted from desire for German unification and constitutional government. Although the leading critics were university professors, their message was spread by students who formed societies that stressed dedication to the fatherland. In October 1817 some 500 students from various states gathered at Wartburg Castle to celebrate the fourth anniversary of the battle of Leipzig (a key part of the liberation of Germany from Napoleonic control) and the 300th anniversary of the Reformation. At the end of ceremonies a group burned the works of reactionary or conservative writers, thereby imitating Luther's burning of a papal bull in 1521.

It was not until the assassination of a conservative dramatist by a deranged student that Metternich sprang into action. In a meeting at Teplitz in July 1819 he convinced Prussian King Frederick William to join in promoting reaction throughout Germany. In September 1819 Austria, Prussia, and eight other states oversaw passage of the Carlsbad Decrees in a session of the Confederation Diet. The decrees imposed rigid press censorship for the next five years and subjected universities and schools to close supervision. Liberal professors and teachers were dismissed or imprisoned, newspapers were suppressed, and student societies were dissolved. To ensure compliance among all the German states, the Diet created an investigative commission and assumed powers to send in troops should governments fail to enforce the decrees.

Metternich then turned to Italy. Although in May 1820 he had supported Castlereagh's rejection of Alexander's call for an international force to intervene in Spain, Metternich's position shifted when revolution broke out in Naples. At the Congresses of Troppau (in November 1820) and Laibach (in January 1821) Metternich played on the Tsar's growing paranoia over international conspiracy to gain support for unilateral Austrian intervention in Italy. The French and British governments refused to attend the congresses, but they accepted that Italy was of particular interest to the Austrians. Troops were soon dispatched to the Kingdom of Two Sicilies and by the end of March 1821 they had restored Ferdinand's absolute rule. They dispersed Piedmontese revolutionaries one month later. Intense repression thereafter drove hundreds of Italians into exile.

Rather than heed the Tsar's call for the Holy Alliance to intervene in Spain, which would have entailed large Russian armies marching across central Europe, Metternich backed French plans for unilateral intervention. In France Liberal attempts to stir insurrection had succeeded only in driving moderates into the arms of reactionaries. In combination with administrative corruption of voter lists, French Carbonari conspiracies had yielded an increasing number of ultraroyalist electoral victories, paving the way for appointment of a government led by the ultraroyalist Joseph de Villèle in December 1821. Villèle initially hesitated over intervention on behalf of the Spanish Bourbon King because he feared he might thereby unleash liberal revolt in France. Eventually, however, he was persuaded by the arguments of the writer François-René de Chateaubriand that a demonstration of military power would appeal to patriotism and enhance the popularity of the Monarchy. A major step was taken when Metternich convinced Alexander that French unilateral action was better than no action at all. Thereafter Chateaubriand overcame British objections by promising that French forces would withdraw as soon as Ferdinand had been restored to full power.

Slim at the outset of the revolution, the chances of intervention had steadily increased. As in the Italian states, the revolutionaries were divided between liberal moderates and Jacobin-style radicals. As at Naples, the King publicly accepted constitutional monarchy while secretly lobbying for foreign invasion to destroy it. Moderates hoped they could convince the King to compromise by modifying the constitution of 1812 through creation of a house of peers, imposing a property qualification for voting rights, and strengthening the powers of the executive. A government minister summarized the Moderate position when he stated: "The ideas of liberty injected superficially in the unprepared masses only serve to create unruly men who disobey legitimate authority."[22] In other regards, however, the Moderates re-instituted the reforms of 1812–13, abolishing seigniorial privilege, ecclesiastical legal jurisdiction, and the Inquisition. Radicals were opposed to any tampering with the 1812 constitution and sought popular approval through opposition to indirect taxes and calls for state expropriation of monastic properties. Following a revolt by the Royal Guards in which the King was implicated, radicals gained control over the government after the elections of 1822. They immediately began plans for more extensive seizure of Church property and drove most the clergy into support of reactionaries.

Counter-revolution led by nobles and churchmen was centered in Navarre, Aragon, Galicia, and Catalonia, where reactionary *juntas* initiated civil war. Lacking funds for arms, the Spanish ultraroyalists could not, however, defeat the regular army. For a time the French sought to convince them to accept a constitution along the lines of the Charter, which would have been acceptable to many liberals, but they were bent on return to the *ancien régime*. Moreover the virtual imprisonment of Ferdinand pushed the French into acting hastily. Like its predecessor, the Spanish revolutionary regime lacked the finances to maintain a large army and promotion had again been based more on nepotism than merit. Loyalty had diminished rapidly and many Spanish generals were inclined to desert in the hope of securing their futures. Thus the French expeditionary force advanced quickly, beginning in April 1823. By September they had re-established Ferdinand's rule. Much to their chagrin, the French were then embarrassed as a vengeful king oversaw a brutal reaction that included massive arrests and executions, and extensive expropriation of property. Thousands of liberals fled to exile as Ferdinand undid all their work, except for abolition of the Inquisition. The King could not, however, restore Spain's colonial empire; all of the latter had been lost, save for Cuba and Puerto Rico in the Americas and the Philippines in southeast Asia.

One last insurrectionary episode remained to be played out in the most unexpected of quarters. Until 1789 Catherine the Great had encouraged Russian contact with western ideas. Freemasonry had spread egalitarian ideals and although Alexander had abolished Masonic societies, some had gone underground as secret societies. Returning officers who had encountered liberalism during the occupation of France grew increasingly restive with Alexander's failure to fulfill past promises. Although many were of the landed gentry, they chafed at domination of the court by conservatives and the inequities of the military colonies. Conspiratorial opposition was divided into two main groups. At Saint Petersburg the Northern Society advocated creation of a constitutional regime that would guarantee civil liberties, abolish social privilege, and respect private property. The Southern Society, composed largely of officers serving in the Ukraine, was more radical, planning to establish a republic and redistribute land so as to abolish class differences.

When Alexander died in December 1825, a succession crisis presented the conspirators with opportunity. Alexander's eldest brother Constantine was the immediate heir to the throne, but Alexander had concluded that his younger brother Nicholas was more suitable and Constantine had privately agreed. After Alexander's death, Constantine initially hesitated to renounce the succession publicly, so that Nicholas was obliged to swear allegiance to Constantine as a temporary measure. Although Constantine made his formal renunciation two weeks later, the Northern Union decided to exploit confusion. Their plan was to intervene in a swearing of allegiance ceremony and convince the Saint Petersburg garrison that Constantine had not renounced his succession and that to swear allegiance to Nicholas would be treason. Encouraged by promises of pay increases, some units did indeed mutiny. The conspirators made little effort to gain popular support, however, and artillery fire by troops loyal to Nicholas soon put a halt to the rebellion. Subsequently a revolt of the Southern Society ended in a single, bloody clash with loyal forces in the Ukraine.

Despite Metternich's claims, the revolts of the early 1820s were isolated and largely the product of local grievances. Nevertheless, they did share certain features. The role of the military was conspicuous, as was the absence of popular support. Even in France, the Carbonari concentrated on subverting army officers rather than promoting mass insurrection. As in Italy, the conspirators were largely middle class, although there was a smattering of lower-class participation. Where the state apparatus was strong and the army remained loyal, revolution could succeed only if elite elements combined with the masses to overthrow unpopular regimes. That foreign intervention had been required to subdue revolt in Spain and Italy was less a demonstration of the strength of revolutionary forces than the weakness of the Restoration regimes. Even so, resentment at privilege, fear of reaction, and misgovernment were facilitating the spread of liberalism.

Conservative Consolidation

The regime of Nicholas I was based on the principles of orthodoxy, autocracy, and official nationality. Orthodoxy gave Russia a messianic tendency that buttressed imperialism: to extend Tsarist rule was to extend the faith. In Poland, the Ukraine, and Byelorussia, Nicholas and the Orthodox Church sought to drive out the Catholic and Uniate (which kept Orthodox ritual but recognized the authority of the Pope) churches. Proponents of autocracy saw the Tsar as a father of his people who rightly expected total submission from his subjects. Official nationality was based on belief that orthodoxy and autocracy gave the Russian nation a specific character that was superior and should be sheltered from foreign influence.

Nicholas was not the brutal tyrant of liberal legend, but he was a determined autocrat and the Decembrist Revolt was soon followed by arrests that brought 121 suspects before a special tribunal. Of the accused, five were hanged and many were given sentences of long penal servitude. In 1826 Nicholas also issued decrees tightening censorship and organizing education so that schools would transmit only the knowledge necessary to each social class. All the same, it was only after the revolutions of 1830 that the Tsar truly earned his reputation as the *"gendarme* of Europe."* Early in his reign Nicholas oversaw much-needed codification of Russian law that sped the legal process and made decisions less arbitrary. Steps also were taken to improve conditions for serfs on Crown lands: taxation was shifted from persons to land, poor peasants gained additional allotments, financial assistance, schools, and medical care were developed, and limited self-government was allowed. Even Nicholas's creation of the notorious Third Section of the Imperial Chancery in 1826 had partly benign origins. The role of the secret police was to harass dissident groups, but attempts were initially made to recruit gentlemen-officers who would serve public interests. Unfortunately, the Third Section soon gained infamy for its employment of entrapment, false accusation, and bribery.

Despite thousands of arrests, the Third Section uncovered few conspiracies prior to its dissolution in the 1850s, and in its incompetence it was sadly typical of the Russian state. Growth in the bureaucracy, from roughly 16 000 in 1796 to at least 82 352 by 1855, was not accompanied by increased efficiency or ability to cope with processes of social and economic change.

If the Russian state was conservative rather than reactionary, so too was the Spanish monarchy. Although Ferdinand was subjected to intense ultraroyalist pressure after destruction of the liberal regime in 1823, the King soon realized that appointment of reactionaries undermined the royal absolutism he prized. Moreover, loss of revenues from the colonies and economic disruption within Spain meant that Ferdinand needed the support of men capable of modernizing the state. Thus he turned again to the moderates upon whom he had relied prior to 1820, issued a partial amnesty of individuals involved in the revolution of 1820, reconstituted the regular army, and sought to bring counter-revolutionary militias under control. In consequence, reactionaries looked to the King's younger brother Don Carlos, who appeared the likely successor to the childless Ferdinand. While Don Carlos did not take part in a revolt that swept much of rural Catalonia in 1827, he was known for his piety and approved of an agenda that included reinstitution of the Inquisition. Ferdinand responded to ultraroyalist challenge by dispatching the army and terminated the revolt, much to the delight of liberals in Barcelona, who rewarded the government with a cheap loan. Yet Ferdinand still would have no truck with political liberalism; the regime also crushed attempts by exiles to rekindle revolution and allowed the Church to recover much of the property lost in 1822–23.

Erosion of the Conservative Order on the European Periphery

For the autocracies, independence movements in the Ottoman Empire posed awkward questions. In the Ottoman Empire the Society of Friends, a pseudo-Masonic order composed largely of middle-class elements, thought initially in terms of revolution throughout the Balkans and hoped for Russian support. When a scheme to begin an uprising in Serbia collapsed in 1817, the Society turned to the Danubian Principalities of Moldavia and Wallachia. Ottoman forces were weak in these Romanian lands, but Tsar Alexander, swayed by the arguments of Metternich, denounced the revolt.

By the time order was restored in the Principalities, insurrection had broken out in Greece, where Ottoman authority was also challenged by the ambition of the provincial governor, Ali Pasha, to install himself as the ruler of an independent state. Although Ali Pasha was defeated by February 1822, Greece was well suited to guerrilla warfare, and Greek ships were able to disrupt Ottoman sea transport while securing foreign contact, trade, and aid. While the rebels could thus maintain control over the Peloponnesus and Rumelia, internal divisions prevented them from extending their positions. The secular liberalism of leading members of the Society of Friends was unappealing to Orthodox Greeks, and attempts to set up a central government ran afoul of military warlords. Thus Greece was wracked by both civil war and a war of liberation, and was scarred by massacres committed by all sides. To break the stalemate Sultan Mahmud II turned in 1825 to Muhammad Ali, Pasha of Egypt, who commanded a modernized army trained by French officers. Beginning in February 1825 the Egyptian Army soon dispersed Greek forces in the south, and Ottoman troops attacked the north, taking Athens by June 1826. Confronted by the probable termination of the Greek revolution, three of the European powers then stepped in.

Much had changed by 1826. For his part, Metternich was consistent in opposing intervention: "Long experience has taught us that in racial denominations there may lie elements of trouble between empires and bones of contention between people and governments. And what a powerful and ever hostile weapon such denominations become in the hands of those who would overthrow, or seek to overthrow, the existing order!"[23] Pressure in Russia to intervene had, however, mounted due to the Tsar's claim to be the protector of Orthodox Christians. Just before Easter in 1821 a group of *janissaries* had publicly hanged the Greek patriarch and then attacked members of the Greek community at Constantinople. Diplomatic ties between Russia and the Porte had been cut in the summer, and it had taken all of Metternich's guile to prevent the Tsar from taking action.

A new British foreign minister, George Canning, was less inclined to take the counsel of the Austrian foreign minister. Although Canning essentially continued Castlereagh's opposition to great-power intervention in the affairs of other states, he was more assertive publicly against the autocracies and less willing to pursue objectives through private negotiation and compromise than his predecessor had been. He thus gained the admiration of many liberals, despite being a Tory. To some extent the British government was influenced by public sympathy for the Greeks stirred by Romantic Philhellenism. Because it was portrayed as a battle against "oriental despotism" by the likes of the poet Lord George Byron, Philhellenism was initially a liberal cause. All the same, Canning was mostly driven by concern that Russia might intervene unilaterally and thereby secure commercial and geostrategic advantages.

When Philhellenism was taken up by other Romantics, most notably Chateaubriand, it took on the guise of a crusade on behalf of Christians. Hence the cause of Greek independence confounded the studied neutrality of Metternich by appealing to royalists. When Tsar Nicholas came to the throne he was less willing to listen to Metternich than Alexander had been and by April 1826 Russia and Britain had agreed to pursue Greek autonomy. For much the same reasons as the British, the French joined this alliance in July 1827, and the three powers established a naval blockade to stop communication between Egypt and Greece. Destruction of a Turkish-Egyptian fleet at Navarino in October then led the Sultan to renounce previous treaties with Russia. As war broke out between Russia and the Ottoman

Empire in April 1828, the French neutralized Egyptian troops by sending a force to the Peloponnesus. With victory achieved by September 1829, Russia gained territory in the Caucasus, confirmation of protectorate status over Serbia and the Danubian Principalities, and Ottoman acceptance of international mediation of the Greek question in the Treaty of Adrianople. Thereafter, in February 1830, the powers guaranteed the independence of Greece.

It would be difficult to argue that the war of Greek Independence was a triumph for the principle of national self-determination. Greek nationalism was confined to a small minority who adopted it mostly to appeal to western sensibilities for aid. Independence was more the product of religious and economic grievance, the weakness of Ottoman rule, and great power geostrategic interests. Still, Metternich had good reason for apprehension: the map of Europe had been altered and a revolution had been sanctioned.

For liberals Greece offered hope. Better yet, Britain seemed an exception to conservative triumph after Liverpool reshaped the cabinet in 1822. Liverpool had previously responded to agitation with repression, but the return of stability in the early 1820s provided a context in which he was willing to encourage younger Tories who favored modernizing reforms that were crucial to the transition to economic liberalism for which British became famous. Revision of the Navigation Acts enabled foreign ship owners to carry goods in and out of Britain, duties on imported goods were reduced, and restrictions that prevented Britain's colonies from trading directly with foreign countries were removed. Other reforms resulted from a mix of humanitarian concern and desire to make provision of law and order more efficient. As Home Secretary Robert Peel oversaw a program of reducing punishments that were disproportionate to the crimes committed so that juries would convict more frequently. As a result imposition of the death penalty dropped precipitously, while the number of convictions entailing imprisonment or transportation (to penal colonies) rose. In 1829 Peel also secured passage of an Act that created a force of 1000 uniformed police who replaced small local forces in London.

Recognition that unduly harsh or restrictive laws were not working could also be seen in revision of the Combination Acts. Despite the fact that the Act of 1799 had forbidden workers from forming unions, they had continued to do so. In 1824 Radical MPs managed to convince a parliamentary commission that the old Act was counter-productive because it prevented workers and owners from rationally bargaining. Thus a new Act legalized unions and strikes, although it also made use of coercion, through threats to property or person, liable to prosecution. Passage of the Act in 1824 was immediately followed by a wave of strikes and pressure from manufacturers led to further revision in 1825. In the later Act workers were permitted to form unions solely to formulate demands as to working hours and wages. Although circumscribed, union activities thus were legal; on the continent governments viewed any form of independent association with a jaundiced eye.

Reform and Revolution in the West

The constitutional monarchies were significantly altered in the early 1830s and by looking at them in combination we can highlight common denominators that produced enduring change.

Reform movements were most impressive in Britain, where Catholics and Dissenting Protestants were excluded from holding public office by the necessity of swearing an oath of allegiance to the Thirty-Nine Articles of the Church of England. The issue was particularly acute in Ireland, where roughly 70% of the population was Catholic. As a result of the Lords defeating a motion for Catholic emancipation in 1821, the barrister Daniel O'Connell formed a pressure group known as the Catholic Association at Dublin in 1823. The Association orchestrated campaigns for Catholics who ran for parliament even though they would refuse the oath and hence not take their seats at Westminster. Such a strategy was well calculated to challenge claims that Ireland was represented within the political system. Public meetings drew numbers in the tens of thousands, and membership soared well into the hundreds of thousands. Despite suppression of the original Association, a New Catholic Association secured the election of numerous Catholics in 1826.

The emancipation issue divided the Tory Party, with reformers recognizing the need for change and traditionalists determined to resist. After Liverpool retired in 1827, two short-lived governments failed to reconcile the two factions, leading to appointment of Wellington as prime minister in early 1828. A hero of the Napoleonic wars, Wellington was of Anglo-Irish descent and was notorious for his fierce opposition to reform. Yet he also knew the value of strategic retreat. Wellington's cabinet also soon fell apart, just prior to O'Connell's defeat of a government minister running in a by-election in County Clare in July 1828. Backed by a Nonconformist pressure group called the United Committee, Lord John Russell, one of several young Whig leaders, then proposed a bill that enabled Dissenting Protestants to hold office provided they swore to do nothing hostile to the Anglican Church. When the bill passed, the exclusion of Catholics appeared all the more anomalous. Thus Peel moved a bill for Catholic emancipation, upon similar terms, in March 1829 and Wellington, recognizing the danger of Irish rebellion, backed him, securing passage in both houses. Tory division, Whig endorsement of reform, and extra-parliamentary pressure would subsequently yield further reform in 1832.

By then revolution had re-appeared on the continent. When Artois succeeded to the throne as Charles X in September 1824, French ultraroyalists seemed to be in the ascendant. Unlike his predecessor, Charles at least looked like a king and he was known for his religious piety and devotion to his family. In Villèle he possessed a shrewd head of the government. Villèle had to cope with rivals whose noble lineage was more imposing than his own, but among ultraroyalist leaders he was the one most capable of binding ultraroyalists into a cohesive force. Better yet for the proponents of counter-revolution, many of the men who had implemented the White Terror of 1815–16 had returned to the Chamber of Deputies – such was the harvest of Liberal conspiracy in the early 1820s.

Triumph was perhaps too complete as ultraroyalists divided into factions based on personal ambition and differing views as to how far to push reaction. In his coronation of May 1825 Charles gave a sign of royal intent: ceremony was medieval in inspiration, with the King receiving sanctification by a Catholic bishop and then "curing" scrofula by the laying on of royal hands. Prior to each parliamentary session, Charles presented Villèle with a list of bills he wanted enacted. Émigrés who had lost lands during the Revolution should be compensated, inheritance laws should be altered so as to favor the eldest son (a step toward primogeniture), and individuals who desecrated sacred objects should be subject to capital punishment. The clerical nature of ultraroyalism could also be seen in increasing Church control over education and state approval of a missionary movement designed to re-Catholicize France.

Extremism provided opportunity. Liberals adopted a defensive posture: they were loyal to the dynasty and their sole wish was to preserve the regime by protecting the constitution from ultraroyalist onslaught. The danger was that the King had fallen under the spell of a clerical cabal. Although claims of theocratic conspiracy were highly exaggerated, they did possess a grain of truth in that a secret organization known as the Knights of the Faith enjoyed great influence in parliament and the government. More important was that legislation designed to favor the former privileged orders gave credence to allegations. Villèle was aware that support for royalism was eroding; he also knew that his position was weakened by factionalism and so he decided on a major gamble. To overcome opposition in the upper house, the King would elevate a large batch of loyal deputies to the Peers and elections would replenish the lower house.

Villèle had overlooked a crucial development in the spring of 1827 when parliament had passed a bill that gave the courts partial jurisdiction over disputes concerning the voter lists prepared by the administration. With the opportunity to redress corruption, Liberals reconstituted a grass-roots network that had been badly damaged in the early 1820s. A consequence was that the electorate grew by about a third. In the elections of November Liberals gained virtually the same number of seats as ultraroyalists, leaving the balance of power in the hands of moderate royalists. In December Villèle's cabinet gave way to one led by the Count de Martignac, who sought to build a centrist base. Unfortunately, in the following year Martignac ran aground when Liberals responded to proposed election of local officials by demanding a broader franchise than the King would grant. Unwilling to abide by strategies based on compromise, in August 1829 Charles appointed a cabinet led by the Prince de Polignac and thereby provoked a crisis. Polignac, an ultraroyalist who reputedly took his political advice from the Virgin Mary, could not pass legislation in a house wherein Liberals and moderate royalists held a majority. Rumors flew that the government would stage a *coup d'état* by refusing to convene parliament, or by revising the Charter by royal edict. When Charles opened the parliamentary session of 1830 with a threatening address, a majority of the deputies called on the King to appoint a new government.

Insistence that a government must be able to command majority support raised the issue of whether France really was a constitutional monarchy with genuine division of powers. Charles sought to resolve the impasse through elections and called on voters to support "loyal" candidates. In a bid to win popularity, the government also sent an expeditionary force to Algiers to "avenge" an incident in which a French diplomat had been struck with a fly swatter. Although the administration and Church threw themselves into the elections much as they had done under Villèle, they were hampered by a judiciary that blocked tampering with the voter lists and a disciplined Opposition strategy based on avoiding any sign of revolutionary intent. The result was the return of an Opposition majority in which Liberal numbers increased. Charles reacted with the July Ordinances, calling for new elections, narrowing the franchise to roughly a quarter of what it had been, and severely restricting the press. The result was three days of fighting that left roughly 150 soldiers and 500 civilians dead. Charles's ordinances had confirmed Opposition warnings of a *coup d'état*; nevertheless, mass rebellion surprised Liberals as much as it did the government.

Popular intervention resulted from material hardship and dislike of a regime still associated with defeat in 1814–15. Economic depression, high levels of unemployment, and a harsh winter had contributed to volatility. Workers in the publishing industry were directly threatened by the ordinance shutting down Liberal presses. Other workers hoped that a new regime would improve their plight, perhaps by price fixing or banishing foreign workers. Yet it was also true that former Napoleonic soldiers shouting "Long Live the Emperor" frequently joined middle-class former National Guardsmen and students in leading the elements of the populace that chose to fight. Although Napoleon had died in exile in 1821, Bonapartism remained powerful among the common people. Three key features then turned Parisian revolt into French revolution. After the initial fighting, the army took a neutral position. While the fighting was still ongoing, a group of Liberal deputies seized the initiative, hailing the popular revolt and creating a provisional government. As word of creation of the provisional government filtered through to the provinces, Liberal committees took over local government, generally without a fight.

In the immediate aftermath of the "three glorious days," Liberals and moderate royalists could agree on what they did not want. Given its association with Revolutionary violence, republicanism possessed few partisans. Moreover, restoration of either the Republic or a Bonapartist dynasty was virtually certain to trigger foreign intervention. Thus Liberals turned to the Duke d'Orléans, making him King by parliamentary vote on August 9. Cousin of the deposed Charles X, Orléans

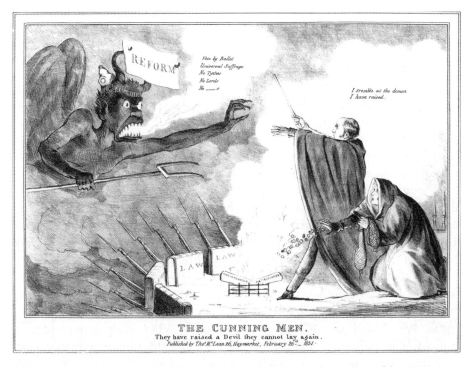

Figure 2.2   The Cunning Men, paper, lithograph, print by Robert Seymour (?), published by Thomas McLean, London, 1831. © The Trustees of the British Museum.

was the head of an illustrious aristocratic family that had aligned with the 1789 Revolution during its early liberal phase. Forced to take flight during the Terror, he had lived abroad until the fall of Napoleon. Despite his reluctance to ascend the throne, in some regards he was a logical choice for liberals and moderates. He was no advocate of violent revolution and would seek to restore order; yet he accepted the basic principles of 1789. Equally important, Orléans was keenly aware that the July Revolution had overthrown a regime installed by the other powers. To counter the threat of intervention, the new King shrewdly appointed Talleyrand as ambassador to Britain. Talleyrand set about reassuring the other powers that France would not seek territorial expansion and, crucially, he secured British recognition of the new regime.

Subsequent alteration of the electoral regime was less generous than radicals had hoped. The national electorate rose from perhaps 90 000 to 166 600 in 1831. Municipal and regional councils also became elective and better than two million men could vote for municipal councilors, but such councils possessed little power. Nevertheless, in other regards the July Revolution brought fundamental change. Louis-Philippe I would rule as King of the French rather than of France, a change of title that recognized national sovereignty, as did re-adoption of the Revolutionary flag, the *tricolore*. In appointing members of the upper house, the King would now select from candidates nominated by the Chambers, and peerage would no longer be hereditary. Catholicism was cited as the religion of the majority, rather than as the official religion of France.

Revolution soon spread and in terms of the states system the most important uprising occurred in the United Kingdom of the Netherlands. Wellington's reaction was typical: "It is a devilish bad business, the most serious affair for Europe that could have arisen."[24] For foreign statesmen what was important was that the United Kingdom had been created as a buffer against French expansion and thus the contentious issue of great power intervention again came to the fore.

Although the causes of revolt were largely the result of domestic politics, they also pointed to flaws within the Vienna Settlement crafted by the powers. The Protestant Dutch King William I tended to rule by executive resolution rather than by passing laws through parliament and several of his measures were unpopular in the Belgian provinces of the south. Creation of state secondary schools produced resentment among Catholic clergymen, as did plans to regulate private Catholic schools. Initially Belgian liberals applauded secularizing measures; thereafter they too were alienated by language policies that sought to replace French with Dutch in all official business. When William responded to criticism with censorship and press trials, liberals and Catholics joined to form the Union, a pressure group modeled on the Irish Catholic Association. A petition campaign for freedom of the press and education gained some 70 000 signatures in December 1829, and another calling for ministerial responsibility achieved the impressive figure of 360 000 in February 1830. Thereafter William offered concessions, but in late August tumult began when a performance at the Brussels opera featured verse such as "Sacred love of our fatherland restore to us our daring and our pride."[25]

Insurgency was also fueled by economic distress. A combination of bad harvests and industrial overproduction had led to bankruptcies and unemployment, sharpening resentment at state taxes. Due to fear of French invasion in the aftermath of the July Revolution, William had concentrated his forces along the frontier, and hence the government could not stop a wave of attacks on government offices and machine smashing in factories. At Brussels the bourgeoisie formed a civil militia to restore order and took over local government. Liberals who dominated the city council then sent the King a list of grievances, including a demand that Belgium be administered separately from Holland. Belgian resistance only hardened when the army tried to take Brussels back in late September. The attack was repulsed amidst fierce fighting, with several hundred lives lost on either side, and the army then fell into disarray as Belgian officers and soldiers deserted. At Brussels an administrative commission assumed the title of provisional government for all the Belgian provinces and called for election of a Constituent Assembly. An array of middle-class deputies then transformed Belgium into a constitutional monarchy with a bicameral parliament.

William called on the powers to reverse the revolution in September. Tsar Nicholas was all for intervention, but Prussia and Austria had revolts closer to home to occupy them and soon Russia would also be distracted by insurgency. Thus at the London Conference in November the powers placed priority on stabilizing the region so as to forestall any designs the French might have on Belgium. In December the powers recognized the separation of the Belgian provinces while stipulating that Belgium must remain neutral in foreign relations. Dissatisfied by the territorial settlement proposed in January 1831, the Belgians initially offered the throne to a son of Louis-Philippe. The new French King did not want, however, to antagonize the other powers and rejected the offer on behalf of his son. Belgian leaders then turned to Leopold of Saxe-Coburg, a more acceptable choice. William attacked again in August 1831 and, much to everyone's surprise, the Belgian army collapsed. Thereafter a French expedition, acting with British approval, intervened to secure Belgian independence, recognized and guaranteed by the great powers in the Treaty of London of November 15, 1831.

There is dispute among historians over the extent to which continental revolution had bearing on the passage of the British Great Reform Act of 1832.[26] Judging by the comments of contemporaries ranging from Wellington to the veteran Whig leader Lord Charles Grey, it would appear that events on the continent did stimulate the British reform movement in the summer and fall of 1830, but that long-term domestic developments and skilful political maneuvering were at least as important to the final outcome. Reformers demanded two basic changes: the franchise should be broadened and made consistent among electoral constituencies, and seats should be distributed so as to reflect population. Radical demand for rationalization had greatly increased due to the efforts of the Union for Parliamentary Reform and Cobbett's *Political Register*. Cobbett's journal specialized in exposing electoral corruption, and the Political Unions, led by wealthy businessmen, acted in a manner similar to the Irish Catholic Association. While the Whigs and the Political Unions viewed each other with mistrust, the Unions did help secure Whig electoral victories and their growing presence could be used by Grey as a warning of the danger of doing nothing.

Adding to perception that change was necessary was severe economic distress, especially in southern rural England, which experienced a wave of arson and destruction of threshing machines. Suppressed in April 1830, the "Captain Swing" riots sharpened the public's sense of crisis. Elections in July–August 1830 revealed the weakening Tory position as the opposition gained roughly fifty seats, and shortly after Wellington made clear his refusal to endorse reform, the government lost a vote of confidence and Wellington resigned.

That power was finely balanced could be seen thereafter in the composition of a new government led by Grey. Young Whigs set the agenda in a coalition that included Radicals and reforming Tories formerly associated with the recently deceased Canning. Convinced by Grey, George IV gave his support to a Reform Act drawn up by a committee on which Russell was prominent. The objective of the bill was to rally middle-class support, or as the committee put it in typically liberal terms: "to satisfy all reasonable demands, and remove at once, and for ever, all rational grounds for complaint from the minds of the intelligent and independent portion of the community."[27] Presented in March 1831, the bill passed the lower house by the narrowest of margins, but subsequent Tory obstruction led Grey to resign and the King to dissolve parliament. Amidst a series of riots, public opinion spoke clearly in favor of reform during the elections of May–June 1831. Passage of a similar Reform Act was thereafter easily secured in the Commons, only to be blocked by the Lords, producing more extensive riots. A period of disorder triggered by a second Grey resignation in May 1832 then convinced Wellington to support reform tacitly by refusing to vote, and forced the King to promise Grey that he would appoint new Lords to pass the legislation should the current house continue to block passage. At that point enough Lords gave in that the Great Reform Act passed on June 4, 1832.

Revision was substantial. Reducing the number of MPs elected by 143 boroughs and transferring the seats to more populous boroughs or counties improved representation. Qualification for voting was made more consistent, though not uniform, and the franchise was extended. The electorate for England and Wales rose from roughly 435 000 to 653 000. In Scotland the franchise expanded from a mere 4579 to 64 447, whereas in poverty-ridden Ireland the increase was only from 75 960 to 92 152. Thus although Britain had again moved in advance of the continent, the regime was far from democratic. All the same, the Tory grip on government had been broken and the authority of the Commons had been enhanced, energizing radicalism.

In the European context, the constitutional monarchies were exceptional in three principal regards: levels of political participation, national coordination of opposition or reform movements, and the ability of elite groups to canalize popular discontent into demand for political change. On their own these three elements were not, however, sufficient to ensure lasting change – the issue of foreign intervention could prove crucial.

Resistance to Change in South, Central, and East Europe

In some regards 1830 was a dress rehearsal for 1848 as revolution in France triggered revolt elsewhere. Nevertheless, conflict was far greater at mid century. Opposition to oppressive or incompetent government was growing, but in the early 1830s it was seldom strong enough to challenge the political order successfully.

In the German Confederation levels of political participation were extremely limited. In the most liberal of states, Baden, the principle of national sovereignty was recognized in that members of parliament swore to represent the interests of all subjects rather than a particular estate. Yet Baden was similar to the other constitutional regimes in that government control of elections meant that parliament exercised little independent power. Censorship ensured that political considerations were confined to expensive academic books as police agents clamped down on pamphlets and newspapers, and sought to prevent political discussion in associations and clubs. It was, however, impossible to block the emergence of political culture entirely. Writers found ways to evade censorship through indirect allusion and allegedly nonpolitical subject matter could be turned to political effect. In certain states news could be gained from foreign journals, and banned writings could be disseminated clandestinely. Nor could governments prevent Germans from gathering in coffee houses, wine shops, or cultural clubs. In such venues associations could be formed that might provide the nucleus for more overtly political activity. Even so, the emerging political public remained confined to educated and economic elites and liberalism developed as essentially a middle-class movement. The vast majority had little interest in such matters. To the extent that they participated, through collective protest over economic issues, the masses remained solely concerned by local interests.

Certain patterns were apparent in the turbulence that followed news of the July Revolution. By and large, the constitutional south German states were free of violence. Nevertheless, opposition candidates gained stronger support in elections and were able to force governments to grant broader freedom of expression. In the Bavarian Palatinate, the Press and Fatherland Association mobilized opinion through formation of 116 affiliated clubs, pamphlet publication, and petition organization. In May 1832 the Association organized a festival of liberty held at Hambach. Some 20 000 listened to speakers call for a united German democratic state.

Elsewhere hardship sparked riots: the targets might be manorial rights, as in Upper Hesse, mechanization, as at Leipzig, high state taxes, as in Hanover, or the presence of Jews virtually anywhere. Middle-class elements might initially sympathize with popular distress, but when demonstrations degenerated into looting they frequently repressed the rioters, forming militias to impose order. In certain instances disorder inspired rallying to the regime; however, middle-class groups frequently used their role in suppressing disorder to press for reform – at Kassel they claimed that a constitution was necessary to avoid a "war waged by the poor against the rich."[28] At times rulers had made themselves unpopular through particular policies, such as the favoritism shown by King Anton to the Jesuits in largely Lutheran Saxony. By flaunting his mistress, William II had antagonized popular and elite elements already angered by his lavish spending on the court and army in Hesse-Kassel.

What was the upshot? Most governments rode out the storm. In Saxony, Hanover, and Brunswick officials convinced rulers to grant constitutions similar to those already in place in South Germany, and in Hesse-Kassel the estates met as a single chamber with extensive legislative and financial powers. Nevertheless, even in these states political change was more formal than real; in practice rulers found ways to evade responsible government. Urged on by Metternich, in 1832 the German Confederation approved measures that signaled a return to reaction, and established that federal law overruled state law. Confederation troops occupied the Palatinate, and concessions were retracted. In April 1833 a coup attempt at Frankfurt by students and teachers from Heidelberg provided a pretext for intensified censorship and police surveillance throughout Germany. At Hanover King Ernst August responded to protests against another purge of the universities with the comment that "professors and whores can always be had for money."[29] What little freedom existed thus was confined to weak parliaments largely isolated from the public. Only Duke Karl of Brunswick was brought down, and even in this instance the Confederation's Federal Diet approved of the transfer of power to Karl's brother, William.

In contrast, revolutionaries in central Italy established new regimes that claimed sovereignty, necessitating military intervention by Austria. Although crowds occasionally carried the Italian *tricolore* of green, white, and red, insurrection was more a product of local grievance than desire for national unification.

Frustrated by the reactionary nature of government under the newly elected Pope Gregory XVI, liberals in Modena, Parma and the Papal Legations began revolts that soon spread to the Marches and Umbria. Economic grievances were linked to political factors: the restoration of internal customs barriers had hampered commercial and industrial development, and high taxes went toward funding extravagant courts. Dissatisfaction was most acute in the Papal States, where secular elite and middle-class elements wanted to participate in government and were deeply alarmed by the regime's inability to provide social order as economic dislocation and population growth combined to create what seemed a tidal wave of urban and rural crime. Metternich pressed the government to include local notables in the administration, but Cardinal Bernetti, Pope Gregory's Secretary of State, refused, arguing that any compromise with secular interests would undermine the divine nature of Papal rule.

By no means did revolt in February 1831 carry all before it. While some towns joined in rebellion, others did not, and much of the countryside remained neutral or hostile. In Parma the leaders of revolt hesitated; a provisional government hoped to force concessions upon Marie-Louise rather than overthrow her. At Modena the Grand Duke lost control due mostly to his failure of nerve. Bologna, where the urban elite could tap into lower-class discontent, was, however, another matter and revolt in the Papal States soon spread all the way to Rome. At Bologna a provisional government organized an Assembly of Notables from towns that had overthrown Papal authority, and the Assembly then proclaimed a new state entitled the United Provinces of Italy. Thereafter the provisional government began to lay plans for a constituent assembly and organized forces for an attack on Rome. However, by late March 1831 Austrian troops had arrived and they rapidly snuffed out the revolts.

Despite the hopes of revolutionaries that the French would block Austrian intervention, Louis-Philippe had no desire to associate his fledgling regime with destabilization of the states system. Thus no military aid was forthcoming, although at a conference of the powers from April to June 1831 the French pressed the Papacy to grant reforms. Bernetti instead focused on creating a volunteer army after Austrian troops had departed. By January 1832 the volunteer army was sufficiently organized that Bernetti could dispatch a force of some 5000 to deal with liberal agitation. Papal troops rapidly defeated liberal forces and then ran amuck, sacking several towns. Austrian troops had to return to restore order, and this time the French sent a task force to Ancona. However, the French merely retained control of Ancona until 1838, when they and the Austrians withdrew from the Papal States. In the meantime the Vatican had instigated another round of repression. Opposition thus was again driven underground. For Metternich the situation was worrisome. Revolution made the Italian regimes all the more dependent on Austrian diplomacy and military force, but refusal to reform meant that trouble could only grow.

Rebellion in Poland had more to do with desire to end Russian domination than demand for social or political revolution. In Poland the roughly 300 000 relatively poor nobles known as the *szlachta* found that Russian rulers refused to recognize their pretensions to special status, and they were hit hard by a slump in international grain prices. With their economic positions declining, Polish nobles were all the more irritated that the constitutional rights they thought they had gained at the start of the Restoration proved meaningless. When in 1820 a couple of liberal parliamentary deputies had criticized the government for muzzling freedom of expression, Tsar Alexander had deprived them of their seats, increased the extra-constitutional powers of Grand Duke Constantine, and refused to convoke another parliament until 1825. Relations had deteriorated further thereafter under Nicholas, partly because several Poles were loosely linked to the Decembrist revolt. When the Polish Senate had failed to convict the accused of treason, Nicholas had annulled the verdict so that the accused were transported to Siberia.

In combination with news of revolution abroad, Nicholas's plan to mobilize troops for a foray into west Europe encouraged a group of army cadets to plot revolt. Nevertheless, the immediate cause of riot in Warsaw in late November 1830 was economic crisis exacerbated by a cholera epidemic. Wanting to avoid bloodshed and hopeful that his Polish Administrative Council would restore order, Constantine withdrew with his Russian troops beyond the border. Far from fulfilling Constantine's expectations, the Council then transformed itself into a governing Executive Commission and sought to extract concessions from Nicholas.

Antagonism escalated as a Russian invasion force assembled in January 1831, and the Polish *Sejm* voted to depose the Romanov dynasty. In February a hastily established government mobilized the Polish army and supplemented it with volunteers so that it numbered 85 000 men. Yet the odds were stacked against the Poles. Attempts to find a European dynasty willing to provide a constitutional monarch ran aground against fear of angering Russia. The refusal of the *szlachta*-dominated *Sejm* to reduce serfdom then ensured that there would be no mass rallying to the new regime. Divisions between radical elements of the *szlachta* and more cautious members of the government and the military command compounded problems and after savage Russian artillery bombardment Warsaw capitulated in September 1831.

The fact that the Poles inflicted serious losses on the Russian army exacerbated retribution. Executions, land confiscation, closure of many Catholic monasteries and nunneries, and banishment of perhaps 80 000 Polish or Lithuanian nobles followed. By tying down Russian forces, the Poles had undermined the ability of Nicholas to push for intervention in the Netherlands, but the costs were high. Congress Poland lost her separate status, constitution, parliament, and army. Russian replaced Polish as the official language, and Poland was placed under Russian-administered martial law. Poland's plight resulted from two vital factors. Despite widespread public sympathy in the west, it was not in the geostrategic interests of the constitutional monarchies to intervene and run the risk of war with the eastern autocracies, all of which had Polish subjects. Without outside aid, the chances of Polish liberation were slender. Worse still, Polish nationalism was almost exclusively the domain of the elite. When the nobility refused to make social or political concessions to the peasant masses the faint possibility of gaining independence disappeared altogether.

Thus the period constituted only a partial success for the statesmen who at the Congress of Vienna had sought to provide stability. The powers had avoided military conflict among themselves but domestic stability had proved more elusive. If revolution achieved lasting change only in France, Belgium, and Greece, revolutionary forces had challenged regimes in Spain, the Italian states, the German states, Russia, and Poland, and there was little reason to presume that matters were settled. Provided they agreed among themselves, the autocracies could stamp out revolts within their spheres of influence. The west was, however, more problematic, given the influence of Britain and France. Nor could liberal contagion be easily confined to the west as communications improved and ideas spread more rapidly.

Demand for change was growing and it sprang from several sources. Desire to be free of foreign domination existed in many countries. Nationalism was, however, in its infancy in most states and was seldom a mass phenomenon. Liberalism, with its emphasis on representative government and calls for freedom of opinion, expression, association, and assembly, was a more obvious challenge to reactionary or conservative regimes. Contemporary liberals were seldom democrats; most believed that political rights should be restricted to men of education and property. If in this regard liberals took a restrictive view of political rights, they nevertheless were fierce critics of privilege. Liberals charged that Restoration regimes were run solely in the interests of the landowning nobility and the upper reaches of the clergy.

While it brandished a stick, liberalism also offered a carrot to Restoration regimes. The stick was apparent in France and Belgium, where monarchs were overthrown due to refusal to compromise with opposition movements. Revolution succeeded partly due to popular unrest, partly because governments had lost the support of part of the socioeconomic elite, and partly because the British opposed repressive intervention by the eastern autocracies. In contrast, by grasping the liberal carrot, Britain managed substantial political change without undergoing revolution. From the standpoint of many Whig reformers, the objective of extending the franchise was less one of recognizing legitimate claims than of buttressing the regime by bringing greater numbers within it and thereby ensuring their loyalty. Liberal emphasis upon capacity meant that an increasing number would have to be included in direct political participation, but a far greater number would remain excluded. There thus were opportunities for compromise with liberalism that conservatives might, or might not, grasp.

Britain was exceptional in possessing a set of institutions and practices that in combination made reform a viable alternative. Parliament and the party system could respond to demand, and demand could be expressed through a free press and organizations acting as pressure groups. Westminster thus served as the focus of debate on national policy, and a good deal of legislation was initially promoted by pressure groups. Despite continued use of patronage to sway voters, voting was largely free of the control exercised by continental governments. Though to a lesser degree, France possessed similar resources for adjusting political systems to social and economic change. Elsewhere, however, the development of civil society remained less advanced as conservative or reactionary regimes sought to preserve order through narrow restrictions on political liberty and repression of those who advocated it.[30]

3

Stability, Stasis
or Decay?
Europe from 1830 to 1848

During the period between the revolutions of 1830 and 1848 peace among the
powers continued. Due to the rhetoric used by leading statesmen, many people
thought that a cultural Cold War divided Europe between the liberal constitutional
monarchies of the west and the autocracies of the east. Historical analysis reveals,
however, that geostrategic imperatives repeatedly trumped ideological considerations in the major confrontations of the era. Partly because four of the powers
shared belief that France remained the chief threat to the states system, the
Concert of Europe held up well despite numerous sources of friction.

In domestic politics liberalism and nationalism continued to spread. They were
not yet an immediate danger to the eastern autocracies, although they did require
increasing state response. It was in Spain and the Italian states that they created
serious problems and the consequence was instability. Liberalism and nationalism
could also pose challenges to the constitutional monarchies of the west, where
politics was further complicated by the emergence of what came to be known as
the "social question." Perhaps the most striking answer to the "social question" was
the new ideology coined socialism. Early socialism gained only a small following
and was not very threatening to the political status quo, but the "social question"
did trigger impassioned debate over what the function of government should be.

Structural Sources of Stability in Inter-State Relations

Why did peace prevail among the powers? Before we turn to specific developments
we can point to several long-term causes that contributed to stability. Memories of
the carnage of the Revolutionary-Napoleonic Wars remained fresh and the costs
involved were still apparent in the financial debts states were obliged to carry.

Europe's Uncertain Path 1814–1914: State Formation and Civil Society, First Edition. R. S. Alexander.
© 2012 R. S. Alexander. Published 2012 by Blackwell Publishing Ltd.

Similarly, statesmen were well aware that foreign war might trigger turmoil at home. Perhaps most importantly, three of the powers (Russia, Britain, and Austria) favored retention of the status quo. While France and Prussia might have wished further revision of the Vienna Settlement, neither was in a position to pursue it.

Perception counts a lot in politics. With an army of roughly 826 000, Russia seemed a colossus. Yet during the Turkish War of 1828–29 Nicholas had found that only 181 000 men were available for campaigning because most soldiers were tied down by provision of security on Russia's vast frontiers and policing in the interior. Mobilization and transportation of Russian forces were painfully slow and took a high toll on relatively limited state revenues. Once assembled, the quality of the rank and file was notoriously poor. Conscription was conducted by peasant communes and, not surprisingly, the village elders made a point of selecting the least promising of men for what, in effect, was a life sentence of 25 years of service. The quality of the navy was also relatively low. Nicholas and his advisors were well aware of these shortcomings and hence their conduct was more cautious than might have been expected.

British policy-makers also confronted limitations. Britain was the first industrial power, was extending her global commercial and financial domination, and had no serious rivals in overseas expansion. Yet Britain was guided by *laissez faire* liberalism and belief that government should be kept to a minimum; there was little likelihood that economic assets would be fully mobilized for pursuit of military-strategic power. Conscription was never seriously discussed and parliament was stingy over funding. Most of the armed forces of roughly 140 000 were stationed far from Britain, and the Royal Navy could not be everywhere, although it was highly active in attacking piracy and the slave trade. All the same, the navy was vastly superior to those of the other powers, and it could concentrate British forces relatively quickly. Perhaps the other powers overestimated British military capacity, or perhaps the fear of Anglo-French alliance drove them into the arms of the British; one way or another, the other powers frequently sought association with Britain, giving Henry Temple, Viscount Palmerston, opportunities to exploit. A pugilist by nature, Palmerston possessed the chauvinism of many nationalists; he believed that the interests of Britain and humanity were one and the same. Nevertheless, Britain's interests lay in preservation of the status quo on the continent and so Palmerston's conduct was less disruptive than it might have been.

France possessed an army of some 259 000 men, and the "Spanish Promenade" of 1823 and intervention on behalf of Belgian independence in 1831 had demonstrated that the French could act forcefully. Nevertheless, French governments were constrained by fear of reuniting the Allied coalition of 1813–15. Orleanist statesmen were also aware that the revolutionary tiger had fed on war in the past, and hence the regime tended to pursue pacific policies. Moreover France was a hybrid power, with interests both on the continent and overseas. France possessed Europe's second leading army and second ranked navy and her statesmen hesitated over priorities.

Metternich also feared the domestic impact of foreign war. Many Austrian officials worried about the loyalty of the various national groups within the Empire, but a more fundamental problem was that the Emperor could not afford a prolonged conflict due to limited financial resources. Of a nominal army of 273 000, only about half were actually in service and any pretence to naval power had been surrendered when Francis sold his recently acquired Venetian fleet to Denmark. The Empire possessed assets: the other powers saw Austria as crucial to stability, and the army could crush revolutionary movements. While the conservative role of the Empire might elicit approval from Nicholas, refusal to reform could, however, undermine sympathy from the western powers.

Prussia was not yet positioned to oust Austrian leadership within the German Confederation. Despite universal conscription, the Prussian army was only 130 000 men strong and Austria enjoyed extensive political support among the smaller German states. A combination of factors did, however, favor an increasingly forward policy. The quality of the Prussian army became exceptionally high as expansion of education prepared soldiers better suited to training and a reforming General Staff carefully studied advances in transport and weaponry. Moreover the apparent revival of French power in 1823 had heightened insecurity among the smaller German states and encouraged entry into a Prussian-dominated customs union called the *Zollverein*. Thereafter conflicts in the Balkans and Italy lessened the ability of Austria to pose as the chief protector of the Confederation, especially during the international tensions that accompanied the revolutions of 1830. Metternich responded with more apparent hostility to the new French regime, but it was Prussia that could provide 80 000 troops for defence of the Confederation. Despite lingering doubts over Prussian intentions, in March 1831 King Ludwig of Bavaria wrote: "I am convinced that safety is only to be found in a firm connection with Prussia."[31]

The Thin Veneer of Ideology

In the 1820s British denunciation of foreign intervention by the other powers had sounded like a matter of principle. All the same, in January 1827 foreign minister Canning had sent an expeditionary force to Lisbon to prevent the reactionary Dom Miguel, regent for his seven-year-old niece Queen Maria II, from seizing the throne of Portugal. Dom Miguel had then promised to respect the Portuguese constitution and the troops had been withdrawn in April 1828. When Dom Miguel subsequently broke his promise, Palmerston allowed Dom Pedro, Maria's father and former monarch of both Portugal and Brazil, to recruit an army in Britain. Defeat of Dom Miguel's fleet off Cape St Vincent thereafter enabled Dom Pedro's army to take Lisbon and reinstall Maria on the throne in September 1833, although Dom Miguel's land forces remained in the field.

So perhaps the underlining ideal was the advancement of what Canning termed "legal-constitutional" (liberal) regimes? By 1833 the Portuguese succession crisis had merged with a similar one in Spain. Prior to his fourth marriage, to Maria Christina in 1829, Ferdinand VII had not produced an heir, giving rise to expectation that his brother Don Carlos would succeed to the throne. Maria then bore Ferdinand two daughters (Isabel and Luisa Fernanda) and in June 1833 she convinced the King to set aside the Salic law that prohibited succession through the female line. When Ferdinand died three months later, Britain and France recognized the regency government of Maria Christina, but Don Carlos and his supporters (Carlists) did not. Instead Don Carlos joined forces with Dom Miguel in Portugal.

To fend off Carlism, Maria Christina needed to secure support from Spanish moderates and liberals. Hence there was apparent ideological consistency when in April 1834 the governments of Britain, France, Spain, and Portugal formed the Quadruple Alliance to expel Dom Miguel from Portugal. There also was a crusading tone to Palmerston's pronouncements: "England, France, Spain and Portugal … will form a political and moral power in Europe which will hold Metternich and Nicholas in check."[32] When read alongside declarations by the autocratic powers, particularly in the Berlin Convention of October 1833, of determination to defend dynastic rights against constitutional reform, such rhetoric suggested that Europe had divided into two camps.

Yet the Quadruple Alliance indicated no great trust between the two powers: Spain would provide troops to help oust Dom Miguel, Britain would provide naval support, and France would send troops only if asked. After Dom Miguel was defeated, in 1834 Don Carlos unleashed civil war in Spain. Maria Christina then asked the French for aid, and the French in turn asked the British for a guarantee of support in the event that intervention triggered war with the eastern powers. Palmerston, however, wanted to prevent the French from gaining influence in Iberia and hence Louis-Philippe had to settle for allowing 4,000 members of the Foreign Legion to volunteer for service. The British responded by permitting recruitment of a 10 000-strong volunteer legion. Ultimately the Spanish government largely on its own overcame the Carlists after six years of struggle. Thereafter neither Iberian regime proved stable or especially liberal. In fact further British intervention to secure an increasingly reactionary regime at Lisbon in 1846 more or less put paid to pretensions of liberal idealism.

By then developments in the Near East had made the pragmatic character of inter-state relations even more obvious. Disappointed that he had gained little during the war of Greek independence, Pasha Muhammad Ali began to exploit the weakness of the Ottoman Empire, expanding Egyptian control into the Sudan and Arabia, and demanding that Mahmud II give him Syria in 1831. When the Sultan refused, Muhammad Ali launched an assault that rapidly drove the Turkish army out of Syria and by December 1832 even threatened Constantinople. All of the powers were deeply interested in these developments; temptation to exploit collapse of the Empire might draw them into direct conflict, or at least alter the balance of power. France stood most to gain by Egyptian expansion, but the last thing Palmerston wanted was a French client state occupying the land routes to India. Given their current engagements in Iberia and the Netherlands, neither of the western powers was, however, well positioned to respond to the crisis, and so it was Russia that seized the initiative.

Extreme peril called for desperate remedies and Mahmud turned to Nicholas, who dispatched warships and troops to Constantinople in early 1833. Well placed to extract concessions, Nicholas played a subtle game. Muhammad Ali would be granted lifetime control over Syria, and the Ottomans were offered a defensive alliance. By the terms of the Treaty of Unkiar-Skelessi, signed in July 1833, Russia would defend Ottoman "independence," and the sultan would close the Straits of the Dardanelles to all ships of foreign states at war with Russia. In a subsequent gesture of good will, Russia withdrew her troops from the Danubian Principalities and canceled reparations stipulated by the previous Treaty of Adrianople. Seemingly magnanimous, Russia thereby secured her interests nicely. The threat posed by Muhammad Ali had not been removed and Turkey remained dependent, giving Russia a dominant influence for future preservation, or destruction, of the Empire. Closure of the Straits would also secure Russian primacy in the Black Sea.

By eschewing territorial acquisition Russia reduced the danger that the other powers might intervene. Nevertheless, Nicholas believed it necessary to shore up Russia's position with approval from the other eastern powers. Reassured by Nicholas's withdrawal of garrisons in the Danubian Principalities, Austria and Prussia then joined Russia in declaring their intent to act in concert concerning the future of the Ottoman Empire. Metternich hoped, however, that the Berlin Declaration might mark a first stage in a process wherein all five powers would reach an accord over Turkey, thereby undermining Russian predominance. Although Palmerston rebuffed Metternich's proposals along these lines, the British and French continued to suspect that Russia planned to seize control of the Straits.

Given the apparent friendship of Russia, it was understandable that Mahmud thought the time had come for dealing with his upstart pasha. Sadly for him, an attack on Egyptian forces in Syria in April 1839 led to a series of defeats. Perhaps it was a blessing that he died before news of these calamities reached his ears, but his sixteen-year-old son Abdul Medjid was left in dire straits. Once again Russian moderation ensured the avoidance of war among the powers. Metternich began the process of collective response by convincing the other powers to join in July 1839 in a statement declaring their intention to resolve the conflict. Wishing to avoid being ensnared by the attempts of Metternich to direct a five-power conference, and especially alarmed by the possibility of France and Britain acting in concert, Russia then reached out directly to the British. Russia would allow the Treaty of Unkiar-Skelessi to be replaced with an international convention whereby the Dardanelles would be closed to all warships during peacetime. Muhammad Ali would be recognized as the hereditary ruler of Egypt, provided that he gave up his recent acquisitions. Although this package would secure Russian domination of the Black Sea, it would restore the status quo in the Mediterranean and the Ottoman Empire more generally, partly by reducing the advances made by France's Egyptian ally. Thus Russian proposals were well calibrated to British interests and the Austrians and Prussians had little choice but to tag along.

The Concert of Europe then reached a critical juncture in July 1840 when France refused to join in presenting Muhammad Ali with an ultimatum that he could maintain hereditary rule in Egypt, and rule over southern Syria for his lifetime; but that failure to agree would mean loss of all of Syria. Adolphe Thiers, first minister of the cabinet, then resorted to saber rattling by mobilizing troops and alluding to a possible attack across the Rhine. The French position was, however, untenable and Palmerston refused "to be daunted by big words and empty vapouring."[33] After a brief bout of patriotic vertigo, Louis-Philippe came to his senses and made clear that no attack was in the offing, thereby enabling Thiers to resign and evade responsibility for his folly. French humiliation increased as Allied forces and internal revolt combined to expel the Egyptians from Syria, forcing Muhammad Ali to capitulate so that he could at least retain Egypt. After the dust had settled, the French were marginally appeased by inclusion in negotiation of the Straits Convention of July 1841, which closed the Straits to foreign warships when Turkey was not at war. All the same, the Egyptian Crisis had demonstrated how little ideological affinities counted against material interests.

The Egyptian Crisis was linked to several other major developments. Concern to recover prestige could be seen in a new French determination to conquer Algeria. Whereas previous expansion beyond coastal cities had been minimal, in late 1840 a large military expedition began a program of conquest in the interior. Clashes with Algerian forces soon spiraled into hostilities with the Sultan of Morocco, who sheltered resistance leaders. More importantly for the European states system, British officials grew alarmed by the prospect of France gaining possession of the Moroccan coast and contesting British control of the Straits of Gibraltar. Fortunately the French and Moroccans settled their dispute by fixing the boundary between Algeria and Morocco in March 1845.

Another indication of the pre-eminence of strategic considerations could be seen in the complex character of relations between Russia and Britain during and immediately following the Egyptian Crisis. Russia had gained predominant influence in Persia by 1828, leading British officials to imagine that Russia had designs on India. To forestall any such threat the British sought to turn Afghanistan into a client state by backing a coup against the reigning Khan in April 1839. Although the coup initially succeeded, the attempt to establish a stable buffer regime then failed amidst chaotic tribal politics, forcing the British to withdraw by the summer of 1842. Nevertheless, the point from our perspective is that Britain was pursuing an overtly anti-Russian policy in one theater, while cooperating with Russia over the Ottoman Empire. Moreover, partly in a bid to restore prestige, and partly due to ongoing suspicion, the British went on to annex Sind in 1843 and the Punjab in 1849.

Utopian Socialism

Socialism first gained notice in the 1830s and 1840s. Karl Marx later termed the early variants "utopian" in order to distinguish them from his own "scientific" socialism and the label has become common. Utopian socialists responded to the "social question" – what to do about the poor families in the towns and cities where industrialization was taking root? Preoccupation with the new proletariat resulted partly from sympathy for men, women, and children residing and working in degrading conditions, and partly from fear that such conditions created "aliens" who shared none of society's values. Living conditions were perhaps worse in rural areas, but the novelty of vast numbers of migrants concentrated in rapidly growing urban slums captured public imagination.

Writers such as Robert Owen, Charles Fourier, and Henri de Saint-Simon argued for a new organization of society. They criticized current economic systems for placing too much emphasis on production, and not enough on distribution, and attributed extremes of wealth distribution to excessive pursuit of self-interest. In place of the free market, they proposed to organize society on the basis of cooperation. Marx considered them utopian partly because they sought change without resort to force, and partly because they viewed poverty primarily in moral terms. Like most of their contemporaries, utopians had been repelled by the violence of the Revolution of 1789, and they rejected the Jacobin tradition of insurrection. Instead they relied on persuasion, linking their arguments to concepts of fraternity, social justice, or Christian brotherhood, and setting up ideal communities as models. While collective responsibility for material welfare was a key to their creed, utopians were not necessarily communist; neither Saint-Simon nor Fourier believed that all land should be collectivized, or that everyone should have an equal amount of property, although all should have enough to provide for their needs.

Diversity was characteristic of socialism from the onset. Saint-Simon's vision would prove highly influential among state planners; he believed that production should be rationally organized by a governing elite of scientists and priests. Fourier proposed the creation of cooperatives in which work would be distributed according to individual characteristics or affinities. Unlike Saint-Simon and Fourier, who needed patrons to put their plans into action, Owen was an industrialist with the means to demonstrate his theories. In the early 1800s Owen bought a cotton mill at New Lanark, Scotland, and set about running it and the attached town on cooperative principles. The results were impressive in that a town with miserable living conditions was converted into a model community with outstanding educational facilities. Whether the transformation could be attributed to cooperative principles or the fact that Owen sunk a lot of money into the venture, was, however, a matter of dispute. Worse still, attempts by Owen and the French utopians to set up ideal communities in America proved disastrous. Nevertheless, Owen's ideas on the value of labor, recognition that mechanization could benefit workers, identification of dangers in the division of labor, and work on behalf of consumer cooperatives did prove highly influential.

Owen had little success in convincing others to follow his example, and French manufacturers were similarly unmoved by utopian arguments. Still, small bands of middle-class disciples of Saint-Simon and Fourier did develop; they sought to spread, and alter, the original message. Without quite reaching full equality, the Saint-Simonians and Fourierists were far in advance of their times in advocating rights for women. Fourier, for example, claimed that "the best nations have always been those which concede the greatest amount of liberty to women."[34] Although Fourier's notions of emancipation from the chains of marriage through "free love" probably did more harm than good to his cause, important advocates of women's rights such as Jeanne Déroin gained political experience within utopian movements. Etienne Cabet, a highly paternalist utopian whose journal le Populaire was widely read among Parisians, developed a stronger following among the artisan males who formed the core of early socialism.

Consolidation and the Constitutional Monarchies: Britain and France in the 1830s

The regimes of Britain and France were similar in structure, but they existed in differing contexts. While the British could read bone-chilling accounts of the Revolutionary Jacobin Terror, they had not experienced it as the French had done. In France foundation of the July Monarchy in 1830 gave rise to great hopes of reform, and immediately thereafter civil disorder fanned fears that enabled conservatives to bring reform to a halt. Meanwhile the British managed to combine a more generous franchise with an impressive body of legislation. The Whigs responded to public expectation that the government would assume responsibility for social legislation, and as government activism increased, bills initiated by private members declined.

After passage of the Great Reform Act, the election of 1832 yielded a large crop of new British MPs. The Whigs and Radicals gained what seemed an overwhelming victory, and some observers thought the Tories had entered into terminal decline. In the event, over the next nine years Robert Peel oversaw a steady recovery of Tory fortunes. He did so by making clear that he accepted the new status quo, and that he was willing to consider further reform. Peel thus took a stance that was calculated to encourage moderate Whigs to stand up against Radical demands, thereby fostering division in the Whig-Radical alliance. The cabinets that dominated the remainder of the 1830s did pass important reforms, but their achievements were insufficient to appease Radical critics, and tactical alliance with O'Connell's Irish MPs caused Grey and the Whig leadership as many problems as it provided solutions.

Several broad trends gave politics a modern cast. Peel's Tamworth Manifesto of December 1834 pointed to advance in party formation. The organization of party clubs at London and party associations in the boroughs and counties, increasing use of party whips and patronage secretaries, appointment of electoral managers at the national and local levels, annual monitoring of electoral registers, and fund raising all contributed to the emergence of an increasingly coherent party system. Another shift could be seen in increased state regulation. In part this trend could be attributed to the influence of Jeremy Bentham's philosophy of utilitarianism, which held that government should be active in promoting the greater good for the greatest number. However, it also derived from increased professionalism in the conduct of government; 1832 began an era of investigative commissions that increasingly were led by experts such as the Benthamite Edwin Chadwick. The findings of the commissions were published in Blue Books that incited public commentary, spread political consciousness, and informed legislation.

Britain was the first nation to undergo industrial revolution and initially it was in Britain that concern over the "social question" was most apparent. At this stage proposed reforms did not produce clear party divisions, but they provoked strong responses from interest groups. Following a harrowing report on child labor, parliament passed the Factory Acts in 1833. The Acts forbade employment of children under the age of 9 in most factories, limited employment of children between 9 and 13 to 48 hours per week, and set a maximum of 12 hours per day for individuals under the age of 18. Children under 13 were required to attend school for two hours per day, and an inspectorate would police factories. The bill, generally supported by landowners and Radicals, was attacked to no avail by liberal economists and manufacturers.

The issue of slavery also stirred impassioned debate. Opposition to slavery derived from a combination of Enlightenment and (especially Evangelical) Christian emphasis on individual liberty. Frustration at the inability of the Royal Navy to prevent continuation of the slave trade had encouraged formation of an Anti-Slavery Society in 1823. Veterans of the campaign that had brought abolition of the slave trade in 1807 such as the MP William Wilberforce joined with more recent additions to the Commons in providing direction to the Society, and the Radical Henry Brougham led the campaign in the Lords. As before, the most impressive feature of reform was the extent of extra-parliamentary mobilization as a network of some 1300 local abolition groups held public meetings, disseminated literature, and gathered petitions. Members of the Society of Friends (the Quakers) and evangelical Anglicans were prominent in the movement, as were women social reformers such as Elizabeth Heyrick, who organized a sugar boycott at Leicester. As in most such movements, divisions arose over strategy as Heyrick clashed with Wilberforce by pushing for immediate emancipation. All the same, the most striking feature of the campaign was that mass mobilization overcame strenuous resistance by MPs who represented the well-funded West Indies planters' lobby.

The immediate catalyst for abolition was a large-scale slave revolt in Jamaica in late 1831. Although the rebellion was quickly repressed, two parliamentary enquiries, and some 4000 petitions for abolition, thereafter prepared the ground for passage of the Slavery Abolition Act in 1833. Emancipation was partial in that the Act did not extend to territories in the possession of the East India Company or the islands of Ceylon and Saint Helena. Moreover only slaves under the age of six were to be immediately freed. Others would have to serve a period of indentured labor called "apprenticeship" under their former owners. Gaining abolition necessitated overcoming concerns over property rights and hence the planters gained the hefty sum of 20 million pounds in compensation. Subsequent resistance by former slaves, however, forced termination of the "apprenticeship" provisions by 1840. Sadly, for former slaves freedom was more often than not accompanied by grinding poverty. Nevertheless, the Act was a landmark in civil rights legislation and the campaign provided experience for reformers who would launch a wide array of subsequent initiatives.

Following the report of a commission in which Chadwick was prominent, in July 1834 parliament passed the New Poor Law. The Old Poor Law Act of 1601 had made poverty relief a parish (local) responsibility and had led to the creation of workhouses for paupers who could not work, due to age or infirmity. Subsequently, in 1795, justices of the peace of the parish of Speenhamland had designed a system wherein impoverished workers had their wages supplemented by relief payments. The Speenhamland system and numerous local variants of "out-relief" then spread and parish rates (taxes) spiraled from two million pounds in the mid 1790s to seven million in 1832. Concern turned to alarm when the Royal Commission of 1832 reported that compensation of the "able-bodied" (working) poor kept wages down because employers exploited it by lowering wages. Moreover the report of the 1834 Commission advocated abolition of all supplemental income because the practice was "destructive to the morals of the most numerous class."[35] Instead, the workhouse system would be expanded; anyone could enter and secure food and a bed, but conditions would be kept at such a miserable level that entry would be a last resort. To a limited extent, the New Poor Law also reduced parish control as state supervision would be undertaken by a Board of Commissioners, inspectors, and auditors. All the same, local parish boards continued to influence administration of the Law and the central government had to make compromises that often led to continuation of "out-relief" in one form or another.

Other reforms provoked partisan combat. The Municipal Corporations Act of 1835 took local government office in the boroughs, except for London, from the hands of Tory oligarchies and made it elective with a franchise that included all male ratepayers. Privilege was also the target in 1836 of legislation that transferred registration of births, marriages, and deaths from the Anglican clergy to the state, and legalized marriages conducted by non-Anglican clergymen. The most contentious of all legislation concerned the position of the Anglican Church in Ireland. Only about 10% of the population was Anglican, and as O'Connell put it: "There never was in the history of the world, so poor a people with so rich a church."[36] In 1833 civil disorder had led Grey to secure passage of an Irish Coercion Bill that enabled the Lord Lieutenant to use sweeping powers to attack subversive organizations. To make this harsh medicine more palatable, the cabinet also brought forward the Irish Temporalities Bill, which reduced the number of Protestant bishoprics, consolidated dioceses wherein there were few Anglicans, imposed a graduated tax on clerical income, and placed Church revenues in the hands of a Royal Commission. That reform was required could be seen in the assent given by the Tories Peel and Wellington. Proposals that funds saved by the reforms should go toward supporting the Catholic Church, however, proved too much for Tories and moderate Whigs to swallow. Thus the issue festered for the remainder of the decade, alienating O'Connell from the government.

Also destructive for the alliance of 1832 was Whig refusal to countenance further franchise reform despite growing popular mobilization. In 1834 radicals led by Robert Owen sought to create a Grand National Consolidated Trades Union, hoping to reorganize industry along cooperative lines. Failure was more a product of noncooperation among the various trades than state repression, although the cabinet sent a hostile message with the transportation to Australia of six "Tolpuddle martyrs" who had tried to organize a friendly society among agricultural workers. More purely political was the Chartist movement initiated by Radicals William Lovett and Francis Place in 1836. Lovett and Place were self-educated artisans who believed that mass mobilization should be used to pressure parliament for reform, although both rejected the use of violence or insurrection. The "People's Charter" called for universal male suffrage, abolition of property qualifications for MPs, and payment of salaries to MPs so that working men could serve. When in 1839 the Commons rejected a Chartist petition backed by perhaps a million signatures, riots broke out. The government responded by arresting Chartist leaders and for the time being agitation ceased.

Expectation of radical change also ran high in France and to secure long-term loyalty the July Monarchy needed accomplishments. Unfortunately after an initial period of instability the regime became excessively cautious and conservative. It did secure passage in 1833 of the Guizot Education Law, a major step in state provision of primary education. Every commune was obliged to set up a school and employ a teacher, and education would be free for those unable to pay, although attendance would not be compulsory. Thereafter, however, reform came to a halt and many early supporters of the regime grew disillusioned.

In the aftermath of the 1830 Revolution the main political groups had reformulated. Ultraroyalists adopted the label Legitimist to underline their refusal to accept what they considered an illegitimate monarchy. The Liberals splintered. Moderates joined with former moderate royalists to form a conservative party of Resistance that maintained that the July Settlement had provided sufficient reform. Although their ascendancy did not become apparent until the appointment of a cabinet led by Casimir Perier in March 1831, the Resistance soon embodied the Orleanist *juste milieu* – a rejection of the extremes of royal absolutism and popular democracy that amounted to stasis. Left-leaning Liberals formed the party of Movement; they considered the reforms of the July Settlement insufficient. Most Movement leaders were loyal to the new regime, but certain elements adopted republicanism. More ominously, among republicans there was a faction that believed the Restoration had been overthrown solely by popular insurrection. They lionized the "people," by whom they meant the urban lower- and lower-middle classes, and they concluded that if suitably mobilized the people could overturn Louis-Philippe.

Economic depression exacerbated by a cholera epidemic heightened discontent. The state responded with subsidies to pay for the distribution of bread and funded relief programs, including workshops that provided jobs. Such measures were, however, far from sufficient to meet demand and were conceived solely as temporary expedients. Initially contacts between republicans and the populace were few; republicans had no solutions to economic problems beyond broadening the franchise and reducing taxes. Nevertheless, criticism of the regime's pacific foreign policy could be used to spark demonstrations, particularly in sympathy with the Poles in 1831.

A regime born of revolution was initially reluctant to repress former allies. Officials at first turned a blind eye as crowds attacked Legitimists conducting a memorial service in Paris and then sacked the archbishop's palace in February 1831. Meanwhile sustained disorder allowed conservatives to exploit fear of social revolution. As early as the summer of 1830 Francois Guizot had called for prohibition of popular societies, and by October the government had banned the republican Society of Friends from holding meetings. Enforcement of an Imperial law that prohibited unauthorized meetings of twenty or more individuals then forced republicans to reorganize as the Society of the Rights of Man and divide into small, secret, cells that recruited artisans and shopkeepers.

A leading banker and industrialist, Casimir Perier had been a combative Liberal opponent of reaction during the Restoration. He was, however, no admirer of the revolutionary crowd and he was determined to put an end to civil order. Already armed with a law that banned large gatherings in early 1831, Perier attacked organizations known as patriotic societies. The latter had been formed to defend France from invasion, but they also served to mobilize Movement supporters. That Perier deliberately set out to polarize politics could be seen in his forcing the resignation of civil servants who were members of the patriotic societies, and in harassment of left-wing journalists. Similarly, Perier deliberately escalated confrontation in crushing a revolt of silk workers at Lyons. By the time that Perier died of cholera in March 1832 he had broken old ties between Restoration moderate and radical Liberals.

Thereafter the July Monarchy followed the course Perier had set it upon. An attempt at revolt by Legitimists in 1832 strengthened support for an increasingly repressive government, and growing concern with order facilitated passage of a law banning all unauthorized associations in April 1834. Aimed principally at republicans, the law also blocked worker attempts to combine for industrial action and triggered another massive rebellion of silk workers at Lyons and a lesser revolt at Paris. Political agitation had been largely absent from strife at Lyons prior to Perier's intervention, but thereafter social grievances had merged with republicanism. The revolts of 1834 provided a pretext for massive arrests in France's two leading cities and during subsequent trials the radical press indulged in coded calls for murder of the King. Such tactics then backfired when an attempt to assassinate Louis-Philippe left forty Parisian bystanders lying dead or wounded on the street in July 1835.

Demand for a crackdown enabled the government to push through laws that outlawed republicanism and eroded freedom of expression. The cost of caution money for the right to publish was increased, street vendors were obliged to apply for permits, restrictions on content were widened, newspapers were repeatedly brought to trial, and trial by jury was removed from press cases so as to secure higher conviction rates. Whether such measures were effective was questionable. Journalists continued to attack the regime, especially through satire and caricature, and while censorship was sufficient to make enemies, it was insufficient to eliminate criticism.

By the time that disorder tapered off in the mid 1830s a new problem had emerged as governments rose and fell in rapid succession. There were several causes of ministerial instability. The Chamber of Deputies became increasingly fragmented due to proliferation of new political groups that had little by way of party discipline. It was thus difficult for cabinet ministers to calculate whether a proposed piece of legislation would pass. The temptation was to do as little as possible; yet doing nothing was unlikely to hold the support of a majority for very long. Further complicating matters was that Louis-Philippe liked to lead the government and he had trouble finding a first minister who was both pliant to his will and able to command a majority among the deputies. The one group perhaps capable of finding sufficient support was called the *doctrinaires*, who were led by Guizot. One of the great historians of the age and a leading political theorist, Guizot was more inclined to lead than follow. In trying to avoid Guizot, Louis-Philippe twice turned to the former Liberal journalist Adolphe Thiers, who avoided contentious domestic legislation and hoped that aggressive foreign policy would rally patriotic sentiment to his advantage.

As we have seen, in his conduct of foreign policy Thiers severely damaged the prestige of the Monarchy and he also was central to an ill-conceived attempt to add lustre to the regime through association with past glory. Galleries at the restored palace of Versailles featured depictions of Napoleonic battle scenes, and several days of commemoration were devoted to the return of Napoleon's ashes from Saint Helena. It is often pointed out that the ultimate beneficiary of such policies was the Emperor's nephew Louis-Napoleon Bonaparte, and certainly it was dangerous for a pacific regime to revive fond memories of a warlord. However, two farcical attempts to seize power in 1836 and 1840 demonstrated that Louis-Napoleon posed little threat to Louis-Philippe. More important was failure to reform. In Britain roughly 32 of every 1000 men could vote in national elections; for France the figure was 5 for every 1000, and meanwhile freedom of association and expression had been severely curtailed.

Liberal Advance and Political Instability: Spain in the 1830s

Despite France's reputation as the home of revolution, Spain was far more tumultuous. Spain became a constitutional monarchy in the 1830s, but there was little reason to assume that the regime would last for very long. The forces of reaction were powerful, little inclined to compromise, and difficult to subdue. Although liberalism gradually gained the upper hand, liberals were divided into warring factions, adding to instability and opening the door to a long line of men on horseback.

The road to constitutional monarchy began when the succession of Queen Isabel II in September 1833 triggered revolt among the reactionary supporters of Don Carlos. Carlist forces in Navarre and the Basque provinces put an army of perhaps 30 000 men in the field, and elsewhere guerrilla forces harassed government troops. All the same, Carlist control seldom extended beyond one tenth of Spain, urban centers were hostile, and lack of international aid rendered purchase of military supplies an acute problem. Thus the First Carlist War of 1833–40 was largely characterized by stalemate, until attrition eroded rebel resolve.

That the war lasted as long as it did was due principally to division among the opponents of Carlism. To defend the throne the regent queen mother Maria Christina needed to broaden support and thus she reached out to liberals with promulgation of the Royal Statute of 1834. The latter provided for a bicameral legislature with an appointive senate and elective lower house (the *Cortes*), but only 18 000 men would be eligible to vote and the government would be responsible solely to the Crown. Worse still, it triggered a tripartite liberal division among Moderates, moderate Progressives, and radical Progressives. Moderates drew their support from the upper reaches of society, feared social revolution, and were troubled by the inclination of Progressives to dispossess the Church. Progressives found their following in the middle or lower-middle levels of society. They were not necessarily opposed to Catholic religious doctrine, but they saw in confiscation of Church property a way to increase the number of property owners and give them a stake in a new liberal regime. Differences between moderate and radical Progressives were partly a matter of degree; radicals were more democratic and more aggressive in their desire to expropriate Church property. Radical Progressives drew their strength from militias and municipal governments wherein their followers were inclined to provoke popular insurrection and prone to anti-clerical violence, especially against the regular clergy.

Despite government attempts to control the elections of 1834, open debate and freedom of the press provided opportunities for a strong minority of Progressives in parliament. A series of radical revolts in leading provincial centers in the summer of 1835 then pushed the Crown further to the left in its quest for support. The government nationalized almost all monastic lands and began selling them off, and the franchise was doubled for elections in 1836, yielding a Progressive majority. Fearing the Progressives intended to reduce royal power, Maria Christina nevertheless appointed a Moderate cabinet. Radicals responded with revolts backed by a group of noncommissioned officers. Maria Christina then gave in to their demands by instituting the constitution of 1812 and calling for yet more elections. While the constitution of 1812 provided for a franchise of all male property owners at the base level, indirect three-stage elections still favored the elite. Moreover, backlash against disorder helped moderate Progressives in the elections of October 1836, giving them control of the *Cortes*.

Moderate Progressives then designed a constitution reflective of their centrist position, replacing the 1812 electoral system with a franchise that granted the vote to 265 000 men. Though hardly democratic, the electoral system was more inclusive than that of France and might have provided the basis for consensus in liberal ranks. Nevertheless, Moderates denounced the "radicalism" of the new constitution and were worried by abolition of the Church tithe and legislation that declared that all Church secular property belonged to the nation. Worse still, many radical Progressives, angered by alteration of the 1812 system, abstained from voting in the elections of September 1837, thereby handing victory to the Moderates. Clashes between the Moderate government and liberal army officers thereafter forced the Crown to call for yet more elections in 1839, which brought a short-lived radical Progressive government that had fallen to a return of the Moderates by early 1840.

The absence of stable government then led to military intervention. General Baldomero Espartero's understanding of politics did not go much beyond platitudes, but he did associate himself with the moderate Progressives and cultivated a populist image among common soldiers by refusing to fight unless he felt certain of victory. Cheap prints in which Espartero struck Napoleonic poses adorned the walls of many homes, and the General's image could also be seen on paper used for rolling cigarettes. Meanwhile liberal factionalism had prevented governments from concentrating their efforts (and tax revenues) sufficiently on the war against Carlism and discontent within the army had reached dangerous levels. Espartero's great achievement came in August 1839 when he negotiated the Peace of Vergara with the commander of the main Carlist army. By allowing Carlist officers to enlist in the Spanish army and granting amnesty to the rank and file, Espartero set the stage for a mopping up of the remaining Carlist forces in the summer of 1840. With his popularity at its zenith, the General was well placed to exploit a Progressive revolt in the fall of 1840 and when the queen regent implored Espartero to back the government, he refused. In exasperation Maria Christina not only appointed

Espartero prime minister, she also made him regent and departed into exile. Military influence had progressed to rule by a general, though not dictatorship.

Below the chaos of events, certain trends emerged. Spain gained its first sustained experience of public debate in parliament and the press, elections, and the formation of loosely organized parties. Much had been done to liberalize the economy: guilds had been abolished, freedom of commerce and industry had been established, and owners had gained the right to enclose woodlands. The experience was, however, deeply unsettling. Governments sought to manipulate the electoral process and party politics often degenerated into struggles over distribution of state jobs. Although land redistribution had been extensive, it worked largely to the advantage of wealthy non-noble elements and poor peasants gained little. That voter turnout steadily declined resulted partly from the frequency of elections; more ominously, it also indicated skepticism over the merits of representative government.

The Volatile Complexity of Emergent Nationalism and Liberalism in Italy, Germany, and the Austrian Empire, 1830–1848

By mid-century the Janus-like (two-faced) character of nationalism was evident – it was a creed both of inclusion and exclusion that in certain circumstances could blend with, or challenge, liberalism. Nationalism and liberalism remained largely elite or middle-class concerns, although expansion of literacy, publishing, and transportation networks facilitated the spread of ideals to less elevated levels of society. Despite censorship, Italian regimes could not prevent discussion of politics in private salons, cafes, universities, and theaters. Criticism ranging from complaints over banditry in the countryside to demand for representative government reflected growing public demand for reform from states that seemed incapable of competent rule. In response Piedmont-Sardinia, the Kingdom of the Two Sicilies, and the Papal States set up consultative bodies during the 1830s and 1840s, but such concessions were an attempt to gain legitimacy without sharing power.

While the crushing of previous revolts had clearly demonstrated that change required liberation from Austrian domination, Italian writers differed over how independence could be achieved. Giuseppe Mazzini gave nationalism a semireligious quality and much publicity. Fond of cigars and guitars, Mazzini was the quintessential Romantic hero, and he was good at securing funding for his cause from wealthy upper-class women. He considered the press "perhaps the only power in modern times. ... it speaks to all the classes; it discusses all questions; it touches all the chords which move in the human soul."[37] Reacting against both liberal individualism and socialism, Mazzini saw the people acting as a nation as the fount of all progress and he stressed that Italians must free themselves. In 1831 he formed the "Young Italy" movement and gained adherents in most Italian states. Nevertheless attempts to stir insurrection fizzled and by 1834 Mazzini had begun a long period of exile. Further attempts at revolt were notable mostly for the execution of nationalist "martyrs" and by the mid-1840s moderate nationalists were counseling against secret societies and insurrection, calling on liberals to engage in constitutional "conspiracy in broad daylight."[38] All the same, Mazzini's cult of patriotic devotion deeply influenced others, Giuseppe Garibaldi among them, who would play a crucial role in future unification.

Mazzini advocated a unitary, republican state, but upon this point other nationalists disagreed. The Turinese priest Vincenzo Gioberti's call for the Papacy to take up the cause of unification seemed to put nationalism on a higher moral plane and appealed to moderates who formed the neo-Guelph movement. Others looked toward Piedmont-Sardinia. When he became king in 1831, Charles Albert was an enigma. His role in the revolt of 1821 perhaps had indicated sympathy for the objectives of the Carbonari, or might have been the product of weakness. Although he cracked down on the perpetrators of revolt in 1833, Charles Albert was not a reactionary, particularly when it came to asserting state primacy over the Catholic Church. His reign was also marked by reforms designed to modernize the economy. In the 1840s treaties entailing reduction of tariffs would trigger high economic growth rates, foster expansion of credit institutions, and encourage industry.

The reign of Charles Albert furthered the spread of nationalism among elite elements that saw in Piedmont-Sardinia a beacon of hope. In neighboring Lombardy economic growth was even more rapid than in Piedmont; yet bourgeois merchants and noble landowners were angered by what they considered high levels of taxation and exclusion from government office. Elsewhere, frustration with protectionist trade policies gave rise to desire for creation of an Italian customs union, and perhaps an Italian federation. Perhaps most volatile of all were the Papal States, where clerical rule continued to resist even the most modest of reforms. While nationalism thus gained ground, the path to unification remained uncertain.

Similar ambiguities were apparent in the German states. After the early 1830s liberalism gradually recovered as economic growth, urbanization, and rising literacy contributed to growing desire for participation in government. The number of books, pamphlets, and newspapers published, and lending libraries established, rose steadily. Associations such as choral or hunting clubs, or scientific, professional or commercial societies, served as forums for discussion of public issues, and universities remained vectors of liberalism. In the early 1830s revocation of a law guaranteeing freedom of the press sparked bitter criticism in the parliamentary lower house of Baden. When in 1837 King Ernst August of Hanover abrogated the constitution of 1833, he triggered widespread protest. Opposition then spread to the parliament of Baden and, although a petition to the Federal Diet failed, the episode brought south and north German liberals into closer contact.

The succession of Frederick William IV in June 1840 initially gave rise to hope among Prussian liberals. More drawn to the arts than to the military, Fredrick William hoped to gain public favor through elaborate royal ceremonial. He was, however, also determined to strengthen monarchical authority and responded to calls for a constitution with the remark that he would never let a piece of paper come between him and his people. When a young radical published a pamphlet arguing that citizens must demand participation in the affairs of the state as an inalienable right, he was arrested. Nevertheless, gathering momentum could be seen in town halls where municipal councillors called for a constituent assembly and criticized state policies. Frederick William sought to take the sting out of agitation by convoking a combined assembly of the provincial estates, hoping that consultation over plans for funding railway expansion would appease liberal appetite for a say in government. Nevertheless, he would have no truck with representative government: "I will not drop the sceptre from my hands. I will not issue a Charter, I will never share my sovereign powers with the estates."[39] Consequent disillusionment soon turned to bitter criticism.

German liberals were gradually drawn toward nationalism as advances in transport and communications contributed to a growing sense of shared community. Moreover, the reactionary nature of petty dynasties in the smaller states led some reformers to hope that German unification might lead to more progressive government. Due to the customs union known as the Zollverein, Prussia played a particular role in the spread of nationalism. Prussian governments had begun in 1818 by abolishing internal tariffs, allowing free import of most raw materials, and limiting duties on manufactured imports. Conversely, heavy duties were imposed on goods in transit to other states, giving neighboring states an "incentive" to join the Prussian system. Initially it was only smaller, adjacent states, enticed by a share of the revenues collected by Prussian customs agents, which joined. However, in 1828 Hesse-Darmstadt negotiated entry while retaining her customs officials. Although attempts to sustain a rival union in central and south Germany were favored by Metternich, Austria did not join due to her position in the Habsburg Empire and when the rival union foundered, Bavaria and Württemberg entered the Zollverein in 1834. Thereafter commercial expansion drew the remaining states like a magnet.

The growth of nationalism became obvious during the Egyptian Crisis of 1840 when Thiers managed to unleash the greatest outpouring of German patriotism since the wars of 1813–14. The way in which nationalism fed upon identification of an enemy "other" could be seen in a famous poem of Nikolas Becker:

> They shall not have it,
> Our free German Rhine
> Though like greedy crows
> They hoarsely cry for it.[40]

Frankreich.
Singt nicht so laut, zum Zeitvertreibe,
Die Laugen Euch aus deutschem Leibe,
Sonst machen wir mit Bomben und Kanonen,
Auf Euer Lied, die Variationen.

Deutschland.
Lärmt, wie Ihr wollt, Ihr links am Rheine,
Nur werft herüber nicht mit Blei;
Sonst schlagen wir Euch Arm' und Beine,
Und Kreuz und Schädel morsch entzwei.

Figure 3.1 German caricature of the Rhine Crisis of 1840 contrasting the calm of the French withf the hysteria of the Germans. SLUB Dresden/Deutsche Fotothek.

The Rhine Crisis also exposed the inability of the German Confederation and Austria to muster sufficient forces to ensure the security of Württemberg, Baden, and Bavaria. The attraction of ties to Prussia was thus once again enhanced (Figure 3.1).

While German nationalism made few inroads in Austria prior to mid-century, liberalism fed on growing belief that the structures of the Empire were obsolete. Emperor Francis had refused proposals to rationalize the state through creation of an advisory legislative state council and a committee of executive ministers, preferring to meet with his ministers on an individual basis. Memoranda advising reform thus piled up while the Emperor dithered. Meanwhile national debt spiraled because the state preferred loans to direct taxation, which would have angered the nobility. Rumors swirled of impending bankruptcy and confidence in the regime fell further in 1835 with the succession of Ferdinand I, whose most profound statement allegedly was "I'm the Emperor and I want dumplings!"[41] Thereafter little came of efforts to improve government. Despite increasing hardship, no serious attempt was made to regulate industrial working conditions, tariffs and taxes drove up prices on articles of mass consumption, and the regime continued to rely on private charity, rejecting proposals to entrust charity efforts to provincial Diets. Censorship remained an irritant; yet elite disapproval rendered it increasingly ineffective. As the sense of malaise grew, civil servants and liberal aristocrats entered middle-class cultural, philanthropic, and economic associations that provided opportunity for discussion and propaganda.

Meanwhile the early stirrings of cultural nationalism could be discerned among various groups in the Empire. From 1815 onwards aristocratic patrons founded Bohemian museums, learned societies, and journals that provided centres for scholars who developed Czech nationalism. Works of history spread notions of common heritage, spirit, and struggle. At least as important were works on Czech language, grammar, and literature. From this language codification process, it was a short step to demands that the "mother tongue" be adopted in schools and state administration. While nationalism gradually spread in Bohemia, it made less progress in Moravia, and had limited impact in the Bohemian Estates, which routinely approved Imperial proposals until the 1840s.

Hungary was a different kettle of fish because the relative autonomy of the Hungarian Estates could be exploited to put forward calls for the replacement of German or Latin with Magyar in public life. At the start of the Restoration Francis I had tried to ignore Hungarian opposition to Imperial policies by refusing to convoke the Estates. Attempts to use state officials, rather than Hungarian county Diets known as congregations, to raise men and money for the army had, however, failed in the early 1820s, necessitating recourse to the Estates in 1825. It was at the latter that linguistic demands were first made; while the Emperor could for a time ignore them, he did have to pledge to respect the autonomy of the Estates by abolishing arbitrary taxation and conscription.

Thereafter demand grew. In the wake of the 1830 revolutions, the Hungarian Estates were better placed to extract linguistic concessions, beginning with public service positions and entry into the bar. Under the influence of Count István Széchenyi, progressive Magyars, generally from the upper levels of the landed gentry, demanded social reform as a means to Hungarian revival. Nobles should relinquish some of their fiscal privileges so as to facilitate state-directed economic development, and feudal burdens and restrictions on peasants should be lessened so as to enhance productivity. Széchenyi hoped that reform could be conducted in cooperation with the Imperial government. Metternich, however, gave no support and in the Estates the Imperial government backed "loyalist" magnates aghast at the thought of social concessions.

By the mid-1830s leadership among Magyar nationalists had been seized by a younger group of radicals who propounded liberal remedies – representative government, ministerial responsibility, and parliamentary control over the budget – to Hungarian backwardness. Foremost among the radicals was Louis Kossuth, a man of formidable persuasive power whose influence derived from editing a journal based on debates within the Estates and congregations. Kossuth was no less socially progressive than Széchenyi; he advocated emancipation of the peasantry and abolition of noble fiscal privilege. Where Kossuth differed was that he saw an end to Hungary's "colonial dependence"[42] on Austria as the essential step toward emancipation. Liberalism and nationalism were thus closely intertwined.

Imperial policy alternated between refusal and concession. In the late 1830s Kossuth and several other radicals were imprisoned, but in 1840 the Egyptian Crisis, and consequent desire to enlarge the army, led the government to take a more conciliatory line. In 1840 the Diet declared Magyar the official language of Hungary, thereby giving the Magyar nobility a virtual monopoly of public office, and imposed Magyar as the language of secondary education. In a more generous spirit, serfs were granted permission to purchase manumission and the right to become free landholders. For its part, the Imperial government granted amnesty to political offenders and relaxed censorship. Expansion of civil society consequently accelerated: toward the late 1840s there were some 250 associations, clubs, and mutual aid societies, and roughly 500 printing companies, including 50 newspapers and journals.

Sometimes there is strength in growing numbers, and sometimes there are weaknesses. Growth in Magyar nationalism brought splintering as Széchenyi attacked Kossuth and entered the Imperial government to pursue his plans for economic development. Meanwhile a group known as the "Centralists" argued for preservation of ties to the Monarchy, though not to Austria, and advocated centralization of power through abolition of the congregations, which they viewed as bastions of aristocratic influence. Reaction against the latter demand actually strengthened the position of conservatives in the Diet and opposition calls for equality before the law, trial by jury, and unification with Transylvania were all rejected in 1843.

A second source of weakness in Hungarian nationalism lay in reaction against Magyar chauvinism. Metternich was quick to grasp this point and decided that tensions among competing nationalist groups should be exploited throughout the Empire. In Hungary Magyar assertiveness over linguistic policies led Croats, Slovaks, Ruthenes, and Romanians to develop their own nationalist movements. Only Croatian nobles possessed much organization, but fear of Magyar domination encouraged all such groups to look to the Imperial government for protection. Outside of Hungary, growing Ruthenian nationalism could be used by the Monarchy to check the separatist inclinations of Poles in Galicia. Similarly, the Bohemian character of Czech nationalism, which had begun to produce opposition to Imperial budget estimates in the Estates, could be used to foster loyalty among Slovenes in Moravia. Yet while licensing the journal *Croat News* might serve to counter Magyar demands, it ran the risk of pouring oil on nationalist fires – in 1847 the Croat *Sabor* (Diet) declared Serbo-Croat the official language of Croatia-Slavonia. Divide and rule was a poor solution to the nationalist problem.

Toward Crisis? The Constitutional Monarchies in the 1840s

Britain seemed to be on the verge of revolt in the early 1840s. The economy was vulnerable to trade cycles in which periods of boom gave way to severe recession, and certain groups were hit hard by increased mechanization and the factory system – the number of handloom weavers, for example, declined from 123 000 to 43 000. Earlier overproduction in the coalmining, cotton, and woolen industries led to severe contraction beginning in 1838 and a run of poor harvests simultaneously drove the price of wheat upwards. Private charity and the Poor Law were stretched to the breaking point everywhere, although the worst was reserved for Ireland, where potato blight led to famine beginning in 1845. The impact of the latter was colossal; by 1849 more than a million had died of starvation or disease resultant from malnutrition, and even greater numbers had sought escape through emigration.

Economic turmoil fortified Chartism and an Anti-Corn Law League. Chartism linked a wide range of political associations with trade unions and was notable for the participation of large numbers of women, although the Charter excluded women from the franchise. While most leaders wished to confine the movement to lobbying parliament, some wanted to attempt insurgency. The Radical Feargus O'Conner, an Irish Protestant landowner, was the chief driving force in an organizational campaign begun in 1840, but he tended to vacillate over whether change should be brought through application of "moral" or "physical" force. Formation of a National Charter Association and a national conference held at Manchester in 1840 were followed by a deluge of pamphlets and lecture tours that culminated in the presentation in May 1842 of a second petition, signed by perhaps as many as three million supporters. Attacked by the government, a franchise reform bill was then easily defeated, setting off a wave of violence. Chartist leaders were seldom responsible for industrial disorders in the summer; nevertheless, the aggressive tone of O'Connor and his followers soon led to a break with moderate Chartists, middle-class elements, and some trades unions.

Another weakness was that mass mobilization was driven by economic grievances for which Chartist leaders had no obvious remedies. As unemployed workers attacked factories and mines and ransacked shops or buildings associated with state authority, a delegation of Chartists rashly called in August 1842 for a general strike of all workers. Even O'Connor denounced this attempt to link economic and political protest. Dozens of Chartists were arrested, although the Crown wisely chose not to grant them "martyrdom" by putting them on trial as a particular group, leaving them to be tried with hundreds of ordinary rioters and receive generally light sentences. Most telling of all was that the interest of many workers in Chartism faded once the economy began to recover.

The Anti-Corn-Law League was more successful. Part of the League's strength lay in the simplicity of its argument: tariffs, particularly those on grain, raised prices to the advantage of landowners and the disadvantage of everyone else. Workers had to pay more for basic staples, and employers had to pay higher wages. Formulated in such terms, the League appealed to a wide range of groups. Urban middle-class elements formed the backbone of the movement and they were joined by Dissenters and Anglican Evangelicals. Led by the Radical MPs Richard Cobden, a Manchester industrialist, and John Bright, a Quaker businessman, the

League's message that free trade would deliver prosperity and secure international peace through the development of trading partnerships had a distinctly religious character. Equally important, the prospect of lower food costs held appeal for working-class elements and free trade could be cast as a means to appease disappointed Chartists.

Despite its assets, the League would not have succeeded had Peel not converted to free trade. When he became prime minister after the elections of 1841, Peel was determined to address the "social question." The means he employed, however, unleashed the equivalent of a civil war among the Tories. Certain measures were not divisive: most Tory landowning MPs backed the Mines Act of 1842 that prohibited employment of girls, women, and boys under ten from working underground. Thereafter laws passed in 1844 excluded children under nine from factory work, reduced the number of hours an older factory child could work to six and half per day, set a 12-hour maximum for women, and required fencing around dangerous machinery. The chief opponents of these measures were to be found among Radicals such as Bright and Whigs who represented the interests of manufacturers determined to preserve laissez-faire. Other measures, however, sowed discord in Tory ranks. Because tariffs on grain imports were fixed in terms of prices on the domestic market, by raising the price level at which tariffs were applied, Peel could open the market to increased imports and thereby encourage the fall of prices. Desire for protection of agricultural interests, however, remained powerful in the countryside and farmers' associations, which often played key roles in Tory electoral organization, were not shy about lobbying their local MPs.

By 1845 impending economic catastrophe and a campaign by the Irish leader O'Connell to sever the 1801 Act of Union had convinced Peel that more must be done. In 1846 the government secured a complete, though gradual, repeal of the Corn Laws. In doing so, it had to rely on support from the Opposition as the majority of Tories voted against the measure. Peel could carry a significant minority of loyalists, and Wellington managed to carry the vote in the Lords, but many Tories would never forgive Peel and his government was brought down shortly thereafter. All the same, repeal demonstrated that the system could act in the best interests of the nation and after Peel's death in 1850 some 400 000 laborers contributed to a memorial to him.

Contrast between Britain and France was stark. Initially France seemed to settle down under the guidance of Guizot, who led the governments of the 1840s. Calm was facilitated by economic growth which the state stimulated through investment in road building, canal digging, and improvements in port facilities. Given the failure of private initiatives to create railways, in 1842 legislation created an arrangement wherein the state built roadbeds, bridges, and tunnels, and then leased concessions to private companies that supplied rails, stations, and working capital. While the state appropriated extensive powers to expropriate property, fix fares, and impose standards, such an arrangement made investment in railways less risky and stirred massive building. The latter boom encouraged coal and iron production, and railways also hastened delivery of mail and newspapers. In combination with development of electric telegraph lines, this communications revolution provided an aura of progress that Guizot exploited in 1846 by asking voters whether they were better off than in 1840. Although he thereby secured a majority of conservatives in parliament, the gambit soon came back to haunt him.

Recession, due primarily to overproduction, first became apparent in industry, commerce, and finance in October 1846 and matters thereafter became far worse due to a succession of bad harvests. As the "social question" returned to the fore, critics asked why a regime that did so much for railway investors did so little for the poor. Little by way of labor legislation had been passed. For factories that employed more than ten workers, a law of 1841 had prohibited hiring of children under 8 and restricted employment of children between the ages of 8 and 16 to eight hours per day. Owners were, however, left to regulate themselves and the image of a regime that cared only for the rich was propagated widely by journalists who gained fodder from political scandals that added to perception that the sanctimonious Guizot ruled by corruption.

Inspired by the Anti-Corn-Law League, in 1847 opponents of the government launched a reform campaign aimed at doubling the franchise. Given restrictions on political assembly, the Opposition resorted to holding some 180 public banquets involving 22 000 subscribers in provincial centers. Guizot would not budge and exasperation at his inflexibility temporarily promoted unity in opposition ranks, so that members of the dynastic (loyal) opposition began to share platforms with quasi-republican speakers. Such a combination, not seen since the early 1830s, was dangerous at a time when works on the Revolution of 1789 were enjoying bestseller status.

Also based on the British model was a campaign for abolition of slavery in the French colonies. Through the 1830s and early 1840s the French movement was small, largely confined to the social elite, and inclined to keep radicals such as the black immediate abolitionist Cyrille Bissette at arm's length. Lobbying was largely confined to parliamentary speeches and sporadic publication that was effectively countered by colonial interests through the purchase of support in the newspaper press. Under such circumstances Guizot could fob off calls for abolition with the argument that while the government favored emancipation in principle, it could not afford the compensation to planters required for immediate implementation. It was not until the mid-1840s that momentum began to gather with a series of petition drives and the growing involvement of the Catholic clergy. Even so, numbers were modest; perhaps 30 000 signatures were gathered in a petition drive launched in late 1847. According to one authority, whereas more than one of every five British adult males probably signed an abolition petition in 1833, less than one man in a thousand signed in France in 1847. Revolution then interceded in 1848 and a provisional government proclaimed emancipation in March. Yet it had chosen to act by decree rather than attempt to pass legislation through a parliament elected on the basis of manhood suffrage. Most French citizens were indifferent to the issue of abolition, but, then again, elite fears of mass political involvement had prevented the sort of mobilization apparent across the Channel.

Ironically, 1848 in Spain saw consolidation of power by the Moderates and relative stability. Few would have guessed such an outcome when Espartero established his regency government in 1840. Espartero was loosely aligned with the moderate Progressives, but he allowed the other parties to continue and initially tolerated criticism in the press. Nor was he a dictator, although he disappointed the Progressives by excluding them from offices reserved for his personal followers even after the Progressives gained a large majority in the elections of 1841. Espartero further alienated radical Progressives with a law extending central government control over the municipalities, and refusal to abolish salt and tobacco monopolies run by rich financiers. Nevertheless the Progressive-dominated *Cortes* was able to put forward plans to sell off the lands of the secular clergy, and expand the franchise to include roughly 500 000 voters by 1843. When a group of Moderates sought to raise revolt in October 1841, radical Progressives formed "public vigilance" commissions and mobilized militias in defence of the regime. Like most members of the military, Espartero viewed the commissions with suspicion, and hence he ordered their abolition shortly after the Moderate revolt had been quashed.

Subsequent relations between the Progressives and Espartero rapidly deteriorated, paving the way for Moderates to recover ascendancy. Rumors that the government intended to sign a free-trade treaty with Britain, at a time of severe depression in Barcelona's cotton industry, sparked a revolt that was subdued only by bombardment of the city. Espartero thereby gained the enmity of radical Progressives and also forfeited the support of moderate Progressives. While the latter were no more pleased by the popular nature of Barcelona's rebellion than Espartero, they concluded that their best interests lay in an alliance with the Moderates. The Moderates had their own *caudillo* (strongman) in General Ramón Narváez, whose popularity in the army had grown upon each occasion that Espartero promoted one of his cronies within the officer corps. Thus when Narváez left exile with former Queen Maria Christina to command an invasion of Spain, he encountered little resistance. After Narváez secured the capitulation of Madrid in July 1843, Espartero took flight.

Narváez thereafter appointed a succession of moderate Progressives as prime minister, but he kept real power to himself while surrounding Princess Isabel with conservative councillors, dissolving militias, and crushing attempts at revolt. There was no question of a return to absolutism, although the regime did seek better relations with the Church as a bulwark against radicalism. Spanish liberalism would, however, have a decidedly conservative cast encapsulated in an alleged statement of Narváez: "I do not think that all men with advanced ideas are rogues, but I do think that all rogues have advanced ideas, just as half of those who do not have advanced ideas are rogues anyway."[43]

There is a tendency to view the period following 1830 solely from the perspective of 1848. In a subsequent chapter we will focus on common denominators in the 1848 revolutions and see that many of the causes of revolt were widespread. Nevertheless the present chapter demonstrates that each state followed its own path and was affected by its own particular circumstances. States such as Britain developed reform traditions that buffered them in 1848. Other regimes, such as those of Spain and Russia, had a sufficiently firm grip that they would not be greatly challenged. Where regimes were weak, and unwilling to adapt to calls for change, trouble was in the offing.

All told, liberalism had made significant strides in the west. Constitutional monarchies had emerged under a variety of circumstances, but their creation had in common two closely related causes. The first was growing conviction that representative institutions must be put in place to ensure that governments acted in the interests of society. The second was belief that regimes must widen their support bases through adoption of some form of representative government. Otherwise revolution would ensue.

In the constitutional monarchies battle lines frequently were drawn over participation in the political system. Many liberals had a highly restrictive conception of what they considered "capacity" and they clashed with radicals who were more democratic. Advocates for enfranchisement of women were few, although several of the utopian socialists did call for enhancement of women's rights. Increasing preoccupation with the "social question" exacerbated political tensions. For some, the remedy was to extend political rights to the masses. For others, the answer was to enhance the repressive capacity of the state. Conservatives used fear of public disorder to justify restrictions placed on publication, assembly, and association, and liberals sometimes wavered in their support of these liberties.

Liberalism was also making inroads in the rest of Europe. Regardless of their inclinations, states simply did not possess the resources to block the flow of ideas from the west. Context was crucial. Liberalism found adherents partly due to the inherent merit of its arguments. However, it also spread because increasing numbers were growing dissatisfied, for a wide variety of reasons, with governments in Italy, Germany, and the Austrian Empire. Liberalism posed the leading alternative to increasingly unpopular regimes, and conservatives had yet to develop counter arguments or strategies capable of blocking the spread of liberalism. Conservatives and reactionaries still ruled most of Europe; even so, many of them felt they were waging a losing battle.

Prior to 1848 liberalism frequently intertwined with nationalism. The two ideologies could be compatible, especially where shared belief in national sovereignty gave liberals and nationalists common ground. Nevertheless, nationalism could also fuse with other ideologies and it was not necessarily compatible with liberal emphasis on individual rights. It was only in the aftermath of the revolutions of 1848 that conservatives began truly to grasp that nationalism could also be used to combat liberalism and the history of Europe altered dramatically from that point onward. Despite Palmerston's rhetoric, liberalism had not greatly affected relations among the powers. Nationalism would prove another matter.

4

The Underpinnings of Politics

Economic, Social, and Cultural Developments up to Mid-Century

For most Europeans material progress was difficult to discern prior to mid-century. Although dynamic forces were at play, they seemed to cause more disruption than improvement and contemporary observers were struck mostly by the large number of desperately poor families gathered in rapidly growing urban centers. Urban poverty was frequently linked by writers to industrialization and it was certainly true that factory "hands" often labored and lived in brutal conditions. Nevertheless the chief source of trouble was to be found in the countryside, where rapid population growth was the main cause of poverty. Agricultural production was increasing, but improvements in productivity were based on changes that concentrated land ownership and reduced the amount of work available for landless laborers.

The industrial revolution was already well on its way in Britain and it gradually spread into continental Europe. In combination with commercial expansion, industrialization would ultimately generate wealth that helped to relieve mass poverty. Unfortunately, in the short term increased industrial productivity often had the same dislocating impact as improved agricultural productivity. While some could adapt to economic change, many could not. The most obvious immediate beneficiaries of economic expansion were the upper levels of the middle classes known as the bourgeoisie. Yet while the middle classes were "rising" in relative wealth, the landowning nobility still dominated high state office, especially in the east. Through the creation or expansion of representative government and the development of civil society power was descending in social terms, but the process was very slow.

Europe's Uncertain Path 1814–1914: State Formation and Civil Society, First Edition. R. S. Alexander.
© 2012 R. S. Alexander. Published 2012 by Blackwell Publishing Ltd.

In the first half of the century, states were far from accepting the idea that they should assume responsibility for the welfare of all citizens or subjects. Nevertheless, they did recognize that there was a link between poverty and civil disorder and therefore they sought to encourage economic growth by reducing encumbrances to production and trade. To a limited extent governments also tried to mitigate hardship through the organization of charity and temporary provision of employment through creation of public works projects. More emphasis was, however, placed on increasing the state's capacity for control and regulation. Police forces grew, more information was gathered for the formulation of policy, and new public health regulations were implemented.

Establishing a direct link between cultural trends and politics is difficult. Romanticism came to the fore in the arts and infused political ideologies with an idealistic yearning for a better world. Romantic artists and writers subjected society and politics to sweeping criticism; yet there was no clear alignment between Romanticism and the various political camps. The period was also marked by religious revival and religious and political struggle frequently intertwined. All the same, renewed fervour did not block the advance of secularism, which enhanced the growth of state power and authority.

Population Growth and Agricultural Production

Dramatic population growth begun in the mid-eighteenth century was sustained (see Table 4.1), albeit with regional variations. Such expansion necessitated greater food supply if Europe were to avoid the appalling crises that had capped demographic growth in the past.

Food supply could be increased by bringing marginal lands under cultivation, or by improving practices on lands already under cultivation. In lowly populated regions such as eastern Germany, Hungary, Russia, and the high plateaus of Spain lands were plowed, farmed to exhaustion, and then abandoned. In the more populous parts of the west dependence on cereal production exhausted the soil and required leaving at least a third of the land to lie fallow. Although they were applied unevenly, three main advances helped to reduce wasteful practices. By rotating grain crops with grasses such as clover or root crops such as turnips, farmers could restore nitrogen levels and use the land continuously. Higher yields from new crop rotation practices were first achieved in Britain and then spread to Belgium, the Netherlands, northern France, the Rhine valley, Saxony, Denmark, and Sweden. Secondly, farmers could reduce dependence on grain by introducing crops such as maize (corn) and especially potatoes, which produced three times as much food per acre. Introduction of potatoes had spread rapidly in Ireland, Germany, Bohemia, and western France after 1780. Maize was grown primarily in the drier climates of the south – in southwest France, central Italy and the Danubian Principalities. The tremendous impact of the

Table 4.1 Estimated population growth, 1800–1850.[a]

	Population, in millions	
	1800	*1850*
Austria	14.0	17.5
Austrian Empire	19.0	30.7
Belgium	3.1	4.4
France	27.4	35.7
Germany	23.0	35.2
Hungary	5.0	13.2
Ireland	5.2	6.6
Italy	17.2	24.4
Russian Empire	40.0	68.5
Spain	10.5	14.0
United Kingdom	17.5	27.2

Source: Raymond Pearson, *A Companion to European Nationalism, 1789–1920* (New York, 1994), p. 237.
© Pearson Education Ltd, 1994.
[a] Statistics for the period should be taken as broad indicators only; they do provide valuable insights as to trends, but the data from which they derive is frequently partial and at times subject to dispute among scholars.

introduction of new crops is particularly apparent in the above table in the dramatic population growth of less developed states such as Hungary. Thirdly, farmers could give up mixed farming and specialize in the crops most suitable to their locality. Dependence on a single crop could, however, prove disastrous if something like the potato blight occurred and specialization also increased vulnerability to market forces.

Such innovations ran up against constraints that limited their application. Innovation required capital to invest and it was no coincidence that productivity was highest in Britain, where enclosure had concentrated landownership and destroyed usage rights. Britain was not unique and enclosure was spreading, but in many areas landowners hesitated to undertake investment where the peasantry exercised traditional usage rights of gleaning (gathering leaves and branches) or pasturing after crops had been harvested. Peasants working small-scale farms dominated many regions and they lacked the resources to invest in new production methods and fought to retain usage rights and common lands that could be crucial to their survival. Nevertheless, production increases saw the incidence of famine drop dramatically.

That Europe left behind previous demographic patterns was also due to enhanced transportation and food distribution. Although there were significant improvements prior to the railway boom of the 1840s, they had limitations that made the coming of the age of rail all the more consequential (see Table 4.2). The main advance in land transport was the hardening (macadamizing) of road surfaces so that roads

Table 4.2 Length of rail line (in kilometers) for select countries.

	1840	1850
Austria-Hungary	144	1579
Belgium	334	903
France	497	2915
Germany	469	5856
Britain	2390	9797
Italy	20	620
Netherlands	17	176
Russia	27	501
Spain	–	28

Source: Carlo M. Cipolla, *The Fontana Economic History of Europe: The Emergence of Industrial Societies* (London, 1973), II, p. 789.

could be traveled in all but the worst of weather conditions. All the same, heavy loads damaged surfaces, making rail transport more effective for carrying bulk goods. Water transport advanced with the introduction of steamboats, development of navigable rivers, canal building, and creation of deep-water ports. Even so, the direction of river systems was more or less fixed by nature; railway lines could more readily be adapted to market forces, thereby reducing dramatic differences in prices. In 1817 a bushel of wheat sold for 16.63 marks in the Prussian Rhineland, whereas the price roughly 400 miles to the east in Prussian Posen was 9.68 marks. By 1855 the price differential throughout Prussia had been reduced to 1.7 marks.

Increased productivity and population growth combined in rural areas to raise the number of landless laborers, requiring new strategies for survival. Overseas emigration rose to an average of 110 000 per year between 1821 and 1850, but such numbers could alleviate distress only marginally. More significant was that early industrial development often occurred in the countryside, enabling some families to find alternative employment in the "putting out" system. All the same, overpopulation frequently led to division of land into small parcels that were insufficient to support peasant families, driving large numbers to towns and cities in search of work.

Rural Society: Peasants, Nobles, and Notables

The majority of Europeans were peasant farmers who lived in isolated farmsteads, hamlets, and villages. Urbanization was more pronounced in the west, yet two thirds of the French still lived in the countryside.

Among peasants a basic division existed between those who were legally free and serfs who endured servitude. Rare in the west, serfdom was increasingly widespread as one traveled into central and east Europe. Western peasants could own land, move about as they pleased, and marry of their own volition; serfs encountered restrictions in all these regards. Serfs also had obligations which varied in kind and degree according to local custom. A serf might have to yield a portion of his produce, provide labor, or perform certain tasks for his lord. Where workers were relatively scarce, landlords generally extracted labor services. Elsewhere absentee landlords tended to rent out their estates and commute labor services into payment of seigniorial dues. On the whole, serfdom was in decline. During the Revolutionary-Napoleonic era the French had abolished the remnants of feudalism wherever they gained control, and in their drive to resist the French the Prussians had also emancipated the peasantry. Nevertheless, in certain regions serfdom was becoming more onerous.

There was great diversity among free peasants. The more successful families had acquired substantial tracts of land through generations of shrewd management; they were able to apply new techniques, owned plow teams, and had the capital to employ others. Below them was a large number of "middling" subsistence farmers who eked out a living on small parcels of often unconnected land. Lower still were peasants whose landholdings were insufficient to sustain a family and required some other source of revenue. On the bottom rung were landless peasants who survived solely on the basis of providing labor to others.

The trends that enhanced productivity increased stratification. Especially in the open fields of the North European Plain, peasant communities traditionally imposed restrictions on property rights – through rights of usage, maintenance of common lands, and regulation of plowing, sowing, and harvesting. In their drive to enhance productivity large landowners, frequently backed by governments, sought liberation from these restrictions. Enclosure had already spread from Britain to the Netherlands, France and parts of western Germany by the close of the Napoleonic era; it would be extended to the rest of west Europe, save for Spain, by mid-century. In Prussia between 1821 and 1870 close to 16 million hectares of land were removed from common usage. The effect was to concentrate ownership in the hands of those who could purchase privatized common land or privately owned land from peasants whose farms no longer proved viable with the loss of usage rights. In Prussia there were roughly two million landless laborers in 1849 and in much of Europe they posed a serious challenge to civil order.

Peasant culture tended to be conservative; strangers and new ideas were viewed with suspicion, although peasants would adapt if advantages were obvious. Having developed in relative isolation, peasant communities could appear remarkably uniform to the outsider in terms of clothing, utensils or implements, food, buildings, physique, speech, habits, and customs. Most clothing remained home-made, although cheap industrial cottons and fabrics were increasingly purchased in the towns. Moreover peasants could draw distinctions that might escape an urban observer – possession of more than one cupboard, or a cabinet with a clock indicated prosperity. Running water was not to be found in peasant dwellings, although in the more advanced villages wells might be supplemented by a fountain.

Also due to isolation, peasant communities varied considerably as a whole. Nevertheless there were common denominators. Housing was primitive and unsanitary; most dwellings consisted of a single room, and doors and windows were kept to a minimum because they were subject to taxation. Fires were an ever-present hazard. Diet was often poor due to reliance on a small number of local staples. Literacy rates were low. Urban cultural movements penetrated the countryside only slowly, although traveling salesmen often combed the countryside selling prints, bric-a-brac, and pamphlets. Farmer's almanacs and religious tracts were the chief reading fare, where it existed. Conscription could, however, alter the perspective of young peasant men and make them a fascinating source of information when they returned to their villages. Market forces in the west, particularly migration in search of work, could also increase ties between town and country. Tradition dominated village culture, providing the rituals that gave each year its rhythm of long days of hard labor interspersed with holidays and festivals, but more recent forms of sociability such as card playing and dancing also made inroads, frequently eliciting the disapproval of clergymen.

Noble landowners were easily the wealthiest and most powerful group in European society. They were, however, a diverse lot and differing legal systems would prove a key variable in the preservation of the estates upon which their wealth, power, and status depended. In Prussia, and in Spain until 1836, perpetual entail prevented the dispersal of noble estates. In Britain noble estates could be preserved by primogeniture, whereas in France the absence of entail and egalitarian inheritance laws led to fragmentation of ownership. In countries where noble titles passed to all heirs, nobles were greater in number and many of them were relatively poor. Magyar nobles comprised 4% of the population in Hungary in the 1820s and the proportion of Polish nobles was perhaps as high as 7%.

Varying legal systems led nobles to adopt differing strategies for maintenance of their positions. Prussian nobles adapted to emancipation of the peasantry and the agrarian depression of the 1820s through the development of capitalistic agriculture. In the Austrian Empire, where seigniorial obligations remained, noble landowners professionalized management of their estates and benefited by the existence of two elite estate training schools. Service to the state remained important to noble status everywhere, although competition from commoners increased. In the rapidly expanding bureaucracies of Prussia and Russia nobles gradually gave way to trained professionals who, more often than not, were commoners. Similar trends were apparent in the Habsburg Monarchy, where emphasis on education and promotion based on seniority of service eroded the influence of old noble families. Domination of governments and the higher levels of the administration thus became all the more desirable, and nobles also were thick on the ground in representative bodies, be they parliaments or provincial diets.

Ultimately noble social dominance was under greater challenge in the west, necessitating greater compromise. In Russia noble magnates could still look down on nonagrarian sources of income and in Prussia the *Junkers* showed little inclination to mix with the bourgeoisie. Disdain for wealth derived from commerce or industry had, however, long been discarded in Britain and in France the elite consisted of "notables" – a fusion of noble and wealthy bourgeois elements frequently joined by marriage, financial and business contacts, and training in the same educational institutions.

Commerce, Industry, and the Emergent Urban Economy

Overseas commerce had been the most dynamic economic sector in the eighteenth century and this trend continued. The period saw less imperial expansion than the second half of the century, but destruction of the Spanish Empire opened markets for other European traders in Central and South America. While the slave trade declined, import of spices, coffee, sugar, and cotton rose, and export of textiles and hardware grew.

No country benefited more by the development of a global economy than Britain (see Table 4.3). Between 1800 and 1850 British imports increased by roughly 400%. Imports of raw cotton, principally from the American South, dwarfed those of other European states (see Table 4.4). Manufactured exports also rose dramatically – roughly 60% between 1800 and 1850. Textiles, especially cheap cottons, led the way; by 1837 foreign sales of cotton exceeded domestic sales by about one third. Investment abroad also dramatically expanded. Between 1815 and 1825 the British invested roughly 6 million pounds abroad annually; by 1850 the

Table 4.3   Relative shares of world manufacturing output.

	1800	1830	1860
Europe as a whole	28.1	34.2	53.2
United Kingdom	4.3	9.5	19.9
Austrian Empire	3.2	3.2	4.2
France	4.2	5.2	7.9
Germany	3.5	3.5	4.9
Italy	2.5	2.3	2.5
Russia	5.6	5.6	7.0

Source: P. Bairoch, "International Industrialization Levels from 1750 to 1980," *Journal of European Economic History* (1982), 11, 296. Reproduced by kind permission of UniCredit Group.

Table 4.4   Average annual raw cotton consumption (in thousand metric tons) in select countries.

	1815–24	1845–54
Austria-Hungary	–	26.5
France	18.9	65.0
Germany	–	21.1
Russia	1.0	21.5
United Kingdom	54.8	290.0

A dash (−) indicates that no figures are available.
Source: Carlo Cipolla, ed., *The Fontana Economic History of Europe: The Emergence of Industrial Societies* (London, 1973), II, pp. 780–1.

figure had reached 30 million pounds per year. The rewards were even more impressive: interest and dividends yielded roughly 8 million pounds annually in the 1830s, and had shot up to about 50 million pounds by the 1870s.

Expansion of markets in Europe was also vital. Prior to 1814 Napoleon's Continental System had sheltered continental industry from British competition. In the aftermath of Napoleon's fall, British exports produced a glut on markets, leading many states to resurrect tariffs. Thereafter such barriers were gradually removed or reduced. British manufacturers, employing the arguments of economists such as Adam Smith and David Ricardo, were keen advocates of free trade and British governments slowly liberalized trade regulations. Equally consequential was Prussia's role in creating the *Zollverein*. Not only did the *Zollverein* eliminate customs barriers to promote economic integration among German states, it also negotiated commercial treaties with other states. In 1831 Prussia reached an agreement with the Netherlands that abolished tolls on the Rhine River. Thereafter trade treaties were signed with the Netherlands in 1839, Britain in 1841, and Belgium in 1844. Meanwhile other states followed the Prussian model in pursuit of internal economical integration. Between 1849 and 1851 Parma, Modena, Hungary, Croatia, Slavonia, and Transylvania joined a customs union previously formed between Austria and Bohemia, and Poland was linked to Russia in a customs union in 1850. Reduction of barriers between states would then accelerate, especially after the signing of the Cobden-Chevalier Treaty between Britain and France in 1860. In the following seven years the French would enter into free-trade treaties with Prussia, Belgium, Italy, Switzerland, Sweden-Norway, Spain, Holland, Austria, and Portugal. The integration of European commodity trade thus proceeded rapidly.

If markets were expanding, capital did not necessarily respond in ways that favored industry. Banks preferred to invest in land, through the offer of mortgages, and in government bonds. Thus the capital for industrial development came largely from enterprising families as industrialists sought to increase their resources through strategic marriages or agreements with associates often drawn from a shared religious community. Self-financing meant that re-investment had to come from profits and hence industrialists gained a reputation for frugality and the heavy demands they placed on employees. It was only with the advent of the railway age in the 1840s that financial institutions began to invest large sums in industry.

In early attempts to define a model of industrialization that consisted of clearly identifiable phases, economic historians drew attention to a pre-revolutionary stage termed "proto-industrialization." Particularly in the eighteenth century, in certain regions merchants began to circumvent guild restrictions by "putting out" raw materials for manufacture by artisans or peasants in their rural cottages. Frequently the finished items were sold abroad, and "cottage industry" thus contributed to development of mass production and markets. Yet, establishing a straightforward link between "proto-industrial" cottage industry and modern industry is not easy. On the one hand, in some regions "proto-industrialization" contributed to the industrial revolution by enabling concentration of wealth in the hands of entrepreneurs who could then invest in plant facilities and machines for factories. On the other hand, in other "proto-industrial" regions cottage industry appears to have hampered adaptation to the factory system. Moreover, the influence of guilds varied greatly and not all urban centers resisted the "putting-out" system. In calico-printing industries at London, Amsterdam, Mulhouse, Rouen, Ghent, Barcelona, and Prague factory production and the "putting-out" system grew simultaneously; at least initially, the two modes of production could be complementary. Ultimately, there were many paths to industrialization, and a wide range of variables determined the paths taken.

A key to the industrial revolution was the way in which productivity was increased by the substitution of machines driven by waterpower or steam for tools operated by hand. Increased productivity lowered prices and, in combination with population growth, created mass markets. Gradually industry's importance within the economy grew, although it still trailed agriculture and commerce by a wide margin at mid-century.

Revolution first occurred in textile production. The process began in 1767 when James Hargreaves, a carpenter and farmer, invented a cotton-spinning machine which could simultaneously turn eight spindles rather than one. Thereafter refinements enabled the spinning jenny to hold hundreds of spindles. The resultant yarn was, however, weak, creating problems for weaving. Richard Arkwright provided a solution in 1769 with his invention of the water frame, a machine that used power generated by a water mill to stretch the cotton prior to spinning, yielding stronger yarn. Ten years later Samuel Crompton combined the two advances in a machine called a mule. Not only did the mule provide yarn of high quality, it was roughly 300 times more productive than a spinning wheel. Resultant increase in cloth production and decline in prices were dramatic, and they became much more so when mules were adapted to the steam engine (Figure 4.1).

Figure 4.1   Mechanized (mule) spinning in a Lancashire cotton factory, 1834. © Bettmann/
Corbis.

The latter mid-eighteenth-century creation of James Watt had initially been used
to pump water out of coal mines. Refinements in coal smelting thereafter enabled
widespread manufacture of superior steam engines made of iron. Although
steam-powered engines were applied to mules from 1800 onwards, it was only
after Richard Roberts developed an automatic steam-powered mule that
application became widespread. The bottom line in this process of innovation
was an immense increase in productivity: it has been estimated that in the
eighteenth century an Indian hand spinner would require 50 000 hours of labor to
spin 100 pounds of cotton; from 1825 onwards Robert's automatic mule could
perform the task in 135 hours.

   Change in textile production illustrated several features of the industrial
revolution. Early inventions solved old problems and also posed new challenges,
stimulating further innovation. While the early inventors were self-taught, Roberts
was a trained engineer and his role was a sign that scientific education would
become increasingly important to development. Advances in one field could
stimulate progress in another, creating reciprocal demand. Growth in the cotton
industry increased demand for steam engines, which in turn relied on improved
iron and increased supplies of coal for power. Some inventions were valuable in
certain contexts, and less so in others. The number of steam engines doubled in
Britain in the 1840s, enabling manufacturers to shift operations from rural water-
driven mills to urban factories. Creation of a turbine engine in 1832 by Benoit
Fourneyron, however, improved use of water power and inclined the French to

continue exploiting abundant river systems, especially given that they had less easy access to coal supplies. Finally, we can note also that while technological innovation had revolutionized spinning, less change had occurred in weaving. For this reason, weaving grew dramatically as a source of employment in the early decades of the century; there were roughly 250 000 handloom weavers in Britain in the mid-1820s. By 1826 technical improvements had enabled mass distribution of powerlooms and begun the displacement of handloom weavers, a process that would play out on the continent in subsequent decades. Industrialization forced change; yet opportunities to adapt varied and the dislocating consequences could be severe.

Britain entered the nineteenth century well in advance of the other European states in industrialization, and her lead would increase dramatically thereafter. The reasons were many. Superior agricultural productivity meant that more resources could be directed to other economic sectors. Superior financial organization helped to provide capital for investment. Maritime commerce fostered production of durable goods and access to overseas markets was provided by the world's leading navy. Especially with the advent of the railway, possession of ample coal supplies was also a major asset, although here one must also take into account willingness to innovate and then develop technological invention. Although the British did not have a monopoly on coal reserves, they were the first to perfect blast-furnace technology so that from the 1760s onwards coke (burnt coal) could be substituted for charcoal (burnt wood) in converting iron to pig iron for the production of wrought iron and steel (see Figure 4.2 and Table 4.5). They thereby freed themselves from reliance on diminishing forest reserves, and blast furnaces produced close to ten times more than the old charcoal furnaces. Except in Belgium, continental iron and steel manufacturers continued to use charcoal forges until the 1850s, partly because they experienced difficulty in adapting British technology, and partly because they had greater access to forests. In the event, at mid-century Britain produced two-thirds of the world's coal and more than doubled the iron production of the rest of Europe combined.

Among continental elites a trip to Britain became an important part of education. While some visitors were horrified by the squalid living conditions of the laboring poor, or the brutal impact of industry on the natural landscape, others returned home determined to emulate the British. It was after a trip to Britain in 1822 that István Széchenyi began to advocate social and economic reform so as to facilitate industrialization in Hungary. The German Alfred Krupp traveled to Britain in 1839 to study industrial production prior to founding a steel factory at Hamburg in 1841. Many Britons, in turn, saw opportunity abroad. The first director of the Krupp steel factory was English, as were 90 of the 150 workers. Britons helped establish the three leading machine-building firms in Bohemia, a pioneering iron works in Moravia, and steamship companies that ran on the Danube and in the Adriatic.

If industrialization was still largely in the offing on the continent, certain long-term patterns were already apparent. Industrialization spread most rapidly in the

Figure 4.2 Coke smelting and the Royal Iron Foundry at Gleiwitz, Upper Silesia, 1841.
© BPK/Lutz Braun.

Table 4.5 Average annual output of pig iron
(in thousand metric tons) in select countries.

	1825–29	1835–39	1845–49
Austria	–	–	146
Belgium	–	126	176
France	212	327	488
Germany	90	146	184
Hungary	–	–	36
Russia	164	177	200
United Kingdom	669	1142	1784

A dash (–) indicates that no figures are available.
Source: Carlo Cipolla, ed., *The Fontana Economic History of Europe:
The Emergence of Industrial Societies* (London, 1973), II, p. 773.

west, where it was concentrated in certain regions. The first ran from northern
France through Belgium into western Germany and included textile manufacture,
mining, and metallurgy. A second, focused on textile production, ran along the
Rhine River, encompassing Alsace, parts of Switzerland, and several towns in

southwest Germany. A third region, also devoted to textiles, could be found in central Europe, stretching from southwestern Saxony into Bohemia.

Industrialization soon became a measure of state power and thus it makes sense to note its progress in national terms. Partly due to ties with Britain and large coal supplies, Belgium led the way in early continental industrialization. Belgium was, however, a small state, and hence France was Europe's second largest industrial producer. Competition with the British forced mechanization and greatly increased productivity in textiles, and in the 1840s development of railroads also spurred industrialization. As before, the French dominated manufacture of luxury goods such as furniture, porcelain, and silk, but production was largely undertaken by artisans working in small shops. Massive adoption of mechanization of spinning could also be seen in emerging industrial centers in the German Rhineland. Elsewhere, however, industrialization was scattered and slow to develop in the German states – some 90% of German weavers still worked at hand-operated looms in 1850. Nevertheless, German governments were quick to build rail systems as a means to absorb surplus labor.

As one traveled eastwards, industrialization became increasingly thin on the ground. Beginning in the 1820s adoption of steam engines led to rapid expansion of cotton factories in Bohemia and Austria. Possession of rich coal deposits also fostered relatively rapid development of rail lines. In contrast, Hungary became a supplier of raw materials for industrializing regions elsewhere in the Empire and nationalists called for customs barriers to protect producers from Austrian and Bohemian competitors. In Russia officials viewed industrialization with suspicion, believing that through enhancement of mobility railway lines posed a threat to civil order. Tsar Nicholas voiced such concerns in characteristic fashion: "The filth which stayed quietly on the bottom will rise to the surface."[44] Reluctance to encourage development of a rail system, in combination with failure to adopt coal forges, meant that Russia fell from being the world's leading iron producer in the eighteenth century to eighth place by 1850.

Urban Society

Unemployment in the countryside led large numbers to search for opportunity in urban centers. Rapid growth in cities such as London, Paris, Vienna, and Moscow (see Table 4.6) was based on internal migration; many major cities were in fact net "killers" in that death rates exceeded birth rates.

Urban centers did generate employment, although opportunities were not necessarily great. Most migrants went to commercial or administrative centers where factories had yet to make their mark. Casual labor, domestic service, manual labor in the construction trades or dockyards, work in sweatshops, prostitution, or crime thus became the leading means by which migrants sought to survive.

Table 4.6 Population growth in select cities (in thousands).

	1800	1850
Amsterdam	201	224
Barcelona	115	175
Berlin	172	419
Budapest	54	178
Glasgow	77	345
Liverpool	82	376
London	1117	2685
Madrid	160	281
Manchester	75	303
Marseilles	111	195
Milan	170	242
Moscow	250	365
Munich	40	110
Naples	350	449
Paris	547	1053
Prague	75	118
St Petersburg	220	485
Vienna	247	444

Source: Carlo Cipolla, ed., *The Fontana Economic History of Europe: The Emergence of Industrial Societies* (London, 1973), II, p. 750.

Population growth rapidly surpassed the capacity of urban centers to provide adequate living conditions. New buildings were poorly built, and old ones were repeatedly subdivided. Families lived in single rooms, sometimes sharing them with as many as 30 others by sleeping in rotation. Nor could sanitation services, garbage disposal, water supply, medical provision, or road building keep up with demand, leading to filthy, poorly lit, crowded slums in which cholera, typhoid, and tuberculosis flourished. New industrial centers provided the worst examples of environmental degradation as city planners sought to concentrate labor close to the workplace. Lakes and marshes were filled, hills leveled, and plants uprooted in radical transformations of rural landscapes. Sewers were left open, waste materials polluted rivers, and coal fumes blackened walls. Response to such conditions varied. Municipal governments began to employ building inspectors, established or expanded fire departments, and commenced installation of gaslights on city streets. Even by the 1830s most French cities were registering more births than deaths and the same trend would become apparent in German cities by the 1840s. All the same, for first-generation migrants the contrast with village life was daunting.

For those who entered the industrial workforce, change was even more shocking. Long hours of labor were also characteristic of rural life, but such toil was conducted in fresh air or at home, tasks were varied, and opportunities for recreation were greater. Labor in factories or mines was a different proposition. Holidays were fewer and breaks were shorter. Idle machines meant losses for owners, and hence they sought to create a disciplined workforce that followed schedules and worked to maximum efficiency. Employers frequently used fines for adult employees, and corporal punishment for children. Factory production also required that workers adjust to the tempo set by machines. Monotonous routine, exhaustion, and absence of safety measures led to accidents for which there was little, if any, compensation. Dust in unventilated textile mills could prove lethal, although reports of harnessed children pulling coal carts through mine shafts were more apt to elicit public concern.

According to testimony given to a British parliamentary committee in 1832, William Cooper, an employee at a flax mill, worked nonstop from 5:00 a.m. until 8:00 p.m., save for a forty-minute respite for dinner, during which he had to clean his machinery. The food or drink that he consumed frequently was covered with dust, and he developed respiratory problems. Having begun work as a child, Cooper's growth was stunted and his body was deformed. He had not been able to attend day-school, although he had learned to read by attending a Sunday-school. By the age of 28 his health had broken down, so that his factory would no longer employ him, leaving him and his family dependent upon parish support. Given such conditions, it is little surprise that employee turnover rates were extremely high.

Since its origins, scholars have debated over the social impact of the industrial revolution. One line of interpretation depicted workers as little more than slaves. Such authors dwelt upon long working hours, low wages, poor living and working conditions, child labor, and worker alienation. A second line of interpretation gave a more positive account, underlining that the industrial revolution produced unprecedented long-term growth that filtered down to the lower classes. By lowering prices, mass production enabled the lower classes to purchase goods that had been beyond their purchasing power in previous generations, and meanwhile *per capita* income rose. Depictions of suffering had been exaggerated; even when higher urban costs of living were considered, factory hands earned higher real wages than rural workers. A factory worker's diet was better, and he or she was apt to be better clothed than his or her rural counterpart.

Such revision helped establish more balanced assessment; yet debate continues. Recent analyses question whether *per capita* income actually did rise in the first half of the century. Industrial workers were more vulnerable to market fluctuations. A slump could leave an unemployed worker with little more than debt and although charities might provide assistance, such institutions could not support large numbers for long periods. Moreover there is no obvious way to measure the impact of industrialization on the family. Mechanization frequently reduced the skills necessary for employment and drew increasing numbers of women and children away from home. Yet the home had been the central place of education for children. Concern with undisciplined factory children would lead to legislation that limited child labor and sought to ensure at least minimal education provision. Britain pioneered legislation early in the century; however, it was only in the 1830s that serious attempts at enforcement began and such developments would not occur on the continent until much later.

Ultimately the industrial revolution was highly disruptive of old patterns of work, social relations, and family life, and neither society nor state was prepared for the dislocations it brought. Yet given population growth, it is fair to ask what the lot of Europeans would have been without the industrial revolution. Previous periods of expansion had been followed by collapse and widespread misery, whereas at mid-century Europe entered a long phase of widening prosperity. Subsequent growth should not be attributed solely to industrialization; yet it did play a crucial part.

Study of the middle classes has also provoked debate. Early descriptions of bourgeois conquest of power have given way to subtler analyses that recognize the staying power of the nobility, emphasize fusion between nobles and wealthy commoners, and recognize diversity within the middle classes. Middle-class elements could be said to share power with the nobility in western states such as Britain and France, but bourgeois presence in the governments of the eastern autocracies was minimal.

Economic growth accentuated differences of wealth and lifestyle within the middle classes. At the top were the bourgeoisie. For centuries, wholesale merchants, financiers, and bankers had constituted the elite of the Third Estate. In the nineteenth century they were joined by industrialists, although relations were not necessarily close. Industrialists came from a broad range of often humble backgrounds, their wealth was recently acquired, and their enterprises appeared volatile rather than secure. Many industrialists had been cloth merchants or small-scale tradesmen; hence they were well attuned to market forces and what especially distinguished them was their capacity for risk taking. The fabulous success of some should not, however, blind us to the reality of the risk entailed; far more enterprises failed than succeeded.

Somewhat below the "grand" bourgeoisie came the liberal professions, wherein status was tied partly to wealth and partly to education. Here too there was great diversity: to be a leading practitioner of law or medicine in Paris or London was one thing; to ply one's practice in a humble backwater was quite another. As states expanded, middle-class elements entered bureaucracies in droves and a leading scholar has concluded that it was state expansion, rather than capitalism, that made the century a "bourgeois" one.[45] In the first half of the century, government expenditure grew by 25% in Spain, 40% in France, 44% in Russia, 50% in Britain, and 70% in Austria. Many civil service positions were poorly paid; nevertheless they conveyed status on "white-collar" workers.

Lower levels of the middle class merged with the popular elements of society and contemporaries saw them as a bridge between the extremes of opulence and poverty. Scholars seeking to define the *petite bourgeoisie* (shopkeepers and artisans) as a social class find the task difficult due to heterogeneity within the group and high levels of social mobility. Not surprisingly, then, expressions of class identity were rare, and observers often viewed the *petite bourgeoisie* as evidence against predictions of social polarization. Small-scale retail merchants were capitalists: they owned their shops, employed workers, and sold goods they had not produced. Yet they also engaged in manual labor, whether by stocking shelves, sweeping storefront entryways, or dealing with the public.

Closely tied to shopkeepers were artisans, whose position was even more liminal. On the one hand, master craftsmen owned the means of production and employed others. On the other hand, they also engaged directly in production, working alongside their apprentices and wage-earners and frequently sharing the same home. Artisans were the group most threatened by mass production. Division of labor undermined the value of skills upon which artisan identity and status depended, and artisans struggled to compete against low-priced confection (ready-made goods). Although mass production never entirely eliminated crafts production, the broad trends were ominous. At mid-century a German observer warned: "amongst the citizens of a town the artisan is the conservative *par excellence*. But he will not remain a conservative if he is pauperized or allowed to degenerate."[46] Literacy was high among artisans and they possessed more political consciousness than manual workers. Hence they played a leading role in riots, revolt, and popular radicalism. Yet artisans were a divided lot, viewing other trades and tradesmen as much as rivals as potential allies. Nor did they necessarily view the demands of manual laborers or the unemployed with any great sympathy. To some extent guild traditions encouraged them to act collectively. Nevertheless, artisans prized independence and they were not easily drawn into a unified labor movement.

In recent times historians have described the middle classes more in cultural than in socioeconomic terms. Definition of, say, the bourgeoisie in terms of values can provide advantages; it helps, for instance, to explain why members of the bourgeoisie (according to socioeconomic definition) often were at the forefront of attacks on bourgeois culture. Nevertheless, there also are problems with the new cultural emphasis, especially concerning its relation to socioeconomic analysis. If an individual who was working-class in socioeconomic terms shared the values defined as bourgeois should we redefine him or her as bourgeois? Or do we resort to the largely discredited idea of "false consciousnesses"?

Attribution of specific values to the middle classes can nevertheless be useful, provided that we do not mistake generalization for unvarying truth. It is true, for instance, that certain middle-class groups prized independence and thrift and eschewed ostentation. In Bradford industrialists were described as "a race of moles that burrowed in the earth and needed not the sunshine of amusement: a generation that was forever hungering and thirsting, scraping and saving."[47] However, some bourgeois aped aristocratic manners, including conspicuous consumption.

That separate gender spheres ideology and idolization of family life were pronounced among the middle classes is well known. Women should preside over

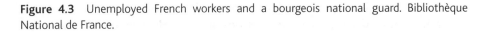

Figure 4.3 Unemployed French workers and a bourgeois national guard. Bibliothèque National de France.

the domestic sphere – managing the family budget, supervising the work of servants and the education of children, organizing social life, and only occasionally entering the public sphere as part of charity associations. Yet it is equally clear that, unlike the popular classes, the middle classes had the means to act upon these ideals. Did such ideals necessarily distinguish the middle classes? Studies indicate that gender norms were also deeply entrenched among the popular elements of society. Family economy dictated that most working-class women work; yet they generally left the public workforce upon marriage, taking up piecework at home. Similar points can be raised concerning privacy, cleanliness, independence, self-improvement, discipline, sobriety, and respectability. When a former factory worker informed a British parliamentary commission that since her husband had given up alcohol he had stopped beating her, paid more attention to the children, become a better worker, and returned to the Church, she was expressing values that transcended class.[48]

Most middle-class prescriptions were aimed at the poor and reflected concern with the number of impoverished families living in urban slums. Compassion and fear both rose as a series of private and public enquiries pointed to worrisome trends. Urban rates of suicide, insanity, crime, and divorce were reported to be higher than in rural areas. To many contemporaries, the urban poor seemed to be alien to the values held by the rest of society. Uprooted from the social bonds of their villages, migrants became the "dangerous classes." Men ignored religion, spent their time drinking or brawling, and showed little respect for authority. Women lived with men out of wedlock, resorted to prostitution rather than earning an "honest" living, and were also prone to alcohol abuse. Family life disintegrated as neither parent attended to the needs of children, who soon took to a life of crime.

Moral depravity allegedly was accompanied by physical decay as malnutrition and lack of hygiene rendered the "dangerous classes" vulnerable to each passing disease. Worse still, they were infectious, particularly prostitutes who transmitted venereal disease. Publication of crime statistics, journals devoted to accounts of crime, and novels serialized in newspapers contributed to exaggerated alarm. Whether crime rates were rising is a matter of debate among scholars; on the whole, it would appear that property crimes were ascending while crimes against the person were declining. There is, however, little doubt that contemporaries perceived a growing threat to social order.

State Formation and Social Control

Central governments generally left poor relief to local government, although they did seek to mitigate hardship during periods of crisis. States frequently sought to organize private charity, to which they contributed, and initiated public works to combat unemployment. Such initiatives were, however, considered temporary expedients; they entailed no recognition of permanent responsibility. Even the English Poor Law was designed to discourage dependency – individuals, or families, must take responsibility for their own welfare. German workhouses gave the unemployed a last resort, but wages were intentionally kept below market rates. While French communes provided hospices for the sick and outdoor relief for the "worthy" indigent, vagabonds were sent to prison and beggars were forced to labor in workhouses.

Poor relief relied heavily on private charity and religious groups played a crucial role in the organization and distribution of aid. In 1833 the Saint Vincent de Paul Society began visiting the poor and sick in France, and in 1848 the German *Innere Mission* commenced similar work. Attitudes to charity differed, however, among the faiths. On the one hand Catholicism taught that charity was a virtue; it brought the poor and wealthy together in Christian community and thus was mutually beneficial. On the other hand certain Protestant sects, notably British Nonconformists, believed that charity must be discriminating; individuals must not be discouraged from making the "right" choices by removal of responsibility. One way or another, charitable institutions such as foundling hospitals, nursery schools, and orphanages provided great opportunity for inculcating the poor with values approved by elite benefactors.

Much effort went into educating the poor and at times educational systems were political battlegrounds. The mutual education system, wherein more advanced students supervised groups of younger students, was developed by the Quaker Joseph Lancaster in the 1800s and it spread to France in 1815, where it was taken up by liberals. French ultraroyalists responded with expansion of teaching congregations. After passage of the Guizot Education Law in 1833, competition between state schools and Catholic private institutions fostered an accelerating drive to gain the minds and souls of lower-class youth that continued throughout the century.

Desire for control also fostered a steady increase in the state's capacity for repression. Many of the traditional institutions of social order (feudalism, church influence, and guilds) had been in decline long before the French Revolution further corroded their authority. Re-establishment of order had then become the means by which Napoleon sought to gain approval for his rule. When Napoleon's Empire fell, many of its institutions were adopted by Restoration regimes and periodic turmoil thereafter fostered demand that the state do more not just to restore order when it broke down, but also to prevent disorder from occurring in the first place.

There were four principal forces for the provision of order. National police forces were created in France in 1798, in Ireland in 1823, and in Spain in 1844. Despite organization of the London Metropolitan Police in 1829, defenders of "English liberty" feared that a national force might be put to political purposes. Thus the civilian police forces organized in England and Wales were placed under the control of local councils. It was not until the 1850s that police forces became mandatory for all boroughs and counties and some remained very small. Even so, growth was sufficient that there were 32 000 policemen by 1881. Similar arrangements were to be found in the German states of Württemberg, Bavaria, and Saxony, although in Prussia the police were directly responsible to the central government. One way or another, concern with state security ensured that local and national police forces were deployed to monitor or repress groups deemed seditious by the central government. A second force consisted of variants of the *gendarmerie* in France, Prussia, Piedmont, and Spain. Designed particularly for the countryside, the *gendarmerie* was composed of former soldiers and organized along military lines. A third force, the regular army, was generally held in reserve for crises. A fourth force, urban militias composed of middle-class property owners, frequently played a crucial role in patrolling streets and breaking up demonstrations, but was notoriously unreliable. They could be dangerous to regimes that had run afoul of elite groups; it was no coincidence that revolts in Bologna in 1831 and 1848 occurred after the Papacy had allowed the propertied classes to form militias. The Prussian government preferred to use military garrisons for crowd control, and elsewhere states would seek to reduce reliance on militias by building up the other instruments of coercion at their disposal.

In urban centers and the countryside police regulations governing behavior steadily increased. Given the limited size of police forces, the state had to rely heavily on civilians for the actual enforcement of such regulations. Moreover, it took a long time to accustom communities to the idea that the state and its agents should have a monopoly over policing. Especially among the peasantry, long-established practices whereby the community imposed social norms through methods such as arson, physical attack, or shaming ceremonies such as "rough music" or "charivari" only gradually gave way. Similarly contentious were police efforts to regulate the behavior of the poor by monitoring drinking establishments or suppressing amusements such as cockfighting.

Inclination to regulate was also apparent in dramatically increased compilation of statistics for the formulation of policy. Budding social scientists were thrilled when in the 1820s the French government began publishing annual reports of crime rates. The natural impulse when given such information was to use it, and calls for legal reform designed to prevent or reduce criminality were not long in coming. Reformers called for measures that were less concerned with retribution than with changing criminals so that they did not repeat their offences. Executions declined as emphasis shifted to imprisonment, with sentences calibrated so as to reflect the gravity of the offence in the hope of securing higher conviction rates. The nature of imprisonment also attracted extensive consideration. According to a leading French advocate of penal reform, discipline was crucial to preventing recidivism; imprisonment should consist of "constant submission to orders, to routines, to obligatory silence – that continuous surveillance that never leaves a man to himself, that demonstrates at every moment both his condition of captivity and the mistrust that he inspires."[49] Measures proposed included separation of first-time offenders from hardened criminals, solitary confinement so that prisoners could reflect on their transgressions, strict daily regimes to instil discipline, and hard labor that would inculcate respect for work. Although a variety of prison models was developed, increasing numbers of convictions led to overcrowding and often made solitary confinement impractical, while complaints about the alleged impact of prison economic production on market prices led to emphasis on work that had no real value. All the same, state institutions were moving in the direction of behavior regulation and by the end of the century half or more of convicts would be imprisoned in individual cells in France and Prussia.

Statistics gathering, often conducted by physicians, was also a feature of public health movements that came to the fore in France in the 1820s and thereafter in Britain. The French pointed to poverty as a key variable in mortality rates, whereas the British emphasized the physical conditions in which individuals lived. While French hygienists could point to their role in passage of a child labor law in 1841, their British counterparts concentrated on sanitation measures. Passage in Britain of the Public Health Act in 1848 then proved a landmark. Local authorities gained a wide array of powers ranging from management of water supply systems and gas works, to regulation of environmentally dangerous trades such as tanneries, to judging the safety of buildings, to the provision of burial grounds, parks, and public baths. Thereafter willingness to act on such powers varied considerably because ratepayers frequently were reluctant to accept the expenses of sanitary reform, and not all continental states would follow the highly decentralized British model. Nevertheless, the path of increased sanitary regulation would be taken by all European states.

Concern with infection was also prominent in a highly contentious example of regulation. Napoleon had led the way in legalizing prostitution so as to assert control over the "oldest profession" in an attempt to reduce transmission of syphilis to soldiers. Prostitution was to be restricted to certain areas and confined to police-monitored brothels. Prostitutes must be licensed, submit to regular medical inspection, and obey regulations designed to reduce their contact with the rest of society. Although rules would vary, and usually be determined at the municipal rather than state level, legalization and regulation of prostitution would spread throughout Europe. The obvious "double standard" entailed (male customers were not regulated) would be a lightening rod for feminist reformers subsequently, but for our present purposes the point to note is that concern with hygiene would open the door to a great deal more state intervention in the second half of the century. In arguing for state-regulated prostitution Giuseppe Sormani made a point that was full of implication: "prostitution is not a crime … but it is a vice, morally and hygienically dangerous to Society. The exercise of prostitution can therefore be considered from the same point of view as that of unsanitary industries, which Society, with every right, subjects to special regulations and special surveillance."[50]

State power (or the lack thereof) was frequently demonstrated by response to disease and epidemic. In the case of smallpox the state could endorse or require preventive measures that ultimately proved effective and gained widespread approbation. Encouragement of inoculation was widespread by the late eighteenth century and by the 1820s recourse was increasingly had to vaccination. Initially states relied on voluntary vaccination; thereafter groups such as soldiers were targeted for mandatory vaccination. By the 1850s the British had made vaccination mandatory for all children. In contrast, France was exceptionally reluctant to intervene so dramatically and vaccination was not made compulsory until 1902.

Cholera posed a more difficult challenge due to uncertainties as to how to combat it. During the initial onslaught in the 1820s and early 1830s, states deployed quarantine measures that had previously been developed to counter the spread of the plague or, more recently, yellow fever. Officials soon recognized that such measures were, however, largely ineffective. Attempts to maintain *cordons sanitaires* on national frontiers and isolate affected internal areas did not stop cholera from spreading, were too expensive to maintain, and harmed commerce. They also provoked dangerous levels of social protest because they frequently fell most heavily on, and violated the customs of, the poor. Thereafter the British swung decisively toward sanitation measures. Nevertheless, the latter could be just as interventionist as the measures propounded by the advocates of quarantine; in 1848 some 48 000 houses in London received inspections. Beyond an obvious increase in the number and presence of state officials, a more subtle development occurred as the state gradually challenged the role of the Church as the chief source of aid and hope during times of affliction.

Cultural Trends: Religious Revival and Romantic Revolt

From the perspective of the recent past, religious revival and the Romantic Movement seem striking departures from the secular rationalism of the Enlightenment. Both looked back to earlier times for inspiration and thus it seems fitting that they flowered during the Restoration. Nevertheless, such a perspective requires qualifications. Romanticism affected high, rather than popular, culture. Similarly, while it is true that religious revival produced mass movements, prior loss of faith was more of a concern for the elite than the common people. Nor is it necessarily accurate to portray religious revival and Romanticism as characteristic of the age; liberalism and secularism continued to gain adherents. Finally, it is also instructive to note that Romanticism and religious faith were not in all regards polar opposites of liberalism.

Religious revival was partly an attempt to counter the challenge posed to Church authority by Enlightenment emphasis on reason and science as the path to understanding. Catholic reactionaries known as *ultramontanes* rejected belief that individuals could gain salvation through rational interpretation of the scriptures, emphasized the corruption of human nature brought by the "original sin" of Adam and Eve, and stressed the authority of the Pope and Church hierarchy. For those who held such views, the Revolution, with its emphasis on individual rights, secularization, and idolization of "Reason" was the work of Satan. Subsequent breakdown of order could be attributed to prior loss of faith and the Piedmontese Joseph de Maistre was just one of many writers who asserted that the Revolution of 1789 was a scourge designed by God to punish humanity. In early 1816 a bishop informed Parisians that: "For over twenty years, we have endured punishment for the failings of our forefathers. … But Providence has made all bow before it, and when the hour sounded … nothing could stop the hand of God from smiting impiety."[51] Impiety soon, however, reared its head again in the form of massive publication of the works of leading *philosophes*, necessitating the organization of a Catholic missionary movement that featured public book burnings.

Protestantism also experienced a dramatic revival that ultimately fostered diversity as the faith splintered into evangelical, orthodox, and liberal wings. An evangelical Protestant "Awakening" had originated in the early eighteenth century in German Pietism and the Moravian Brethren, prior to spreading to England in the form of the open-air preaching of John Wesley and Methodism. After 1815 British Evangelicals then spread "the word" to the continent by founding missionary and bible societies in Norway, Denmark, France, Switzerland, and Holland.

For British Evangelicals and German Pietists religion was a matter of the "heart" rather than the mind; they emphasized experience and sentiment while urging listeners to interpret the bible for themselves and model their lives on that of Christ. In doing so they sparked intense enthusiasm, particularly among peasants and artisans, but they also posed a challenge to the authority of formal theological learning, sacrament, and Church hierarchy. By the 1830s traditional Calvinists, Lutherans, and Anglicans had begun to respond to the "Awakening" with their own revival. While the latter shared emphasis on spiritual renewal, the confessionals were more inclined to remain within the confines of doctrinal orthodoxy. Competition among evangelicals, orthodox confessionals, and liberals who continued to emphasize rationalist theology would thereafter provoke numerous schisms within Protestant churches.

Renewed fervour posed challenges to states, established churches, and religious minorities alike. In the aftermath of the Revolutionary era regimes generally sought to promote revival, seeing churches as buttresses to social order and the Restoration settlement. However, states also sought to manage the churches and curb religious zeal when it ran counter to state interests. In theory Orthodoxy was part of official Russian identity, but the extent to which the state sought to impose Orthodoxy varied in a diverse Empire. While the Tsarist regime might be surprisingly pragmatic with it Muslim populations, intolerance led to confinement of Jews to a Pale of Settlement on the western border of the Empire, termination of the Uniate Church in the Ukraine, and harassment of Catholic officials in Poland. In the west militant Catholicism lay behind revival of the Jesuit order in Spain, Piedmont-Sardinia, and Austria. Anti-semitism could be seen in re-confinement of Jews to ghettoes in the Papal States and the kingdom of Sardinia, and expulsion from the German free cities of Bremen and Lübeck.

For monarchs close ties with the Church could prove a double-edged sword. Although the Church might provide sanction, it might also pose a rival source of loyalty, place restrictions on state prerogative, and prove politically divisive. The revolutions of 1830 in France and Belgium partly resulted from state religious policies. On the reverse side of the coin, certain theologians drew the conclusion that close ties to the state did not necessarily benefit the faith. Félicité de Lamennais, a former ultramontane champion of Papal reaction, converted to liberal Catholicism after 1830. In stressing religious liberty Lamennais helped to found a wing within Catholicism that was not resolutely opposed to modern developments such as civil equality, representative government, and freedom of expression. For the Papacy sovereignty, however, rested solely with God and his agents on earth – the Church and legitimate monarchs. Thus Lamennais's writings were condemned in a papal encyclical of 1832. Yet close ties to the state did not come without cost. Although the concordats negotiated by Rome with various states offered a measure of security and funding, they also entailed increasing state control over the appointment of bishops. In 1829 some 555 of 646 diocesan bishops were appointed by the state rather than the pope.

Revival did not carry all before it. Liberal theologians often were entrenched in the theological faculties of the established Protestant churches and fought against revivalist emphasis on emotion and orthodox emphasis on traditional dogma. Fortunes varied; while the Calvinist national Church of Geneva returned to the orthodoxy of its founder, liberal Protestants remained dominant in France. Similar struggles occurred in Britain and the German states, with a tendency for social elites to adhere to the established churches, while large numbers of the masses turned to the more charismatic preachers of the "Awakening."

Not all returned to the fold. In France recently recruited peasant priests repulsed as many as they attracted with their aggressive zeal. More constructive was the work of women who entered religious congregations or lay organizations and devoted their efforts to provision of charity, nursing, and education; between 1815 and 1850 the number of nuns in France rose from 15 000 to 66 000. Urbanization posed problems; often there were neither churches nor priests nor pastors to attend to the growing ranks of urban poor. In the countryside hostility or indifference to organized religion was less apparent. Disruption of official Church practices in the 1790s had, however, facilitated the revival of pagan rituals, often intermixed with Christianity, with which the Church had long been in combat. Among the peasantry, belief in magic and witchcraft remained widespread.

It is a well-worn convention to begin discussion of Romanticism by emphasizing that it eludes precise definition. One can identify characteristics that perhaps typified Romanticism, but in so doing one encounters numerous contrary examples. Given the inclination of Romantics to defy convention, differences among at least three generations of artists, and varied national contexts, it is perhaps inevitable that description of the movement requires constant qualification.

The origins of Romanticism can be traced back to dissent with what was considered excessive Enlightenment emphasis on reason and material progress as the means to achieve a better world. Romantic preoccupation with spirituality was notorious. It could take the form of religious faith in the works of Chateaubriand, a search for the divine in nature in the paintings of Caspar David Friedrich, or emphasis on eliciting emotional response in the musical compositions of Ludwig von Beethoven. The appeal to sentiment and imagination, so marked in the novels of Charles Dickens, was well suited to the mode of melodrama, and differed radically from the tone of detached objectivity generally associated with the *philosophes*. Fascination with the middle ages and Gothic art was particularly apparent in the works of Walter Scott and Victor Hugo, and reflected longing for an ideal time when faith and honor had bound all individuals in a community of shared belief. Nevertheless, Romanticism was not necessarily reactionary, and especially in central and east Europe it was closely intertwined with confidence in the power of human reason. Rather than expressing desire simply to return to the past, Romanticism reflected belief that something valuable had been lost. Future progress, rather than stasis in an ideal past, required regaining what had been lost.

Enlightenment *philosophes* had expressed a linear conception of progress wherein all peoples advanced along the same path. Difference indicated that some had progressed more than others. German Romantics, especially Johann Gottfried von Herder, challenged this conception of progress, arguing that different peoples advanced along different lines, and that wisdom from past experience was embodied in age-old local customs, laws, and tradition. The true repositories of wisdom were the people, or folk – the peasant and, to a lesser extent, urban masses who remained untarnished by the cosmopolitanism of elite culture. Toward preserving and spreading this wisdom, the brothers Jacob and Wilhelm Grimm initiated a vogue of publishing folk tales, while other scholars recorded or "rediscovered" the "pure" language of the people. In Poland in 1816 Zorian Dolega Chodakowski called on scholars to "undertake a search for information among our own people … One must go to various remote localities and stoop beneath the peasant's thatched roof. One must be present at his feasts, at his play, and at the various events of his life."[52] Herder had not ranked European peoples in a hierarchy and had believed that they should develop along their own paths, free of foreign influence. Subsequent thinkers such as Johann Gottlieb Fichte were, however, more inclined to proclaim the superiority of their culture, and a messianic strain soon emerged in most variants of early nationalism. Why should a superior culture not lead the rest?

Inclination to exalt an idealized construct of the "people" to some extent clashed with a second characteristic of Romanticism – individualism. Romantics became celebrated for their willingness to break out of the confines of classical or neo-classical artistic strictures. What mattered was that the artist found the best means to evoke the sentiments he or she wished to convey and old rules should be dropped if they hindered self expression. As Friedrich put it, "The painter should paint not only what he sees before him, but also what he sees in himself."[53] Romantics also made a convention of tales of individual protagonists struggling heroically against social restraints that prevented personal fulfilment. As Romanticism began to blur into social realism, the French novelist Honoré de Balzac filled his novels with such characters and the motif became so standard that it was suitable for satire in Lord George Byron's epic poem *Don Juan*:

> Let us have Wine and Woman, Mirth and Laughter,
> Sermons and soda-water the day after.[54]

Emphasis on individual expression and willingness to challenge convention also helped to open space for women writers such as George Sand (Amandine Aurore-Lucille Dupin), who produced a steady stream of widely-read confessional novels, and Mary Shelley, whose *Frankenstein* challenged belief that science could conquer nature, rather than work in harmony with it.

All of the leading political ideologies were reflected in Romanticism. Nationalism took some of its character from Romantic emphasis on the "people" and the cultures that were ascribed to them. Utopian socialists and reactionaries could extract something from Romantic yearning for a golden age wherein communities had lived in harmony. If early Romantic British poets William Wordsworth and Samuel Taylor Coleridge found that the Revolution spoiled their initial enthusiasm for liberty, a later generation led by Byron would defy the conservative regimes of the Restoration era. When Germane De Staël, a leading liberal who had introduced German Romanticism to France, died in the early Restoration, leading Romantics Chateaubriand, Alphonse de Lamartine, and Hugo were either conservative or reactionary royalists; by 1848 Lamartine and Hugo had passed from royalism to republicanism and Chateaubriand had flirted with liberalism. Ultimately Romanticism was characterized by a search for ideals that could overcome social and cultural divisions. For some, such aspirations would seem to be fulfilled during the "springtime of the people" that immediately followed the revolutions of 1848. Material realities would soon, however, reassert their political ascendancy and Romanticism became a movement of the past in the west. Nevertheless, because it was so closely tied to cultural nationalism, Romanticism would persist in central and eastern Europe throughout the nineteenth century.

The period of 1815–48 was one of gradual, often painful, transition. Population growth, in combination with increased agricultural productivity, was creating widespread unemployment in the countryside. Neither overseas emigration nor rural cottage industry could absorb such large numbers, and hence urbanization accelerated. The industrial revolution had not developed to a point where it provided an answer to these problems, and in its early stages it frequently added to dislocation, particularly in the form of sharp cyclical slumps that deepened misery and heightened insecurity. Migrant workers often confronted desperate circumstances when they moved, entering factories where they existed, working in construction or service industries elsewhere, performing whatever odd tasks might come their way, or slipping into crime. Towns and cities could not keep pace with the influx in provision of infrastructure, leading to horrifically degraded living environments. Yet urban migration continued because prospects were better than in the countryside.

Alarm over the "social question" and exaggerated fear of the revolutionary potential of the "dangerous classes" led to increasing calls for action to maintain or restore order. The most striking response was growth in the state's capacity to police and regulate, although events would soon reveal the limits of state power in these regards. A more complex trend involved inculcation of the masses with values espoused by the elite. Whether such values were entirely foreign to the masses is questionable; what is clear, however, is that only the wealthy could afford to put ideals such as separate gender spheres into practice. One way or another, greater attention, apparent in a deluge of prescriptive literature, was directed toward the masses by private and public organizations. Growing involvement in the organization of charity and provision of education pointed toward greater state efforts in regard to social control, and already such encroachments were provoking clashes with religious authorities. To a limited extent, states also expanded their regulatory powers, particularly in regard to public health, but also regarding child labor.

Still missing was recognition that the state could play a greater role in seeking to mitigate the dislocation brought by economic change. The causes of unemployment were not fully understood and too frequently unemployment was attributed to moral qualities such as irresponsibility rather than structural change within the economy. Moreover, even in its early stages, socialism raised questions about property rights. As the revolutions of 1848 would demonstrate, fears concerning destruction of private property would make reform more difficult to achieve. Romantic and religious aspirations for communities in which all members shared in a sense of collective responsibility would shatter as political and social divisions opened wide.

5
Europe in Transition
The 1848 Revolutions and the Crimean War

Unlike during the Revolution of 1789, when one country spread revolution elsewhere, in 1848 revolt broke out more or less simultaneously throughout Europe. Although each insurrection was shaped by particular context, the European character of the 1848 revolutions could be seen in a common pattern. Initially the revolutionary tide carried all before it; Louis-Philippe lost his throne and other monarchs agreed to opposition demands. Far from occurring in isolation, uprisings were triggered by news from abroad; as listeners at a popular assembly in Mannheim were told: "One idea flashes through Europe. The old system shakes and falls into pieces."[55] Collapse of the old regimes then created space for political participation and competing demands soon divided moderate and radical reformers. From June 1848 onwards conservatives exploited such divisions to roll back revolutionary accomplishments. Repeatedly, news of successful counter-revolution elsewhere encouraged monarchs to seize the initiative at home. By the end it seemed that little had been accomplished; yet politics had gone through a major transition. Brief as it was, the "springtime of the peoples" had encouraged a flowering of civil society that expanded political consciousness, and lasting social or political change had occurred in several states. While the "social question" dominated, the "woman question" also came forward, and meanwhile two new creeds, "scientific" socialism and anarchism, were being formulated.

Little had changed in the states system by 1852. Nevertheless, in France the 1848 revolution had led to the establishment of a regime that was determined to revise the Vienna Settlement. French challenge to Russian influence in the Ottoman Empire thereafter contributed directly to the outbreak of the Crimean War of

Europe's Uncertain Path 1814–1914: State Formation and Civil Society, First Edition. R. S. Alexander.
© 2012 R. S. Alexander. Published 2012 by Blackwell Publishing Ltd.

1854–56. War among the powers severely damaged the Concert of Europe and paved the way for subsequent dramatic alteration of the states system.

Origins

Revolt resulted from a combination of short- and long-term factors. We have discussed these factors separately in previous chapters, so here we can focus solely on how they combined. Population growth put pressure on food supply and rural overpopulation led to increasing unemployment. Large-scale riots in East Prussia, Silesia, and Posen in the early 1840s were harbingers of looming challenge. Tension was also building in urban centers where factories, mechanization, and overcrowding engendered resentment among artisans.

Long-term sources of conflict were exacerbated by a recession that commenced in 1845 with a potato blight. In the following year a hot, dry summer yielded the worst grain harvest in three decades. Scarcity of basic foodstuffs led to a doubling of prices by 1847, producing market riots and threatening bands of beggars demanding aid. Fortunately the harvests of 1847 and the years following were bountiful and prices declined until the mid-1850s. Except in Ireland, famine was averted; yet elite and mass elements had been traumatized. Worse still, previous over-production in manufacturing and excessive extension of credit had rendered the financial, commercial, and industrial sectors vulnerable, and the reduced purchasing power brought about by high food prices then tipped the balance.

Economic crisis gave urgency to the demands of opposition groups calling for reform. Here too there was a combination of long- and short-term factors at play. Provision of education and expansion of literacy increased political consciousness, particularly among artisans and shopkeepers. Gradual expansion of the press had a similar impact, and the increasing rapidity of communications meant that news traveled more swiftly. Civil society could also be seen to be expanding in the formation of clubs and associations. In combination, economic crisis and rising political opposition raised questions over the legitimacy of existing regimes. Corrosion of loyalty existed at both elite and popular levels, and it increased as governments refused to grant reform.

The Initial Wave

Two developments were precursors of revolution. In 1846 election of Pope Pius IX encouraged Italians to hope that the Papacy would take the lead in a peaceful unification of Italy in the form of a federation. Thereafter reforms appointing layman to state office, reducing censorship, creating a civic guard, and forming a customs union among the Papal States, Tuscany, and Piedmont-Sardinia seemed to confirm expectations. Then illusions were shattered in 1847 when Pius told a Consultative Assembly that Papal sovereignty derived from God and could not be compromised by a profane constitution. A second precursor was more threatening. In March and April 1846 attempts by Polish patriots to trigger a war of liberation led instead to a peasant onslaught on noble landowners. Perhaps a thousand mutilated corpses were piled onto carts in the province of Galicia. Despite nationalist charges that Habsburg officials had connived in the attacks, it would appear that the slaughter resulted solely from peasant antagonism toward their noble masters. One way or another, the episode led the Imperial government to abolish the *robota* (a feudal labor service) in Galicia, provoking demand for liberation elsewhere.

Revolution began in January 1848 with an uprising at Palermo that soon spread to the mainland of the Kingdom of the Two Sicilies. At Naples King Ferdinand II reluctantly conceded to pressure by publishing a new constitution based on the French Charter. His actions placed pressure on other rulers and by February 8 Charles Albert had granted Piedmont-Sardinia a constitution (the *Statuto*), also based on the Charter. The Grand Duke of Tuscany followed suit by granting a constitution on February 17 and within a month the Pope would do the same, though the legislative powers of a proposed secular parliament were very limited. In contrast, Austrian authorities remained unbending. At Milan in January reformers had organized a boycott of gambling lotteries and tobacco sales that were a principal source of state revenue. Austrian soldiers responded by smoking ostentatiously in public, leading to combat with nicotine-deprived crowds that led to six deaths and declaration of martial law throughout Lombardy-Venetia on February 25.

Developments in Italy were less influential than events in France, which remained the focus of conservative fear. When the Guizot government banned a reform banquet at Paris, most opposition politicians acquiesced because they too feared that the combination of economic hardship and political protest might spark revolt. Several radicals, however, ignored the ban and organized a demonstration on February 22. Clashes between troops and demonstrators spiraled out of control on the following day when nervous soldiers fired a fusillade on a crowd of protestors. Barricades were soon erected and the forces of order began to collapse. The civil militia known as the National Guard actually joined in the revolt and many soldiers hesitated to open fire. At first Louis-Philippe sought to appease his opponents by dismissing Guizot; thereafter realization that he had lost the support of the middle-class National Guard convinced him to take flight.

Parliamentary opposition leaders such as the Romantic writer Alphonse de Lamartine then demanded creation of a republic. Lamartine read out a list of names of parliamentarians and journalists for a provisional government, while the crowd shouted out its acceptance or rejection. With a ministry of moderate republicans thus chosen, the deputies and crowd marched to the *hotel de ville* (city hall) to proclaim the new government to the people, only to be confronted by a group who intended to proclaim a list of men known for advocating social reform. Jubilation at the overthrow of the Monarchy facilitated compromise and thus several radicals, including the socialist Louis Blanc, formed a minority in a revised list otherwise dominated by moderates.

Confusion soon reigned in the Austrian Empire. On March 3 the lower house of the Hungarian Diet voted for a reform program that gave Hungary autonomy within the Empire. Shortly thereafter Austrian liberals at Vienna called for dismissal of the government and creation of a Diet in which peasants and the middle classes would be represented. While the government hesitated, crowds gathered in the streets of Vienna and events took a familiar course. Harassed troops fired on angry crowds, middle-class Civil Guards refused to restore order, and the court capitulated. Meanwhile Hungarian radicals put forward a program of "Twelve Points" that called for freedom of the press, the executive ministry and a National Assembly to be based at Budapest, equality of religious and civic rights, equal taxation, abolition of seigniorial taxes, national armed forces, and union with Transylvania. Under attack at so many points the court gave in; Emperor Ferdinand accepted the resignation of Metternich and by March 15 he had promised to grant a constitution to Austria and concede greater autonomy to Hungary. Within three days revolt began at Milan; after five days of fighting Marshal Radetzky withdrew his army to a fortified zone between Lake Como and the River Po known as the Quadrilateral. Imperial forces also withdrew from Venice and most of mainland Venetia to Verona, enabling the republican lawyer Daniele Manin to proclaim re-establishment of the Venetian Republic.

In Prussia Frederick William reacted to news of insurrection with the remark: "Satan is on the loose again."[56] Unnerved by the success of opposition forces elsewhere, and by disorders throughout the German states, he then announced his willingness to participate in drawing up an all-German constitution. All the same, fighting between troops and crowds broke out at Berlin on March 18. Disturbed by the loss of perhaps 200 lives, the King ordered the Army out of the city. Effectively the prisoner of an aroused populace, Frederick William was thereafter forced to watch while corpses from the street fighting were tossed on a pile. He agreed to election of a Prussian constituent assembly based on universal male suffrage, but public humiliation was unlikely to reconcile him to the bourgeois liberals whom he was forced to appoint to government. With no support forthcoming from Berlin or Vienna, rulers of the smaller German states appointed liberals to government and granted constitutions where there was none, or enhanced parliamentary powers where there were.

What was most striking was how little fighting had been required. The initial revolts were largely confined to urban centers and often rulers capitulated after relatively small demonstrations. Fear generated by memories of 1789 doubtless played a part in undermining the confidence of conservatives who believed that momentum lay entirely with their opponents. Nor was fear confined to conservatives; very few political leaders wished to see a repeat of the Terror. Even among supporters of the revolution in France, establishment of a republic brought a mixture of joy and alarm; as the novelist Flaubert put it, "the sound of the guillotine made itself heard in every syllable of the word 'Republic.'"[57]

The Springtime of the Peoples

In the aftermath of the revolutions state control contracted, allowing previously repressed groups to come forward. The constitutions of 1848 advanced freedom of expression, assembly, association, and petition, and greatly increased the number of individuals who could vote.

The press rapidly expanded. In the Austrian Empire the number of newspapers with political content rose from 19 to 306, and in Paris total press runs went from 50000 prior to the revolution to 400000 in May. Amidst expansion, groups previously linked by common opposition began to enunciate their differences. While liberals emphasized maintenance of civil order, radicals sought to build mass followings. Pursuit of support among artisans, agricultural laborers, and impoverished peasants then led some radicals to advocate social revolution. Radical writers did not, however, have the field to themselves; conservatives soon proved themselves equally adept by the propagation of monarchist journals.

The principal forms of freedom of assembly were mass demonstrations and political clubs. The line between peaceful protest and insurrection was, however, a thin one, and while such occasions might be useful to revolutionaries, violence increasingly provoked counter-revolutionary sentiment among a public worried by disorder. Political clubs served several functions. Through the reading of newspapers and speech making, they provided opportunity for information gathering, discussion, and indoctrination. Debate tended to produce homogeneity as like-minded members continued to attend while those who disagreed went elsewhere. Clubs thus took on the colorings of the political *blocs* in parliament. Through correspondence they formed networks and in Germany clubs organized federations and national congresses. At election time the clubs were centers for voter mobilization, and while parliament sat they organized petitions.

Given their advocacy of male democracy, it is not surprising that radicals were at the forefront of political association. Their efforts did not, however, go unchallenged as royalist societies could be found in France, Germany, and Italy. Prussian landowners were quick off the mark in forming an organization dubbed the *"Junker* Parliament"* and their efforts were effective in sidelining agrarian reform legislation in the summer of 1848. *Junker* mobilization was a sign of things to come in terms of the organization of interest groups, but it was too obviously tied to social privilege to have much mass appeal. More consequential were the Prussian conservatives who shrewdly gave up openly championing absolutism and social hierarchy while simultaneously playing on fears of Jacobinism among the armed forces, state officials, and the clergy. By the spring of 1849 there were roughly 300 conservative patriotic societies with 60 000 members.

Perhaps the most remarkable development of the period was the organization of associations for promotion of women's rights. Women's political participation in 1848 occurred mostly within mixed groups. They took part in insurgency and some male clubs allowed women to attend, although few allowed them to speak. In certain instances women held their own public meetings or joined men to express support for various causes, and often they formed associations to aid the casualties of street fighting. Gender specific initiatives were more striking and frequently they resulted from exclusion by men from associations. Women formed political clubs in cities such as Berlin, Vienna, and Paris to press for improved educational and employment opportunities, control for married women over their own property, or legalization of divorce. At Paris Eugénie Niboyet, edited *The Voice of Women* and Jeanne Déroin called for women to gain the vote. In Saxony the novelist and social reformer Louise Otto founded the *Women's Newspaper*, calling on women to enter the realm of freedom.

Through its advance toward male democracy, 1848 clearly exposed the patriarchal nature of politics. Women did gain entry to the Frankfurt parliament as spectators, but when they began to interject their opinions into the debates, they were forced to depart. In France a contributor to *The Voice of Women* warned: "In the Republic of 1848, which has for its mission the abolition of privilege, there still exist pariahs, and these pariahs will be you [women]!"[58] Déroin argued that although men and women were different, such differences were equally worthy of representation in government. Mothers fulfilled their duties to society and hence should not be denied rights. Not all feminists claimed the right to vote, however, as divisions emerged over priorities. For George Sand, establishing the French Republic had to come first. After posing the question of whether women should participate in politics, Sand answered: "Yes, some day … but is that day near? No, I think not, and in order for women's position to be transformed, society must be radically transformed."[59]

Governments responded with repression. Women's clubs were closed in France in June 1848, women's political activity was banned in Austria in March 1849, and Prussian women were prohibited from entering political associations in 1850. Part of a broader process of reaction, denial of rights for women was all the easier in that it reflected a general current of male hostility. Not all men advocated repression and some male associations were supportive of women's organizations, but caricatures of "unnatural women" in the press, calls for women to confine themselves to domesticity, and physical disruption of meetings were more typical.

The most widespread political experience was voting. As one would expect, levels of politicization varied regionally. Austrian liberals made rapid advances in transforming voluntary associations into political clubs; yet organization at the state level was rudimentary and voter turnout low. Party formation was more advanced in Germany where elections for the parliaments of the smaller states were complemented by creation of an all-German parliament. Hopeful that an all-German state would prove more progressive than the smaller ones, 51 liberals met at Heidelberg on March 5 and elected a committee of seven men. The latter, in turn, convoked a gathering at Frankfurt of some 600 deputies of the current state assemblies who formed a pre-parliament. The pre-parliament then decided that elections should be held for a German constituent assembly. Significantly, the deputies did not specify franchise qualifications and left the individual states to determine their electoral systems. Disappointing to democrats, this decision revealed the desire of moderates to cooperate with the existing authorities. Much thus rested on the evolving character of the current regimes, but the hope invested in the Frankfurt parliament could subsequently be seen in some 17 000 petitions signed by three million people.

The Crucible: Politics up to the June Days

Revolution did not sweep through all states. Although Chartism revived in Britain, it was racked by internal division. Early on, officials deployed troops and enrolled special police constables, but they avoided direct confrontation. In Ireland starving populations were too preoccupied with survival to challenge the 34 000 troops concentrated there. Moreover, abolition of the Corn Laws reduced frustration with a regime that seemed capable of change. As violence continued on the continent, support for the Chartists diminished amidst allegations of forged signatures for another reform petition. The sympathy of many Chartist leaders for the social democratic policies of French radicals created friction with British middle-class liberal reformers, and in June the government arrested Chartist leaders with little difficulty.

Where revolution had occurred, it was soon followed by dispute. In France moderate republicans believed in *laissez faire* and held that establishment of male democracy was sufficient to ensure that government represented the interests of all, whereas radicals called for state intervention to secure more equitable distribution of wealth. Initially moderates had felt obliged to make concessions and thus on February 25 the provisional government had issued a decree proclaiming it would secure work for all by creation of national workshops. The term "national workshop" had particular connotations for workers who had first encountered it in Louis Blanc's *The Organization of Labour*. Blanc thought the state could put an end to capitalism by organizing cooperatives called national workshops which would be run and owned collectively by workers. When the creation of national workshops was announced workers expected something along such lines. Moderates in the cabinet, however, had no intention of attacking capitalism and in fact the national workshops were little more than make-work projects designed to keep workers busy until economic prospects improved.

A hike in taxation to fund the workshops provoked riots, particularly in the countryside, where peasants saw no reason why they should have to support urban "loafers." More contentious still were the arguments of some radicals that the state should eliminate or restrict property rights. Although few clubs were communist, the press focused on occasions when extremists such as Louis-Auguste Blanqui called for war on the rich. An inveterate, middle-class conspirator, Blanqui had vaguely socialist aspirations, but he was more preoccupied with the process of revolution than its results and his main contribution was to foster the idea of a revolutionary vanguard that would achieve revolution with minimal reliance upon popular insurrection. It was not difficult under such circumstances for conservatives to stoke alarm over a "red menace" to private ownership.

Radical leaders were at times compromised by the actions of militants acting at the street level. The Left worried that manhood suffrage might work to their disadvantage and demanded that elections to a constituent assembly be postponed until the peasantry had been "enlightened." On March 17 a demonstration of over 150 000 Parisians organized by the clubs "convinced" the government to set the election date back by two weeks. A second march on April 16 was, however, dispersed by an increasingly hostile National Guard. Radical fears were then confirmed as some 500 seats went to moderate republicans, another 300 to former Orleanists and legitimists whose loyalty to the Republic was suspect, and only 100 to radicals. Radicals were correct in thinking that patronage ties had induced peasants to vote for local notables, but in focusing on urban workers they had almost entirely forgotten the rural elements that formed the majority of the population. Selection of a new government more in conformity with the Constituent Assembly confirmed the leadership of Lamartine and led to the departure of Blanc. Militants responded with a demonstration on May 15. Of some 20 000 initially gathered, perhaps 3000 invaded the National Assembly and applauded while Blanqui demanded a huge tax on the rich and removal of troops from Paris. Thereafter a group of revolutionaries proceeded toward city hall to proclaim a new regime, but the National Guard then arrived to disperse the crowd and arrest the leaders of revolt.

At that point the fate of the national workshops hung in the balance. Moderates were convinced that the workshops were "a permanent center for insurrection"[60] and swept aside arguments that keeping 100 000 workers occupied promoted civil order. The government decided to abolish the workshops and a decree of June 21 ordered workers under the age of 25 either to enter the army or work in the provinces draining swamps. Older workers would be paid a token indemnity. By June 23 barricades had gone up, and the minister of war General Cavaignac allowed them to spread while he concentrated his forces. Hand-to-hand combat between perhaps 15 000 insurgents on one side, and the army and Mobile National Guard on the other, was fierce until the army's artillery fire decided matters. There were perhaps 10 000 casualties by the time fighting ended on June 26.

Some contemporaries saw the June Days as an opening salvo in a war between the upper and lower classes. Certainly social tensions abounded, especially as some

100 000 National Guardsmen poured in from the provinces to aid in a restoration of order that included summary execution of roughly 3000 insurgents and the arrest of 12 000 more. Yet the civil war is better interpreted as republican fratricide. Most workers stayed out of the fray. National Guardsmen fought on both sides and the main government civil force, the Mobile National Guard, was lower-class in composition. Radical leaders were torn in their allegiance, uncertain whether the revolt constituted an attack on the Republic, or an attempt to save it. One way or another, the June Days marked a watershed in the history of the revolutions.

Outside France divisions between the Left and Right were generally complicated by nationalism, but elections to the Frankfurt Parliament clarified differences in Germany. Partly due to restricted franchises, the elections favored liberal constitutional monarchists and conservatives, although radical democrats also gained significant numbers of seats. After gathering on May 18, the deputies formed into *blocs* and began to debate. They created a provisional government (the German Central Government) that would be responsible to the Assembly and led by the Austrian Archduke John as Imperial Vicar, and also voted to create an army and navy. The economic liberalism of the deputies, most of whom were landowners, businessmen, or members of the liberal professions, soon became apparent in refusal to follow the example of the French in proclaiming a right to work – such a guarantee would be "a sanction of laziness."[61]

More problematic were the issues of defining the nature and boundaries of a new German state. Most parliamentarians preferred a constitutional monarchy, raising the question of who should be the ruler. A majority backed the *Grossdeutch* (Big German) solution which entailed full integration of the German parts of the Habsburg Empire and exclusion of the non-German parts. This option pointed toward the Emperor as ruler. A second faction advocated the *Kleindeutch* (Little German) solution, which linked the lesser states to Prussia and pointed to Hohenzollern rule. For the time being the deputies chose to concentrate on designing a constitution; yet issues of nationalism continued to haunt them. Despite initial expressions of sympathy for Polish nationalism, the deputies soon supported the Prussian government's decision to partition the Grand Duchy of Posen and incorporate a questionably large "German part" into Prussia. A more complicated source of trouble had arisen in March when the German populations of Schleswig-Holstein revolted against Danish rule. When the Prussian liberal government dispatched troops, the Assembly joined in declaring war on Denmark. Nationalism thus initially revealed itself as a source of unity.

The way in which the "springtime of the peoples" could descend into "a nightmare of nationalities"[62] was most evident in the Austrian Empire. Hoping to exploit Austrian retreat in March, Charles Albert of Piedmont-Sardinia declared war on Austria. His troops entered Lombardy and Venetia and soon thereafter plebiscites secured approval for unification, thereby terminating the radical governments that had driven out the Austrians. Expansion appealed to Charles Albert, but he also wanted to undercut democratic forces by leading unification

Figure 5.1   Revolution in Vienna, 1 May 1848: Soldiers fire on the mob during a revolutionary uprising against the Habsburg Austrian Empire. Getty Images.

along lines of his own choosing. Unfortunately the conservative nature of his rule undermined support, and the King hesitated to attack the remaining Habsburg forces in the Quadrilateral and Verona. Meanwhile the Pope, arguing that he could not sanction a war between Catholic states, reversed an earlier decision to send troops in support of Italian liberation. King Ferdinand, having initiated a coup against his opponents at Naples, also recalled his forces to overcome a revolt in Calabria and a bid for secession in Sicily. The Austrian commander Radetzky thus gained breathing space to strengthen his forces.

The reluctance of Charles Albert to engage resulted partly from calculation that there might be no need; the Empire was under attack on many fronts. With the Imperial government in disarray, the Hungarian Diet moved to Budapest. Shortly thereafter Magyar deputies passed the March Laws, creating a separate Hungarian government and transforming the Diet into a parliament with control over its own army, the state budget, and foreign policy. To rally support the Hungarian parliament then abolished serfdom in April, although relatively little land was provided to the peasantry and the franchise for parliamentary elections was restricted to roughly seven percent of the population. The motives of the Imperial government for abolishing serfdom in Galicia were similarly political, but here the intent was to maintain antagonism between Polish nationalists and the Ruthene peasantry.

Figure 5.2   A Paris women's club in 1848. © Photo 12.

With the support of Tsar Nicholas, Imperial forces then landed a first blow against nationalism later in the month by bombarding Cracow and destroying a Polish nationalist committee.

The fortunes of the Imperial government plummeted in mid-May when demonstrators at Vienna forced the resignation of conservatives from the government and secured broadening of the franchise for elections to the promised Austrian constituent assembly. The Emperor and court conceded these demands while they were taking flight to Innsbruck, leaving control over Vienna to a radical Committee of Public Safety. Imperial prospects did not appear much brighter in Bohemia, where nationalist rivalry led to a Czech boycott of elections for the Frankfurt parliament. At Prague Czechs singing "Forward against the Germans, forward against the murderer, against Frankfurt"[63] prevented Germans from voting and in early June they organized a Slavic Congress. Delegates of the Slavic nationalities called at the Congress for creation of an Imperial federation wherein a Slavic province would gain the same autonomy as Hungary.

Flickering ambition in court circles to restore absolutism was revived in June. Prior to the Slavic Congress clashes between Czechs and Germans had provided pretext for the recall of Prince Alfred Windischgrätz to command of the Prague garrison. An aristocratic Bohemian landowner, General Windischgrätz was an unreconstructed reactionary. Radicals thus viewed his doubling of military street patrols and emplacement of artillery on the hills overlooking the city with chagrin. Demonstrations on June 12 soon turned into battles with soldiers – exactly the excuse Windischgrätz wanted for bombardment. Surrender by the leaders of perhaps 1500 insurgents followed within a week, enabling the General to place the city under martial law, purge the National Guard, and send delegates to the Slavic Congress packing.

Incomplete Conservative Recovery, July–December 1848

The June Days precipitated polarization in France. In parliament at least 300 crypto-royalists formed the Party of Order and began to attract moderate republicans alienated by social turmoil. The Lamartine government gave way to one led by Cavaignac, who accelerated a crackdown on radical clubs and newspapers. Desire for strong government could also be seen when the deputies completed a new constitution; the Republic would be led by an elected president who, like parliament, could claim to represent the nation, though he would be restricted to a single, four-year term of office. Meanwhile radicals regrouped to form a democratic-socialist bloc known as the Mountain and united provincial clubs in an electoral organization named Republican Solidarity for the presidential campaign that began in November.

For many the most astounding event of 1848 was the return of a Bonaparte to power as a result of the elections. Yet Louis-Napoleon possessed powerful assets. He had a band of personal supporters who built a broader following through propaganda based on platitudes concerning former greatness, the necessity of national unity, and benign intentions toward all. Perhaps more valuable was that Louis-Napoleon was not associated with the carnage of the June Days. All the same, the extent to which he rose above others was a sign of the effect nationalist sentiment could have on the masses. Whereas Louis-Napoleon racked up 5 534 520 votes, his nearest rival, Cavaignac, had to settle for 1 448 302, and candidates such as Lamartine gained derisory figures.

France was free of fighting in the second half of 1848; elsewhere much of Europe was convulsed. Calabrian insurrection in the Kingdom of the Two Sicilies was suppressed in June and in the following month Austrian forces routed the troops of Piedmont-Sardinia. Italian soldiers fought bravely, although poor leadership apparently led Radetzky to tell his gunners: "Spare the enemy generals – they are too useful to our side."[64] Resultant armistice enabled the Austrians to reoccupy Lombardy and mainland Venetia in August, although Venice held out. In September the Neapolitan army invaded Sicily and it would force a truce with Sicilian separatists in October. Against such currents there were counter-currents. Elections held in Tuscany in June and subsequent demonstrations at Florence forced the Grand Duke to appoint Giovanni Montanelli, a democrat who advocated an all-Italian constitutional assembly, as prime minister in October. At Rome the assassination of a liberal prime minister on November 15 sparked a demonstration organized by democratic clubs and the civil guard and Pius IX fled to the Kingdom of Two Sicilies. Rome became the haven for radicals such as Mazzini, who established a central committee of Italian clubs while calling for an all-Italian Constituent Assembly in December.

As time passed, foreign policy intertwined with domestic politics. Pressure applied by Britain and Russia led the Prussian government to negotiate an armistice with Denmark in August. Frederick William signed without even consulting the German Central Government at Frankfurt, a sign of growing resolve at the Prussian court. Although the Frankfurt parliament initially denounced the armistice, shortly thereafter conservatives and constitutional monarchists voted to reverse the condemnation and nationalist attempts to stir revolt in Frankfurt, Cologne, and Baden were suppressed by troops.

The crucial role of military loyalty became even more obvious when Frederick William appointed Count von Brandenburg, a conservative cavalry general, as prime minister. In November Brandenburg called the army back into Berlin and placed the city under state of siege. The Prussian Constituent Assembly called for a tax revolt; Berliners, many of whom were frightened by demands for social revolution, however, remained quiescent. By December 5, Frederick William could dissolve the Constituent Assembly. The King did, however, sugar coat this pill by issuing a constitution that proclaimed basic civil liberties and provided for a bicameral legislature, while guaranteeing the supremacy of the monarch. Parliament would have important rights in voting taxes and the lower house would be elective, although property qualifications ensured that 15% of the population would choose two-thirds of the deputies. Prussia had left absolutism and the society of orders behind, satisfying some liberals while denying democratic aspirations.

Would conservative revival also issue from conflict in Habsburg lands? Nationalist antagonisms grew in June during elections for an Austrian Constituent Assembly and Hungarian and Croatian National Assemblies. While the first two posed challenges to Imperial authority, the third turned all power over to the government of Ban (Viceroy) Josip Jelacic, a loyal Imperial appointee who considered the Magyars more a threat to Croatians than the Emperor. Already troubled by clashes in Transylvania and the Banat, the Hungarian government sought removal of Jelacic by offering aid to Imperial forces fighting in Italy. Hungarian constitutional monarchists still wished to retain their ties to the Habsburgs, although radicals denounced the offer. In its moment of peril the Imperial government dismissed Jelacic from office. Nevertheless, Radetzky's victories over the Italians in the summer soon ended willingness to compromise and by late August Jelacic had been reinstated as Ban and commander of the border forces. Conservatives could also note that cracks were appearing among Viennese revolutionary forces as nationalists and liberals in the National Guard fought workers demanding higher wages. When the court returned to Vienna in August, the government soon set in motion plans for the destruction of Hungarian autonomy.

As Jalacic led 40 000 troops into the Hungarian interior, the Hungarian National Assembly voted for armed resistance and appointed Kossuth to lead a National Defence Committee. Efforts by Kossuth to raise an army were then facilitated by looting conducted by Jelacic's troops as they advanced toward Budapest. Angry peasants threatened Jelacic's supply lines, and roughly 50 000 Hungarian regular forces drawn from the old Imperial army gained several victories by early October. Jelacic was thus forced to retreat toward Vienna. Although clashes with Romanian nationalists in Transylvania and the Banat were less favorable for the Hungarians, matters then took a dramatic turn for the worse for the Imperial government.

Viennese democrats viewed the prospect of Imperial re-imposition of absolutism on Hungary with misgiving. Thus on October 6, crowds surrounded the Vienna garrison and called on the troops to refuse marching orders. Encouraged by detachments of the National Guard, soldiers mutinied and a mob seized and lynched the minister of war. Once again the court fled, this time to Olmütz in Moravia, where they soon were joined by most the government and the majority of the Constituent Assembly. As before, radicals seized control of the capital. However, they gained only limited aid in other Austrian towns and cities, and virtually none in the countryside, where peasants wrongly attributed abolition of serfdom in September to the Emperor. With forces led by Jelacic and Windischgrätz converging on the city, the Viennese radicals could only hope for intervention by the Hungarians. After initial hesitation the Hungarian army did advance, but it was driven off by Imperial forces on October 30. One day later bombardment and infantry assaults began. Some 2000 insurgents died in fighting and Viennese radical leaders were summarily executed.

The fact that liberals had divided from radicals over the revolt in Vienna gained them little gratitude at court as constitutional monarchists in the government were replaced in November by conservatives such as the new prime minister, Prince Felix Schwarzenberg. A diplomat, advisor to Radetzky, and brother-in-law of Windischgrätz, Schwarzenberg soon demonstrated himself to be an extremely able, though not overly scrupulous, leader. When the Constituent Assembly finally reconvened, it was abruptly informed that Emperor Ferdinand had abdicated in favor of his young nephew Francis Joseph. The deputies had not been consulted and would have no influence over future policy. Windischgrätz and an army of 70 000 men drove the Hungarian government into flight from Budapest in December, but Hungarian forces continued fighting.

In the Balance: A Second Revolutionary Wave and Conservative Response, January–October 1849

Louis-Napoleon was opportunistic and circumstance in early 1849 favored adoption of conservative policies. Thus he appointed a former Orleanist to head a government that banned Republican Solidarity, driving radical associations underground. In April the president sent a military contingent to Rome, ostensibly to mediate between the Roman Republic and the Papacy. Few were fooled; the action was designed to woo French Catholics. Elections to the National Assembly in May enabled conservatives to increase their representation to roughly 450 seats. Nevertheless, observers were more struck by the perhaps 250 seats won by the Mountain. That radicals performed well in urban centers was expected; that they also extended their reach into the countryside came as a shock. Since the June Days radicals had distanced themselves from association with the "red menace" by avowing respect for private property and desire to spread ownership. They had also applied their ideas to a rural context by advocating state support for agricultural cooperatives and low-interest loans. Radical advance was then compromised when Louis-Napoleon ordered an assault on Rome and militants responded with demonstrations. At a time when parts of the press were calling for insurrection, the demonstrations were easily dispersed in June. Anything but predictable, Louis-Napoleon thereafter confounded expectations. After French troops had taken Rome, the president "leaked" a letter to the Pope demanding reform of the "evils" of Papal government. Catholics were scandalized and the government resigned, enabling the president to appoint a more Bonapartist one.

French intervention rubbed salt into self-inflicted Italian nationalist wounds. January elections in Piedmont-Sardinia, the Papal States, and Tuscany had favored radicals. In February a constituent assembly in the Papal States had proclaimed the Roman Republic, and demonstrations by Tuscan democrats had forced the Grand Duke into flight. At the Piedmontese court Charles Albert decided again to try to canalize nationalism for his own dynastic ends, but when Piedmontese forces renewed war with Austria in March they gained little support from the other Italian states and were rapidly defeated. Charles Albert then abdicated in favor of his son, Victor Emmanuel II, leaving behind a government forced to sue for peace. What followed was as much a mopping up operation as a war. Attempts to raise taxes and conscript troops by the revolutionary government triggered virtual civil war in the southern Papal States as conservative notables and peasants attacked republican forces. At Florence counter-revolutionary demonstrations soon enabled the civil guard to engineer the return of the Grand Duke. Return of the Austrians partly motivated Louis-Napoleon's decision to send a force to Rome and while Garibaldi managed to turn back the initial French attempt to take the city in June, Rome subsequently fell after a month-long siege. Under Austrian bombardment,

Venice capitulated in August and meanwhile Ferdinand stamped out the last of the revolutionary embers by permanently suspending parliament at Naples and defeating a second Sicilian attempt at secession.

Like the first Italian war of liberation, the second had been launched during a time of crisis in the German states. German democrats had shifted their focus from Frankfurt to elections for state parliaments and registered notable gains. Even in Prussia conservatives had gained only a narrow majority in January, necessitating revision of the electoral law so that the franchise became even more the preserve of landowners, wealthy bourgeoisie, and state officials. By March the Frankfurt parliament had finished drawing up a liberal bill of rights, but any lingering hope for a *Grossdeutch* solution was put to rest when Emperor Francis Joseph I issued a decree confirming the unity of his Empire. The deputies then turned to Frederick William, until he too refused to take an "imaginary crown baked from mud and clay"[65] (Figure 5.3) and added his intention to dissolve the parliament. When the hostility of the two powers was further demonstrated by orders to Prussian and Austrian delegates to cease attending, several of the smaller states issued similar directions and most liberals retired. Nevertheless, radical resistance flared in the south and west of Germany. In May democratic insurgents seized power in Dresden and similar events occurred in the southwestern province of the Palatinate and in Baden, where the army went over to the side of the rebels. Prussian troops crushed the revolts and by July resistance had collapsed.

With the second revolutionary wave rolled back in Italy and Germany, only the Austrian Empire remained. Although the Imperial winter campaign had begun well, Hungarian armies were able to drive the Austrians back from Budapest in April. With their troops again advancing toward Vienna, the Hungarian National Assembly proclaimed Hungary's independence and appointed Kossuth interim president of the new regime for the duration of the war. Imperial attempts to counter these reversals with a conscription drive produced riots and hence the court had to resign itself to asking Tsar Nicholas for aid. Whether the 140 000 Russian troops that joined in the counter-offensive launched in May were critical to the fighting is doubtful, given only 500 Russians died in battle, whereas 11 000 expired of cholera. Nevertheless, Russian presence affected the morale of exhausted Hungarian forces. In late July the Hungarian government emancipated the Jews from legal restrictions, legitimized mixed marriages between Jews and Christians, and passed a nationalities law that gave minorities the right to use their mother tongue in administrative and legal matters and in primary schools. Progressive as they were, such measures were far from sufficient to overcome the hostility engendered by previous Magyar chauvinism. Fighting continued until October, with the Austrians and Hungarians both losing perhaps 50 000 men, and reprisals soon followed. Kossuth was fortunate to escape; some 150 rebel leaders were executed and 1765 individuals were given long terms of imprisonment.

Figure 5.3 Frederick William IV contemplates an Imperial Crown: "Should I? Shouldn't I? Should I?" © BPK.

Conservative Consolidation and the Spanish Exception

When measured against the expectations of the spring of 1848 the revolutions had clearly failed; yet significant changes had occurred. In terms of mass impact, the most profound development was the abolition of serfdom in the Austrian Empire. Elsewhere limited advance in representative government was preserved in certain states. Constitutional government would continue in Piedmont-Sardinia. In Prussia modification of the electoral law yielded the intended conservative triumph in elections in June 1849 and in January 1850 parliament granted the king absolute veto power over legislation while allowing him extensive authority to rule by decree. All the same, creation of a parliament wherein voting rights were determined by wealth and not by corporate privilege brought an end to the estates as political bodies.

Elsewhere constitutional government was pushed back. The Habsburg government dissolved the Austrian constituent assembly and issued a "temporarily suspended" constitution that proclaimed the unity of the Empire and centralized power in the hands of Imperial authorities at Vienna. After the death of Schwarzenberg in 1852, a disillusioned liberal lawyer named Alexander Bach became the chief architect of a neo-absolutist drive that concentrated power in the monarchy. Traditional local autonomies and noble privileges were swept aside and replaced by uniform (Austrian) laws and a single system of taxation. Hungary was divided into five administrative units and German was made the language of the state. Where Austria led, client states in Italy followed: the Kingdom of the Two Sicilies, Tuscany, and the Papal States all terminated constitutional government while repressing political association and censoring the press.

Despite the destruction of the Frankfurt parliament, the issue of German unification almost triggered war between Prussia and Austria. In 1849 and 1850 Prussian diplomats and constitutional monarchists in the lesser states pursued a proposal known as the "Erfurt Union," basically the *Kleindeutch* solution shorn of any democratic pretense and calculated to ensure the dominance of the Prussian monarchy. Austrian annoyance was extreme and by late 1850 war appeared imminent, until Tsar Nicholas forced Fredrick-William to back down in what became known as "the humiliation of Olmütz."

In France the subsequent history of the Second Republic was dominated by a duel between Louis-Napoleon and opponents who wished to confine him to a single term of office. Although many members of the Order Party were willing to cooperate with the president, constitutional revision was made difficult by the necessity of securing approval from four-fifths of the deputies in the National Assembly. Meanwhile former Orleanist leaders sought to combat radicalism by passing a new press law directed against socialism, increasing clerical influence over primary education, and disenfranchising close to three million voters by imposing a requirement of three years fixed residence.

Given this scenario, Louis-Napoleon shrewdly adopted a middle position. On the one hand he exploited fear of radicalism, so that parliamentary conservatives allowed him to appoint whomever he wanted to key positions in the government, administration, and military. On the other hand he burnished his populist credentials by calling on the National Assembly to restore full manhood suffrage. Meanwhile he drew up plans for a revision of the Republic that would entail an additional ten years of rule for the president and a sharp reduction in parliamentary powers. To justify these steps, a plebiscite would be held to ask the nation for approval. By the time Louis-Napoleon launched "Operation Rubicon" on December 2, 1851 the elements of the Order Party that had voted against a second term of office were discredited. They were among the 220 deputies arrested during a coup in which many members of the military, civil administration, and police participated. Radicals were also rounded up. While their incarceration sparked fighting that took 160 lives at Paris, resistance proved greater in the provinces.

Democratic-socialist organization for forthcoming elections was transformed into an uprising of peasants and rural artisans, frequently led by middle-class radicals. Over 70 000 took up arms, mostly in central and southeastern France, and roughly 30 000 took part in fighting. Such widespread resistance shocked contemporaries. In fact most rebels submitted as soon as they were confronted by superior force and there were only 120 fatalities; nevertheless the fears generated by 1848 boiled over as conservatives meted out wildly disproportionate repression. Of some 27 000 arrested, 15 000 were summarily sentenced by special judicial commissions and roughly 10 000 were transported to the colonies. Little of this pleased Louis-Napoleon, who had expected a smooth takeover of power. He could, however, seek to justify the coup by portraying resistance as a sign of social revolution, and he could claim that conducting a plebiscite proved his commitment to democracy. Voting on December 21 was subject to official pressure; yet the results added up to an overwhelming endorsement – 7.4 million gave their approval, 1.4 million abstained and 600 000 refused.

As most the continent left revolt behind, Spain spun toward it. Commenced in 1843, Moderate rule was heavily reliant on the ability of General Narváez to use the army to stamp out rebellion. Constitutional revision in 1845 weakened parliamentary authority by giving the Crown absolute veto power over legislation, and reduced the electorate to perhaps 100 000 wealthy property owners. Conservative consolidation was, however, undermined by factionalism among the Moderates, a series of scandals at the court of Queen Isabel, and the hankering of "neo-absolutists" to be rid of Narváez. As the threat of rebellion seemingly receded, Narváez was pushed aside in early 1851. Subsequently prime minister Antonio Bravo Murillo ruled by decree while formulating a constitution that would have limited the *Cortes* to an advisory role and reduced the electorate to roughly 7000. In March 1851 the government concluded negotiations with Rome and agreed to a Concordat that recognized the legitimacy of previous sales of Church lands and confirmed the rights of the Crown in Episcopal appointments. In return, the state would pay the salaries of clergymen, support seminaries, affirm that Catholicism was the sole religion of Spain, and guarantee that teaching in all educational institutions would conform to Catholic doctrine. Fears of a return to the *ancien régime* and alarm over agitation caused by economic recession in 1854 then sparked a small-scale military revolt led by liberal Moderate generals. Although the military revolt was quashed, the regime was thereafter engulfed by popular insurrection at Madrid and a series of provincial rebellions in July 1854.

New Departures on the Left: Scientific Socialism and Anarchism

Largely unnoticed during the events of 1848, a singularly important development occurred when two middle-class Germans published a program for the Communist League, a small, secret, international organization based in London. In the *Communist Manifesto* Karl Marx, a writer and journalist, and Friedrich Engels, son and representative in England of a textile manufacturer, called on workers to unite in a revolution that would overthrow the ruling classes. Scientific socialism had issued its first challenge.

Already in 1844 Engels had published *The Condition of the Working Class in England*, one of a growing number of works that provided rich detail of the poverty of industrial workers. To such materials Marx added analysis derived from study of economic, social, and political history. According to Marx, history was determined by struggle between those who owned the means of production and those who worked for them. Beginning in the middle ages, capitalism had gradually brought a change in economic production that destroyed feudalism. As commerce and, later, industry surpassed agriculture in wealth generation, the bourgeoisie pushed aside the nobility and seized control of government, most notably in 1789. The tendency of capitalism was, however, to concentrate wealth in the hands of large-scale producers and eliminate social stratification so that society ultimately would consist of just two classes: the bourgeoisie and the proletariat. Moreover, the seeds of its own destruction were imbedded within capitalism. Increased production intensified competition among owners, leading them to cut wages, which in turn reduced demand, leading ultimately to collapse of the entire system. For the proletarians, the short-term prospect was increasing poverty; yet their concentration in factories would endow them with class consciousness – recognition that their shared plight was the result of exploitation by owners. Once enough workers had gained class consciousness, they would revolt, seize control of the state, and create a new social and economic order. Class distinctions would then disappear as private ownership would be abolished, work would be organized along cooperative lines, and all would become equal. Once socialism reached its highest stage – communism – there no longer would be a need for the state.

Marx's emphasis on material power and allegedly scientific approach held appeal at a time when the "woolly" idealism of Romanticism seemed *passé*. Relatively simple in its basic premises, Marxism would become more sophisticated in subsequent elaboration in works such as Marx's *Capital*, the initial volume of which appeared in 1867. Concepts such as "the labor theory of value" (that workers created the total value of a product) and "worker alienation" (that the division of labor stripped the worker of self-esteem), although not original to Marx, would become highly influential due to his writing. Moreover, because the revolution did not unfold as soon as he initially expected, there was plenty of opportunity for Marx to build more flexibility into the original theory. The result could, however, create ambiguity. Marx believed that the role of socialists was to enable proletarians to unite as a class party so that they could bring about revolution. How the revolution would enfold would depend upon circumstances that could not be predicted, and hence there was no clear formula or program for proletarian revolution. Because he died prior to the emergence of mass socialist parties, Marx thought mostly in terms of popular insurrection, arguing that "no great movement has been born without the shedding of blood."[66] By the early 1870s he seemed, however, to accept that socialism could be advanced by democratic means, and in the 1890s Engels went perilously close to endorsing entirely peaceful strategies. Yet the element of violent confrontation remained central to Marxist rhetoric and planning. Moreover, while Marx believed that a period of proletarian dictatorship would be required to liquidate capitalism, he said little about how such a government would "wither away" into simple administration that presumably would require no coercion.

As a political movement, "scientific" socialism had certain basic weaknesses. A fundamental point of Marx's theory was undermined because capitalism did not unfold along the predicted lines; economies grew and social stratification remained, albeit in new forms. With its focus on urban industrialization, Marxism said relatively little about the countryside, where the vast majority lived. With its economic determinism, Marxism left little space for individual will or belief systems that did not conform to the new orthodoxy, and the concept of "false conscious-ness" left Marxists blind to the class-crossing appeal of religion and nationalism. Marxism did provide workers with a system of belief around which they could mobi-lize, and organization would prove crucial to pursuit of rights and improved material circumstances. Whether Marxism's association with violence and funda-mental rejection of pluralism was an asset for workers is doubtful.

"Scientific" socialism was immediately challenged by anarchism. Although anarchism shared the belief that revolution was necessary to achieve social justice, the two creeds differed in attitudes to power and authority. Marxists were political in that they wanted to gain control of the state. Especially as it aged, Marxism also tended toward a centralized chain of command within the party structure. Anarchists viewed authority as inherently corrupting, eschewed party politics, and saw the state as an enemy, regardless of who controlled it. While Marxists would seek to use trade unions for political purposes, anarchists thought the bourgeoisie should be fought solely through industrial conflict.

Pierre-Joseph Proudhon was perhaps the father of modern anarchism. He first gained notoriety with a pamphlet wherein he argued that property was theft. Despite this opening salvo, Proudhon's ideal was akin to that of the independent peasants and artisans whom he admired – everyone should possess (though not own) enough property to fulfil their needs. No one should have more than they needed, and they should possess property only in so long as they worked on or in it. What was most valuable was labor, the sole determinant of the value of any product. Proudhon shared little of the enthusiasm of liberals and some utopian socialists for increased production, and he saw mechanization as a means by which the dignity of labor was removed and workers were exploited by bourgeois employers. Because he prized the autonomy of individual workers, Proudhon took particular aim at the state: "To be governed is to be watched over, inspected, spied on, directed, legislated at, regulated, docketed, indoctrinated, preached at, controlled, assessed, weighed, censored, ordered about, by men who have neither the right nor the knowledge, nor the virtue."[67] Something of a moral puritan who mistrusted basic instincts, Proudhon was very much an advocate of separate spheres gender ideology, and hence he was primarily concerned with state intrusion upon the liberties of males, although he saw in the family the crucial institution of society.

Proudhon advocated federalism as the solution to state and bourgeois oppression. Work should be run by autonomous worker associations and produce could be exchanged by what amounted to barter. Small communities or collectives should regulate themselves, although they would need to band together loosely for common purposes such as defence. Perhaps because he was an autodidact, Proudhon was not the most systematic of thinkers and when combined his ideas do indeed seem anarchic. Nevertheless, his desire to enhance freedom through removal of authority, in combination with his desire to promote equality through cooperative production, struck a chord with workers steeped in artisan traditions, and his refusal to divorce individual morality from politics gave his thought a religious quality that appealed to certain peasant communities.

Proudhon's dislike of coercion meant that he was deeply ambivalent over the likely effects of revolution; other anarchists were less shy about the application of force. Mikhail Bakunin, a former junior officer in the Russian army of noble extraction, believed that the state was "the most flagrant, most cynical, and most complete denial of humanity."[68] In pursuit of social revolution, Bakunin adopted Blanqui's strategy of organizing secret societies led by a vanguard which would seek to provoke revolt whenever states underwent crisis. Whereas Blanqui restricted himself to France, Bakunin took part in conspiracies in various European states and in certain regions, principally in Italy and Spain, anarchism made inroads into peasant communities. Marx saw Proudhon, Bakunin, and later anarchists as heretics and he would fight their influence when the workers of the world finally began to unite in the First International in the 1860s.

The Return of Great Power Rivalry

Within a year of his seizure of power, Louis-Napoleon had transformed the Second Republic into the Second Empire with himself as hereditary monarch. The new regime was modeled on that of the First Empire and, for the sake of dynastic continuity, the new Emperor took the title of Napoleon III. A veneer of democracy was maintained in that all males could vote in elections for the lower house of a parliament that possessed little power. Only the Emperor could propose legislation, the legislature's right to amend proposed law was narrowly restricted, parliamentary discussion was kept secret, and Louis-Napoleon could veto any bill. Given state patronage of "official" candidates, muzzling of the press, and banning of associations, opposition in the legislature was initially slight. Amidst economic recovery much of the public accepted the substitution of order for liberty; the plebiscite of November 1852 asking for approval yielded 7.8 million votes in favor, and only 250,000 against.

What did the other monarchs think of the "upstart" who proclaimed that "The empire means peace"[69] in October 1852? They were unimpressed by his checkered past and disliked the championing of his uncle that formed the basis of his propaganda. Limited toleration of the new regime was hedged with suspicion; Palmerston speculated that Louis-Napoleon planned to strike a "stunning blow" and the Russian foreign minister concluded that his "absence of principles"[70] required constant vigilance.

No one had done more to maintain the status quo than Tsar Nicholas and hence Russia was an obvious target for a revisionist power. Louis-Napoleon probably did not intend war, but certainly French demands in 1852 that Roman Catholic, rather than Orthodox, monks be given guardianship of the Holy Places in Jerusalem were better calculated to anger Nicholas than the Ottoman Sultan. The Turkish government perhaps viewed the demands as an opportunity to play the French against the Russians; one way or another it sent contradictory messages to both sides, angering each. In May 1852 Louis-Napoleon contravened the Straits Convention by sending a warship through the Dardanelles. In February 1853 Nicholas sent an envoy to Constantinople with instructions to intimidate the Sultan into making further concessions over Russia's "right" to protect Orthodox Christians. Encouraged by the French and a Russophobe British ambassador, the Turks refused and in response the Russians occupied the Danubian Principalities in July 1853.

Although there were many points at which conflict could have been resolved through negotiation, there were also vital interests at play, making compromise more difficult. Russian domination of the Ottoman Empire would threaten the interests of the other powers throughout the Middle East, Balkans, and Black Sea regions, and perhaps serve as a base for penetration of the Indian subcontinent. As he aged, Nicholas became less inclined to make concessions and meanwhile Palmerston leaned toward terminating the threat of Russian expansion once and for all. Louis-Napoleon grew anxious over reports of limited support for war; yet he was eager to secure alliance with Britain. No power sought more vigorously to preserve peace than Austria. On the one hand, Russian domination of the Ottoman Empire ran against Austrian interests and aligning against the western powers would jeopardize possession of Austria's Italian provinces. On the other hand, war against Russia would open up a vast front of fighting that Imperial finances could not sustain, and might trigger renewed revolt among the Poles and Hungarians.

Hopes of avoiding conflict ended in November 1853 when a Russian squadron destroyed an Ottoman fleet on the southern coast of the Black Sea. In late December the British cabinet decided to send the British fleet to the Black Sea, where they would join the French, and in February 1854 the western powers issued an ultimatum demanding Russia evacuate the Principalities. Austria then made the best of a bad hand by announcing it would occupy the Danubian Principalities so that the western powers did not. Embittered as he was by "perfidious Austria,"[71] Nicholas could only agree; Russia could not afford addition of Austria to the forces arrayed against her. All the same, Russia could not be certain of continued Austrian neutrality. The Austrians simultaneously pressed the British and French to define moderate peace terms while pressuring Russia with the threat of entry into the war. Meanwhile Prussia adopted a stance that tended to favor Russia as Frederick William and the German Confederation joined Austria in a defensive alliance while refusing to mobilize their forces.

The main theater of operations became the Crimean peninsula, where Sevastopol was the key Russian naval base on the Black Sea. Neither side distinguished itself in the siege of Sevastopol. The British army gained a reputation for incompetence, and while the French fought better, they too suffered from outbreaks of cholera and dysentery that demonstrated poor preparation. Nevertheless, matters were far worse on the other side. The absence of rail lines south of Moscow and the primitive character of roads made the journey from central Russia so difficult that perhaps only 10% of soldiers dispatched in the winter of 1854–85 actually arrived at their destination. Supplies were equally difficult to provide and the quality of outdated weaponry was low. When Nicholas died in March 1855, Alexander II came to the throne determined to maintain the war effort. However, the fall of Sevastopol in September, the loss of some 480 000 lives, the entry of Sweden into the allied coalition in November, and warnings from Prussia that she too might have to join the opposing side convinced him that capitulation was necessary by February 1856.

War weariness in the west, mutual suspicion between the British and French, and determination on the part of Austria to end conflict ensured that the Treaty of Paris of March 1856 was relatively lenient. Russia surrendered a section of Bessarabia at the mouth of the Danube to Moldavia and the fortress city of Kars (south of the Caucasus Mountains) to Turkey, and agreed that the Danubian Provinces would be placed under the protection of all the powers while remaining part of the Ottoman Empire. Such losses were made more acceptable when the Sultan issued a decree promising to respect religious liberty, enabling Alexander to claim that Russia had achieved her objective. Neither was acceptance of freedom of navigation and trade on the Danube and in the Black Sea particularly disagreeable. Annexed to the Treaty was, however, a convention with Turkey that barred both from maintaining naval bases on the Black Sea and this concession was far more humiliating. More devastating still was recognition that Russia was slipping from the ranks of the great powers. Grand Duke Konstantin Nikolayevich drew the obvious conclusion when he stated: "We cannot deceive ourselves any longer; we are both weaker and poorer not only in material but also in mental resources, especially in matters of administration."[72]

Taking Stock

Europe seemed to have changed remarkably little by the end of 1856. Despite fears of republican France leading a revolutionary crusade throughout the continent, the powers had not gone to war during the 1848 revolutions. Indeed, in so much as it had occurred, military intervention, whether by Russia or France, had worked in favor of restoring the pre-revolutionary status quo. Even when the Crimean War broke the years of great-power peace, there was little territorial redistribution. Liberal hopes for constitutional monarchy had made limited progress in Piedmont-Sardinia and Prussia; elsewhere they had been crushed. The flowering of political association and freedom of the press, in combination with pent up social grievance, nationalist rivalry, and economic turmoil, had produced more by way of conflict than tolerance, and pluralism had soon given way to levels of violence that favored the advocates of strong government.

All the same, profound forces were at work. In much of Europe, serfdom and the old order of social estates were destroyed. Previously excluded from power, liberal and radical proponents of change had gained experience which would subsequently influence their ruminations over how the Left had been weakened by division. That nationalism too had gained ground could subsequently be seen in inclination to commemorate 1848 as a national, rather than European, phenomenon. The eruption of mass politics also forced governments to take the general public into consideration in new ways. Whether by increasing repressive capacity, or by seeking to ensure better provision of material supplies, or by seeking to entrench social order through educational systems and urban renewal, governments would develop policies with broad public opinion increasingly in mind. Louis-Napoleon provided an example in all of these regards; unfortunately he also set precedents for overcoming domestic division by appeal to aggressive nationalism.

6

Wars of National Unification and Revolution in the European States System, 1850s–1871

After the uproar of the 1848 revolutions, the 1850s initially brought calm as states concentrated on economic expansion and imposition of order. The Crimean War then ushered in upheaval as defeat removed Russia from the camp of powers that sought to maintain the Vienna Settlement. Opportunities thus arose for statesmen to pursue revision, generally at the expense of the Austrian Empire. Louis-Napoleon played the role of catalyst in a series of conflicts that led to the unification of Italy and Germany, although in the end France was as much a victim as Austria. Whereas success in warfare enabled victors to create new states, defeat forced regimes to undertake reform in a bid to regain credibility. Whether the reforms conducted in Russia and Austria were sufficient to restore loyalty remained to be seen; in France liberalization of the Second Empire could not save it from the foreign policy failures of the Emperor. France would then undergo the uprising of the Paris Commune and while a new republic would stagger on, it would be seriously damaged by the experience.

Even in states that did not engage in war, the period was eventful. Britain continued along the path of gradual reform and provided a context in which a relatively advanced women's movement could press for further change. Spain remained tumultuous, lurching from one regime to another in a failing search for consensus among elite factions. Even victory could not ensure stability; the unification of Italy created a new set of problems that led to massive discontent, conflict, and violence. If in certain regards the period seemed to fulfil some of the early promise of 1848, in others it appeared to herald yet more volatility.

Europe's Uncertain Path 1814–1914: State Formation and Civil Society, First Edition. R. S. Alexander.
© 2012 R. S. Alexander. Published 2012 by Blackwell Publishing Ltd.

Domestic Politics in the 1850s: Liberalism in the West

If the early 1850s were notable mostly for reaction, there were exceptions in Britain and Piedmont-Sardinia, and the character of the French and Spanish regimes was anything but fixed. In Britain imperial policy dominated and nothing came of plans for franchise expansion; nevertheless key figures were pondering further reform. Given the continental context, the fact that constitutional monarchy took root in Piedmont-Sardinia was striking, and it furthered the prospects of the Savoyard dynasty seizing the lead in Italian unification. Under Louis-Napoleon the Second Empire remained authoritarian, but the regime's search for popularity suggested a basic instability. Where Spain might be headed remained unclear. Despite an attempt at the sort of compromise required to establish stability, the resultant government achieved little.

British government was generally conducted by coalitions of Whigs, Liberals, and free-trade Tories. Apparent Whig ascendancy, however, masked tensions within the government formed in December 1852 by the Earl of Aberdeen, leader of the free-trade Tories after the death of Peel. Russell and Palmerston entered the cabinet and soon clashed over the former's proposal for franchise reform. Against this backdrop of bickering titans, the standing of chancellor of the exchequer William Gladstone rose as he gained a reputation for frugality. Initially a Tory, he had followed Peel in converting to free trade, and thereafter he would gain popularity as a champion of franchise reform. Gladstone well understood the popularity of tax reduction, especially when taxes were perceived to be socially inequitable. He thus contributed to a trend that saw indirect taxes (on basic consumer goods) fall from 70% to 60% of general taxation between the late 1840s and the early 1880s. Meanwhile young Conservatives such as Benjamin Disraeli sought to develop alternatives to traditional protectionist policies that seemed outdated. A Jew who had converted to Anglicanism, Disraeli was an anomaly among Tory landowners, but he was a gifted writer, original thinker, and acerbic speaker. Brief minority governments enabled Disraeli and the Earl of Derby to demonstrate that the Conservatives were at least capable of governing, and Disraeli too began to advocate franchise reform.

Foreign policy dominated politics. Florence Nightingale's fame for bringing organized nursing to military hospitals was an indictment of the government for its mismanagement of the Crimean War. According to Palmerston the officer in charge of the Army's Commissariat Department was "opposed to every new resource and improved practice"[73] and criticism leveled by parliamentary commissions was such that Queen Victoria was forced to replace Aberdeen with Palmerston in 1855. Thereafter trouble began when East India Company administrators intervened against the Hindu practices of *suttee* and *thugee*, creating tensions that were exacerbated by land reform based on British concepts of private property. Discontent over terms of service in the army had long been simmering among the roughly 200 000 sepoys in the army, and revolt was set off by suspicion that new cartridges were wrapped in paper greased with cow or pig fat. Use of the cartridges required biting off the wrapping with the mouth, which would have been a violation of religious principle for Hindus (for whom the cow is sacred) or Muslims (for whom consumption of pork is forbidden). The Indian Mutiny of 1857 soon extended beyond the troops, building on religious and proto-nationalist grievances, although there was little unity among the groups involved in rebellion. In early 1858 reinforcements, in combination with the large number of Indian soldiers who remained loyal, enabled the British to turn the tide, but fighting entailed indiscriminate slaughter on both sides. In 1859 Palmerston announced abolition of the East India Company. The government would rule directly, with a Secretary of State for India in the cabinet and a Viceroy to represent the Crown in the colony. More troops would be stationed in India, and command would be centralized under the Crown.

The way in which imperialism and nationalism intersected was apparent in Palmerston's dealings with China. British merchants long had sought full access to Chinese markets, particularly to profit by the opium trade, and the Chinese government had been forced to grant "treaty ports" such as Shanghai and Canton on the mainland, and to lease Hong Kong to British control. In 1856 a shipping vessel, registered as British and owned by a Hong Kong merchant, was boarded by Chinese officials and 12 of the crew were arrested as pirates. Although the men were subsequently released, Chinese officials refused to issue a public apology. Hoping to force concessions, the Governor of Hong Kong ordered naval bombardment of fortifications at Canton, triggering riots as enraged Chinese attacked the British enclave. Palmerston chose to support the Governor, leading parliament to pass a motion of censure against the government. Challenged by Disraeli, the prime minister then called a general election, arguing that the government must respond when an "insolent barbarian wielding power at Canton has violated the British flag."[74] The campaign was a triumph for him, as the governing coalition gained a sizeable majority in 1857 and entered into war with China. Ironically, Palmerston was then hoist upon his own petard in February 1858. In response to French requests for repression of conspirators in London, Palmerston sought passage of a Conspiracy to Murder Bill that would have made such activities a felony. The bill could be portrayed as kowtowing to France, and Palmerston resigned rather than accept an "unfriendly" amendment that passed the lower house. Aided by the French, by 1860 the British had forced the Chinese government to make further commercial concessions and pay a large war indemnity. The political danger of using foreign policy to court public approval was, however, clear.

In France the Second Empire brought transition to modern industrial society as production doubled, foreign trade tripled, and railway expansion carried market forces and urban culture to the countryside. Growth was largely a product of international trends, although it was true that Imperial governments stimulated

Figure 6.1   Removal of a portion of the Latin Quarter, Paris 1860. Roger Viollet/Getty Images.

expansion. Louis-Napoleon's policies have been linked to the influence of utopian socialism; yet similar approaches could be seen in autocratic Prussia and liberal Piedmont-Sardinia. What linked these regimes was statism, not socialism. In France statist policies could be seen in guarantees of minimum interest rates on railway securities, creation of joint-stock clearing banks to facilitate supply of credit, and massive reconstruction programs.

Louis-Napoleon wanted to turn Paris into a showcase of Imperial grandeur. Under the direction of Baron Georges Haussmann medieval slums were replaced by broad boulevards illuminated by gaslight and lined by spacious apartment buildings. Road and rail systems were coordinated so as to reduce congestion. Increased light and open space complemented improvements in sanitation brought by updating sewer systems and water supply, and green space was enhanced by development of public parks. Not everyone was pleased. For the writer Victor Hugo, Imperial preference for neo-classical style was almost as reprehensible as destruction of the medieval past. For revolutionaries, the ease with which troops could transport artillery along broad boulevards was an ominous portent. "Gentrification" drove up property values, creating a paradise for speculators, and allegations of corruption flew, launched by Haussmann's dubious accounting. For the poor, increasing prices, taxes, and rent meant departure to the outskirts of the city, creating a "red belt" that surrounded an increasingly conservative core. In the short term such concerns could be brushed aside. Although the image of an Empire of crass *parvenus* took root, the regime was acting on widespread desire for pursuit of prosperity.

The value of stability could be seen in the contrasting examples of Spain and Piedmont-Sardinia. In 1854 rebellion led by General Leopoldo O'Donnell and popular insurrection at Madrid forced Queen Isabel II to call on General Espartero to lead a provisional government. Neither Espartero nor O'Donnell had any plans, however, for social reform that might have benefited the masses. The franchise for elections to a constitutional *Cortes* was broadened to include close to 700 000 voters, and the latter chose a chamber composed largely of Progressive lawyers and land-owners. The main impact of the revolution was to trigger further expropriation of Church property and widespread sale of common lands. Although they provided a boost to state revenues, property sales were of little benefit to impoverished agricultural laborers because purchase required a substantial initial deposit.

Once inclined to pose as a modern Napoleon I, Espartero came to see himself as a martyr to the extremes of Spanish politics: "To the throne I am presented as a demagogue, to the people as a deserter from their sacred cause."[75] For his part, O'Donnell cultivated his standing among the officer corps and at court. Pious in all matters except adultery, Isabel resented the anti-clericalism of the Progressives and hence in 1856 she dismissed Espartero and turned to O'Donnell. Revolts in Madrid and Barcelona then produced hundreds of casualties and in the *Cortes* moderate Progressives, frightened by the violence, acquiesced. Although militias were dissolved, subsequent reaction was mild and O'Donnell sought compromise with an "Additional Act" that made the Senate elective and established jury trials for press offences. By 1858 O'Donnell had formed a "long ministry" that actually endured until 1863.

O'Donnell based his government on a "Liberal Union" of centrist Moderates and Progressives. Unlike Narváez, O'Donnell sought to rule with parliamentary approval and accepted election of radical Progressives and Democrats to the *Cortes*. All the same, reform came to a halt, the Church regained its influence in education, and censorship of the press remained persistent. Although the regime focused on developing communications infrastructure, endemic rural poverty gave rise to frequent riots, and rail expansion was troubled by shoddy construction and financial corruption. Hoping to foster patriotic support, O'Donnell involved Spanish land and naval forces in a series of imperial engagements that yielded few benefits. Moreover, foreign policy developments broke the Liberal Union. Progressives were alienated when Isabel refused to recognize the newly unified Italian Kingdom in 1861, and Moderates were angered when Isabel refused to sack General Juan Prim after he had clashed with Louis-Napoleon and a French expedition in Mexico in 1861. O'Donnell resigned in February 1863, bringing an end to the sort of compromise required to establish stable rule.

Under Camillo Benso di Cavour, coalition gave solidity to Piedmontese government. Prior to his entry into politics in 1848, Cavour's travels abroad had given him an appreciation of liberal political and economic systems apparent in his contributions to *Il Risorgimento* (The Resurgence), a journal which later provided the Italian unification movement with its name. Although he was a proponent of reform, Cavour rejected the democratic republicanism of Mazzini and, while he would labor for Italian independence under Piedmontese leadership, he knew that too aggressive an approach would replicate the failures of the past.

Despite pressure from the Austrians, Victor Emmanuel had refused to revoke the *Statuto*; he thereby appeased liberals while securing a constitution wherein the monarchy remained powerful. Nevertheless, criticism of the peace settlement with Austria in 1849 forced prime minister Massimo Taparelli d'Azeglio to dissolve parliament and call on voters to elect a Chamber less hostile to the King. "Encouraged" by state intervention, voters provided the government with a majority. As a cabinet member Cavour subsequently enhanced liberal prospects by driving a wedge between conservatives and moderates with legislation that eliminated ecclesiastical courts, reduced the number of religious holidays, and gave the state the right to veto gifts bequeathed to the Church.

Piedmont-Sardinia's image was enhanced by reaction elsewhere. Austrian government in Lombardy-Venetia was marred by vindictive repression of Italian patriots. At Rome Pius IX refused administrative reform and after a trip to Naples Gladstone castigated the Bourbon regime as "the negation of God erected into a system of government."[76] Thus Mazzini could again bestir revolt; his insistence on creating a republic, however, splintered his following as increasing numbers accepted that expansion of the rule of Victor Emmanuel offered the best prospect for unification.

As prime minister after November 1852, Cavour prepared for future expansion. Piedmont-Sardinia entered into free trade treaties and underwent dramatic rail expansion. Commerce and agriculture were stimulated by reforms that enhanced the supply of credit. Yet, more than economic growth was required to overcome Austrian presence in the peninsula. The Crimean War initially posed a challenge in that the British and French were more interested in wooing Austria, but ultimately the King's desire to enhance the dynasty's military tradition led him to send a contingent. While participation led to few immediate benefits, Cavour did begin discussion with Louis-Napoleon over the "Italian question." Equally significant, in August 1857 a group of former followers of Mazzini issued a manifesto expressing their support of the Savoyard dynasty and calling for the creation of a unified Italy. Never more than 2000 in membership, the National Society contained many writers who aggressively promoted unification throughout Italy.

Autocratic Politics in the 1850s

After they had regained control from the revolutionary forces of 1848, the regimes of central Europe sought to maintain order through repression of dissent, increase in the coercive capacity of the state, and promotion of economic growth. The

Federal Diet set up a "committee of reaction" to monitor the German states, and called for abolition of political societies and institution of draconian press censorship. To underline their independence of the Diet, middle-sized states frequently ignored such injunctions; all the same, on their own initiative many of them cracked down on freedom of assembly, association, and the press. Police forces harassed radicals and state control over educational institutions was tightened.

In the Austrian Empire governments pursued modernization by encouraging railroad building. State ownership was reduced as rail lines were sold to private companies and provision of capital was boosted by creation of the *Creditanstalt* bank, which helped finance long-term capital projects. Despite these initiatives, resources remained meager. Attempts to reduce debt failed due to military expenditures triggered by foreign policy crises and hence state fiscal demands drained the private sector. Mobilization of the army during the Crimean War and the costs of maintaining large numbers of troops in Hungary contributed to an 1859 budget wherein 40% of revenue was devoted to servicing the interest on state debt.

Economic growth was pursued as a means to gain approval; nevertheless, rule was by no means based on consent. Officials paid closer attention to the public than before 1848, higher pay and better conditions for civil servants improved an expanding administration, and judicial procedure became more uniform and less arbitrary. Yet the military still provided order in much of the Empire, and a recently organized *gendarmerie* gained a reputation for mistreatment of civilians. Police spies remained thick on the ground, and with the Concordat of 1855 the Catholic Church gained control over education and extensive influence in censorship and family law.

In Prussia state formation was guided by minister-president Otto von Manteuffel. A highly experienced state administrator trained in law, Manteuffel was a determined opponent of representative government who concentrated on increasing the size, reliability, and influence of the bureaucracy. Ministerial authority was enhanced by creating a category of political officials among the judiciary and civil service who must rigorously follow government policy and refrain from expressing any support for opposition opinion. The state also increased its provision of civil order, reducing reliance upon the military. Between 1848 and 1855 the *gendarmerie* and border guards increased from 1500 to 2500. More strikingly, the Berlin police force rose from roughly 250 to 4000, was given military discipline, and was directed to scrutinize public life. Although the force became notorious for identity checks, press seizures, and deportations, the police chief also shrewdly courted favor by opening public baths, establishing a fire department, and improving street cleaning.

Economic development also dominated politics in Prussia. Rapid industrialization was facilitated by the founding of large joint-stock banks, and railroad building enabled coal, iron, and metal industries to boom. While the Prussian government acted conservatively in supporting guilds and granting nobles the right to entail estates, state-sponsored banks provided loans for peasants to pay off their remaining feudal dues. In combination with population growth, termination of the manorial system facilitated the flow of labor to urban centers. Moreover, by making itself Germany's largest owner of coal mines, the Prussian state gained significant influence over industrial production generally.

Having already created a three-tier voting system for the parliamentary lower house in 1849, the Prussian state in 1854 converted the upper house into an appointive body of peers dominated by the nobility. Yet parliament retained legislative and budgetary powers, partly because the state was dependent on middle-class elements for loans. Muted political life continued in choral societies and shooting clubs, and liberalism revived in 1858 when Crown Prince William became regent after Frederick William was incapacitated by a stroke. William appointed a government of moderates who promised to respect civil rights, and moderate liberals responded favorably. Given their rapid wealth accumulation, upper-middle-class interests were actually favored by the franchise and when William forbade officials from interfering in elections in 1858 liberals gained a large majority. A decade characterized by reaction thus finished with a looming challenge to autocracy.

The Quixotic Foreign Policy of Louis-Napoleon: Italian Unification

When Felice Orsini tried to assassinate Louis-Napoleon in January 1858 he set in motion a train of events that destroyed European stability. A former follower of Mazzini, Orsini targeted the French Emperor as a bulwark of reaction blocking Italian unification. Although he missed his target, killing eight and injuring over a hundred in the process, Orsini's attempt convinced Louis-Napoleon to take action. The Emperor had in fact been a member of the Italian Carbonari in his youth and he felt some sympathy for the arch-conspirator, although this did not save Orsini from execution. Louis-Napoleon wanted to rectify what he considered an abnormal situation in Italy and frequently referred to the principle of national self-determination, but mostly he wanted to substitute French for Austrian influence on the Italian peninsula.

It says much about Louis-Napoleon's diplomacy that he kept discussions with Cavour in July 1858 secret even from his own foreign minister. Cavour would manufacture a conflict so as to provoke Austria into a declaration of war. French intervention would thus appear to be motivated by defence of Piedmont-Sardinia and with luck the other powers would remain on the sidelines. Defeat of Austria would then enable territorial redistribution designed to strengthen Piedmont-Sardinia in the north and cement French influence elsewhere. While Cavour was willing to use the French, he pursued differing objectives. He expected that war would unleash revolution in central Italy, providing further opportunities for Piedmont-Sardinia. In the meantime the agreement would be sealed by the

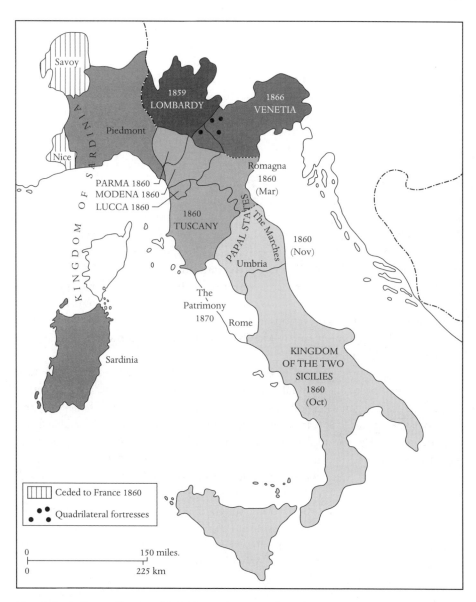

Map 6.1 Italian unification. F.R. Bridge and Roger Bullen, *The Great Powers and the European States System 1814–1914*, 2nd edition (Harlow: Longman, 2005), p. 143.

marriage of Victor Emmanuel's pious 15-year-old daughter to Louis-Napoleon's cousin Prince Jerome-Napoleon, a notorious rake. Hence Princess Clotilde became the first casualty of war.

Although the other powers pressed for resolution of the Italian situation by negotiation, Cavour's scheme succeeded due to Austrian financial inability to maintain a protracted war footing. On April 21, 1859 Austria delivered an ultimatum demanding that Piedmont-Sardinia demobilize. Cavour happily refused and Austria declared war. French and Italian forces had the better of early engagements, but high casualty rates made Louis-Napoleon nervous about response in France. A growing tide of nationalism in the German states also gave cause for alarm, although the hopes of Francis Joseph that "that ignominious scum of Prussia"[77] would come to Austria's aid were illusory. Nor was Louis-Napoleon pleased when pro-unification insurrections broke out in Tuscany, Modena, and the Papal Legations. He therefore chose to work out a deal unilaterally with Francis Joseph in July. Austria would cede most of Lombardy to France, and Louis-Napoleon would hand the province over to Victor Emmanuel. Austria would retain Venetia, and France would forego previously agreed upon acquisition of Savoy and Nice. Shocked, Cavour resigned in protest. Because Louis-Napoleon made clear that he would not allow Austria to intervene in central Italy, the game was not, however, over. In August and September Italian revolutionaries oversaw the election of national assemblies that lobbied for annexation by Piedmont-Sardinia. Britain and Russia favored such a solution and, given these circumstances, Louis-Napoleon offered approval of the annexations in return for Savoy and Nice. Cavour returned to negotiate the agreement, and in March 1860 plebiscites in the affected areas gave a veneer of public approval.

Fortune had favored Cavour in his dealings with Louis-Napoleon and his luck would hold in subsequent manipulation of the great patriot Garibaldi. The unification of southern Italy began when followers of Mazzini commenced revolt in the Kingdom of Two Sicilies in April 1860. Initially crushed at Palermo, insurgency, based partly on peasant demand for land redistribution, then spread. The Bourbon regime probably would have survived had it been able to reassure social elites by restoring order. However, by intervening with a volunteer army of 1000 "Redshirts," Garibaldi managed to seize control of Sicily by June. The poorly armed Redshirts were at first vastly outnumbered by Bourbon troops, but Garibaldi's superior leadership, support from the insurgents, and a second rising at Palermo gave Garibaldi command of the island. He then consolidated his position by conscripting peasants while patriotic mainland associations sent funds, weaponry, and medical supplies.

Garibaldi proclaimed he was fighting to unify Italy under the rule of Victor Emmanuel; yet from Cavour's perspective he presented two problems. Firstly, Garibaldi was a democrat and his victories enhanced his ability to influence the nature of a new Italian regime. Secondly, in his plans to take Rome and Venetia Garibaldi risked drawing France and Austria back into the fray. To overcome these dangers, Cavour convinced Victor Emmanuel to send his forces south, annexing the Papal Marches and Umbria. To secure acceptance by Louis-Napoleon, Cavour promised that Rome would be left untouched. Although Garibaldi's forces initially progressed rapidly when they launched their mainland campaign in mid-August, Bourbon resistance then stiffened. In contrast, troops led by Victor Emmanuel quickly defeated the Papal army in September and soon thereafter entered the

Kingdom of the Two Sicilies. It was the Piedmontese army that finished off Bourbon forces, thereby weakening Garibaldi's ability to make demands. There would be no election of a constituent assembly to negotiate terms of union, although plebiscites would sanction annexation. Although the new Kingdom of Italy was proclaimed in parliament in March 1861, radicals and supporters of regional autonomy would never be fully reconciled to the regime.

Nevertheless, most of Italy had been united. The means by which unification had been achieved – duplicity, subversion of established regimes, and resolution of conflict through force – signaled that a new era had begun. Nationalism had played a part; yet it was the nationalism of part of the elite, not of the masses, and the character of the new regime would reflect this basic reality. No one had done more than Cavour to create the Italian Kingdom, and it did not augur well when he died in June 1861.

Partial Unification of Germany

Few events affected nineteenth-century Europe as much as the unification of Germany under Prussian direction. To some extent the previous undermining of the Concert of Europe apparent in the Crimean War and unification of Italy helped pave the way by weakening Austria. It was also true, however, that Prussia's victory came about due to the opportunism of a leader whose conduct of diplomacy was just as clever and unscrupulous as that of Cavour.

Otto von Bismarck-Schönhausen was determined to advance Prussia's place within Germany and he would prove a master of *realpolitik*: belief that politics consists of the pursuit of power rather than ideals. An ambitious, well-educated and domineering *Junker*, Bismarck detested liberalism. Nevertheless, he recognized that some sort of accommodation must be reached between the monarchy and constitutionalism and he saw in nationalism a means by which the monarchy could cultivate support. In September 1859 liberals from a variety of states had founded the *Nationalverein* to lobby for creation of a unified German state. Composed largely of Protestant professionals and businessmen, the *Nationalverein* built a membership of roughly 25 000. In combination with organizations such as the German Rifleman's Confederation, the German Gymnastic Society, and the German Singing Confederation, the *Nationalverein* brought the "German question" back to the fore of politics.

Bismarck was made minister-president of the government in 1862 amidst a constitutional struggle. Prince William had succeeded his brother as King William I in 1861 and was determined to expand the Prussian standing army. Liberals suspected that the intent of proposed reforms was to secure unquestioning loyalty to the Crown so that the army could be used against parliament, and tensions were exacerbated when radical liberals broke with moderates to found the Progressive Party, which soon became the largest party in the Prussian *Landtag*. The Progressives wanted to control how reform was conducted and so they

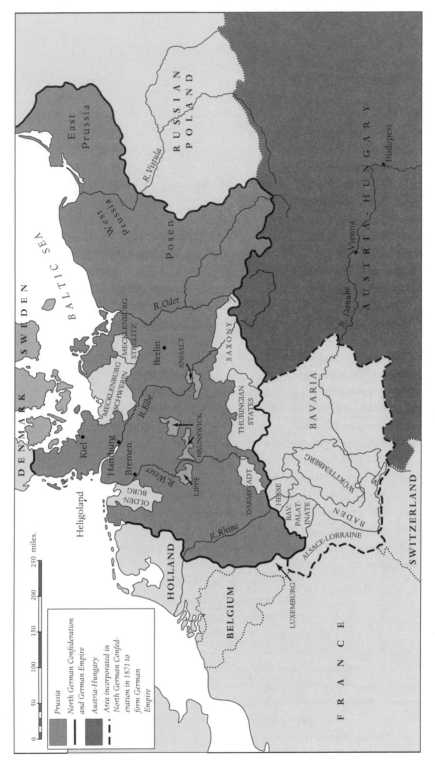

Map 6.2 German unification. William Carr, *A History of Germany* (London, Edward Arnold, 1972), next to p. 117.

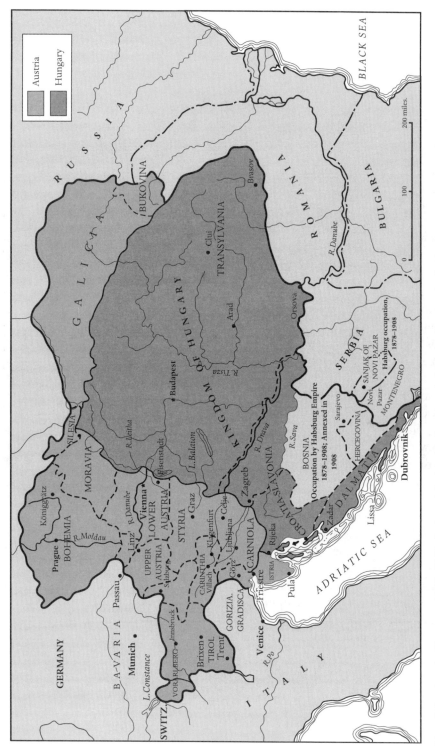

Map 6.3 Austria-Hungary, 1867–1918. Barbara Jelavich, *Modern Austria* (Cambridge: Cambridge University Press, 1987), p. 68.

Austria
Hungary

BLACK SEA

200 miles.

100

0

R U S S I A

BUKOVINA

ROMANIA

BULGARIA

Brasov

G A L I C I A

TRANSYLVANIA

Clui

Arad

Orsova

K I N G D O M   O F   H U N G A R Y

R.Tisza

Budapest

R.Danube

SILESIA

MORAVIA

Königgrätz

BOHEMIA

Prague

R.Moldau

R.Raitha

L.Balaton

Eisenstadt

SERBIA

Belgrade

SANJAK OF
NOVI PAZAR

Novi
Pazar

Habsburg occupation,
1878–1908

MONTENEGRO

BOSNIA
Occupation by Habsburg Empire
1878–1908; Annexed in
1908

Sarajevo

HERCEGOVINA

Zagreb

R.Drava

R.Sava

C R O A T I A - S L A V O N I A

Dubrovnik

DALMATIA

Zadar

Lissa

Rijeka

ISTRIA

Pula

Trieste

ADRIATIC SEA

GORIZIA

GRADISCA

CARNIOLA

Görz

Ljubljana

Celje

Klagenfurt

CARINTHIA

Villach

STYRIA

Graz

Vienna

LOWER
AUSTRIA

UPPER
AUSTRIA

Linz

R.Danube

Salzburg

GERMANY

B A - V A R I A

Munich

Passau

L.Constance

Innsbruck

VORARLBERG

Brixen

TIROL

Trent

SWITZ.

Venice

R.Po

I T A L Y

convinced the lower house to insist on line-item budgetary approval so as to direct how credits would be spent.

Lurking within this wrangle was the issue of whether King or parliament would rule Prussia. If Bismarck hoped initially to conciliate liberals, his remarks were poorly calibrated: "Germany does not look at Prussia's liberalism, but at her power. ... The great questions of the age are not settled by speeches and majority votes ... but by iron and blood."[78] When the lower house persisted in altering the budget, Bismarck convinced the upper house to reject the amended budget and then prorogued parliament. Assured of the loyalty of the army and bureaucracy, Bismarck decided the state, acting on emergency powers, would continue collecting taxes and conducting the military reforms. Much as they opposed the government, liberals could do little; after 1848 very few had any appetite for revolution.

It was not until Danish nationalism reignited conflict in Schleswig and Holstein that Bismarck's qualities as a statesman were truly revealed. As part of a series of agreements with the great powers, the Danish Monarchy had promised that the two duchies would have their own constitutions and would be consulted in the drawing up of a common constitution for all the King's possessions. Schleswig would not be incorporated into Denmark and Germans and Danes would have equal rights. Yet in parliament nationalists pressed for the union of Denmark and Schleswig and by September 1863 they had drawn up a constitution that integrated the duchy. When King Fredrick VII died in November 1863, he left no direct heir. Although the claims of Prince Christian of Glucksburg were recognized by the powers, when he (as Christian IX) signed the constitution, Frederick of Augustenburg proclaimed himself the Duke of Schleswig-Holstein and appealed to the German Confederation. A wave of patriotism swept through the German states as liberals called for immediate recognition of Duke Frederick and entry of Schleswig-Holstein into the Confederation.

From the onset, Bismarck thought in terms of Prussian annexation of the duchies. He saw no advantage in allowing liberals to establish another independent north-German state. Nevertheless, he was also fully cognizant of the need to tread cautiously among the other powers. The situation was even more complicated for the Habsburgs, who feared any alignment between Prussia and German patriotism. Thus the Austrians were receptive when in January 1864 Bismarck proposed joint action and mutual determination of the future of the duchies. The Danes then made matters worse for themselves by rejecting an ultimatum to conform to previous agreements and Austrian and Prussian forces occupied Schleswig in early February. In April the other powers intervened, leading to an armistice and a conference at London. Danish refusal to accept compromise proposals then alienated Britain, Russia, and France, leaving Prussia and Austria free to resolve the issue by force. Renewal of fighting secured the defeat of Denmark by July and the upshot was that Denmark surrendered the duchies to joint-management by Austria and Prussia in October 1864.

To further her influence in Germany, Austria promoted recognition of Duke Frederick's claims to Schleswig-Holstein. The cause was popular with groups like the *Nationalverein* and a motion of recognition put forward by Bavaria and Saxony was carried in the Confederation Diet against Prussian opposition in April 1865. Tensions were alleviated in August by an agreement that Austria would administer Holstein and Prussia Schleswig, but Bismarck had not given up on annexing both. The drift toward war then recommenced when Austrian authorities allowed a demonstration in favor of Duke Frederick at Altona in January 1866. Bismarck had not been idle in the interim. Russia was unlikely to back Austria after the Crimean War, and Britain, even if so disposed, would not intervene without a continental ally. Louis-Napoleon believed that a clash between Prussia and Austria would be a long drawn-out affair and that France would have opportunity to intervene as a mediator and secure advantages. To encourage such thoughts, Bismarck hinted that France would be compensated in the event that war with Austria led to Prussian expansion. Any chance of an Austro-French alliance was thereby scuttled. Better yet, Louis-Napoleon helped convince the Italians, eager to take Venetia, to ally with Prussia in April 1866.

Bismarck's attempts to harness nationalism were less successful and a proposal by the Austrians that the Diet determine the future of Schleswig-Holstein was carried. In response Prussia declared the Confederation dissolved and called on the other states to follow Prussia in founding a new German nation. Most the states were unwilling to conceive of nation building on such terms and hence war commenced with Prussian invasion of Saxony, Hanover, and Hesse-Kassel on June 16, 1866. Many contemporaries expected a Habsburg victory; yet since 1860 Prussia had doubled military expenditure while Austrian expenditure had been halved. Worse still, 100 000 Habsburg forces had to be deployed in the south against Italy, leaving 175 000 Austrian and 32 000 Saxon soldiers to confront 250 000 Prussians.

Superior military planning, particularly exploitation of opportunities for rapid deployment of troops provided by rail systems, then gave Prussia a series or rapid victories. It took only three days to secure control over the three smaller German states. Thereafter on July 3 the defeat of Austrian forces commanded with "awful ineptitude"[79] at Sadowa soon terminated resistance in the south German states. Peace terms would have been far worse for Austria had the wishes of King William been fulfilled, but Bismarck realized that humiliation of the Habsburgs might invite armed intervention on the part of the French or Russians. Prussia would annex Schleswig-Holstein, Hanover, Hesse-Kassel, Frankfurt, and Nassau. The Confederation would be abolished and replaced by a North-German Confederation which would include Saxony but exclude Austria. The southern states of Bavaria, Baden, Württemberg, and Hesse-Darmstadt would remain independent, with the option of forming their own confederation, and a plebiscite would be held in north Schleswig, enabling the Danish majority to join Denmark. The sole territorial loss for the Habsburgs would be Venetia, which would be handed over to Italy.

Had Louis-Napoleon let matters rest with the preliminary Peace of Nikolsburg, the War of 1866 might have proved less a watershed than it did. By demanding compensation in the Rhineland in August, the French Emperor drove the south German states into a series of secret alliances that placed their armies under Prussian command in the event of war. The chances of forming a truly independent south German confederation thus were compromised. After the Peace of Nikolsburg had been formalized as the Peace of Prague on August 23, Louis-Napoleon decided to offer Prussia an alliance in return for support of French acquisition of Belgium. He gained nothing in doing so and the French foolishly provided Bismarck with a document outlining their designs on Belgium.

To the victor went the spoils as elections in Prussia yielded strong conservative gains. Bismarck then initiated an indemnity bill to compensate for illegal collection of taxes since 1862. He thereby recognized that the government had violated the constitution. Nevertheless, most liberals put expansion above constitutional principles; in 1867 right-wing liberals would form the National Liberal Party to press for further unification immediately, and constitutional reform later.

There was not much in the constitution of the North German Confederation to encourage liberals in the short term. There was no declaration of rights. The Prussian King became president of the Confederation, assuming complete command of foreign policy and the army. The princes of the 24 states within the Confederation retained their positions and controlled the choice of representatives to a Bundestrat (federal council). All the same, Prussia provided 17 of 43 representatives to the Bundestrat and chose the federal chancellor, who presided over Bundestrat meetings. Bismarck was thus well placed to dominate. The Confederation also had a Reichstag elected on the basis of universal manhood suffrage, but legislation had to secure the consent of the Bundestrat, and neither body had much control over spending on the army, which constituted 90% of the Confederation budget. Bismarck intended "to destroy parliamentarianism by parliamentarianism";[80] the system he designed was more elaborate than that of Napoleon I, but in spirit it differed little.

The Early Stages of the Women's Movement

In the aftermath of 1848 opportunities for women to organize were extremely limited on the continent. British liberalism was, however, less hostile and by the end of the 1850s a host of associations, frequently linked to a group of reformers known as the Langham Place Circle, had been formed. In a manner that was to become characteristic of the women's movement, the associations drew attention to a broad range of subjects – legal rights, education, employment, and suffrage. During the following decades relaxation of restrictions would enable French, German, and Italian women also to organize associations and publish journals that championed reform. The "woman question" was thus launched throughout Europe, although the women's movement remained strongest in Britain.

The legal subordination of women was an early focus of activists. In Britain a petition by some 2600 women, including many leading writers, contributed in 1857 to passage of a parliamentary act that made divorce less difficult to achieve. Nevertheless the act did not redress the common law custom of coverture, which subordinated married women to their husbands in all legal matters, including possession of property. Hence the campaign would continue until 1882, by which time married women had gained control over their earnings and property. Similar concerns over women's legal status led Maria Desraismes and Léon Richer to found the periodical *The Rights of Women* at Paris in 1868, but progress came more slowly.

Roughly the same pattern could be seen in opposition to state regulation of female prostitution. In 1869 Josephine Butler, a devout Christian activist previously involved in efforts to gain access to higher education for women, launched a campaign against the British Contagious Diseases Acts. She attacked the violation of civil rights entailed in police detainment and forced inspection of women and challenged the double standard involved in not inspecting male clients of prostitutes. By tapping into long-established radical networks in which nonconformist Protestants were prominent, Butler's National Association organized 17 000 petitions containing two and a half million signatures. Not long thereafter Butler's arguments were echoed in Paris and Milan, and subsequently Butler built an international alliance against the "white slave trade." Yet while the Contagious Diseases Act was abolished in Britain in 1886, battle against state-run female prostitution had only begun on the continent.

British women were also on the forefront in pressing for the vote. In 1865 the Langham Place group organized the Women's Suffrage Committee, which later became known as the National Society for Women's Suffrage. Among the candidates for MP whom the Committee supported in 1865 was the liberal philosopher John Stuart Mill. Upon entering parliament Mill raised the issue of granting women the vote and the subject was aired in a full debate. Although women were not enfranchised, feminists were encouraged that women's suffrage had gained 73 votes in favor (against 196 opposed). Thereafter feminists questioned why only men should qualify on the basis of tax payment. They gained partial satisfaction when women ratepayers (widows or single women) gained the vote in local government elections, and by the mid 1870s women had become eligible for election to school and Poor Law boards.

With his publication in 1869 of *The Subjection of Women*, Mill called for removal of all barriers to women's development as human beings. The work was part of a shift in feminist thought toward arguments based on the right to individual self-realization, and Mill's point that no one could know whether women were "naturally" subservient or independent until artificial social constraints were removed stirred controversy throughout Europe. Proponents of separate spheres ideology counter-attacked by claiming that in straying from their role of "angel of the hearth" women would harm themselves and corrupt the public sphere. In perhaps the most notorious instance of debate, the anarchist Proudhon provided a "calculus" that he claimed demonstrated the inferiority of women in physical, intellectual, and moral capacity. Although expressed in a bizarre fashion, Proudhon's beliefs were in fact widespread. They were, however, now being challenged intellectually and meanwhile the increasing number of women in the workforce raised questions about whether males could or should be the sole family breadwinner.

The British women's movement was also precocious in a less favorable regard as the issue of whether to join Butler in her campaign against the Contagious Diseases Acts provoked division within the suffrage movement. Conservative leaders, such as Millicent Fawcett, prized respectability and feared that association with Butler would tarnish their standing, thereby diminishing their ability to rally support. Unlike the more radical leaders of other suffrage societies, especially at Manchester, Fawcett and the London Society also were unwilling to promote suffrage for married women. Splintering over priorities and tactics thus weakened the suffrage movement in the 1870s, and the same problem would emerge on the continent in subsequent decades.

Domestic Politics in the 1860s: Reform in the Autocracies

War was the ultimate gamble for statesmen. Cavour and Bismarck had triumphed and hence they were able to shape the new states they had created. Conversely, defeat in war could severely damage the prestige of a regime and force it to undertake reform. Designed to reduce criticism, reforms initiated in Russia and Austria more often than not created as many problems as they resolved.

When Alexander II came to the throne in 1855, Russia gained a Tsar who was trained in governmental affairs and seasoned by travel. Although he was determined to maintain autocracy, he was also convinced of the need to broaden support by opening channels of communication between the state and the public. Unfortunately a chasm soon opened between cautious state officials and intellectuals who called for sweeping change. Given recognition that great power status required modernization, it was to be expected that the state would seek to develop a rail system. Russians preferred, however, to invest in commerce and foreign investment had to be induced by guarantee of profits; thus the state frequently became the leading investor in private lines. Gradually building accelerated, but funding required sale of Alaska to the USA and complicated the most dramatic reform of the era – emancipation of the peasantry (Figure 6.2).

Advocates could cite many reasons for abolishing serfdom. Poverty was endemic among all peasants, although state peasants were marginally better off than privately-owned serfs (perhaps 38% of the population). Though not as massive as in the past, rebellions continued, adding fear to humanitarian considerations. Moreover the Crimean War had highlighted military and economic arguments.

Figure 6.2 Alexander II addresses Moscow nobles on the emancipation of the serfs. John Massey Stewart Picture Library.

Inability to read made Russian peasants poor soldiers, and because they had little incentive to improve, low agricultural productivity hindered industrial development – a key to military power.

Liberal nobles who supported abolition were a small minority among a group upon whom the regime depended and it took five years of consultation with noble committees before the Emancipation Statutes were proclaimed in 1861. In general, serfs would be freed of bondage and receive close to half the land they had previously been allotted. Nobles would retain the other half and be compensated for their losses with state treasury bonds. Because the state was in no position to fund compensation, peasants would have to make 49 annual redemption payments to the treasury. Until the payments were complete, land would be held in trust by the *mir* (village commune), which would collect payments. The *mir* could redistribute lands according to need, and could also impose travel restrictions on peasants who fell behind in payments. Thus, though personal bondage had been removed, ties to the land remained. In 1866 state peasants received a similar deal: they could purchase the lands upon which they toiled through redemption payments, or they could remain as tenants.

The Tsar Emancipator gained little gratitude as rebellion and refusal to pay redemption testified to continuing peasant discontent. Many nobles also were angered. Some would modernize their estates and hire peasant labor to expand production; others could not adjust and moved to the towns while renting their lands. A sizeable number of peasants supplemented their earnings by working as hired labor. A much smaller number managed to purchase more land and employ capitalist methods, while others left for urban centers. The entire process proved deeply unsettling for decades to come, and the continuing restrictions placed on the peasantry slowed improvement in productivity.

Further reform soon followed. Partly due to the decline in noble authority entailed in peasant emancipation, and partly due to recognition that the state bureaucracy was incapable of providing adequate government in the provinces, 19 provinces in 1864 gained a measure of self government when local assemblies called *zemstva* were formed. The *zemstva* were given responsibility for roadbuilding, economic development, and provision of public health, welfare, and education institutions. Membership was elective, though franchises reflected social hierarchy and corporatism. At the district level, nobles, townsmen, and peasants would separately elect representatives, but representation was weighted so that nobles held roughly as many seats as the peasantry. At the provincial level, representatives would be chosen from the members of the district *zemstva*. Nobles would chair elected executives at both levels and their influence predominated throughout the system.

In other regards, reform was less impressive. When demonstrators criticized state policies in 1861, student organizations were broken up, and further protests led to massive arrests. Alexander then took a different tack in 1863. Statutes granted the universities self-administration, degree requirements for professors were tightened, and increased support was provided for needy students. Student enrolment rose thereafter, until a former student tried to assassinate the Tsar in 1866, enabling conservatives to reverse liberalization. Entry into the universities was restricted, reducing the number of middle-class students, and discipline was handed over to the police.

Conservatives viewed the universities as hotbeds of sedition and they lumped together all proponents of change as nihilists. Nihilism held that state and society were so corrupt that any means used to hasten their destruction was justified. There was, however, great diversity of thought among the leading advocates of change. Alexander Herzen believed that the Russian peasantry was inherently communist and hoped the Tsarist regime could be convinced to remodel society along the lines of the village commune. By the 1860s he had lost much of his following to the journalist Nikolai Chernyshevsky, an advocate of social revolution. Still, while Chernyshevsky recognized that revolution required the application of force, he was no advocate of random acts of violence. The latter position was left to the student Sergei Nechayev, who outlined his views in his *Catechism of the Revolutionary*. Revolution would not occur until the people were driven to it by utter despair. Those who sought improvement should be eliminated because they retarded the necessary progress of misery. Although Nechayev managed to build a small network of cells, his ordering of the execution of a dissident member in 1869 led to discovery of the organization and his imprisonment for life. Reading of the *Catechism* in court produced a public backlash and the revolutionary movement went into remission.

Reform also took a chequered course in Poland. In 1862 Alexander restored limited autonomy. Nationalists then demanded full independence and in January 1863 a rebellion carried insurrection as far as Lithuania and White Russia. Crushed in 1864, the revolt led to harsh reprisals: roughly 400 insurgents were executed after trial, tens of thousands were deported, and the estates of over 3000 landowners were confiscated. After retracting autonomy, the Tsar then instituted a series of politically motivated social and cultural reforms. Peasants, generally untouched by nationalism, were emancipated on favorable terms, whereas landowners received little compensation. Russian became compulsory in Polish schools and in the Russian borderlands use of Polish was banned.

The close relation between defeat and reform was also apparent in the Austrian Empire. After the loss of Lombardy, the Imperial regime needed to restore loyalty. Hence the February Patent of 1861 gave the nationalities of the Empire a bicameral parliament. Nevertheless, elections for the lower house ensured German domination because qualification was based on landowner-ship, and in truth Francis Joseph had not changed his view of representative government: "We shall have a little parliamentarianism, but power will remain in my hands and the whole thing will be adapted to Austrian realities."[81] Far from reconciling non-German groups, the February Patent led to election boy-cotts. Worse still, German liberals pressed the monarchy to yield more power and sought support from Hungarian nationalists. To undercut such maneuvers, the Emperor opened discussions with moderate Magyar leaders Ferencz Deák and Count Gyual Andrássy. After defeat in the Austro-Prussian War in 1866, alarm at German nationalism made the Imperial government even more willing to compromise.

Creation of the Dual Monarchy in 1867 seemed to mark the triumph both of Hungarian autonomy and Austrian liberalism. The *Ausgleich* (Compromise) divided the Empire into Austrian and Hungarian Monarchies, with both ruled by Francis Joseph. Unity would be maintained by the Emperor's appointment of a Common Council of ministers responsible for foreign policy, war, and the financing of common government. Each realm would have its own constitution, parliament, and government for domestic affairs. Common problems and eco-nomic issues would be discussed by representatives of both parliaments, and Hungary would have the right to renegotiate tariff policy, currency regulations, and financial contributions every ten years. Croatia would become part of the Hungarian state, but would retain a separate parliament (the *Sabor*) and government, unlike Transylvania.

The new Austrian Basic Law formally recognized rights championed by liberals, but Imperial practices sometimes vitiated them. The various national groups were supposed to be treated equally; yet a new electoral regime for the lower house favored German representation in the *Reichsrat*. Freedom of assembly and association could be denied by the government on the basis of alleged threat to public security, and Francis Joseph simply ignored ministerial responsibility to parliament. Furthermore, the Emperor could veto legislation and rule by decree when parliament was not in session. All the same, constitutional government had advanced with the new arrangements and Austrian liberals were thereafter able to secure legislation to their liking: elementary education and military service became compulsory. In 1870 the Concordat with Rome was abrogated, leading to the restoration of civil marriage, removal of the education system from Catholic control, and granting of equal civil rights to non-Christian groups. Moreover, elected communal and municipal councils gained control over a wide range of responsibilities, including education, health, welfare, transport, and public amenities, although they would work in cooperation with state officials who concerned themselves mostly with the police. Whether the government could be held accountable by parliament, or whether the new institutions would represent the interests of all national groups, however, remained in doubt.

In Hungary governments were responsible to parliament; yet the latter was utterly dominated by the Magyar elite and restrictions on political association and press laws suggested little shrift would be given to the aspirations of non-Magyars or, for the matter, the masses generally. In 1868 a nationalities law sought to establish equal legal treatment of all groups and provided for education at the primary and secondary levels of education. Nevertheless, it recognized no collective rights for minorities and was in truth designed to facilitate assimilation into a Magyar nation. Discontent with the Compromise of 1867 thus simmered among the non-German and non-Magyar nationalities of the Empire.

Domestic Politics in the 1860s: Reform in Britain and France

Male democracy made significant strides in curiously different ways in the western powers in the 1860s. Because parliament held real power, possession of the vote was meaningful in Britain and, partly due to miscalculation on the part of Liberal and Conservative leaders, the franchise was greatly extended in a Second Reform Act. France already possessed universal manhood suffrage. Still, genuine democratization did not commence until Louis-Napoleon began to woo the Left with a series of concessions that transformed the Second Empire.

The last period of government under Palmerston began in 1859 with an agreement that united free-trade Tories, Whigs, moderate liberals, and Radicals, and essentially founded the Victorian Liberal party. Although at times the Liberal Party seemed little more than a loose collection of interest groups, Liberals were linked by certain core values. Many of the latter derived from earlier Radicalism: emphasis on individual independence (though not necessarily individual liberty when community interests were involved), suspicion of the state but belief in the law as an instrument of social mediation, support for free trade, and (secular or dissenting) anti-clericalism. The influence of Nonconformity gave Liberalism a democratic tendency that strengthened popular liberalism and ensured that the Party transcended social class. For Liberal leaders the key to success was to find a balance between emphasis on independence and expectation that government would be active. Although necessary, discipline must be applied loosely. Gladstone described the art of management nicely when he stated "Liberalism has ever sought to unite freedom of individual thought and action ... with corporate efficiency," but he added that this aim was "difficult."[82] Economic liberalism dominated policy; while Cobden negotiated free trade treaties, Gladstone reduced taxation. Foreign minister Russell largely avoided conflict in foreign lands and the period saw no major domestic initiatives.

Plans for reform soon emerged, however, when Russell formed his last government, after the decease of Palmerston in 1866. As Leader of the Commons, it was Gladstone who introduced a bill that would have enfranchised roughly 400 000 new voters. It also would have eliminated many small borough seats, some of which were held by Whigs, and hence a combination of Liberal dissidents and Conservatives rejected reform in June. Russell resigned and Derby then formed a minority Tory government. The key to what followed was Disraeli's conjecture that the working classes were more conservative than the middle classes. Although initial debate among Tories led to several cabinet resignations, growing public support for reform enabled Derby to press on in 1867. In a welter of amendments discipline broke down on both sides and the result was a much more sweeping Second Reform Act than either Disraeli or Gladstone had intended. Some 1 150 000 new voters were added and many seats were redistributed. Disraeli was pleased that the Tories had passed reform before the Liberals did; yet he had misjudged what Derby termed "a leap in the dark."[83] General elections in 1868 widened the Liberal majority and it was Gladstone who formed the next government. Gladstone was the son of a wealthy merchant and had been educated at Eton and Oxford, but he excelled at articulating, and shared the values of, popular liberalism and was seen as the leading opponent of elite privilege. Hence "the People's William" was the chief beneficiary of Disraeli's gamble.

Over the next five years Gladstone initiated an impressive series of reforms. Gladstone feared that the Liberals might be viewed by the public as a collection of various interest groups rather than a party capable of representing the nation. In essence he was confronting a central dilemma of mass politics – how to give coherence to a party that is composed of various, at times divergent, interests? His strategy was to prioritize certain problems as great moral issues before which other concerns, however worthy, must yield precedence. For the most part, it proved an effective strategy. Disestablishment in July 1869 put the Irish Anglican

Church on the same legal footing as the Catholic and Presbyterian churches. In 1870 an Irish Land Act was passed in an attempt to reduce agrarian discontent. The powers of landlords to evict tenants were restricted, evicted tenants were to be compensated for any improvements they had made, and government loans were made available to tenants who wished to purchase their lands. Intended to reconcile the Irish to British rule, such measures were perhaps too little too late and they ran aground against Irish alienation; 1870 saw creation of a Home Government Association that would push for establishment of an Irish parliament.

Other reforms proved more effective. Although the Education Act of 1870 did not found a unified national system, it marked a major step in state intervention. Where provision of education was deemed inadequate, local boards could be established to levy taxes, build schools, and hire teachers. School boards could make attendance compulsory and parents would have to pay, although fees could be waved for the poor. In addition, several acts advanced the principle of careers open to talent. Virtually all permanent appointments in the civil service would be based on competitive examination, and officer's rank in the army could no longer be obtained by the purchase of commissions.

In France the key to relatively peaceful regime alteration was Louis-Napoleon's decision to appeal to the Left in a bid to compensate for eroding conservative support. Catholics were appalled by the Emperor's Italian policies. The business community was alarmed by the costs of the Italian war and an ill-conceived attempt to establish a satellite state in Mexico between 1861 and 1867. Many businessmen were also alienated by the signing of a free trade treaty with Britain in 1860. The plan behind lowering tariffs was that costs would be reduced for consumers while competition forced French producers to improve efficiency. Unfortunately, implementation coincided with a sharp economic slump in 1862 and many firms went bankrupt. Thereafter decline in growth rates gave ammunition to advocates of protectionism and critics of deficit financing.

From the inception of his regime, Louis-Napoleon had tried to detach workers from republicanism and in the 1860s this strategy was intensified. In 1862 the Emperor sponsored a workers' delegation to London to observe English labor conditions and in the following year he set up an agency to held fund the establish-ment of cooperatives. In 1864 workers were granted the right to strike, provided they did not form permanent associations. In 1868 Louis-Napoleon let it be known that the state would tolerate unions, although they were not given legal sanction. Labor began rapid organization and in the face of a wave of strikes the position of the state remained ambiguous. While the Socialist International was permitted to organize, its leaders were repeatedly prosecuted. Thus the regime gained little gratitude among working-class leaders.

Political liberalization also came incrementally. In 1860 the legislature was granted the right to present an annual address to the Emperor, its sessions were opened to the public, and publication of debates was legalized. In 1861 deputies gained the right to vote on each section of the budget and to amend bills. In 1863 a minister was assigned the task of defending government policies in the legislature, and four years later deputies gained the right to interpolate (formally question) ministers. Also in 1867 press laws and restrictions on public meetings were relaxed, allowing opposition groups to criticize the government more freely, and organize their followers publicly. Here too, the results were alarming. In 1857 Opposition candidates, a combination of conservatives, liberals, and republicans, had garnered 750 000 of the votes cast in elections. In May 1869 they reached 3.3 million – over 40% of the total.

In theory, all 40 republicans sitting in the legislature in late 1869 were hostile to the Empire. Yet in practice they were divided over the stance to take regarding a regime that was shedding its authoritarian origins, and liberals were similarly uncertain. In the legislature, a bloc known as the Open Left was composed of moderate republicans such as the barrister Emile Ollivier. Like a group of liberals led by Thiers, they were willing to work with the Emperor for reform. A second bloc known as the Closed Left included future republican luminaries such as Jules Simon, Jules Favre, and Léon Gambetta; they would not cooperate under any circumstance. None of these groups, however, advocated insurrection.

If republicanism posed little immediate danger, diminishing confidence raised questions about the future of an ailing Emperor and his dynasty. Nevertheless Louis-Napoleon continued along the path of reform when in January 1870 he called on Ollivier to form a government and undertake constitutional revision. The resultant system consolidated previous measures and furthered liberalization, but it was fraught with ambiguity. The Emperor would retain wide powers in foreign policy and there would be no prime minister. Whether ministers were responsible to the Emperor or to parliament remained unclear. Despite such uncertainties, when the public was asked to approve the new constitution in May an overwhelming 83% voted positively. Such an endorsement marked a triumph and Louis-Napoleon had shown remarkable resolve in transforming his regime from authoritarian to liberal.

Domestic Politics in the 1860s: Instability in Italy and Spain

If the first task of government is to provide civil order, neither the Italian nor the Spanish regimes could be judged a success in the 1860s. Given the limits of mass nationalism, the task of integrating the diverse peoples of the Italian peninsula was always going to be difficult and it was made virtually impossible by ill-conceived state policies. In Spain the central problem was a familiar one – the failure of elite factions to establish a regime capable of providing stability while accommodating reform.

When Cavour died in 1861, Louis-Napoleon commented: "The driver has fallen from the box; now we must see if the horses will bolt or go back to the stable."[84] In fact more horses entered the stable as diplomacy enabled the Kingdom of Italy to continue the unification process. Alliance with Prussia in 1866 allowed Victor

Emmanuel to add Venetia, and in 1870 war with Prussia forced the French to remove their garrison from Rome, enabling the Italian Kingdom to seize control.

Territorial acquisition said little about the ability of the regime to govern effectively. The Kingdom was a genuine constitutional monarchy. Although ministers were in theory responsible solely to the King, Victor Emmanuel established a convention of appointing governments that could secure majorities in the lower house. Parliament held real power: financial measures had to be introduced in the Chamber, deputies could initiate legislation, and ministers could be summoned for votes of confidence. Power inevitably fell to groups tied to the *Risorgimento*. While the Right predominated, the Left occasionally entered into coalition government and absence of party discipline tended to blur division between the two main parliamentary *blocs*. Neither the ultraroyalists of the extreme Right nor the democratic radicals of the extreme Left posed much of a challenge to the regime. Nevertheless, the franchise was restricted to about 2% of the population, raising questions about whether parliament could represent the interests of the vast majority.

D'Azeglio spoke for the regime when he stated: "Now we have made Italy, we must make Italians."[85] That unification had been achieved by annexation meant that Italians would have to accustom themselves to the political, administrative, and legal systems developed in Piedmont-Sardinia. Implementation of the Napoleonic administrative model meant that power would be centralized, with little consideration given to local autonomy. Toward developing a national culture the state encouraged creation of a foundation myth that glorified the *Risorgimento* by stressing heroism while ignoring division. Nationalist construction of the past, reflected in maps, museums, monuments, and public ceremonial, then ran up against material realities. Although mass education systems could be used to inculcate patriotism, funding for expansion was lacking; most of the children who did attend school did so for less than two years.

Obstacles to national integration were many. Loss of the Papal States drove Pius IX further along the path of reaction; in 1864 his *Syllabus of Errors* denounced nationalism and in 1868 the Church issued a decree ordering Italian Catholics not to participate in political life. After the annexation of Rome, in May 1871 parliament passed a "Law of Papal Guarantees" that ensured papal independence in the Vatican, largely separated Church and State in Italy, and provided the Pope with substantial annual revenues. Pius would have none of it. Although the "Papal Guarantees" helped ensure there would be no foreign intervention on behalf of a Pope who was seen as hopelessly intransigent, reconciling Catholics to the new regime was going to prove difficult.

As troublesome as cultural grievances were material ones. The wars of unification had been costly and to address spiraling debt the government decided to increase indirect taxes that fell largely on the poor. In the south resultant resentment was heightened by adoption of free trade policies that reversed former protectionism and made dire poverty worse. Failure to act on earlier promises of land redistribution, dissolution without compensation of Garibaldi's volunteer forces, and conscription deepened alienation. Widespread brigandage on the mainland was at times coupled with support for restoration of the Bourbons, and in Sicily brigandage took on an unalloyed social character, pitting landless peasant bands against landowning elites. The new state found itself confronted by guerrilla-style civil war and responded by garrisoning the south with some 120 000 troops. Fighting flared until 1865 and then smoldered in episodic banditry. As one commentator put it, union between the north and south was "like going to bed with someone who has smallpox."[86]

In 1870 the house of Savoy appeared set to profit also by the decline of the Spanish Bourbons when Amadeo, second son of Victor Emmanuel, was made King of Spain. To some extent, Isabel II had been the author of her own misfortunes. After forcing the resignation of O'Donnell in 1863, she had appointed prime ministers who could not find a working consensus amidst the absolutist pretensions of the court and the deeply divided social elite. In the absence of coherent government, old problems grew threatening. O'Donnell's foreign policy had greatly increased debt while state revenues declined in the midst of a recession. Exports and foreign investment fell sharply, triggering a collapse of Spanish lending agencies and a slump in industrial production. Worse still, drought ruined the harvests of 1866 and 1867. Economic crisis sharpened questions about the regime's viability and an important development occurred in November 1867 when O'Donnell died of typhus. O'Donnell's followers, including the Moderate General Francisco Serrano, shifted their support to General Juan Prim, a Progressive who harbored few illusions about Bourbon rule.

The "Glorious Revolution" of 1868 briefly put Spain at the forefront of democratic politics. When Serrano commenced revolt at Cadiz, he was soon joined by disaffected Unionist generals, and most Spanish towns, cities, and military garrisons came out in support of the rebels. By October 3 Serrano had entered Madrid and the Queen had fled to France. Democrats had played little direct role in the overthrow of the monarchy, although they had triggered insurrections that established revolutionary *juntas*. The latter established militias, plundered churches, and banned collection of consumption taxes. Among the various forces involved in revolt there was little agreement beyond opposition to the old regime; nevertheless a provisional government led by Serrano acted on a prior agreement by organizing elections based on universal male suffrage. Of the roughly 3,800,000 qualified, about 70% voted, yielding a constitutional *Cortes* of 130 Progressives, 90 Unionists, 70 Republicans, 45 Democrats, and 17 Carlists. If politics could have been reduced to a system, the Spanish might have been well served by the constitution drawn up in 1869. The latter proclaimed commitment to civil and political liberties, including freedom of religion, and established the basic institutions of a constitutional monarchy. Still, systems are one thing; practices are another.

Prim formed a government and immediately had to deal with revolt in Cuba. Spanish sugar and tobacco planters opposed granting concessions to the rebels, who were composed largely of poor peasants and runaway slaves, and the government resorted to repression. It was, however, difficult to track down irregular forces in mountainous countryside and jungle. Worse yet, Cuban revolt meant that Prim had to set aside plans to reduce conscription and taxation; some 100 000 troops were stationed in Cuba by 1870. In combination with the disbanding of revolutionary *juntas* and civilian militias, retention of conscription played into the hands of republicans. Although revolts in Zaragoza and Valencia were quashed by the army, they also signaled that instability would continue, partly because republican leaders soon lost control over their followers. At least one republican deputy drew the obvious conclusion, though he did so in exile: "Feverish agitation, barricades, shots and murder will always benefit the government more than us."[87] In a sign of things to come, in October minister of the interior Práxedes Sagasta suspended the constitutional guarantees of freedom of assembly and speech.

For Prim the order of the day was to find a dynasty to crown the constitutional edifice. While the French Duke de Montpensier enjoyed conservative support from Unionists, and the Savoyard Amadeo was popular among anti-clerical Progressives and Democrats, Prim favored a centrist Hohenzollern candidate. When Montpensier shot his cousin in a duel he also killed his prospects for the Spanish Crown, and thereafter pressure from the French forced Prim to abandon plans to put a Prussian on the throne. Hence Prim opted to back Amadeo. The latter was elected in the *Cortes* in November 1870, shortly before Prim was assassinated in December. Whether Prim had rendered the house of Savoy a service could be questioned and the French would have even less cause to be pleased by their part in the affair.

Birth and Death: The Franco-Prussian War and Paris Commune

War between Prussia and France was not inevitable after creation of the North German Confederation in 1866. Louis-Napoleon was not eager for conflict; he knew that parliament's watering down of military reforms raised doubts about the army. Given previous foreign policy failures, he was, however, poorly placed to deny a rising tide of chauvinism apparent in the press and parliament. Nor was Bismarck necessarily dissatisfied with the status quo. Prussia's domination of the north might be complicated by addition of the largely Catholic south, and Prussia already possessed influence throughout Germany due to transformation of the *Zollverein* into an elective *Zollparlament* that determined common commercial policies. Still, Bismarck's position was built on using nationalism to neutralize liberalism. After the threat posed by French calls for compensation receded, the inclination of the south German states to assert their independence recovered. Criticism of taxes for army reform mounted and anti-Prussian candidates gained a majority in elections to the *Zollparlament* in 1868.

War with France could yield dividends provided the French found no allies and Bismarck was a master at isolating his opponents. Austria-Hungary was in no shape to undertake another war. Past French expressions of sympathy for Polish nationalism had alienated the Russians and in 1868 Russia and Prussia reached an agreement of mutual aid in the event that either was attacked by two powers. Victor Emmanuel looked on France fondly; yet it was Prussian victory that had delivered Venetia and the French were obstructive over Rome. That left Britain and Louis-Napoleon had already provided Bismarck with a means to neutralize any sympathy from that quarter.

Spain provided the pretext for war. The French could not accept the possibility of a Hohenzollern attack from both the Rhineland and the Pyrenees and their pressure led to the renunciation of the candidature of Prince Leopold of Hohenzollern-Sigmaringen to the Spanish throne. Bismarck was disappointed, until the French pushed matters too far. In July 1870 the French ambassador pressed King William, who was taking the waters at the spa town of Bad Ems, to guarantee the candidature would not be renewed. William refused, but he also privately expressed his approval of Leopold's renunciation. By then Bismarck wanted to force matters and so he resorted to subterfuge after William had sent an account of the meeting. Bismarck edited the Ems telegram so as to give the impression that William and the ambassador had clashed, leaving both parties aggrieved. Thereafter he handed the altered version to the German press, knowing their reports would inflame French opinion. As Parisian crowds bellowed "To Berlin!" war was declared "with a light heart"[88] by the Ollivier government on July 19. Any possibility of British involvement soon disappeared when Bismarck published earlier French proposals for annexation of Belgium. That the French sought to invade through the Bavarian Palatinate then ensured that the south Germans rapidly fell in line behind their Prussian commanders.

As the General Staff well knew, the Prussian army had by no means demonstrated invincibility against the Austrians in 1866. Thus the army had adopted a quick-firing Krupp breechloader that improved its artillery and effectively neutralized the advantages of the superior French Chassepot rifle. Prussian organization, again manifest in use of rail lines, stood in stark contrast to chaos on the French side as soldiers moved in one direction and supplies went in another. When battle commenced in early August the Prussian officer corps out-classed their French counterparts in coordinating resources and seizing opportunities. French refusal to fall back on Paris then led to the capture of 130,000 men and the Emperor at Sedan on 2 September. That the writing was on the wall could be seen in a note sent by Louis-Napoleon to the Empress: "I would have preferred death to witnessing such a disastrous capitulation."[89]

Bonapartists put up little resistance on September 4 as republicans Gambetta and Jules Favre led a march to city hall to proclaim a republic and organize a Government of National Defence. Republicans were soon, however, disabused of belief that they could easily negotiate peace; Bismarck's terms were harsh. The government thus resolved to continue the fight and with Paris under siege in October Gambetta departed by hot air balloon to organize resistance in the provinces. The surrender of a second army of 173 000 at Metz on October 27 thereafter triggered an attempt to seize power at Paris by Blanquists; although the National Guard restored order, moderate republicans were reminded of how war could play into the hands of extremists. Gambetta managed to throw several makeshift armies into the fray, but a series of inconclusive skirmishes failed to relieve Paris.

With Parisians reduced to dining on animals from the zoo, on January 28 the government signed a three-week armistice that entailed the surrender of Paris and allowed for election of a National Assembly that would meet at Bordeaux. Deputies would then choose a government that could claim to represent all of France in negotiating what were bound to be unpalatable peace terms. The choice of the French on February 8 shocked republicans. By continuing the war they had acquired the image of "hawks" in a country that wanted peace. The result was an Assembly wherein Orleanist and Legitimist deputies held a large majority over republicans, independents, and a rump of Bonapartists. For the moment the deputies vowed to set aside their differences and concentrate on securing peace and toward the latter end they elected Thiers to run the government as "head of the executive power."

Thereafter the deputies approved the peace negotiated by Thiers and Favre with Bismarck. By the terms of the Treaty of Frankfurt, signed in early May, France would lose Alsace and much of Lorraine, and pay an indemnity of five billion *francs*. Bismarck's terms partly derived from pragmatic considerations: reparations were set at a level designed to cripple the French economy in the years following defeat so that the means to pursue revenge would not exist. Still, there was something more at play when Bismarck allowed the French to keep the fortress of Belfort in return for permitting the German army to parade down the Champs Elysées. Unlike in 1866, Bismarck rubbed salt into the wounds of a defeated opponent.

Already on January 18, William had been proclaimed Kaiser (Emperor) of all the German states in a ceremony conducted at the Palace of Versailles. In negotiations conducted in the previous months, the various princes, states, and parties had extracted concessions concerning their place in a new German state. The Empire thus was a reformulation of the North German Confederation in which the rights and differences of the smaller states gained substantial recognition. Moreover, in the future declarations of war would require approval by the Federal Council, wherein the dominance of Prussia would be reduced by inclusion of 15 new votes for the southern states. All the same, patriotic fervour trumped particularism and the position of Prussia remained dominant.

As victory united Germany, defeat threatened to tear France apart. The episode known as the Paris Commune was a tragedy born of error and delusion. During the fall radicals had formed a network of "vigilance" committees, published journals, and gained election into the officer corps of the National Guard. With the regular army engaged on the front, defence of Paris had been left in the hands of perhaps 300 000 National Guardsmen. After months of siege, near starvation, epidemic, and bombardment had produced some 40 000 deaths, radicals felt

Figure 6.3 The Oath at Versailles. "The Proclamation of Wilhelm as Kaiser of the new German Reich, in the Hall of Mirrors at Versailles on 18th January 1871," painted by Anton Alexander von Werner, 1885. Schloss Friedrichsruhe, Germany / The Bridgeman Art Library.

betrayed by the armistice and the unwillingness of the provinces to continue fighting. The February elections then sharpened the apparent contrast: radicals, including Blanc, Gambetta, and the neo-Jacobin Georges Clemenceau, swept the board in Paris. As royalist deputies at Bordeaux voted to shift their meetings to

Versailles rather than the capital, suspicion of betrayal mounted and National Guardsmen formed a quasi-political Republican Federation. When news that the Assembly had agreed to the treaty arrived, Guardsmen seized rifles and cannon and carried them off to working-class districts. Thereafter attempts by the government to shut down radical newspapers and legislation terminating payment to National Guardsmen added fuel to the fire.

When Thiers ordered troops to retake the cannon in mid-March 1871, crowds intervened and two officers were shot. Thiers and the government then fled to Versailles, leaving Paris in the hands of radicals. Negotiations between the central government and the National Guard Federation thereafter failed, leading to election of a municipal assembly known as the Paris Commune. Suspicion immediately arose that Thiers had abandoned Paris so that militants could discredit themselves and hence justify subsequent elimination. Well-known radicals, Gambetta, Clemenceau, and Blanc among them, wisely distanced themselves from the fray. For his part, Thiers did little to discredit rumors that made his actions appear calculated rather than panic-stricken.

Marxist description of the Commune as a proletarian revolt was misleading, although social tensions played a significant part. Upper-middle-class and moderate elements mostly boycotted the election of the Commune, which in turn chose an executive committee. The Committee was composed of a wide array of militants – Blanquists, Proudhonians, a single Marxist, and anti-clerical Jacobins – who possessed little ideological coherence and divided over whether to impose a revolutionary dictatorship. The Commune was popular in character and it briefly gave power to men drawn from outside the elite, but far from constituting an industrial proletariat, the support base for the Commune covered the broad range of social categories typical of the revolutionary crowd from 1789 onwards. The Commune's social program was modest: a moratorium on debt would be extended, articles pledged at pawnshops would be given back, abandoned factories would be turned over to worker cooperatives, albeit with compensation to owners, and education would be removed from the Church. There would, however, be no attack on private property; the Commune was anxious to maintain good relations with commerce and the Bank of France, upon which it depended for funds. Meanwhile Thiers, with help from Bismarck, reassembled an army of 130 000 that was smarting from defeat and willing to reassert authority. As the inevitable assault loomed, post-revolutionary euphoria turned to a hunt for traditional enemies in Paris: churches were ransacked and the Archbishop and several priests were taken as hostages.

Five weeks of siege preceded a "Bloody Week" of street fighting that began on May 21. Haussmann's transformation of Paris meant that barricades were no longer effective; all the same, the army advanced gradually, securing areas with at times indiscriminate slaughter. As they retreated, Communard fighters torched public buildings and shot hostages. The army responded with summary execution of anyone found with a gun. Perhaps as many as 25 000 Communards died in the fighting and summary executions; another 40 000 alleged Communards were imprisoned.

The combined impact of the Franco-Prussian War and the Paris Commune was complex. Conservatives had been terrified by the Commune and their loathing of the "dangerous classes" would make them unreceptive to arguments for social reform. Working-class organization would go into steep decline over the next decade. Division from radicals improved the prospects for moderates determined to establish a democratic republic, but the Third Republic would have to be socially conservative. Former advocates of political decentralization such as Ferry came to the conclusion that "a unitary and centralized state"[90] was crucial to the preservation of France, although republican emphasis on the importance of municipal institutions to citizenship would continue. For socialists, destruction of republican fraternity meant that internationalism based on class allegiance, rather than nationalism, seemed the way forward.

The period 1854–71 was thus one of enormous change. War had convulsed the states system, raising the question of whether further conflict was in the offing. Why should nationalists in other parts of Europe not try to follow the examples set in Italy and Germany? Potentially as corrosive was the way in which diplomacy had been conducted. In evaluating Bismarck's treatment of the French during negotiations of the Treaty of Frankfurt, Disraeli shrewdly assessed the new reality: "there is not a diplomatic tradition that has not been swept away. You have a new world, new influences at work … The balance of power has been entirely destroyed."[91]

Britain seemed an island of stability. Avoidance of international conflict after the Crimean War doubtless fostered domestic stability; Russia, the Austrian Empire, and France all provided examples of the volatility that defeat could produce. While the Romanov and Habsburg dynasties sought to repair damaged prestige, it was by no means clear that they had succeeded in strengthening support amidst growing opposition. Although the most far reaching political reforms had been conducted by Louis-Napoleon, defeat by Prussia proved more than his revamped regime could survive.

Gladstone had good reason to fear alienation in Ireland; yet what was truly singular about Britain was the combination of stability with political advance. Spain was an object lesson that reform without stability achieved little. After unification Italy was similarly tumultuous as the process of integration proved far more difficult, and less satisfactory, than nationalists had imagined. Wealth generated by industrial revolution, overseas empire, and global commerce doubtless contributed, but it was also true that the deepening maturity of their civil society fostered British ability to combine stability with progress. Acceptance of the right to association could be seen in the precocity of the British women's movement, and meanwhile leading politicians sought to identify and act upon public opinion rather than repress it. Simultaneously the British were progressing toward a coherent party system, facilitating passage of legislation. Many continental states possessed parliaments by 1871; combining representative with effective government would, however, prove the great challenge of the future.

7

Europe from the Paris Commune to the Fall of Bismarck, 1871–1892

Arms, Alliances, and Inter-State Relations in the 1870s

The wars of German unification had demonstrated how much could be gained by rapid concentration of mass armies, forcing states to build the size and readiness of their forces. Table 7.1 demonstrates the marked trend of military expansion.

Contemporaries were convinced of the importance of employing the most recent innovations and hence technological advance also encouraged increased spending. Britain participated in naval races with France and Russia in the 1880s and 1890s, and thereafter with Germany. By the latter date all the major navies had competed in the development of torpedo-boats, torpedo-boat destroyers, submarines, warships, and battle cruisers. The race between armour and armour-piercing guns made rapid obsolescence acute in naval construction and it was also problematic on land. Between 1874 and 1884 the French constructed 166 forts to stop German invasion, but by 1886 the development of a delayed action high explosive meant that artillery shells could penetrate masonry before exploding. Thus the French had to remodel the forts, lowering their elevation and re-inforcing concrete with steel. Thereafter further advances continuously increased destructive capacity. Whereas a field gun of Napoleonic vintage could fire 150 rounds a day and have an effective range of up to 1200 meters, by 1914 it could fire 300 rounds and reach 7000 meters. A Napoleonic musket could perhaps fire five times a minute, whereas a machine-gun could unleash up to 400 rounds a minute.

Europe's Uncertain Path 1814–1914: State Formation and Civil Society, First Edition. R. S. Alexander.
© 2012 R. S. Alexander. Published 2012 by Blackwell Publishing Ltd.

Table 7.1   Military and naval personnel of the powers, 1870–1914.

	1870	1880	1890	1900	1914
Russia	716 000	791 000	677 000	1 162 000	1 352 000
France	454 000	543 000	542 000	715 000	910 000
Germany	410 000	426 000	504 000	524 000	891 000
Britain	345 000	367 000	420 000	624 000	532 000
Austria-Hungary	252 000	246 000	346 000	385 000	444 000
Italy	353 000	216 000	284 000	255 000	345 000

Source: Adapted from Quincy Wright, *A Study of War*, 2nd edition (Chicago, 1965), pp. 670–1. Reproduced by kind permission of University of Chicago Press.

Figure 7.1   The dream of the inventor of the Needle Gun. © Bettmann/Corbis.

Given these trends, why did peace prevail among the powers? The key was that Bismarck wished to consolidate the German Empire and became an advocate of the status quo. He calculated that none of the powers could afford to enter unilaterally into conflict with two or more of the others and that if one could count on two allies, one could rest secure. Bismarck assumed that the French longed for revenge, and thus he negotiated alliances designed to isolate them. Desire to avoid continental entanglement meant the British were unlikely to ally with France, but what if conflicting interests drove either Austria-Hungary or Russia into the arms of the French? Part of Bismarck's genius lay in recognition that alliances could be used to restrain allies, but binding the other two eastern powers was akin to herding cats.

Tension was already evident in the early 1870s. Russia had exploited the Franco-Prussian War to repudiate the Black Sea clauses of the Treaty of Paris of 1856, raising alarm over Tsarist intentions toward the Ottoman Empire. Both Russia and Austria-Hungary wished, however, to cultivate friendly relations with Germany. Thus meetings begun in September 1871 culminated in a military convention between Germany and Russia and loose agreement between Russia and Austria-Hungary over military cooperation in the event that either was attacked. In combination the agreements came to be known as the *Dreikaiserbund* (Three Emperors' League).

Bismarck's determination to maintain peace was then demonstrated during another flare up of the Eastern Question. Most diplomats recognized that preservation of Ottoman rule offered the best hope of preventing the powers from fighting over conflicting regional interests. Yet to some extent the powers could thank themselves for disorder in the Empire. Ottoman attempts at reform were hampered by insufficient state revenue, partly due to the powers' imposition of low customs tolls. When the Empire had declared bankruptcy in 1857, the powers had imposed a Council of Public Debt, which administered one-fifth of Imperial revenues in the interests of European bondholders. Moreover, the "Capitulations" that gave European states a say in treatment of religious minorities encouraged the latter to look abroad for support.

Although Slavophiles sent aid to Christian rebels in Bosnia-Herzegovina and called for military intervention in 1875, Tsar Alexander followed advice that Russia must avoid a repeat of the Crimean War. When in 1876 Serbia and Montenegro declared war on Turkey, Russia opted for diplomacy, hoping that pressure by the powers would force the Ottomans to grant concessions. Unfortunately, Turkish slaughter of Bulgarian rebels in June upped the ante, and thereafter division among the powers at an international conference held at Constantinople in late 1876 convinced the Turks that they could act with impunity. Promises to Austria-Hungary that Russia would not seek to create a large client state then paved the way for armed intervention, beginning in April 1877. Initially stout Turkish resistance crumbled, and the Russians soon advanced toward Constantinople. Subsequent negotiations led in March 1878 to the Treaty of San Stefano, in which

Russia unwisely extracted major concessions, including creation of a large Bulgarian state. Russia thus drew the ire of Austria-Hungary and Britain.

Bismarck did not believe that the Eastern Question was "worth the healthy bones of a single Pomeranian musketeer."[92] Nevertheless, with the Three Emperors' League crumbling, he reluctantly accepted the role of power broker at a congress assembled at Berlin in June 1878. By then calmer heads had prevailed at St Petersburg. The campaign against the Turks had again revealed inadequacies in the Russian army and hence Alexander made broad concessions. While Bulgaria proper gained independence with Prince Alexander of Battenberg as ruler, Eastern Roumelia and Macedonia remained under Ottoman rule. Serbia, Montenegro, and Romania gained recognition as independent states. Austria-Hungary was given a mandate to occupy Bosnia-Herzegovina, while the British occupied Cyprus and secured agreement that passage through the Aegean Sea and the Straits would remain free during times of peace.

Despite Russian disenchantment at having been forced to make so many concessions, by June 1881 Bismarck had managed to induce the three Emperors into a new agreement of benevolent neutrality should any of them enter into war with a fourth power. Although the agreement did not apply to war with the Ottomans, attached clauses allowed for enlargement of Bulgaria and closure of the Straits in time of war, both of which pleased Russia, and agreed to future Habsburg annexation of Bosnia-Herzegovina. The Three Emperors' Alliance would then be renewed in 1884. By then deteriorating Franco-Italian relations had facilitated formation of a Triple Alliance of Italy, Germany, and Austria-Hungary in May 1882. For Italy and Germany the Alliance entailed joint defence in the event of attack by France. Austria-Hungary would join in defence of Italy from French attack and in return Austria-Hungary could count on Italian neutrality in the event of war with Russia. Thus French isolation appeared deeply entrenched.

The Coming of Male Democracy

The ideological spectrum had broadened to include six main groups: reactionaries, conservatives, liberals, radicals, socialists, and anarchists. All contained a variety of subgroups, and they frequently divided over the issue of male democracy.

There were several reasons why democracy advanced. Observers of the wars of German unification believed that high literacy rates among common soldiers had played a part in Prussian success and such reflections encouraged increased state provision of primary education. States were also keen to encourage industrialization and arguments concerning the relation between education and productivity had salience in that regard too. Increased literacy fostered growth in the publishing trades, and the development of communication and transportation systems facilitated the flow of information to the countryside, expanding political consciousness.

Moreover, much of the continent began to catch up with the British in associational life as commentators remarked on a "mania" for forming clubs. Such associations might or might not be explicitly political in character; one way or another, their profusion made state control more difficult and the increasing entry of the masses into civil society broadened demand for democracy.

A common feature of the main political groups was, however, their reluctance to grant women the vote. Several women's groups had supported the Paris Commune, and an enduring legend had developed of crazed women torching public buildings. It thus was no coincidence that studies of crowd psychology linked irrational behavior to "feminine" characteristics. In the aftermath of the Commune many women's groups sought to disassociate themselves from "unwomanly" radicals; yet exclusion from the franchise was made explicit in Denmark in 1871 and in France in 1874.

Thereafter the women's movement began to recover. In 1878 Richer and Deraismes, leaders of the French League for Women's Rights, organized an international congress at Paris. Most participants were French, but a significant contingent came from other European, North American, and South American states. Although suffrage was excluded, much of the discussion was political in nature, encompassing calls for legal and educational reform, and abolition of state-regulated prostitution. Meanwhile Josephine Baker's crusade against the "white slave trade" established its base in Switzerland, which would be the scene of five international conferences between 1877 and 1887. In 1888 a conference specifically on suffrage was held at Washington, and in the following year a second general congress was held at Paris.

As the women's movement grew, it became more complex. In Britain suffrage was high on the agenda, apparent in the combining of smaller groups in the National Union of Women's Suffrage Societies (NUWSS) led by Millicent Fawcett. Whereas the NUWSS restricted its efforts to suffrage, the German Woman's Association founded by Louise Otto-Peters focused on education and working conditions, largely eschewing the issue of the vote. In France division emerged between the League for Women's Rights and more radical feminists such as Hubertine Auclert, a superb publicist who argued that women should refuse to pay taxes until they gained political rights. The League advocated an incremental approach, hoping to build momentum by concentrating first on legal reform and appealing to the male republican establishment. Somewhat like Sand several decades earlier, Richer feared that large numbers of women would follow the directions of Catholic priests and in 1882 he put the matter thusly: "If they voted today, the Republic would not last for six months."[93] Despite her notoriety for anti-clericalism, Auclert rejected such concerns and wanted to push immediately for enfranchisement as the means by which other reforms could be achieved. Her rejoinder was typically forceful: "man and woman should together govern this society that they form part of, and share in exercising the same rights, as much in public life as in private life."[94] She sought support from American and British feminists, and tried to work with socialists, putting her beyond the pale for most middle-class women's groups. Already present, issues of religious and class identity would further complicate divisions over strategy in the future.

Domestic Politics in the 1870s: Britain and France

Britain and France had recently made significant advances toward democracy. In the former the Second Reform Act initially favored the Liberal Party, spurring the Conservatives to improve their party structure in a successful drive to regain power. Although both parties encountered problems while in office, they were highly active, demonstrating that democratic advance need not impede effective government. Matters were more complicated in France: recovery from defeat by Prussia had to be the first order of the day, and meanwhile the exact nature of the regime remained uncertain.

After an impressive beginning, in Britain Gladstone's first government ran out of steam. In 1871 Nonconformist desire to reduce working-class alcohol consumption led to passage of a Licensing Act that was generally unpopular and provoked division in Liberal ranks. Thereafter growing trade unionism produced even deeper fissures. After its foundation in 1868 the Trades Union Congress (TUC) had grown dramatically, reaching a membership of 1 192 000 in 1874. The TUC was dominated by skilled workers and eschewed ties with revolutionary socialism; yet Liberal attitudes toward labor were mixed. Acts passed in 1871 gave trades unions legal recognition; however, they also made picketing illegal, with unions subject to criminal prosecution. Meanwhile the Tories had been busy, holding annual conferences wherein local activists mixed with leading MPs, and building a National Union of Conservative Associations that could claim 791 affiliated bodies by 1877. Having badly lost a general election in 1874, Gladstone concluded, "We have been borne down in a torrent of gin and beer,"[95] but he was understating the problems his party faced.

Despite the rise of a Home Rule Party of some 58 members determined to establish separate Irish government, Disraeli could at last form a majority government and the first two years of Tory government saw passage of a significant body of legislation. Unions gained the right to picket; while they were liable to civil damage suits for breach of contract, they were no longer subject to criminal penalties. The boroughs gained powers to clear slums and rehouse inhabitants; use of injurious drugs in food was forbidden, and schooling for children between the ages of five and ten became mandatory. Such enactments built bridges with advocates of "municipal socialism" such as Joseph Chamberlain. Mayor of Birmingham, Chamberlain was also a founder of the National Liberal Federation (NLF) in 1877. Although the NLF was designed to strengthen ties between the parliamentary leadership and local activists as a means to establish a more radical party program, it had little impact on Gladstone and Chamberlain grew frustrated.

Disraeli also set out to associative Conservatism with robust imperialism. According to Disraeli the choice lay between empire and "a comfortable England, modeled and moulded upon Continental principles and meeting in due course an inevitable fate."[96] Yet once again he was too far in advance of future trends. His desire for creation of a South African federation of British colonies and Boer (Dutch) republics led the British to defend the Transvaal from the kingdom of Zululand and in January 1879 over 800 British soldiers were killed in battle. By June the British had destroyed the Zulu army, but shortly thereafter news arrived of another slaughter of British soldiers at Kabul in Afghanistan. Public discontent then rose further due to Turkish massacre of Bulgarian Christian nationalists in the latest flare up of the Eastern Question. Gladstone exploited alarm by simultaneously attacking Disraeli's overseas expansionist tendencies and his refusal to take action against Ottoman repression. In his "Midlothian campaign" during the election of 1880, Gladstone went "on the stump," speaking to crowds in the tens of thousands while outlining policies. Much as Queen Victoria might disapprove of such direct appeal to the electorate, Gladstone reaped the harvest. The Liberals gained a large majority despite the return of roughly fifty Home Rulers now led by the firebrand Charles Stewart Parnell, a Protestant landowner of Anglo-Irish heritage.

In France Adolphe Thiers was an unlikely founding father of the Third Republic. Rotund, verbose, and disputatious, "Monsieur" Thiers was liberal in ideology and authoritarian in temperament. He was loathed in Paris for his crushing of the Commune, but he was venerated in the provinces, and he was respected among foreign statesmen and financial interests. Thiers had concluded that a republic would least divide the French and best accommodate democracy. His past peregrinations gave him contacts with all the main political camps, and at a time when defeat made unity necessary, Thiers was the man of the hour. For two crucial years he would combine the offices of president and prime minister.

Given their majority in the National Assembly, royalists seemed well placed to bring about a restoration. They were, however, divided into three bickering camps. Although Bonapartists had little representation in parliament, they retained a redoubtable popular base. Legitimists supported the Bourbon pretender, the Count de Chambord; they tended to reaction, but needed to work with Orleanists, who constituted a larger bloc in the Assembly. Orleanists were troubled by the ultramontane tendencies of the legitimists and were determined to establish parliamentary government. Nevertheless dynastic lines suggested a potential agreement: Chambord was childless and next in line to the throne was an Orleans. Fine in theory, compromise ran aground when in a manifesto published in July 1871 Chambord insisted that he would not ascend the throne unless the French replaced the tricolor flag with the Bourbon white standard. He thereby symbolically rejected all that had unfolded since 1789. For dismayed legitimists and appalled Orleanists there was nothing to do but wait and hope.

In August 1871 Thiers gave a first public sign of his new allegiance by pushing the Assembly into electing him president of the Republic. By then he had already floated the first of two massive bond issues, enabling him to rebuild the standing army so that it was equal in size to that of Germany by 1875. Better yet, he could also repay the war indemnity and negotiate an end to German occupation by the end of 1873. By setting France on the road to recovery he had, however, undercut royalist reliance on him and hence Thiers was forced into resignation in May 1873. Election of Marshal MacMahon then secured a president willing to turn the reigns of power over to a monarch and MacMahon, in turn, appointed the Duke de Broglie as prime minister. A distinguished writer with experience in the diplomatic corps, Broglie was keen to promote unity among royalists and to establish elite rule under the guise of what was termed "moral order."

Coined the "Republic of the Dukes," noble-led government was always on the defensive. After a period of self-imposed exile, Gambetta returned to push for a strategic combination of his followers with moderate republicans and Orleanists. His plan to secure the Republic first, and republicanize it later, gained his bloc the unflattering title of "Opportunists" and entailed a break with radicals such as Clemenceau, but it did enhance republican prospects. There was only so long that royalists could forestall determining the nature of the regime, and thus in January 1875 Gambetta and Broglie secured passage of the "Wallon Amendment," which established the constitutional foundations of the Third Republic. To secure the latter, Gambetta had to agree that parliament would become bicameral. Elections for a senate would be weighted in favor of rural voters, and 75 of the 300 Senators would be elected for life by the lower house. The "Wallon Amendment" thereby established a check to radicalism in the Chamber of Deputies. Moreover, the president of the Republic would be chosen by parliament, not the nation. It was understandable that memories of Louis-Napoleon haunted liberals and republicans; all the same, such measures reduced the likelihood of effective government.

Elections held in 1876 demonstrated that the previous Chamber had been a product of exceptional circumstance. The three republican camps (radicals, Opportunists, and moderates) gained 360 seats; Bonapartists recovered to win 75, and other royalists fell to 76 in the lower house. MacMahon initially temporized, but by May 1877 he had appointed another government led by Broglie. Although Broglie could not hope to gain a parliamentary majority, he could deploy the resources of the state in pursuit of royalist victory in elections held in October. Purge of republican administrators, prosecution of republican newspapers, measures to prevent republican meetings, and aggressive support of "official" candidates by the Catholic Church duly followed. Republicans closed ranks and in the end they retained a majority of 317 seats to 199. Senate elections in January 1879 then gave them a majority in the upper house as well. MacMahon held no illusions that a seizure of power could work for anyone other than a Bonaparte, and hence he resigned. Republicans could at last set about creating the regime they desired and they began by replacing MacMahon with Jules Grévy, whose chief qualification was that he had voted against creating a presidency in 1848.

Domestic Politics in the 1870s: Spain and Italy

There were various ways by which elites could maintain control while seeming to accommodate demand for expansion of political rights. Creation of parliaments that possessed little power was one means; another was for the state to direct the outcome of elections. During the 1870s Spain and Italy both possessed parliaments with considerable powers; unfortunately they also became characterized by political systems that sought to negate genuine electoral contestation.

From his arrival early in 1871 until his abdication in 1873, Amadeo I lived in what he considered a Spanish madhouse. Although he respected the constitution and, unlike his predecessor, did not undermine attempts to build consensus within the political elite, there was no consensus to be found. Soon after Amadeo took the throne, "Carlos VII" rekindled civil war. Neither Carlism nor support for Isabel's son Alfonso was, however, much of a threat; the main culprit was rampant factionalism. Spain became a republic in February 1873 because the parties that had founded Amadeo's regime could not cooperate enough to provide effective government.

Republicans seemed to triumph in elections for a constituent *Cortes*; yet only about a quarter of the electorate had actually voted, indicating that support for republicanism was thin on the ground. Worse still, when the *Cortes* assembled in June 1873, republicans splintered into a faction that favored extreme federalism, a bloc that wanted to maintain a unitary state, and a third group that floated between the other two. Francisco Pi y Margall, a distinguished writer and philosopher, led the latter group. Inspired by the writings of Proudhon, Pi had provided the theoretical underpinnings for a fusion of republicanism with federalism that capitalized on discontent with the power of the central government, the political influence of the army, and the close ties of the Church and state. When he formed a government Pi planned to combat Carlism, stabilize finances, grant Cuba autonomy, separate Church and state, and enable the poor to purchase privatized Church lands. Despite such intentions, the need to crush Carlist revolt soon forced Pi to shift away from the anti-militarist republican Left and by the end of June he had proposed to suspend constitutional liberties in an attempt to reassert state control. He thereby ruptured relations with "intransigent" republicans and triggered rebellions in a large number of provincial cities and towns. With the army occupied fighting the Carlists, intransigents used militias to seize control and declare independence. Unfortunately their version of federalism consisted of little more than pursuit of office or plunder of the Church. They possessed little popular support and when small detachments of the army arrived, most of the *juntas* soon fell.

The principal result of federalist revolt was to drive republicans who wished to preserve Spanish unity toward cooperation with the parties of the Center and Right, and into the hands of the generals. In January 1874 conservative generals staged a coup and placed Serrano at the head of a new government. Alas Serrano soon proved inept and when the army suffered a defeat by Carlist forces in December, a second coup was led by General Martínez Campos, a veteran of the wars in Cuba. More importantly, in back of Martínez Campos stood Antonio Cánavos del Castillo, who had united most of the senior command in support of a restoration of the teenager Alfonso. Republicans had accomplished little, but they had frightened their rivals into a consensus.

A historian and former schoolmaster, Cánovas possessed clear ideas of how a Bourbon Restoration should function. The monarchy must shed pretensions to absolutism and share power with the socioeconomic elite. Within the elite, political groups must give up notions of excluding rivals permanently from power; such struggles provided undesirable elements with opportunity. Cánovas held that "universal suffrage means the dissolution of society"[97] and claimed that only the elite wished "to defend property, to re-establish the social order, to give the security and guarantee of law."[98]

As premier, in early 1875 Cánovas assembled a cabinet composed of Moderates, Unionists, and Progressives, and put forward a draft constitution. The latter gave the king the right to nominate government ministers, who would be responsible to a bicameral parliament. Senators would gain their posts by election, appointment, or through possession of high offices in the state or Catholic Church; the *Cortes* would be elective. Basic civil and political rights were acknowledged, but they were subject to unspecified regulations that rendered them meaningless. Although freedom of religion was proclaimed, Catholicism remained the religion of the state. Non-Catholics could not conduct public ceremonies, and the Catholic Church regained extensive, though not complete, control over education. The state then deployed intimidation to secure a *Cortes* which would ratify the constitution.

Thereafter matters unfolded according to plan. In the *Cortes* two main blocks emerged. Most Moderates, Unionists, and Progressives joined a Conservative Party led by Cánovas, while a minority of Progressives led by Sagasta went into loyal opposition. Universal suffrage was replaced with a franchise that restricted the electorate to about 6% of the population. Better yet, in January 1876 Cánovas and Sagasta established a convention whereby the dynastic parties agreed as to which electoral seats would actually be contested, and which would be considered the domain of one of the two dynastic parties. By such means each party could ensure that even if it "lost" the campaign, it would still retain a certain number of seats while awaiting its chance at power.

To ensure that the system functioned, the government invested extensive authority in the hands of local power brokers called *caciques*. The latter were members of the landowning elite, often the owners of properties that had been taken from the Church in the 1820s and 1830s. Frequently they were appointed as mayors and their essential task was to secure election of deputies who would be obedient to the government. Power was highly centralized in the Restoration, with all local and provincial appointments held by the Crown, and hence the *caciques* were well placed to dispense patronage to themselves and their clientele. They also had recourse to intimidation, violence, and fraud when the offer of local office or economic advantage proved insufficient. Although the system had to be propped up by repression, it went a long ways toward keeping conflict within the bounds of what the elite considered appropriate.

Political struggle of course continued; not all previous division could be papered over. Prior decades of onslaught by liberals had strengthened ultramontanism in the Church and the concessions made by Cánovas were never enough to appease zealots bent on removing even the slightest vestiges of toleration. Nor could individual ambition be entirely subordinated. Carlism was decisively beaten in early 1876 and so Cánovas dispatched Martínez Campos to Cuba with a force of some 15 000 men. With a combination of force and the offer of amnesties, Martínez Campos secured an armistice with Cuban guerrillas in February 1878. Order appeared to have been restored until he returned from Cuba as a champion of reform, triggering a cabinet crisis. Upon the suggestion of the King, Cánovas resigned in March 1879, but he blocked proposals for reform and thus brought about the fall of a Martínez Campos government in December. Martínez Campos and his followers therefore joined with Sagasta in a newly formed Liberal Fusionist Party. Despite the fact that Cánovas managed to secure abolition of slavery in 1880, by February 1881 Alfonso had decided to ask Sagasta to form a government. Still, while Cánovas was thus cut out, the system he had created remained.

It had taken chaos to produce elite consensus in Spain; no such threat was required in Italy. Known as the Extreme Left, a handful of democratic MPs formed a caucus that lobbied for franchise enlargement, but they opted for legal opposition and generally cooperated with the more centrist Left. Prior to the elections of 1876, Left leader Agostino Depretis, a former follower of Mazzini, announced a program that struck many as radical. The Left would establish free, compulsory, lay education, widen the franchise, reduce taxes, and stimulate the economy of the south. Yet government by the Left thereafter spoke more of continuity than change. A law passed in 1877 provided for free and compulsory education for children between the ages of six and nine; however, it also made provision for religious instruction when requested by parents and was only loosely implemented. Little came by way of state investment in the south and taxation remained high. It was not until 1881 that suffrage was extended, so that the electorate rose from 620 000 to over two million. The urban lower middle classes, concentrated in the north, thus entered into the political system while the impoverished south remained grossly under represented.

Depretis then adopted a policy which held that differences were so slight that right-wing groups could join left-wing groups in government. Known as *transformismo*, Depretis's system was designed to neutralize criticism by stripping politics of ideological content, and meanwhile ministers of the interior manipulated the electoral system with promises of patronage to rally support for favored candidates. By reducing parliament to a collection of small groups focused solely on entry into government, "transformism" fostered instability – there were not enough offices available to keep everyone happy. Cabinets came and went rapidly in the late 1870s, although Depretis usually remained at the center of them. Skepticism about the system inevitably grew, providing opportunity for the political extremes.

For the mass of the population there were various means of protest. By the late 1870s brigandage no longer posed a threat to the state, but rural riots aimed at tax collectors, and urban market riots triggered by high prices, continued. Officials were more perturbed by strikes; especially when aimed at excessive working hours, strikes could gain public sympathy. Perhaps more corrosive was that fear generated by perceived growth in crime rates led to sharp criticism of the regime's failure to deal with the "social question." Disillusioned by the failure of the *Risorgimento* to bring progress, the historian and future senator Pasquale Villari wrote: "Too great a part of our people is brutalized by misery, oppression, and abjection. It is only this abjection that keeps them tranquil. But its existence constitutes an enormous weakness for our country as a whole."[99]

Whether anarchism could be considered a popular movement seems doubtful. Based at Naples between 1865 and 1867, Bakunin had formed a local chapter that claimed a membership of 4000. While anarchism found a limited base among urban artisans, more conspicuous among its ranks were students and young intellectuals. By 1873 anarchists were claiming a membership of 26000; yet a march on Bologna by 150 anarchists was easily crushed in 1874. Attempts to stir rural revolt west of Naples in 1877 proved farcical; peasants could make little sense of the strange visitors who distributed guns but did not pay their bills. Thereafter anarchism descended into "propaganda by the deed." An attempt to assassinate the King and the bombing of a patriotic procession in November 1878 triggered repression and convinced some that scientific socialism provided better prospects than anarchism. Others, including the Extreme Left, instead rallied to the liberal regime.

Domestic Politics in the Eastern Autocracies in the 1870s

During the 1870s it seemed that German and Austrian liberals might be able to bring about the creation of parliamentary regimes. By the end of the decade it was apparent that no such transformation had occurred. In Hungary the situation differed; parliament was an effective instrument, but elections were largely controlled by a governing party. In Russia discontent with the limits of previous reform produced agitation; yet revolutionary movements fostered reaction rather than reform. Taken in sum, the 1870s thus brought little by way of democratic progress in central and east Europe.

In constitutional terms, the German Empire was an ambiguous hybrid. Foreign policy was exclusively the domain of the federal government, which, like the army, was responsible solely to the Kaiser. The *Reichstag* possessed considerable powers of approval concerning taxation and the federal budget, but it could exercise little control over state or military policy. Moreover, the broad sweep of domestic government was conducted by the individual states that composed the Empire. Prussia was easily the most powerful of the states and Prussian interests predominated at the federal level; nevertheless, the lesser states retained their own sovereigns, constitutions, and voting systems. That the *Kaiser* was also the King of Prussia enhanced his power, but it also meant that he was perceived as simply the first among equal sovereigns.

In pursuing German unity Bismarck enjoyed major advantages over his Italian counterparts when it came to nation building. He exaggerated in stating "I am the master of Germany in all but name,"[100] but he did wield enormous power as the leader of the Imperial and Prussian governments. Over time Bismarck gradually developed the *Reich* government, creating a series of offices headed by secretaries of state. There was, however, no cabinet; officials reported directly to the chancellor, who, in turn, reported to the Kaiser. Ultimately, Bismarck's power derived from his ability to influence the Kaiser, upon whose support he depended.

Germany was prosperous, industrialization was developing rapidly, the education system was the envy of other states, and the Empire enjoyed great-power status. Yet the process of integration was complex and the results of Bismarck's efforts were mixed. That work remained to be done could be seen in low voter turnout (51%) for the first *Reichstag* elections in 1871 and in the distinction Theodor Georgii, president of the gymnasts' association, drew between the "German Empire of our hopes and dreams" and "the real German Empire."[101] The principal obstacles to integration were residual loyalties to the smaller states, dislike of a constitution that privileged *Junker* interests, and continued longing for the *Grossdeutch* solution of 1848.

Whereas popular nationalism steadily spread, state-sponsored nationalism was problematic. In the south German states antagonism toward the French had trumped animosity toward the Prussians in 1870–1 and thereafter Bismarck sought to enhance patriotism through adoption of a new German flag, annual celebration of the victory at Sedan, and monuments commemorating the war and unification. All the same, resistance to Imperial construction of nationhood could be seen in abstention by disaffected groups (especially Catholics and Socialists) from Sedan Day celebrations, a counter-current of monuments that linked 1870–1 to the contributions of particular states, and disinterest in a cult of the Emperor that had trouble spreading beyond Prussia.

Ability to manage the system he had created was important to Bismarck's status at court, and to secure legislation he could exploit the gratitude of the National Liberals for his role in unifying Germany. As the largest party in the *Reichstag* (holding 155 of 399 total seats in 1871), the National Liberals helped pass legislation that included adoption of uniform coinage and currency, creation of an Imperial *Reichsbank*, standardization of the legal system, and removal of internal restrictions on trade and industry. However, attempts to centralize rail systems ran aground, ensuring that a major source of revenue remained in the hands of the states rather than the Imperial government. Moreover, the Liberals found that Bismarck offered little aid when they sought to reduce provincial press restrictions through creation of national laws. The chancellor was opposed to any concentration of power at the national level that might affect conservative dominance in Prussia.

Despite the fact that it was limited by concern for the interests of the Prussian elite, Bismarck's desire to nurture unity still led to major conflicts. German Catholics, concentrated in the south, had formed the Center Party in 1870, leading Bismarck to suspect that Catholicism provided the basis for ongoing opposition to the Empire. He found confirmation in the tendency of Danish, Polish, and Alsatian minorities to align with the Center Party, but what was crucial was that Bismarck believed that Catholics were more loyal to Rome than Germany. Led by the former minister Ludwig Windhorst, the Center Party supported confessional schools, opposed civil marriage, and favored decentralization, with more autonomy for individual states. Perhaps most importantly, by 1871 the Center Party had 58 members in the *Reichstag*.

Coined the *Kulturkampf* (Struggle of Civilizations), Bismarck's attempt to subordinate the Church consisted of measures passed in the Prussian *Landtag* and Imperial *Reichstag*. In Prussia between 1872 and 1875 laws removed schools from clerical (whether Catholic or Protestant) control and placed them under state supervision, subjected all church appointments to veto by the state, and introduced civil marriage. During the same period the *Reichstag* banned Jesuits (seen as being the chief auxiliaries of papal authority) from setting up establishments in Germany, gave states the right to expel individual Jesuits from the Empire, and transferred birth and death registration from the Church to civil officials. In 1875 conflict reached its peak. While a papal encyclical declared all the measures invalid, further laws enabled Prussia to suspend subsidies where clergymen resisted legislation, and to ban all monastic orders, except those involved in medical service. By 1876, 10 of 12 bishops were in exile or under arrest, roughly 1400 parishes lacked incumbents after clergymen had been expelled or imprisoned, and some 16 million *marks* of property had been seized. Nevertheless, the Center Party doubled its vote in 1874 and by 1881 held 100 seats in the *Reichstag*. Bismarck drew the obvious conclusion about the counter-productive nature of policies that provoked mass resistance and began to back away from anti-clerical policies.

Thereafter economic concerns encouraged Bismarck to change direction. Competition from American and Russian wheat exporters threatened Prussian landowners, and in 1873 industrial overproduction and excessive speculation led to a stock market crash. To secure the interests of the *Junkers* and industry, Bismarck decided to abandon free trade policies. Given that most National Liberals advocated free trade, he thus would have to find support elsewhere. While he could count on a new Conservative Party formed in 1876, it was not until the death of Pope Pius IX in February 1878 that Bismarck could seek an accommodation with the Center Party. Leo XIII was willing to compromise, although negotiations were slow.

In May 1878 an anarchist fired two shots at the Emperor, providing Bismarck with opportunity to appeal to patriotism while launching a crusade against the Social Democratic Party (SPD). Formed in 1875, the SPD was neither anarchist nor large. Although it had a Marxist wing, was affiliated to the International, and was dedicated to social revolution, in its founding Gotha program the SPD had rejected use of illegal means to achieve its ends. Nevertheless, Bismarck considered all international associations a threat to national unity. He therefore called on the *Reichstag* to pass laws making calls for class warfare in the press a punishable offence. Fearing that they might too fall victim to censorship, the National Liberals and Center Party rejected the legislation. When, shortly thereafter, a second assassination attempt wounded the Kaiser, Bismarck called for elections, knowing the public was shifting toward reaction. While the Center Party held up well, the National Liberals and their more radical allies the Progressives lost 38 seats, enabling the Conservatives to gain 37. Moreover the National Liberals managed to avoid greater decimation only by agreeing to anti-socialist legislation during the campaign. Bismarck thus gained a *Reichstag* more to his liking. A new law banned socialist meetings, societies, and publications, police were given powers to expel agitators, and states gained the right to declare state of siege where uprisings occurred. Still, there were limits as to how far the National Liberals would go: individuals could still run for election as socialists and speak freely in the *Reichstag*, although they would not have the support of a party apparatus.

The chancellor could then turn to a new general tariff law. Negotiations with the Center Party would not secure a complete end to *Kulturkampf* until 1887, and even then civil marriage remained compulsory and the Church had to submit all appointments for approval by state authorities. Otherwise, however, the earlier laws were repealed, enabling Bismarck to secure support from the Center Party over tariffs. By pushing protectionism as a patriotic measure, Bismarck secured passage of a new tariff bill in July 1879 and broke from his marriage of convenience with liberalism. Cracks apparent in the debates over free trade then splintered the National Liberal Party. While Liberals committed to free trade and parliamentary government fused with Progressives to form a Radical Party in 1884, the remaining Liberals orbited round Bismarck.

Austrian Liberals encountered a similar fate. In the aftermath of the Franco-Prussian War, manifestations of German nationalism led Francis Joseph to explore the possibility of basing Austrian government on the support of conservative Slavic landowning elites and German conservatives offended by Liberal anti-clericalism. When Bismarck made clear that he had no desire to add 12 million Austrian Catholics to Germany, Francis Joseph decided instead to appoint Prince Adolf Auersperg as minister president in late 1871. A Bohemian landowner and former army officer who enjoyed friendly relations with the Liberals, Auersperg in 1873 oversaw a reform that established direct parliamentary elections, rather than delegations from the provincial diets. Nevertheless the franchise continued to be based on property ownership, restricting the electorate to about 6% of the adult male population. Moreover deputies were elected by the *curia* system, so that they represented specific constituencies – large landowners, chambers of trade and commerce, towns, and rural communities.

Liberal influence depended on an increasingly shaky parliamentary majority. Secularizing measures were not necessarily popular, and several Liberals were tied to fraudulent financial schemes that produced major scandals in 1873. Even so, the Auersperg government could have carried on had Liberals not opposed occupation of Bosnia-Herzegovina in 1878. Liberals argued that parliament had a right to approve foreign policy measures that entailed increased expenditure, threatened to refuse tax credits, and demanded reduction in the armed forces. In back of their argument was fear that the introduction of more Slavs would undermine German leadership. Although Auersperg managed to secure acceptance of the Treaty of Berlin, the Emperor never forgave Liberals for intruding on foreign policy and he happily accepted Auersperg's resignation in early 1879. Elections thereafter saw the Liberals and their more radical allies the Progressives gain 140 seats, whereas roughly 160 seats fell to German, Czech, and Polish conservatives. Francis Joseph thus could turn to Count Eduard Taaffe, his close personal advisor since childhood, to run a new government.

In Hungary political life was dominated by the issue of the Monarchy's place in the Empire. Moderate liberals such as Andrássy and Deák sought to defend the 1867 Compromise and initially led the governing party. Kálmán Tisza, a Calvinist nobleman who had participated in the parliamentary government of 1848, headed a wing of liberals, known as the Resolution Party, who wanted establishment of a separate Hungarian army, budget, currency, and tariff system. Further to the left was the Independence Party, which called for severing all ties with Austria, though not necessarily with Francis Joseph. Occupying the political right was the Catholic People's Party, a group that featured opposition to liberalism rather than populism. When Deák retired from politics and Andrássy departed to become the Imperial minister of foreign affairs, the governing liberal party went into decline. Tisza thus gained the initiative and fusion of the government liberals with the Resolution Party as the Liberal Party in 1875 put him in the driver's seat. Elections held in the same year gave the Liberals 333 of the 408 seats in parliament. Thereafter the state administration would be entrusted with ensuring that elections yielded Liberal majorities through the familiar means of patronage, intimidation, and fraud.

Given the existence of the Independence Party, Tisza could pose as a moderate in negotiations with the Imperial government and he thereby secured rapid expansion of a state bureaucracy that provided thousands of jobs for the Magyar gentry. Nevertheless, he understood that an angered Emperor might align with the other nationalities against Magyar rule, and that Francis Joseph possessed an army more than willing to crush dissent. Tisza thus set aside demand for increased autonomy and concentrated on assimilation of non-Magyars. The limits of his liberalism could be heard in a speech to electors in 1878: "By liberalism I have never understood [that] we should abruptly and at any price choose to implement the most liberal course, whether or not it corresponds to our circumstances."[102] All the same, a moderate line with the Imperial government was bound to disappoint some of his followers. Thus Tisza was confronted by the formation of a splinter center-left "United Opposition" that, for a time, seemed to threaten his government.

Although Magyar assimilation policies in education laws and official language rights stirred resentment, the Slavic peoples were weakened by division. The Compromise had secured limited Croatian autonomy, but Croatian deputies in the Hungarian parliament were a small island in a Magyar sea whenever it came to voting on taxation, conscription, defence, commercial treaties, and communications. Appointed by the Emperor, the Croatian executive (the *ban*) had to be approved by the Hungarian parliament and in consequence he was usually a Magyar. At least the Croats did have autonomy over internal administration, local education, and judicial affairs; thus they were better placed to assert rights denied to Romanians.

In Russia revelations in the trial of Nechayev, though frightening, did not terminate desire for change. Instead, *nihilism* gave way to Populism, a movement based on belief that educated individuals should carry their knowledge to the people and enable them to bring about revolution. Populism was expounded by intellectuals in works such as Petr Lavrov's *Historical Letters* and once again it was students who responded. Populists formed study circles and beginning in 1874 perhaps 3000 of them sought to establish contact with workers and the peasantry. Communicating their beliefs to people who still viewed the Tsar as sacred proved difficult, however, and years of effort produced meager results. Meanwhile infiltration by police spies led to hundreds of arrests and deportations to Siberia.

Failure to stir the masses enhanced the idea of forming a vanguard of dedicated radicals who would overthrow the state first, and educate the people second. In 1876 a new revolutionary organization known as "Land and Liberty" established secret cells wherein command was highly centralized, and one section was dedicated to murder. Assassination of a leading police official then triggered the usual cycle of reprisal as the state put political crimes under the jurisdiction of the military. Thereafter divisions arose within Land and Liberty and in 1879 members who wished to widen the application of terror broke off to form the People's Will, a society that contained perhaps 500 members. More anarchist than populist, the People's Will became obsessed with assassination of the Tsar.

Meanwhile the regime hesitantly returned to the path of reform. The Third Section was abolished and its operations were transferred to the ministry of the interior, where Count Michael Loris Melikov, a distinguished cavalry officer and civil administrator of Armenian descent, tried to focus attention on the few who were truly dangerous among the roughly 31 000 individuals under surveillance. Loris-Melikov believed the state must institute "measures which would facilitate the trustworthy elements of society, and defending their lawful interests, revive their weakened trust in authority."[103] He convinced the Tsar to accept establishment of an advisory General Commission, some of whose members would be elected by the *zemstva* and city councils. Such developments were, however, cut short when terrorist bombs thrown on March 1, 1881 found their mark, mortally wounding the Tsar and signaling the end of reform.

Inter-State Relations in the 1880s: The "New Imperialism" and the Demise of the Bismarckian Alliance System

Historians frequently cite the 1880s as commencing an age of "new imperialism" in which Europeans seized larges swathes of Africa and Asia. If we ask what was new about the "new imperialism," we can answer that the difference was mostly one of degree. Between 1815 and 1870 expansion had been intermittent and conducted mostly by three states. The British had increased their possessions in India and annexed New Zealand, made Natal a colony, and added naval bases or trading stations at Singapore, Aden, and Hong Kong. Russian expansion had been more extensive: in central Asia Turkestan had been taken, and Bukhara and Khiva had been made protectorates. To the east, the Chinese had been forced to cede the left bank of the Amur River and the lands between the Ussuri River and the Pacific Ocean. The French had enlarged territorial bases in Algeria and Senegal, and made inroads into Cochin China and Cambodia. Otherwise, there was not much by way of expansion. There were signs in 1875 of rising interest, manifest in a geographical congress where it was decided to organize exploration of the African area between Zambezi and the Sudan. Nevertheless, it was in the 1880s that European influence widened at an astonishing pace; as Belgium, Italy, and Germany entered the field, the more established imperial states increased their efforts.

If we turn to why the "new imperialism" occurred when it did, the main conclusions to be drawn are that imperialism varied according to where one looks, and that a complex phenomenon was unlikely to stem from a single cause. Early explanations posited that imperialism was an extension of capitalism. Due to the industrial revolution, European markets became saturated and hence entrepreneurs sought new markets and raw materials overseas for their surplus capital. Such arguments have not held up well under empirical examination: most capitalists showed little interest in colonies and businessmen did not necessarily influence the officials who made decisions as to state involvement. Yet while they cannot on their own provide an adequate explanation, economic considerations cannot be simply dismissed. Pressure groups did lobby governments successfully at certain points in time, and to some extent they represented economic interests. Moreover, it was not a coincidence that expansion coincided with a shift to protectionism. Fear of being shut out of European markets could motivate states to pursue colonies.

In certain regards "new imperialism" looks like an extension of European national rivalries. For some of the French, overseas expansion was a means to

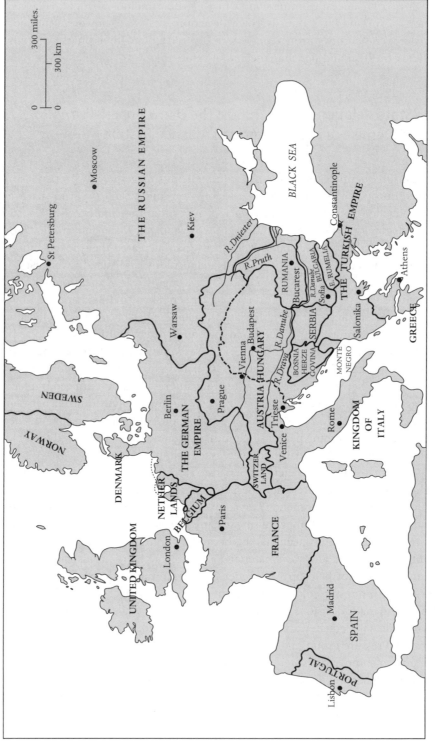

Map 7.1 Europe in 1880. J.M. Roberts, *Europe 1880–1945*, 2nd edition (London: Longman, 1989), p. 598.

restore prestige lost in 1871 and for some Italians empire offered an opportunity to establish Italy as a great power. For the British, "new imperialism" was primarily a reaction to perceived threat to previously established interests and informal steadily gave way to formal empire. Notions of Social Darwinism frequently led thinkers, and sometimes statesmen, to reduce global relations to a battle for survival in which races must expand or perish. In an article in the *Saturday Review* Lord Salisbury wrote: "Eat and be eaten is the great law of political as of animated nature. The nations of the earth are divided into the sheep and the wolves – the fat and defenceless against the hungry and the strong."[104] Others saw colonies and emigration as safety valves for domestic social pressures. In its more virulent form, imperialism envisaged overseas peoples simply as resources to be exploited, although imperialism also drew on less inhumane secular and religious beliefs that "advanced" peoples should carry "progress" to the less "civilized."

Individual pursuit of glory, love of adventure, and the allure of allegedly more liberal sexual conventions also drove imperialism. In many situations it was possible to argue that an unstable frontier threatened a colony and necessitated the extension of (European) provision of order. While communications were improving, it remained difficult for metropolitan governments to assert control over agents in the field, allowing for a great deal of local initiative. A metropolitan government could thus be presented with a *fait accompli* long after the action had occurred.

If some Europeans had the will to expand, they also had superior means with which to do so. Modern rifles and machine guns gave imperial armies an overwhelming advantage on land, just as the development of the gunboat (an armed steamboat) enabled shelling of targeted populations along coastlines or river banks. Equally important were improvements in medicine such as the use of quinine to combat malaria, and the development of cartography. Once established, rail and communications systems could enhance European power on land, while improvements in navies and merchant marines sped the supply of colonial and military outposts.

Given that the "new imperialism" coincided with the emergence of mass politics, it was inevitable that imperialists sought to make their beliefs popular. In doing so they often faced an uphill battle. Criticism of imperialism might be based on humanitarian, nationalist, or economic grounds, but a greater problem lay in public indifference. Britain, where Empire became increasingly important to identity, was not necessarily typical; Jules Ferry's remark that French interest in Empire did not extend beyond the belly dance seems more suggestive where the continent is concerned. In most continental states one could find imperialist groups organizing conferences and exhibits, or publishing journals and books. All the same, they were small in membership and few Europeans had a direct economic interest in the colonies. Public interest thus fluctuated, though it was growing.

Prior to 1900 the principal impact of imperial rivalry on the European states system was to drive a wedge between Britain and France. At the Congress of Berlin

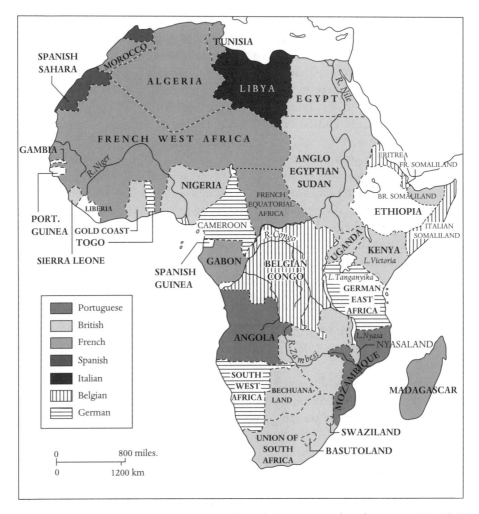

Map 7.2   The partition of Africa. H.L. Wesseling, *The European Colonial Empires 1815–1919* (Harlow: Longman, 2004), p. xv.

in 1878, France and Italy had been obliged to settle for hints that the other powers might accept their acquisition, respectively, of Tunis and Tripoli. When in 1881 the French occupied Tunis they began the "scramble for Africa." Britain's desire to secure passage to India via the Suez Canal and Red Sea led in 1882 to combat with Egyptian rebel forces angered by European control of the khedive's finances and eager to seize control of the Canal. Although they were not willing to join the British in occupation of Egypt, the French were incensed when Gladstone decided to convert Franco-British joint management of the khedival debt into a six-power control commission that included Italy. For Bismarck, matters unfolded nicely as Franco-British relations soured.

The "scramble" accelerated after the Berlin Congo Conference of 1884–85 established guidelines for effective occupation of a territory and internationalization of the Congo and Niger Rivers. King Leopold of Belgium was untypical in his preoccupation with the interior of equatorial Africa as France joined Britain, Germany, and Italy in establishing colonies along the coasts of West and East Africa. Expansion in Asia was less rapid: the British took the northeastern frontier of Burma, and the French annexed the whole of Annam up to Hanoi. Perhaps the most striking departure was Germany's participation between 1884 and 1885, although appearances were deceptive. For domestic purposes, Bismarck needed the backing of a Colonial League and he wanted to secure German overseas trading interests. Hence he supported state protection of trading companies in South West Africa, the Cameroons, Togoland, East Africa, and numerous Pacific islands. After the elections of 1887 Bismarck, however, no longer needed the League. Moreover Bismarck expected chartered companies to bear the costs of colonial commercial development and government. When they proved incapable of doing so, he grew "weary of colonies"[105] and turned against further expansion.

In the 1880s overseas imperialism generally enabled the Europeans to compete without much likelihood of a major conflagration; the Near East was another matter. In September 1885 revolutionaries staged a coup and proclaimed the union of Eastern Rumelia with Bulgaria. When Serbian forces, seeking compensation for their neighbor's expansion, attacked Bulgaria, they were soundly defeated. Thereafter peace was negotiated in March 1886; the Bulgarians made no territorial claims on Serbia and the powers rewarded them by recognizing Prince Alexander as personal ruler of Eastern Rumelia. Had matters rested at that point, solidarity among the eastern powers might have prevailed. However, the Russians then backed a coup that ousted Prince Alexander in August 1886. Worse still, Russia sought to control the election of a successor and Tsar Alexander III contemplated military occupation. In November the Habsburg foreign minister Count Gustav Kálnoky von Köröspatak in effect threatened war should Russian troops intervene. When British prime minister Lord Salisbury made similar statements, Tsar Alexander backed down. Deeply angered, he thereafter refused to consider any further alliance with Austria once the Three Emperors' League had lapsed.

Given the absence of German backing during the Bulgarian Crises, Kálnoky began to look for support elsewhere. The provisions of the Triple Alliance thus were extended with a protocol for Italian cooperation with Austria-Hungary in the preservation of the status quo in the Ottoman Balkans. Better yet, ties to the Italians drew Austria-Hungary closer to Britain. In February 1887 the British and Italians had reached an accord aimed at preserving the status quo in the Mediterranean, principally from Russian or French depredations, and Austria and Spain joined the First Mediterranean Agreement shortly thereafter. Britain's entry into a continental agreement revealed declining confidence in the Royal Navy's capacity to deal with a combination of two potential opponents (France and Russia) and offered the Central Powers some security against potential conflict with Russia.

Bismarck sought to compensate for the loss of the Three Emperors' League with complicated maneuvering. In June 1887 he negotiated a secret Reinsurance Treaty with Russia wherein the two powers promised to remain neutral should either be attacked by a third power. Although the Treaty did not necessarily conflict with Germany's other agreements, Bismarck did not reveal its existence to the Austrians. Moreover, Bismarck committed Germany to support Russia's position in Bulgaria and the Straits. Relations became even murkier in December 1888 when a Second Mediterranean Agreement was aimed more specifically at Russia. Triggered by Russian naval build up in the Black Sea, the Second Mediterranean Agreement envisaged possible naval and land action in the Ottoman Empire, and was recommended to the British by Bismarck. Given growing tensions, it is difficult to see how Bismarck could have honored all of Germany's commitments; in the event fraying relations with Russia resolved apparent contradictions. Economic depression forced Bismarck to yield to *Junker* demand for high tariffs against Russian grain imports, and the Russians retaliated with increased duties on German manufactures. As the two states drifted toward a tariff war, criticism of the German government's underwriting of loans to Russia reached a crescendo and the German state guarantee was withdrawn in November 1887. German businessmen unloaded Russian securities, which were snapped up by the French.

Bismarck's attempt to avoid rupture with Russia became even more difficult when William II took the throne in June 1888. During a state visit by Francis Joseph in July 1889 the new Kaiser informed the Emperor that: "whatever reason you have for mobilizing, whether Bulgaria or anything else, the day of your mobilization will be the day of mobilization for my army, whatever the chancellors may say."[106] Contemporaries would learn that William's assurances did not always hold water, but in this case they did accurately signify decline in Bismarck's control over policy. In March 1890 Bismarck resigned. His successor, Count Leo von Caprivi, judged that Bismarck's juggling act ran a serious risk of alienating Austria-Hungary and the Reinsurance Treaty with Russia was not renewed. The alliance systems that had dominated inter-state relations for close to two decades were in the process of a dramatic transformation.

West European Domestic Politics in the 1880s: Britain and France

Economic recession meant that all states had to deal with mass discontent, but the "social question" did not exist in a vacuum. At times nationalist agitation or religious controversy pushed the "social question" into the background; more frequently the issue of mass poverty was intricately bound with other preoccupations, making resolution all the more complex. Britain in the 1880s brought frustration to Gladstone. Despite a major reform of the franchise, the decade was characterized by imperial problems, cleavages within the Liberal Party, and failure to resolve the "Irish problem." Conversely, in France republicans passed a good deal of significant legislation. Many of the measures were, however, highly divisive and here too pursuit of overseas empire created trouble. Most importantly, nationalist agitation fused with economic discontent to create a "New Right" that prefigured fascism. Thus republican hopes to put their regime on a solid foundation were dashed by the first of a series of crises that gave the Third Republic an aura of permanent vulnerability.

Given the attacks he had made on Disraeli in his "Midlothian campaign," the public expected that upon his return to power Gladstone would extricate Britain from imperial conflict. The occupation of Egypt thus struck many as the opposite of what had been promised. More troubling still, the subsequent collapse of the Egyptian government triggered a revolt in the Sudan led by a religious leader called the Mahdi (the Messiah). After Gladstone accepted Sudanese independence in 1881, General Gordon, dispatched to oversee withdrawal of Egyptian garrisons, instead tried to overthrow the Mahdi. When Gordon was subsequently surrounded at Khartoum, the government was slow to organize a relief mission, and Gordon and his men were slaughtered in early 1885.

Gladstone also had trouble marshaling disciplined support in domestic politics. Radical Liberals such as Chamberlain wanted social reform, whereas Gladstone preferred to rely on Whigs who opposed social legislation. Similarly corrosive was the strategy of Irish MPs of obstructing legislation with marathon speeches. While obstruction gained attention and helped to maintain support for Parnell in Ireland, it produced a mixed response among Liberal MPs. Gladstone was well aware of deteriorating conditions in Ireland; yet the "Irish problem" was becoming increasingly intractable as the poverty of tenant farmers led to an accelerating number of evictions. Mass resistance took two main forms: violent action or ostracism of targeted landlords organized by a Land League. At a political level, grievance could be channeled in two directions. Whereas secret societies sought an independent republic and were not shy of violence, a second option lay in support of the Home Rule Party in the Commons. Because he was also leader of the Land League, Parnell seemed well positioned to establish a unified movement, but there were divisions and confusion in Ireland over whether the objective of Home Rule was self government or social amelioration.

Gladstone combined repression with encouragement in 1881 when the Coercion Act suspended *habeas corpus* while a Land Act enabled judges to set "fair" rents. Unfortunately the immediate impact of the Land Act was limited because tenants compromised by arrears in rent payment could not seek arbitration. Gladstone thus entered into a pact with Parnell to secure passage of a further law that would enable tenants in arrears to take advantage of the Land Act. Yet the issue was so sensitive that Gladstone did not inform even his Irish ministers of the negotiations and the Irish viceroy and chief secretary soon resigned amidst recriminations that Parnell had been rewarded for sedition.

Relations plummeted further when the new chief secretary and a second official were assassinated in May 1882 in Phoenix Park, Dublin.

Despite friction within the Liberal Party, cooperation between Gladstone and Salisbury, Tory leader in the Lords and likely successor to Disraeli after the latter's death in 1881, extended the vote to large numbers. Whereas the Liberals wanted to make franchise qualifications uniform in the counties and boroughs, the Tories wanted redistribution of seats. The net effect of combining the two objectives was that after 1885 about 66% of adult men in England and Wales possessed the vote and the figures for Scotland and Ireland were roughly 60% and 50% respectively.

Parnell, speculating that a Tory government might be more cooperative, soon thereafter caught the Liberals off guard by voting with the Opposition, leading to formation of a minority government under Salisbury. The following months consisted mostly of campaigning prior to the election of 1885. Although electoral results indicated that expanding the county franchise had benefited the Liberals, the real winners were Parnell's Nationalists, who saw their numbers jump to 86 MPs. Neither the Liberals nor the Tories could be certain of a majority, and hence Salisbury's government continued until the new parliament met in January 1886. Gladstone's son Herbert then dropped a bombshell – his father had converted to Irish Home Rule.

Gladstone's decision proved a watershed. Parnell terminated his dalliance with the Conservatives, enabling Gladstone to form a new government. Salisbury adopted an anti-Nationalist stance and thereby encouraged the defection of conservative Liberals, many of whom were Whigs. Radical Liberals also splintered; after the prime minister brought forward a bill for creation of an Irish legislature in April, Chamberlain went into revolt. When the proposal was defeated, Gladstone chose to resolve the issue through another general election. The result was brutally clear: while the Conservatives rose to 316 seats and the Irish Home Rulers held their own, Gladstone's Liberals plummeted to 191 MPs, and Liberal Unionists (who had defected) held 78 seats. Salisbury thereafter appointed a Liberal Unionist as the new chancellor of the exchequer and began a process that would see a significant number of former Liberals cross over to the Conservative Party. The Tories also enjoyed good fortune in Ireland as Parnell's reputation was tarnished when his wife divorced him for adultery. In the midst of fighting to retain his leadership, Parnell then died in October 1891, leaving behind two warring Nationalist parties.

The chief legislative contributions of the Salisbury government consisted of the introduction of free elementary education and the Local Government Act of 1888. The latter established elected county councils, while giving urban centers of over 50 000 in population the right to elect their own, separate, governments. The newly established councils could raise revenues through local rates, controlled their own police forces, and gained responsibility for state schools and provision of local welfare. In social terms the bill shifted power away from aristocrats and the gentry, and opened the doors to working-class participation. Although such legislation gave some substance to the claims of "Tory democrats" and attracted Chamberlain, continued economic recession and extensive labor militancy undermined the government. Elections in 1892 in which the Tories adopted the title "Unionists" saw sufficient Liberal recovery that in August Gladstone, with Irish Nationalist support, formed another government.

In France republicans set about regime consolidation in the early 1880s. They moved parliament back to Paris, adopted the *Marseillaise* as the national anthem, and made Bastille Day (July 14) a national holiday. Laws previously used to combat republicanism were terminated: restrictions on the press and public assembly were removed, trade unions were legalized, and life membership within the Senate was abolished. More contentious were measures designed to undermine the influence of the Catholic Church. Re-establishment of divorce could be interpreted as an act of liberalization, but it had strongly anti-clerical overtones. Laws that established state secondary schools for girls and made primary education free and compulsory were accompanied by clauses banning religious orders that had not been authorized by the state. In removing religious teaching from the syllabus of state schools, republicans claimed that elimination of "obscurantism" cleared the deck for education based on science and reason, thus providing opportunities for workers and peasants to better themselves. Nevertheless, the reforms failed to prevent the elite from patronizing Catholic secondary schools, and offered only limited opportunity for social mobility.

The Opportunist Jules Ferry emerged as the key figure in government, although he was troubled by the rivalry of Gambetta and cabinets seldom lasted a full year. Ferry was determined to avoid further conflict with Germany and he championed imperialism as the means by which France could recover lost prestige and power. His pursuit of overseas expansion drew criticism, however, from the Radicals led by Clemenceau, who joined the Right in arguing that resources should be directed instead toward regaining Alsace-Lorraine. When the combined effects of economic depression and a defeat of French forces in Indo-China toppled a Ferry government, the Radicals and the Right made major gains in the election of 1885. Thereafter Opportunist government depended on cooperation with the Radicals, who insisted on inclusion of General Georges Boulanger as the minister of war.

Crisis soon arose, exposing several of the regime's basic weaknesses. Boulanger cultivated the image of a strongman who would stand up to Bismarck and due to aggressive rhetoric at the time of a border incident his popularity soared. Fears both of war with Germany and of the General's intentions then led Opportunist and Radical leaders to remove him from office in late 1887. Shortly thereafter the "Wilson scandal" (based on revelations that the President's son-in-law was trafficking in military honors) encouraged Boulanger to pursue a more aggressive course. After he had been dismissed from the army, his followers put him forward as a candidate in multiple by-elections and in 1888 Boulanger won seven times. He could not, of course, hold seven seats, but his victories demonstrated the extent of his support throughout the country.

Boulanger's militarism, nationalism, and populism fit within certain Jacobin traditions and almost all the early organizers of his campaigns were revolutionaries or Radicals calling for social reform. The journalist Henri Rochefort, a Communard returned from exile in 1880, lent his vitriolic pen to the cause, and Blanquists and several Marxists also cooperated. All the same, much of the mass base and grassroots organization of the Boulangist movement came from the League of Patriots. Founded by Paul Déroulède in 1882, the League encouraged gymnastics and military training in schools and it soon numbered some 30,000 members. Members were eager for revenge against Germany and many would later become part of the xenophobic New Right. A third element became important as the movement developed – to gain funds Boulanger traveled to Switzerland, where he secretly gained the backing of royalist leaders.

Boulanger was shrewd enough not to put forward a clear program, which would have broken the fragile unity of his following. Instead he focused on a vaguely defined revision of the constitution that would have strengthened the executive allegedly as a means to eliminate parliamentary corruption. After another electoral victory in the republican heartland of Paris in January 1890, some of his supporters began to push for a coup; Boulanger preferred instead to wait for general elections in September. The plan was that candidate lists, with Boulanger at the head, would be put forward in every department. Thus Boulanger would be elected everywhere – in effect a national plebiscite. To combat this possibility, the government changed the electoral system to single-member constituencies and banned candidates from standing in more than one. Although some members of the League then prepared a coup attempt, at the planned time Boulanger either lost his nerve or decided it was better to stick to legal means. One way or another, inaction proved fatal as the government learned of the plot and brought legal proceedings against members of the League. When the minister of the interior hinted that Boulanger was next in line for arrest, the General took flight. Subsequent court procedures brought to light Boulanger's secret dealings with royalists and this revelation ruined his career. He never did return; instead Boulanger shot himself on the grave of his mistress in 1891. By then the crisis had subsided; yet Boulangism's combination of anti-parliamentarianism and nationalism had yielded 43 seats in 1890 and marked a vital stage in the emergence a new, proto-fascist, political Right.

Spain and Italy in the 1880s

Although the Spanish and Italian states stabilized in the 1880s, neither made much progress in addressing poverty. Stability resulted more from the weakness of opposition than the effectiveness of government, and failure to address demands provided opportunity for groups seeking to mobilize mass discontent.

Spanish government was dominated by the Conservatives led by Cánovas and the Liberals led by Sagasta. A former engineer, Sagasta was a convincing orator, but he was known more for political opportunism than dedication to the principles he espoused. Between 1881 and 1883 Sagasta gave the appearance of advocating social reform: consumption taxes were lessened, press censorship was lightened, and the length of military service was reduced. Yet change in the tax structure actually benefited landowners while placing increased burden on shopkeepers, popular movements were crushed, and the control of the *caciques* was tightened. Also troubling was the return of factionalism apparent in the formation of a new party named the Dynastic Left and led by Serrano. Wishing to free himself of Sagasta, the King turned to the Dynastic Left, but efforts by Serrano to secure universal manhood suffrage failed in January 1884, leaving little option other than to recall Cánovas.

Subsequent elections saw the Conservatives score a massive victory, partly because many Moderates, clericals, and some Carlists had joined them. Cánovas wanted to block reform, but a wave of social unrest left him fearful that Spain might fall into revolution upon reception of news that the King was dying of tuberculosis. He therefore offered the premiership to Sagasta. After the death of Alfonso in 1885, the regent queen Mariá Cristina agreed to dissolve the *Cortes*, enabling the Liberals to gain a wide majority by the usual corrupt means in April 1886, and re-absorb most of the Dynastic Left. More superficial reform followed, including freedom of association in 1887, and universal male suffrage for elections in 1890. Yet democracy meant nothing when elections were still controlled by the *caciques* and freedom of association was negated by a ban on protest demonstrations or meetings.

If the Restoration was not yet in serious trouble, security had mostly to do with the weakness of the regime's enemies. The attempts of one of several warring republican factions to raise revolt failed abysmally. Toward the end of the decade anarchists divided between revolutionary syndicalists (who fused Marxist focus on the industrial proletariat with continued rejection of political parties) and terrorists, whose "propaganda by the deed" (individual acts of violence) brought repression down on all and sundry. Meanwhile what one historian has described as "Decaffeinated Marxism"[107] percolated slowly as a new Socialist Party managed to gain only 4000 votes in the parliamentary elections of 1891. On the other end of the political spectrum, Social Catholicism emerged in the form of a lay organization, Catholic Action, which encouraged formation of peasant cooperatives while denouncing liberalism. Nevertheless, divisions among Catholics were such that efforts to found a specifically Catholic political party foundered.

In Italy prime minister Depretis concentrated on retention of power through *transformismo*. While Francesco Crispi, the organizer of Garibaldi's famous "Redshirts," drew attention by his attacks on the government, he soon entered Depretis's system when offered the ministry of the interior in 1887. Crispi became the obvious successor when Depretis died later in the year. The Church feared him and many charitable institutions were in fact subsequently secularized; nevertheless Crispi's legislative record was less radical than expected. A new penal code that abolished the death penalty, reduced punishment of crimes against property, and tacitly recognized the legality of strikes did constitute a liberal advance. Yet authoritarian features remained: groups wishing to organize meetings still had to notify the police in advance, and the police retained the power to send individuals into internal exile without trial.

Although he had once advocated decentralization of power, recognition of the obstacles to integration had led Crispi to conclude that a strong, unified state was necessary to inspire nationalist sentiment. Liberal institutions were insufficient to bestir patriotism and hence Crispi propagated the cult of *Risorgimento* heroes, of whom he was one. More ominously, he viewed war as an instrument for creating nationalism. He had called for a "baptism of blood"[108] at the time of the Austro-Prussian War, and it was in his conduct of foreign relations that Crispi was truly radical. He deeply resented French "theft" of Tunisia and sought compensation with plans for expansion in Ethiopia. Italy had occupied Massawa in 1885, but the port on the Red Sea was of little value unless the Ethiopians conducted their trade through it. In May 1889 Crispi signed a treaty of friendship with the Sudanese King Menelik of Shoa, one of several contestants for power in war-torn Ethiopia. When Menelik, aided by Italian rifles and loans, became Emperor, Crispi concluded that Italy had gained protectorate status over Ethiopia. Thereafter the Italians expanded their Red Sea possessions to form "Eritrea," and began conquest of Somalia, leaving Menelik mistrustful. Crispi's imperial fervour then got the better of him in January 1891 when he charged conservatives with having backed "a policy of servility to the foreigner."[109] One of Crispi's cabinet ministers resigned at this outrage, prior to the government being brought down by a vote of nonconfidence.

Illusions of imperial grandeur exacerbated flawed economic policies. Increased military expenditure meant that government deficits soared and thus there was little room for investment in agriculture, where productivity remained low. Nor did governments possess a comprehensive industrial strategy. Although tariffs favored northern industrial interests, protectionism triggered dramatic commercial decline in the early 1890s. Worse still, banks were poorly regulated and vastly overspent their reserves on dubious projects, leading to collapse and consequent widespread unemployment beginning in 1889. A government-commissioned private enquiry revealed extensive political corruption; yet its report was neither published nor presented to parliament as the government sought to hush up what nevertheless emerged as a major scandal. Many Italians would have concurred with the sociologist Vilfredo Pareto when he wrote: "a band of brigands is governing our unhappy country."[110]

Against this backdrop, socialism gained ground when Filippo Turati and Anna Kuliscioff founded the Milanese Socialist League. Turati and Kuliscioff stressed a gradualist approach based on propaganda, party organization, and reform, and in October 1892 their arguments proved central to the foundation of an Italian

Socialist Party. A wide array of production and consumer coops, credit banks, and mutual-aid societies already existed; yet most of these associations cut across class lines and had elite or Church patrons. Thus one of the first tasks of the Socialist Party would be to eliminate "bourgeois" influence by creating "autonomous" mutual-aid societies and encouraging formation of single-trade unions.

The Eastern Empires during the 1880s

The eastern empires were reluctant to grant political rights, but Bismarck blazed a path by instituting a social welfare program and to a limited extent Austria followed. Designed to buttress authoritarian rule, social reform failed in its primary objective; yet it was progressive in comparison to the repression employed by Hungarian and Russian governments to impose unity on dissident nationalities.

Despite the arrest of some 600 members during the electoral campaign of 1881, repression had failed to break the SPD. In consequence Bismarck turned to provision of social welfare in a bid to prevent socialism from spreading among industrial workers. Universal social insurance for industrial workers was introduced by acts that covered medical treatment (in 1883), accident insurance and burial grants (in 1884 and 1886), and old-age pensions (in 1889). Funding for the individual components varied: workers and employers jointly carried the costs of medical treatment, employers bore the full cost of accident insurance, and employers, workers, and the state all contributed to pension funds. To secure the legislation the chancellor relied on support from the Conservatives, the Center Party, and some 50 National Liberals who accepted Bismarck's argument that social welfare would secure a docile workforce. Nevertheless socialism continued to grow, partly because Bismarck dismissed calls for workplace regulations.

Bismarck found parliament increasingly difficult to manage. In 1881 proposals for increased indirect taxation were defeated, forcing the state to go deeper into debt to finance military expenditure and social welfare. Conflict reached its apex in 1887 over the seven-year army grant because parliament wanted to review expenditures every three years. Bismarck's reply was that the army must not be dependent on the *Reichstag*. In a subsequent electoral campaign the chancellor exploited international tensions to brand his critics as unpatriotic and thereby gained a majority for an electoral alliance of the Conservatives and Liberals, but the result masked a substantial rise in the number of opposition votes. Thereafter Bismarck contemplated replacing parliament with some sort of corporatist body and matters did not improve when William II came to the throne in June 1888. The young Kaiser wished to pose as progressive at a time when Bismarck was returning to reaction. Although William and Bismarck agreed that the anti-Socialist law should be made permanent, they divided over whether municipal authorities should retain the right to expel agitators. When Bismarck's proposals were rejected by the *Reichstag* in 1890, the chancellor dissolved parliament, only to find the Kaiser promising more welfare legislation during the electoral campaign. The obvious breech cost the Right at the polls, and when a further quarrel erupted over William's anti-Russian tendencies, Bismarck resigned.

As minister president of Austria, Count Taaffe relied on a coalition of Poles, moderate and conservative Czechs, and German Catholic conservatives to secure social legislation. Reforms passed between 1883 and 1889 included limitations on the daily hours of factory and mining labor, abolition of child labor, compulsory Sunday rest, workers' health and accident insurance, and establishment of inspectorates to enforce regulations. Although coverage was partial rather than universal and enforcement was frequently lax, the laws put Austria well in advance of much of Europe.

Legislation sprang from a variety of concerns. As agricultural depression forced smallholders to sell off their lands and move to urban centers, Austria gained an industrial proletariat that comprised roughly one-fifth of the workforce. Initially anarchism dominated activism, but thereafter it was dislodged by three rival parties that threatened to build mass opposition movements. Georg von Schönerer's German National Association initially focused on social reform, although it subsequently degenerated into anti-Semitism. More formidable was a Christian Socialist Movement that argued for reorganization of production along corporatist lines. Under the direction of the lawyer Karl Lueger, the Christian Socials also adopted anti-Semitism to woo craftsmen and peasants. Finally, in 1889 Viktor Adler united several small labor groups in founding a Marxist Social Democratic Party that pledged to seek its objectives through democratic means.

Legislation also resulted from illusory hope that attention to social issues might counteract nationalist division. Shortly after assuming office Taaffe turned to the Czechs, who were divided between groups known as the Old and Young Czechs. Although the latter were just as nationalist as the former, they had concluded that boycotting the *Reichsrat* failed to advance Czech interests. Cooperation with the government then yielded laws that increased use of the Czech language in state administration in Bohemia and Moravia, increased Czech representation in the Bohemian *Landtag*, and created a Czech section at the University of Prague. In return the Young Czechs backed a law that extended the franchise for parliamentary elections in the urban and rural communes. Enfranchisement of large numbers of peasants and lower-middle-class elements was intended to weaken the influence of big business and high finance (bastions of liberalism), and in 1885 elections duly gave the various factions of the Right a sizeable majority.

Given the advantages they had traditionally held, it was perhaps to be expected that German Austrians would be reluctant to transfer their allegiance away from the Habsburg Imperial state. Nevertheless, the 1880 language ordinances fostered growth in the number of Slavs in the imperial and provincial bureaucracies, and the suffrage reform of 1882 greatly increased the number of non-German deputies elected to the *Reichsrat*. The Liberal Party had been largely untouched by nationalism until Schönerer broke with it to form the German National Association and call for union with Germany in 1882. Schönerer carried few deputies with him, but his calls in parliament for "legal restrictions on the Jewish exploiters of the people"[111] reverberated in athletic clubs and the German School Association. After the loss of 15 seats in 1885 the Liberal Party splintered, with a moderate group identifying itself as "German Austrian," and a radical wing basing its program solely on German interests and rejection of parliamentary government.

Inability to find some sort of compromise between German and Czech leaders, and the Emperor's alarm over growing German discontent, ultimately brought Taaffe's fall. When a state decision favored German interests in a district of Bohemia, angry demonstrations forced declaration of a state of siege in Prague, and Czech parliamentary deputies began to exercise the obstructive tactics for which Irish Nationalists had become famous. To break the parliamentary impasse, Taaffe put forward an extension of the franchise that would have quadrupled the electorate from its current size of roughly 1 725 000. Given that the lower classes were thought to be less affected by nationalism than the middle classes, the bill was not illogical; however, Taaffe overlooked the crucial point that his conservative coalition would object to such extensive democratization. When the bill was rejected in November 1893, Taaffe's period of office abruptly ended.

Under Tisza's government, social reform was extremely limited in Hungary. While amendments made in 1884 to labor law declared worker associations and strikes legal, they also made incitement to strike a punishable offence and mandated that all associations must be nonpolitical in character. Despite the latter prohibition, 1890 saw formation of a Social Democratic Party. The party cultivated ties with unions, but it was small and stood little chance of representing workers in parliament until the franchise was expanded. In the absence of reform, discontent frequently took the form of Anti-Semitism. Relatively large numbers of Jews had immigrated to Hungary since the eighteenth century and the role they played in finance, commerce, the professions, and the arts drew hostile attention. In the early 1880s dozens of anti-Semitic organizations formed and by 1884 they had elected 17 deputies to parliament. Partly because his opponents tried to use anti-Semitism to attack the Liberal Party, and partly because the Magyar nobility was generally tolerant of the Jewish population, Tisza denounced anti-Semitism as "shameful, barbaric and injurious to the national honor"[112] and cracked down on the organizations, leading to their disintegration.

The focus of Tisza's government remained assimilation and concomitant harassment of nationalist groups that dared to object. Opportunities to force assimilation were limited at the primary level by the right of the recognized Churches to provide schooling, but the state could ensure that education in secondary and higher levels was conducted in Magyar. While the Serbs remained largely quiescent, a Romanian National Party formed in 1881 demanded autonomy. Francis Joseph refused, however, to hear a presentation of grievances in 1892, and thereafter the Hungarian government arrested 15 members of the Party prior to shutting it down. Meanwhile the Ban of Croatia, Count Károly Khuen-Héderváry, played a classic game of divide and rule to undermine Croatian nationalists. Kheun deployed patronage and electoral corruption to build a party that gained a narrow majority in the *Sabor*, and then developed an alliance with the Serbs by allowing them into the administration.

The principal opposition to Tisza thus came from within Magyar nationalist circles. The left-center Moderate Opposition led by Count Albert Apponyi and the Independents wanted to push harder than Tisza in securing constitutional revision and in 1889 and 1890 debates over the Imperial Defence Bill turned rancorous. Worse still, many Liberals followed Apponyi in demanding that Magyar replace German as the language of command in Hungarian regiments. Tisza gained passage of the bill; yet he was sufficiently embarrassed that he soon resigned.

Nationalist discontent, often triggered by policies of assimilation, was also on the rise in Imperial Russia. Upon coming to the throne in 1881, Alexander III made clear that he would not compromise. Known for his physical prowess, Alexander tried to convey an image of autocratic strength; unfortunately the firm direction he provided was based on stubbornness and an unwillingness to continue his predecessor's attempt to broaden support for the regime. Concerning the proposed General Commission, Alexander followed the advice of his former tutor Constantine Pobedonostsev: "We suffer quite enough from talking-shops, which, under the influence of worthless journals, simply stoke up popular passions."[113] Calls for a unified cabinet were also rebuffed, moderates departed the government, and the Tsar turned to conservatives.

As Over Procurator of the Holy Synod, Pobedonostsev advocated a hard line policy based on autocracy, Orthodoxy, and Russification to combat the pernicious effects of western ideas of democracy, liberalism, and individual rights. Emphasis on state security then became infected by conspiracy mania as formation of the Okhrana, a political police that specialized in spying and entrapment, led officials to overestimate the strength of revolutionary groups. In fact the terrorist "People's Will" soon fell apart. While some former Populists went on to help form the Socialist Revolutionary Party, Georgii Plekhanov put down the foundations for a Russian Social Democratic Party. Unlike the Social Revolutionaries, who continued focus on the peasantry, the Marxist Social Democrats sought to establish links with factory workers.

Several of the reforms of Alexander II were rolled back. Press regulations were tightened, a Statute of 1884 virtually abolished university autonomy and banned student organization, the role of the Orthodox Church in primary education was expanded, and the office of land captain was created in 1889. Appointed by the minister of the interior, land captains were drawn from the gentry. Their task was to administer the peasantry and they also took on the judicial role formerly exercised by justices of the peace. Desire to strengthen the authority of the elite could also be seen in changes in the *zemstva* system that made the gentry a separate voting block and greatly increased their representation.

If Imperial Russia was not quite the "prison of peoples"[114] later described by Lenin, it was highly diverse and intensification of Russification was apt to stimulate resistance. In 1897 a census revealed that ethnic Great Russians constituted only 45% of the roughly 122 million inhabitants of the Empire.

In the west, Poland remained especially troublesome for Russian imperialism. Use of Polish was prohibited in secondary schools, and kept to a minimum in primary schools. Poles were blocked from entry into the state bureaucracy, and replaced by Russians when the Warsaw-Vienna Railway was nationalized. For their part, Polish nationalists frequently adopted socialism, but divisions among revolutionary groups made them easy prey for the police. As elsewhere, nationalism became increasingly xenophobic as anti-Semitism became a means for rallying mass, including peasant, support. In the Ukraine nationalism was less pronounced. Although immigration by Russian industrial workers and Russian domination of the administration angered some intellectuals, they were largely isolated due to an extensive ban on publication in Ukrainian. In the Baltic provinces, Russification was aimed particularly at the German elite as the Imperial state helped fund an Orthodox drive to uproot Lutheranism, replaced German with Russian in the schools, and introduced Russian judicial courts. Lower-class Estonians and Latvians were largely unaffected; nevertheless many of them were moving into the towns and some would thereafter enter socialist and nationalist movements.

In central Asia resistance sprang from several sources. A conversion campaign conducted by the Orthodox Church angered Muslims in Tatar regions, as did Russian settlement on nomadic lands converted to cotton farming. Relations between the Imperial state and Armenians were especially complex. Armenians were divided by the Russian and Ottoman Empires, and many hoped that Russia would unite all Armenians through conquest. They thus were disappointed by the results of the Berlin Congress and subsequent Imperial attempts to improve relations with the Turks. When Armenians continued their anti-Turkish activities, Russian officials began to encourage neighboring Azerbaizhanis to harass them. Equally troublesome was the development of a Georgian nationalist movement triggered by the claims of the Russian Orthodox Church to supervise the Georgian Orthodox, Russian domination of the administration, dislocation resultant from emancipation of the serfs, and Armenian domination of finance and commerce. Georgia would prove especially fertile ground for revolutionary socialism.

Misguided though it was, Russification was intended to render non-Russians loyal, whereas the Jews of the Empire were treated as aliens. Anti-Semitic literature abounded and the state contributed by funding publication of a book alleging the existence of a Jewish international conspiracy to take over the Empire. The state did little to repress extensive pogroms (mass attacks on Jewish persons and property) that followed the assassination of Alexander II, and local officials often connived in the violence. While Alexander III disapproved of the pogroms, subsequent legislation was the opposite of sympathetic: new Jewish settlers were banned from residing in rural areas of the Pale, Jews could not own property or run businesses outside the towns of the Pale, and Jews could not conduct trade on Christian holidays. In consequence Jewish rural businesses had to be sold for a pittance, and many Jews were forcibly expelled from their homes.

Few regimes are entirely bereft of saving graces. Tsar Alexander wanted above all to maintain Russia's position as a great power and he recognized that his objective required economic modernization and pursuit of peace. As minister of finance from 1881 to 1887 Nicholas Bunge established a Peasant Land Bank to complement a similar institution set up for the gentry, abolished the head tax, and introduced an inheritance tax. Bunge also introduced labor legislation that limited daily working hours for juveniles, banned night work for women and children, and sought to regularize payment of factory workers by restricting employers from using fines to reduce wages. To enforce the new laws a factory inspectorate was established. Bunge's efforts soon, however, gained him the label of "socialist" among employers and he was forced to resign. Subsequent ministers would focus solely on industrial expansion.

Discontent rose sharply due to the famine of 1891–2. Partly a product of state requisitioning of grain for export so as to prop up the value of the *ruble* on world markets, the great famine was compounded by cholera and typhus epidemics and ultimately took at least 330 000 lives. After an initial period of neglect, the state finally responded with relief funds used to supply seed grain, fodder, and food, and sought to coordinate private charity efforts. Intervention and a good harvest in 1893 managed to stave off a complete collapse; yet the famine cruelly exposed the limits of the state's administrative capacity at a time of massive suffering. The absence of state institutions at the local level made efficient distribution of aid difficult, and meanwhile often poorly informed land captains clashed with *zemstva* members over priorities. Physicians hired by the *zemstva* blamed their employers for unwillingness to spend money on sanitary education and regulation to combat the spread of disease. Peasants, suspicious that the state had planned the epidemic, attacked medical personnel and were further convinced of conspiracy by the army's frequently brutal suppression of riots. All in all, the great famine severely damaged the regime's prestige and stimulated demands for radical change.

Given what followed, it is tempting to see the fall of Bismarck as a watershed, but such a perspective understates how little had been resolved by 1890. Despite escalating arms races, two factors had facilitated peace among the powers: Germany had become an advocate of the status quo in Europe, and overseas expansion had enabled the powers to compete with relatively little chance of war breaking out among them. However, the safety valve effect of the "new imperialism" diminished each time a European state staked yet another overseas claim, and no solution had been found to conflicting Russian and Austro-Hungarian interests in the Balkans. Based on the assumption that the French would pursue a war of revenge, Bismarck's strategy of keeping France in diplomatic isolation had heightened insecurity in the Third Republic, and engrained a belief that subsequently would contribute to equal insecurity in Germany. Although it had gained two decades of peace, Bismarck's alliance system was based on fear rather than trust and it had fallen apart by the time of his fall, initiating a new phase of rising tension.

In domestic politics a broad pattern had begun to emerge. All states were confronted by a variety of challenges: calls for change in political systems, demands for social reform, rising nationalism, battles between the advocates of secularism and religious groups, and the early stirrings of the women's movement. What was crucial was that the challenges were interrelated and thus difficult to address separately.

Governing elites responded in differing ways. For a period during the 1870s it appeared that liberals might be able to further representative government in Germany and Austria by increasing the powers of parliament; by the 1880s it was clear that they had failed. In his battle against parliamentary government Bismarck relied on manipulation of nationalism and provision of social welfare. Though to a lesser extent, Taaffe also sought to use provision of social welfare as a means to buttress Habsburg rule. In terms of state formation, the development of state social welfare was a remarkable achievement; yet it did not serve the political objective of undercutting the growth of opposition groups. Moreover, in Austria nationalism greatly complicated politics: on the one hand rivalry between Czechs and Germans threatened to tear the state apart; on the other hand it made parliamentary government virtually impossible, strengthening the position of the Monarchy as the sole source of unity.

Volatility was, if anything, even more pronounced in Hungary and Russia. Within the confines of the Compromise of 1867, the Hungarian parliament possessed significant power, but the principle of representative government was weakened by the narrowness of the franchise and vitiated by state control of elections. In its pursuit of unity the Magyar elite stirred antagonism by forcing assimilation upon other nationalities, and equally troubling was a recrudescence of Magyar nationalism bent on renegotiating the terms of the Compromise. State policies of assimilation were also a source of growing instability in the Russian Empire. Worse still, rejection of reform and return to repression was a poor antidote to the revolutionary hydra, especially when misguided economic policies contributed directly to a stunningly widespread famine.

As in Hungary, elite political ascendancy in Spain and Italy was partly achieved by manipulation of the electoral process. Given Spain's tumultuous past, it is not difficult to understand the desire of Cánovas to design a system that would provide order. Unfortunately, the Canovine system was similar to the *juste milieu* of France's July Monarchy in that *stasis* was mistaken for stability; no regime can endure unless it is capable of adaptation. That a similar system evolved in Italy was especially disillusioning given the earlier aspirations of the more democratic elements of the *Risorgimento*. Creating "Italians" proved more difficult than had been expected and state policies frequently exacerbated divisions that were deep and bitter. Crispi thought that he could emulate Bismarck in fostering unity through territorial aggrandizement, but imperial aspirations would prove to be just as damaging for domestic stability in Italy as they were in Spain.

By contemporary standards France was on the forefront of democracy; parliament was powerful and virtually all adult males could vote. The essential problem in France lay in combining a powerful parliament with effective government. As one crisis succeeded another, republicans would repeatedly demonstrate that they could act forcefully in defending their regime; yet their record in addressing the "social question" was uninspired. Across the Channel, the British were gradually moving toward full male suffrage and the woman's movement was becoming an important proponent of reform. Due partly to the development of a relatively coherent party system, advancement of the representative principle had not been as detrimental to effective government as it had in France, where 60 governments rose and fell between 1870 and 1914. Nevertheless British governments were not making progress in resolving the "Irish question" and they were well behind the Germans in addressing the "social question."

That much of Europe was volatile rather than stable should not surprise us. As we will see in the next chapter, Europe was undergoing fundamental economic, social, and cultural changes that created new aspirations while triggering fear and uncertainty. Adapting political systems to these profound forces was bound to be difficult.

8

The Underpinnings of Politics

Economic, Social, and Cultural Developments from Mid-Century to 1914

From the 1850s onwards the transformative nature of commercial expansion and industrialization became increasingly apparent. On the whole, the effects were positive as growth improved the material conditions and life expectancy of a rapidly expanding population. Nevertheless, disparities in wealth distribution increased and trade cycles wherein periods of growth were followed by recessions added anxiety to discontent.

The impact of economic growth was complex. Industrialization increased the number of factory workers and placed pressure on crafts production. Meanwhile significant progress was made in organizing workers in labor movements. All the same, the majority of workers did not join unions and, even among those who did, most did not take part in strikes or align with the political groups that claimed specifically to represent the working classes. Moreover, countervailing trends ensured that society remained highly diverse. Most Europeans remained engaged in agriculture and while in some areas land ownership became more concentrated, in other regions the reverse was the case. More strikingly, the most pronounced development of the period was the emergence of a service sector composed of a broad range of lower-middle-class elements. While some "white-collar" organizations were politically conservative, others leaned toward the Left.

States responded to such change with massive expansion. Motivation sprang from two main sources: international rivalry led governments to pursue modernization, and the collapse of the old society orders created a vacuum into which the state entered in pursuit of social order and/or national unity. Growth in power

Europe's Uncertain Path 1814–1914: State Formation and Civil Society, First Edition. R. S. Alexander.
© 2012 R. S. Alexander. Published 2012 by Blackwell Publishing Ltd.

inevitably fostered conflict as the importance of control over the state became more and more apparent in day-to-day life. Increasingly such struggle could be seen in the formation of voluntary associations. Although not all such associations were political in character, many were organized specifically to influence state policy.

Economic growth, expansion of the provision of education, improvements in communications and transportation, and the rapid growth of associations all made European culture more complex. Especially in the west, Romanticism went into decline after the revolutions of 1848 and for several decades high culture was characterized by optimism that science would bring progress to all. Thereafter, however, the cult of science and reason expressed in the philosophy of positivism was steadily eroded. By the turn of the century high culture was remarkably volatile as developments in the arts, philosophy, and science challenged old certainties and reversed earlier confidence. In contrast, mass culture revealed less pessimism about the future, and state policy adhered to lines that broadly conformed to the basic tenets of positivism. Education should be expanded, material improvement should be pursued through economic growth, and government should be rationalized through employment of scientifically trained professionals.

Rising Population

A hallmark of the period was sustained population growth. In 1850 there were roughly 275 million Europeans; by 1913 the figure was close to 481 million. Whereas birth and death rates remained high until the mid-1870s, thereafter they both declined and the key was that death rates fell more sharply. Improved nutrition (especially consumption of protein), provision of public sanitation, and food hygiene (especially the pasteurization of milk) all contributed to longer life expectancy (see Tables 8.1 and 8.2).

The extent to which medical advances contributed is less clear, although increased provision of vaccination against contagious diseases did help. Meanwhile increased use of contraception reduced birth rates. Beginning in the 1880s women had their last child at an earlier age, with the average age dropping from 40 to 35. Hence families became smaller, especially in the west. By 1900 the average Prussian family had five children, the average English family four, and the average French family fewer than three. Not surprisingly, there were significant regional, social, and cultural variations. Birth and death rates remained higher in the south and east, diseases such as cholera and tuberculosis were more deadly in urban areas, industrial working-class men and women tended to start families earlier than peasants and artisans, and Catholics and the Orthodox took to birth control less readily than Jews and Protestants.

A second feature of the age was increased mobility as improvements in transport made travel and relocation more feasible. The majority set off in search of

Table 8.1   Life expectancy at birth.

	1860		1875		1900–13	
	Men	*Women*	*Men*	*Women*	*Men*	*Women*
England	39.5	42.7			51.5	55.4
France	38.2	41.3			45.4	48.9
Germany			36.0	38.0	45.0	48.0
Austria			31.0	34.0	39.0	41.0
Italy			35.0	36.0	44.0	45.0

Source: Adapted from Theodore Hamerow, *The Birth of a New Europe: State and Society in the Nineteenth Century* (Chapel Hill, 1983), p. 81. Reproduced by kind permission of University of North Carolina Press.

Table 8.2   Estimated population growth, 1850–1900.[a,b]

	Population, in millions	
	1850	*1900*
Austria	17.5	26.2
Austrian Empire	30.7	45.5
France	35.7	38.9
Germany	35.2	56.4
Hungary	13.2	19.3
Ireland	6.6	4.5
Italy	24.4	33.0
Russian Empire	68.5	130.0
Spain	14.0	18.6
United Kingdom	27.2	41.0

[a] Statistics for the period should be taken as broad indicators only.
[b] For statistics of earlier growth, see Table 4.1 in Chapter 4.
Source: Taken from Raymond Pearson, *A Companion to European Nationalism, 1789–1920* (New York, 1994), p. 237.
© Pearson Education Ltd, 1994.

improved material prospects, although certain minorities, most notably the Jews and Poles of east Europe, also departed to escape persecution. The extent to which industrial development could absorb rural surplus labor frequently determined departure points and destinations. Until the 1890s most overseas migrants departed from the German states, Britain, and Scandinavia; thereafter the main centers of emigration were in the Mediterranean states and the east. Whereas between 1800 and 1845 roughly 1.5 million Europeans had departed the continent, nine million left in the following three decades. Between 1871 and 1891 some 27.6 million emigrated and in the decade prior to 1914 the annual average was 1.4 million.

While international emigration thus provided a demographic safety valve, migration within Europe and within individual countries was also dynamic. There were over three million foreigners resident in France in 1914 and it has been estimated that in 1907 roughly half of the German population lived relatively far from their birthplaces. Such movement did not necessarily prove permanent; most large cities developed "floating" populations of migrant workers who might or might not put down roots and join more settled working-class communities. Moreover nationalist and geostrategic considerations led certain states, especially Germany but also France, to place restrictions on the entry of foreign workers and reduce opportunities to gain permanent residence.

Economic Expansion

The economic history of the period can be divided into three main phases, but before we turn to them, it is worth underlining that global economic ties became increasingly important throughout the entire period. One measure of the latter trend can be seen in the proportion of gross national production that consisted of exports. European exports rose from 9.4% in 1860, to 12.6% in 1890, to 14% in 1913, a level not again achieved in the twentieth century.

Various improvements contributed to commercial expansion. Replacement of the paddle wheel with the screw propeller made steamships quicker and reduced freight costs. European ownership of steamships rose from 186 000 tons in 1850 to 1.5 million tons in 1870 and thereafter the days of the sailing ship soon drew to a close. Declaration of the Danube and Rhine Rivers as freeways for all ships also facilitated transport, as did opening of the Suez Canal in 1869. Railroads provided similar advantages on land (see Table 8.3).

Table 8.3   Length of rail line (in kilometers) for select countries.

	1860	1880	1910
Austria-Hungary	4 543	18 507	43 280
France	9 167	23 089	40 484
Germany	11 089	33 838	61 209
Britain	14 603	25 060	32 182
Italy	2 404	9 290	18 090
Russia	1 626	22 865	66 581
Spain	1 917	7 490	14 675

Source: Carlo Cipolla, ed., *The Fontana Economic History of Europe: The Emergence of Industrial Societies* (London, 1973), II, p. 789.

Meanwhile communications and exchange were revolutionized by the development of postal systems, encirclement of the globe by telegraph lines and submarine cables, and, to a limited extent, introduction of telephone networks, which were used mostly by business men. In regard to transport and communications, states often could see mutual advantage in cooperation. Hence the International Telegraph Union was founded in 1864 and ten years later all European counties were connected by the Universal Postal Union, which delivered some three billion letters and postcards in its first year of operations. International conventions were established for the laying of cables, agreements were reached for conveying commercial goods across frontiers, and international express trains began to run in the 1880s. Facilitated by the discovery of gold in North America and Australia at mid-century and in South Africa in 1886, conversion to the gold standard by virtually every European state by 1908 also fostered commerce by providing fixed rates of exchange and stabilizing prices.

Mid-Century Prosperity

From the early 1850s until the early 1870s the European economy grew rapidly as a second wave of the industrial revolution was triggered by the construction of rail networks. Railway construction led to rapid growth in the iron, steel, mechanical engineering, and coalmining industries, and encouraged the development of steam-powered production. Because they reduced the costs of bulk transport, railways also facilitated the substitution of coke for charcoal and the use of blast furnaces in iron smelting and steel manufacture. Pig iron output was already high in Britain at mid-century (see Table 8.4) and in the 1850s Germany, France, and Belgium began rapid growth due to replacement of charcoal with coke. Production moved from forested regions to coal mining centers and became more concentrated than in the textile industry. As in the first industrial wave, development tended to be regional rather than national, and the north and west developed much more

Table 8.4 Average annual output of pig iron (in thousand metric tons) in select countries.

	1860–64	1885–89	1910–13
Austria	216	540	1 655
France	1 065	1 626	4 664
Germany	613	3 541	14 836
Hungary	93	217	549
Russia	297	616	3 870
United Kingdom	4 219	7 784	9 792

Source: Carlo Cipolla, ed., *The Fontana Economic History of Europe: The Emergence of Industrial Societies* (London, 1973), II, p. 773.

quickly than the south and east. While others would develop on the continent later in the century, the region running from northern France, through Belgium, to the German Ruhr Basin became easily the most important.

Agriculture prospered as prices rose slightly and stabilized. Rail systems enabled farmers to expand their markets, allowed supply to respond more readily to demand, and encouraged specialization in cash crops. Productivity improvements were primarily a consequence of specialization: in southern France farmers concentrated on viticulture, whereas in the German Münsterland farmers raised pigs to supply ham and sausage to coalminers and steelworkers in the Ruhr. In Britain, where cereal prices were declining, farmers switched to raising cattle and throughout northern Europe farmers increasingly grew "industrial" crops such as rape (for oil), hops (for beer), and sugar beet (for sugar and alcohol).

There has been some debate among historians over the importance of the creation of joint-stock or corporate banks, beginning with the foundation of *Crédit Mobilier* at Paris in 1852. Such banks were more adept than traditional merchant banks at raising large amounts of capital quickly to meet the financial needs of the second industrial wave, which required far more investment than textiles. The older banks, however, remained powerful and were more willing to adapt than initially recognized. Moreover, even the new joint-stock banks often showed the same reserve concerning industrial investment as the older banks. Ties between finance and industry gradually grew closer, but inclination to fall back on investment in government bonds or real estate remained strong. Moreover, industrialists often were leery of joint-stock organization, fearing loss of control to shareholders or banks.

Economic Slowdown

Whether the period from the early 1870s to the mid-1890s truly constituted a "Great Depression" has also produced academic dispute. Perception varies according to where one looks; yet on the whole the term depression appears an exaggeration. International and domestic commerce continued to grow, albeit at lower rates. Due to declining prices, real wages also improved, although such gains were offset by rising unemployment. One way or another, in comparison to the preceding and following phases the period was undoubtedly a difficult one.

From the 1870s onwards the arrival from abroad of vast supplies of raw materials drove down prices. Agriculture was hit especially hard, initially by the entry onto the market of grain from the Americas and Russia, and then by the arrival of meat products from the Americas, Australia, and New Zealand due to development of refrigeration technology. Moreover, unintended import from America of the parasitic insect phylloxera virtually destroyed French wine production. Although for a time Italian and Spanish producers reaped the benefit, eventually they too would have to undergo the painful process of uprooting diseased vines,

Table 8.5 Average tariff levels in 1914 on
industrial products in select countries (%).

Austria-Hungary	18
France	20
Germany	13
Italy	18
Russia	38
Spain	41
United Kingdom	0

Source: Adapted from Sidney Pollard, *Peaceful
Conquest: The Industrialization of Europe 1760–1970*
(Oxford, 1981), p. 259. Reproduced by kind
permission of Oxford University Press.

applying sulphur to the soil, and grafting indigenous vines onto disease-resistant
American rootstocks.

Falling prices triggered decline in land values and forced many laborers to depart
for urban centers. Nevertheless, farmers could try to cope with international
competition through several means. Growing knowledge of organic chemistry
enabled farmers, especially in Germany, to improve crop yields through application
of artificial fertilizer. Others could follow the British example of switching from grain
to livestock and dairy production, or purchase new technology such as the reaper-
binder or (usually horsedrawn) threshing machine. Individually, the vast majority
lacked the wherewithal to undertake new types or techniques of production, but
the rapid spread of the cooperative movement, principally in the form of rural
savings banks and consumer cooperatives, provided opportunities to undertake
improvements. All the same, the main strategy among continental agricultural
interests was to lobby governments for tariffs, tax breaks, and subsidies. Virtually
everywhere they succeeded.

Agriculture was not alone in pressing for an end to free trade. The period saw
notable advances in industrial productivity as mechanization was largely completed in textiles and technical advances enabled use of low-grade iron ore in blast
furnaces for steel production. While steel production increased dramatically to
meet demand in shipbuilding, armaments, railways, and machine making, prices
remained low and profits were slender. The British were notably slow in establishing large, mechanized steel plants, and had been surpassed in steel production by
Germany in 1893. Prices for textiles also remained low and growth in production
of British cottons came to a virtual halt. Below the surface of short-term sales
figures, radically different trends were emerging. Investment in steel would pay off
handsomely subsequently, whereas textile production would gradually migrate
away from its initial centers in search of cheap labor, initially to Italy and Russia,
and subsequently to Asia. Given small or declining profits, industrial interests frequently joined agricultural groups in lobbying for tariffs and by the mid-1890s only
Britain and the Netherlands had bucked the trend of protectionism (see Table 8.5).

The Return of Rapid Growth

In the mid-1890s Europe entered another expansionary phase wherein profits grew, real wages and consumption increased, unemployment declined, and prices rose. For continental farmers, rising prices and increased productivity were combined with the advantages of high tariffs that provided shelter from competition. Matters were different for British farmers as maintenance of free trade produced stagnation.

By the turn of the century several shifts were apparent in industry. As textile production declined in importance, prior investment in steel manufacturing paid off. The emergence of the chemical and electrical industries as motors of growth was, however, the main departure of the period. Mass production in the chemical industry could be seen in pharmaceuticals, household products, synthetic dyes, chemical fertilizers, and the refining of crude oil to produce petroleum. Growth in the electrical industry was largely attributable to the development of power grids that enabled introduction of subway systems, tramcars, electric street lights, and electric motors. All the same, fulfilment of electricity's potential remained far from complete; only a small percentage of private residences were attached to power grids. Similarly, while the motor industry attracted much attention, techniques such as the assembly line had yet to be introduced and production runs were small. Whereas there were 3.5 million bicycles, there were only 125 000 motor vehicles in France, the leading European center of automobile production in 1914. Use of petroleum as a source of energy was increasing as navies and ocean-liners adopted it, but the industry was still in an early stage of development on land.

As before, industrialization was concentrated along regional lines – in northern Britain, northern and eastern France, the German Rhine and Ruhr, northern Italy, southern Russia and the Baltic strip, and the Spanish Basque coast. If industrialization was thus broadening, it nevertheless remained the case that the south and east mostly played the role of supplier of raw materials to the north and west.

For contemporaries, the most striking development was that by 1913 Germany had virtually caught Britain in industrial production. There were several causes. Having been the first to industrialize, the British possessed old facilities and were reluctant to invest in new ones that made their previous investments obsolete. Perhaps more salient was that formal scientific training became increasingly important in the second and third industrial waves. Continental competitors, especially the Germans, created education systems that produced more scientists and professionally trained managers in secondary schools and universities. Prussia had blazed a path in establishing first-rate chemical laboratories at the Universities of Berlin and Bonn, and thereafter German companies led the field in creating laboratories with research teams

Figure 8.1   Advances in transport: the automobile, French colour poster, 1902. Getty Images.

that excelled in the mass application of innovations frequently discovered elsewhere. Although it was a Briton, Henry Perkin, who made the key discovery that led to production of artificial dyes, by 1900 roughly 80% of the industry was located in Germany.

Economic concentration gathered pace, although relatively small family firms remained the norm. Concentration was especially pronounced in Germany, partly due to exceptionally close ties between banking and industry. Banks frequently purchased company shares and placed agents on boards of directors and by 1915 Germany's top 16 bankers controlled 437 industrial directorships. They encouraged vertical and horizontal integration and also fostered the formation of cartels (associations of independent enterprises that combined to set production quotas and determine prices). The net result was to create huge, powerful, companies and minimize investment risk. In 1904 the average German steel manufacturing company was four times the size of its British counterpart.

While Germany became a significant exporter of capital from the 1870s onwards, far more British investment flowed overseas, where returns were higher. British strategies made sense in general terms: in 1914 Britons invested 2.8% of their wealth abroad, and earnings from overseas investments constituted 10% of national income. Nevertheless, concentration on foreign investment meant that British industry became increasingly uncompetitive and hence Italy, Russia, and to some extent Austria looked to the German model when it came to industrial finance.

Social Change: Urbanization

Many of the trends discussed in Chapter 4 accelerated after 1850, although the rates at which they progressed varied from region to region. Urbanization followed the pattern of economic growth – very rapid until the 1870s, continuing at a slower pace until the 1890s, and then accelerating again. Migration became even more closely linked to industrial development as steam-powered factory production displaced rural industry. Rail connections were essential to expansion and, once established, industry could spur other sectors, especially the building trades. By 1914 close to 80% of the population of England and Wales lived in urban centers; for Germany the figure was roughly 60%. At the other end of the spectrum, only 13% of Serbians lived in urban centers, and for Russia the figure was 18% (see Table 8.6).

It was the vast capital cities that first caught the eye, especially as rapid transit (trams and trolleybuses) enabled them to develop sprawling suburbs. The expansion of industrial centers was, however, at least as considerable. Whereas Essen (in Germany) possessed some 6000 inhabitants in 1850, by the turn of the century it had a population of 300 000. Between 1860 and 1897, Lodz (in the former Congress Poland) expanded from 31 500 to 315 000. When Germany was united in 1871, there were only four cities with a population of 100 000; by 1910 there were 44.

Table 8.6   Population growth in select cities (in thousands).[a]

	1880	1910
Amsterdam	317	567
Barcelona	346	560
Berlin	1122	2071
Budapest	371	880
Glasgow	587	784
Liverpool	553	746
London	4770	7256
Madrid	398	572
Manchester	341	714
Marseilles	360	551
Milan	322	599
Moscow	612	1481
Munich	230	595
Naples	494	723
Paris	2269	2888
Prague	162	225
St. Petersburg	877	1907
Vienna	726	2030

[a] For statistics of earlier growth, see Table 4.6 in Chapter 4.
Source: Carlo Cipolla, ed., *The Fontana Economic History of Europe: The Emergence of Industrial Societies* (London, 1973), II, p. 750.

Rural Society

Despite its relative decline in terms of national wealth, agriculture remained vital to the economy and employment. Even in Germany and France, between a third and a half of the population gained their livelihood from farming. For Italy, Spain, and Austria-Hungary the percentages were between a half and two-thirds, and in Russia close to four-fifths of the population worked on the land (see Table 8.7).

For Europe as a whole, the decline in relative wealth and power of the landed nobility continued. Yet there were dramatic variations and one should not underestimate the staying power of the nobility, who generally remained the wealthiest of citizens or subjects up to the Great War. The decline of the British aristocracy could be measured in the decreasing percentage of landowners who were millionaires; while landowners constituted 73% of this exclusive club during

Table 8.7   Shares of national output by sector in 1910.

	Agriculture	Industry	Transport/ commerce
Britain	6	34	29
France	35	36	7
Germany	25	43	15
Russia	60	29	12
Italy	42	22	23

Source: Adapted from Clive Trebilcock, "The Industrialization of Modern Europe," in T.C.W. Blanning (ed.), *The Oxford History of Modern Europe* (Oxford, 2000), p. 56. Reproduced by kind permission of Oxford University Press.

the period 1858–79, by 1900–14 they had been reduced to 27% as the combined impact of agricultural depression, death duties, and income tax forced massive land sales. In political terms diminishing influence could be seen in the replacement of appointive governmental offices with elective bodies and in the introduction of examination and open competition as the basis for entry into, and promotion within, the civil service. Roughly the same pattern could be discerned in the declining position of the French, Italian (except the Piedmontese) and Spanish nobilities.

Matters were less clear cut in central and east Europe. In Germany the rise of the industrial bourgeoisie was symbolized by the vast fortune acquired by Alfred Krupp; when she took over the family dynasty Bertha Krupp became the richest individual in Prussia. To some extent Imperial policy did favor the bourgeoisie in that Poor Law legislation forced eastern agrarian interests to help pay for labor migration to the industrial west at a time when agricultural labor was excluded from social insurance policies Yet the continuing power of the *Junkers*, who still held 78% of high state Prussian offices in 1911, could be seen in the retention of high agricultural tariffs in Germany even when major industrial interests had begun to question the efficacy of protectionism. Noble domination of high office also remained the norm in the Habsburg and Russian Empires, although commoners increasingly made their way into the ranks of state administrations. In Hungary landed nobles dominated governments and composed 41% of MPs even in 1914.

In central and east Europe the wealth and power of noble landowners was partly determined by the terms under which serfdom was abolished. Whereas abolition in Poland was designed to weaken the nobility, in Russia and Austria-Hungary it was conducted on terms that were more favorable for the nobility. Much thereafter depended on whether nobles successfully adopted commercial farming practices. While *Junker*, Bohemian, and Magyar magnates generally prospered, between 1870 and 1905 noble ownership of arable land in Russia fell by about a third. For the lesser nobility of central Europe, the agricultural depression of the 1870s brought a period of rapid decline in land ownership and hence large numbers entered into rapidly expanding state bureaucracies. Between 1867 and 1910 the number of civil servants in Hungary rose from 16 000 to 120 000, of whom roughly 47% were of noble origin. Even so, there were limits as to the number of jobs debt-ridden states could create, and hence the gentry still went into relative economic decline.

As before, noble strategies for retaining status varied from country to country. In France the fusion of nobles and the upper bourgeoisie continued. In 1900 nobles possessed a third of the directorships of railway companies and a quarter of the directorships of large banking and steel firms. The classic act of fusion remained marriage. While Spanish aristocrats entered domestic mergers with Catalan banking and industrial families, lesser Italian nobles joined forces with wealthy merchant families at Naples. British aristocrats frequently intermarried with merchant banking families in London, and between 1870 and 1914 no fewer than 60 British lords wed American women. In central and east Europe such lines were less readily crossed; Russian and Prussian nobles steered clear of ties with the bourgeoisie. Elements of the gentry who had entered public office tended to retain their prejudice against commerce as ignoble, and hence they formed few ties with the middle classes.

For the peasant/farming community, it is difficult to offer any generalization that does not require immediate qualification. For Europe as a whole, agriculture was of diminishing importance as a source of employment; yet this point holds more for the west and north than the south and east. Urbanization and growth in nonagricultural economic sectors were more effective in easing rural overpopulation in the north and west, a trend that was reflected in emigration. Rising material standards also were more evident in the north and west, although progress could also be seen in parts of the south and east. Signs of improvement took many forms: among them were replacement of thatch with slate in roofing, adoption of glass windows, purchase of crockery, chairs, and more fashionable (factory-made) clothing, and improved nutrition. Material progress followed the broad economic pattern and the alleged "Great Depression" was especially hard for the agricultural community. Conversely, rising prices for agricultural goods from the turn of the century to 1914 were especially good for farmers, although they brought complaints from urban interests troubled by annual inflation rates of close to 3%.

Employment in agriculture could still be linked to variations in the forms of land tenure. Farmers in Britain generally possessed relatively large holdings and security of tenure, had adopted commercial farming, and produced high crop yields. In France and western Germany peasant holdings were smaller, but entry into commercial farming was gathering pace. As one traveled south and east, the ranks of small-scale, independent farmers decreased. In certain regards the Russian case was exceptional as a Peasant Land Bank founded in 1883 enabled communes or cooperatives of relatively wealthy peasants to buy up lands sold by nobles. Most former serfs were, however, tied to the village *mir* and bound by redemption payments. They had little opportunity to expand their holdings and little incentive to increase productivity until redemption payments were abolished in 1907. All the same, the existence of the *mir* meant that there were fewer landless peasants than in other eastern states.

Peasant society remained relatively conservative. Peasants were not oblivious to modern developments, but they maintained their old attachments. Those who were most likely to embrace change, the young, frequently moved to urban centers, leaving behind aged communities that preferred older ways of doing things. Thus while change did occur, it was relatively slow. Despite massive attempts to gather information by the state, peasants still seemed "foreign" to officials, and frequently peasants were able to evade attempts to regulate or "modernize" their lives. Conservatives, who lauded peasant traditionalism as morally superior, found they could rally rural support by championing protectionism, which enabled peasants to maintain inefficient modes of production, and in certain regions anti-Semitism could be deployed to gain a rural following.

There were, however, exceptions, especially where politicians adjusted their policies and rhetoric to suit peasant interests and culture. In parts of Germany, France, Italy, and Spain socialism and anarchism made some inroads into rural society. To some extent the cooperative movement also encouraged adoption of collectivist principles, although credit cooperatives generally financed individual, rather than collective, peasant initiatives. Voluntary associations such as firefighting corps, livestock insurance and mutual aid societies, and threshing coops held appeal for peasants because they provided opportunities for risk management in the daily struggle for survival. Such associations introduced peasants to democratic practices and gradually encouraged growing confidence in science. At a more general level, expansion of education, increased literacy, and improved communications and transportation increased political consciousness among peasants. Elections, in particular, provided opportunity to negotiate with, or influence, politicians who, in turn, could use control of the state to benefit peasant communities. Entry into national politics might or might not entail ideological conversion. When peasants in the relatively undeveloped southern Massif Central rallied to the French Republic in the 1890s, they did so not because they had adopted anti-clericalism, but because they wished to benefit by the services the state could provide. Conversely, participation in voluntary associations in the Loire Valley does appear to have promoted secularism among the local peasantry.

Urban Society

Marx's prediction that society would become increasingly polarized was confounded by increasing complexity within the middle class. At the top, bourgeois wealth advanced much more rapidly than that of the landowning nobility. As discussed previously, the extent to which wealth translated into political power varied from state to state. Where middle-class elements tended to predominate was in municipal government, enabling them to focus attention on reconstruction of the urban environment.

In the upper reaches of the bourgeoisie there was a tendency toward stratification as wealthy financiers, industrialists, and businessmen turned away from older ties to shopkeepers and craftsmen and instead associated with leading members of the liberal professions and senior state officials. The trend toward spatial segregation increased with the massive urban renewal projects of the period, and while the inclination of wealthy middle-class groups to cluster in fashionable suburbs was more pronounced in Britain, it could also be seen on the continent. The creation of huge business firms with large units of employment also reduced personal contact between workers and owners.

The fate of other middle-class groups varied considerably. Crafts production went into slow decline. In the decades immediately following 1850 the continued expansion of outworking by merchants posed the main threat to artisans. Thereafter the spread of mechanization into production of consumer goods such as shoes, furniture, and kitchenware began to take a toll. In Germany the proportion of workers employed in shops with five or fewer employees dropped from 43% to 32% between 1895 and 1907 and a similar trend developed in England. Alarm over the spread of mass production had led in 1882 to formation of the General Union of German Artisans and a similar Belgian association was founded in 1900. Despite such initiatives, traditional artisan culture was steadily eroded by the emergence of mass consumer culture. Whereas the more prosperous artisans were apt to join clubs that emphasized self-improvement and respectability through reading, lectures, and concerts, the less prosperous joined working-class groups in attending drinking establishments and music halls.

Like artisans, shopkeepers experienced a decline in wealth relative to the rest of society, and they were troubled by the development of department stores and cooperatives. In France in 1888 they formed a lobby group that demanded higher taxes be imposed on large-scale retail enterprises. Yet the sheer volume of increasing sales enabled continued growth in the number of retail shops, alongside expansion of department stores, chain stores, and consumer cooperatives. Generalization is difficult, but on the whole it can be said that after 1848 the *petite bourgeoisie* gradually dropped its ties with popular radicalism and shifted toward the political center or right, seeking defence of property in liberal regimes or lending support to nationalist movements.

In terms of future development, the salient feature of the period was growth in the tertiary sector as provision of services created a new lower-middle class of "white-collar" salaried employees who did not provide manual labor.[115] It has been estimated that the lower-middle class rose from roughly 7% of the British population in 1850 to 20% by 1900, at which point more than 5% of the French labor force was employed by the government in white-collar jobs. While fathers of the traditional *petite bourgeoisie* derided such positions because they lacked the independence of self-employment, their sons and daughters entered the tertiary sector in droves. A high proportion of service-sector positions, particularly in clerical work and retail commerce, went to women. Salaries were typically low; yet such jobs did provide new opportunities and alternatives to domestic service, which fell into decline.

There was no over-riding link between the new lower-middle class and political orientation. The line between salaried employees and manual workers was sharp in terms of status, earning power, and security in countries such as Germany and Austria, and the German Federation of Salaried Commercial Employees, formed in 1893, was notoriously conservative. Part of the appeal of white-collar work in fact lay in a traditional distinction between manual and nonmanual labor that was re-inforced by the wearing of formal attire. Yet in France relatively low salaries and discontent triggered by inflation in the early 1900s led some state employees, particularly postal workers and school teachers, to launch strikes and demand entry into radical unions. Similar left-leaning trends could be seen among British white-collar workers.

Growth within the middle classes drew considerable commentary, but more attention was directed toward the working classes as industrialization swelled the number of blue-collar workers and working-class activism became more prominent. Between 1882 and 1907 the number of German factory workers rose from roughly five to nine million, and in Russia the number of factory workers doubled between 1890 and 1914. Even by the 1890s, better than half the labor force in Germany, Britain, and Belgium was employed in firms with more than 20 workers.

Numbers meant little without organization. Worker association tended to unfold along national lines and the character of labor organization was markedly influenced by immediate relations with owners and the state. For these reasons the development of the labor movement is traced largely in the narrative chapters; here we will settle for noting several broad characteristics. Beginning in the 1860s a succession of states began to loosen restrictions on unions and strikes. Until the 1890s craft unions composed primarily of skilled workers remained predominant within the labor movement. Most craft unions were more concerned with education, self-improvement, and respectability than revolution; they preferred to use collective bargaining to work for limited gains and used strikes sparingly. A major breakthrough in unionizing semiskilled or unskilled labor then occurred in the west from the early 1890s onwards, and it brought forward the organization of industrial unions. The latter united all types of workers in an industry locally and then linked local unions into national federations. By 1914 there were perhaps 4.14 million unionized workers in the United Kingdom, 2.5 million in Germany, 1.1 million in France, and 840 000 in Italy.

Industrial unions were more inclined to initiate strikes than craft unions had been, although their initial radicalism diminished over time. Lost strikes cost money and could sharply reduce membership. The key to loyalty was ability to improve wages and working conditions and hence a broad trend toward reformism

Figure 8.2 Preparations for a strike in Hungary. Hungarian National Gallery, Budapest, Hungary/The Bridgeman Art Library.

became evident even in anarchist-syndicalist organizations. As unions grew, they developed increasingly elaborate administrations composed of officials who sought to clarify objectives and formulate plans in terms of the likelihood of success. Unlike in the past, when worker protests had mostly broken out during hard times, unions tended to strike during periods of prosperity, when owners were more likely to make concessions. Following the example of the industrial unions, craft unions initiated strikes more frequently and also grouped nationally.

While the labor movement thus made impressive gains, important limitations remained. Partly due to uneven industrial development, diversity remained the norm among workers and finding common ground among them was not easy. Many paternalist owners shrewdly formed company or "yellow" unions among their employees and secured loyalty by providing pension benefits and housing. Even where independent unions had been formed, coordinating their activities under a single, central, direction proved immensely difficult. While some unions were linked to political parties, others eschewed such association as a distraction from the main (often pragmatic) objectives of the membership. Moreover, prejudice meant that unions were not good at recruiting women or immigrants, and nationalism and religion could negate attempts to unite workers. Thus unions never came close to organizing the majority of workers. Immediately prior to the Great War the rough figures of unionized workers were 25% in Britain, 15–16% in Germany, and 10–11% in France and Italy. Given the resistance of continental state administrations and employers, it was perhaps not surprising that it was only in Britain that a functioning system of collective bargaining was established by 1914.

In broad terms the period brought improved conditions for workers – rising real wages, increased consumption, better nutrition, declining food and clothing prices, a shortening work week of roughly 55–60 hours, and increasing leisure opportunities. Yet conditions remained harsh. Workers seldom possessed much property, placing them in a vulnerable position when they could no longer provide labor due to old age, illness, or injury. When business cycles brought unemployment, working-class families could rapidly fall into destitution. Unions and mutual-aid or friendly societies could provide only limited insurance, and hence for workers the most promising development of the period was creation of state social insurance programs. The latter were, however, established only in the more advanced states and available to relatively small numbers. Nor were conditions improving rapidly in all regards; housing was frequently inadequate. Few families now lived in single-room tenements in England, but such was not the case elsewhere. Prosperity was "trickling down" to workers, but most were well aware that disparities in the distribution of wealth were actually increasing.

State Response to Economic and Social Change: Increasing Intervention

Contemporaries were not wrong in thinking that government was growing by leaps and bounds, although states in fact extracted relatively less from gross national product than they had in the past. States enjoyed dramatic increase in revenues due to population increase and economic growth, but what was crucial was that they altered how they spent their revenues. Given that wars were relatively rare, and that reserve systems cut the costs of maintaining large armies, states were able to direct more of their funds toward civilian expenditure. The main "growth industries" were increase in the state bureaucracy, development of transportation and communications infrastructure, and provision of national (mostly primary) education systems. It was only in the final decades prior to 1914 that the more advanced states began to establish rudimentary social welfare systems, and the British were exceptional in instituting a limited measure of pro-gressive income taxation as a means to redistribute wealth. Nevertheless, there was no mistaking the overarching trend: between 1870 and 1900 the number of civil servants in Germany, Britain, and France rose, respectively, from 210 000 to 405 000, 99 000 to 395 000, and 224 000 to 304 000.

Why did states shift so dramatically to civilian expenditure? Desire for moderni-zation was a major cause, and it had much to do with international rivalry. Modernization, whether in increased economic productivity, enhanced infrastruc-ture, increased literacy, or improvement in the general health of the population, was perceived as directly linked to military power and state survival. Similarly influential was growing conviction that an essential role of the state was to manage social relations. Frequently driven by fear of socialism, states increasingly intervened in the economy in pursuit of national harmony. Proponents of *laissez faire* sometimes managed to limit reform; yet even liberals increasingly accepted that the state must play a greater role.

Collapse of the old society of orders had produced a vacuum into which the state moved in pursuit of social order. Primary education became the principal means of inculcating the masses with desired values, although state provision of free and compulsory mass education for boys and girls was much more developed in the north and west than in the south and east. By 1901 the German state spent 12% of its budget on education, whereas Spain spent only 1.5%. At the turn of the century illiteracy rates in Russia, Serbia, and Romania were still well over 75%, whereas they had been reduced to 14% in Britain and France by 1906.

Given its role in inculcation, educational policy frequently was a political battleground. Much of the initial impulse for expansion of mass education came from liberals and as states increased funding of primary education, they also sought to assume control over curricula and teacher training, provoking clashes with religious groups. Outcomes varied. Whereas in France and Germany emphasis on secular education entailed more time spent on reading, writing, and arithmetic, and less on religious instruction, such trends were less apparent in Britain and Russia, and the influence of the Catholic Church remained formidable in Spain. At times shared opposition to socialism led to compromise with the Church, as was the case in Italy.

Where secularism was most advanced, nationalism began to supersede Christian morality as the main value system propagated in state schools. Courses in history, geography, and even the natural sciences were designed to bolster patriotism. While the impact of such efforts has been well documented for France and Germany, it is, however, doubtful that state-directed nationalist instruction was uniformly effective. Attempts to spread patriotism were largely ineffectual in the Italian south. Moreover, promotion of a single national language could spawn disintegration rather than integration. Imposition of Russian in primary schools in Poland led to creation of an underground school system wherein perhaps a third of the population learned how to read Polish. In Hungary assimilation policies produced mixed results. Between 1880 and 1910 the percentage of Hungarians who listed themselves as Magyar on censuses rose from 46.6 to 54.5. Urbanization contributed, as did higher rates of emigration among non-Magyars. Most of the roughly one million assimilees were, however, of German or Jewish descent, and meanwhile resistance hardened among Slavic groups. Conversely, in Austria the relative autonomy of local governments enabled nationalist groups to compete in the founding of schools and the language of instruction, creating endemic friction. As before, nationalism provided opportunities and challenges according to context, and states could never entirely master it.

Secondary and higher education remained largely the preserve of male elites. In 1890 less than 3% of the age group of 10–19 years attended secondary school (except in Switzerland) and in the same year less than 1% of the age group of twenty to twenty-four years attended university. Emphasis on knowledge of the classics as the main qualification for entry into higher education served to favor the elites and as late as 1890 43% of classroom time in French secondary schools was devoted to Latin and Greek. Education for women was designed to restrict them to the "domestic sciences" (sewing, cooking, and cleaning) rather than to prepare them for entry into the public sphere. Nevertheless as the economy diversified and created new jobs, public demand for increased opportunity steadily rose and by the turn of the century several of the barriers to social mobility through higher education had crumbled. By 1902 universities in Germany and France had begun to accept students from secondary schools that taught modern (modern languages, science, mathematics, technology, and modern history) subjects. Similarly, the medical and legal professions dropped knowledge of Greek or Latin as a requirement for entry. At roughly the same time women began to enter the universities in small but significant numbers. In 1914 the proportion of women in German, French, and British universities was, respectively, 7%, 10%, and 10%.

State authority was also extended in the domain of public health. State provision of medical care slowly grew and intertwined with private charity, producing pluralist systems. In 1888 French hospitals were placed under the control of a state-administered council and their activities were extended with neighborhood dispensaries. Nevertheless, the French medical association viewed the development of a national system with skepticism, and responsibility for medical provision remained primarily the purview of local governments. Provision of medical care in Germany was also largely a local responsibility, but in the 1890s private charity was given an increasingly national direction by the foundation of patriotic leagues that were headed by high-ranking state officials and their wives. Such organizations developed tuberculosis and infant welfare schemes, establishing clinics and dispensaries throughout the Empire.

From the first cholera epidemics in the 1830s, through vaccinations against smallpox, to the measures taken against syphilis late in the century, European states developed their own preventive strategies to combat contagious disease. Initially there was a rough correspondence between political systems and prophylactic strategies. Autocratic states were more apt to employ invasive measures such as quarantine, whereas liberal states such as Britain emphasized sanitary measures. Nevertheless, the British eventually fell into line with the continental states in a "neo-quarantinist" approach to cholera that combined selective inspection (especially of travelers and ships), isolation of the ill, and disinfection, a trend that was re-inforced by identification of the *comma bacillus* as the cause of cholera in 1893. Ultimately state policy was influenced by a host of factors ranging from concerns over economic impact, to geographical considerations, to fears and anxieties about certain groups within society, to administrative capability. It was the combination of these factors within a specific context that determined decision-making and led to differing systems.

Such differences were over forms of intervention rather than reluctance to see an increase in the role of the state in public health. Theoreticians called for states to create centrally coordinated, total systems of public health, replete with medical policing. At times the advocates of prevention through improved sanitation could be just as draconian as the proponents of quarantine; the Scot John Robertson called for "the entire destruction of many houses"[116] to prevent the spread of disease. A key feature of sanitation measures was, however, that they often were expensive to implement, which was one reason why less developed states were more inclined to resort to quarantine. Much of the responsibility for public health was in fact left in the hands of local governments. All the same, the number of public health officials steadily grew as states passed legislation enabling medical officials, building inspectors, or police and judicial officers to inspect homes and their residents.

Intricately linked with issues of public health, urban development was also left largely to local officials. Baron Haussmann's transformation of Paris was not necessarily typical in this regard; he was appointed by the central government, whereas it was elected mayors such as Joseph Chamberlain of Birmingham and Karl Lueger of Vienna who subsequently gained fame for their promotion of "municipal socialism." In the decades leading to the Great War, German municipal governments took the lead in institutionalized urban planning, often as a means to counter the state administration. Expansion of municipal authority and provision of services, particularly in transportation, gas, and water, sprang from a mix of motives – idealism, self interest, and bourgeois civic pride. Although at times it was restricted by liberal sentiment, urban planning led to increased encroachment on the private economy, especially when private companies failed to provide satisfactory services.

Physical and moral hygiene were linked in public perception, and crime prevention remained a central state preoccupation. In a bid to professionalize law enforcement, officials increasingly called on experts in the sciences to help track down criminals, standardize means of identification, and provide testimony during trials. The period also saw the rise of criminal anthropology and a great deal of debate as to the origins of criminality. In 1876 Cesare Lombroso published *Criminal Man*, in which he claimed he could identify a "race" of criminals by analysis of cranial and facial irregularities. Members of the criminal "race" were primitives who had not evolved any sense of moral responsibility and should be eliminated. Similar notions were later floated in Spain, where gypsies were identified as an atavistic group that refused to integrate with the rest of society and thus failed to adopt more civilized norms. Although it was Enrico Ferri who first coined the term "born criminal,"[117] under his guidance Italian criminologists described their work as "criminal sociology," a term that suggested criminality was a product of both environment and heredity. Moreover by the late 1880s Lombroso's ideas were under vigorous attack by French scholars who argued that crime was a social, rather than hereditary, phenomenon.

Belief in moral and physical degeneration as the source of crime nevertheless remained powerful among medical experts. In assessing the claims to madness of a man charged with murder in 1891, a leading Parisian alienist observed that the defendant's face was asymmetrical and noted that such physical "stigmata are often associated with individuals who demonstrate a variety of intellectual and moral defects." He concluded that society must be protected from such "a danger-ous disabled person."[118] In 1913 Charles Goring's *The English Convict: A Statistical Study* dealt a fierce blow to theories about physiological distinctions; yet even Goring took up eugenicist notions of regulating the reproduction of the "socially unfit." By then sterilization of "degenerate" offenders had already been employed in Switzerland and several American states, although European criminologists generally refrained from endorsing such measures.

Theoretical debate easily crossed national borders, and to a limited extent police officials began to explore the possibilities of sharing information on an international basis. Perhaps not surprisingly, the first efforts were directed against political refugees following the revolutions of 1848. Thereafter the wave of anarchist assassinations in the 1890s led to agreements for international surveillance. The latter were then further developed in response to public alarm over the "White Slave Trade" of prostitutes, and by 1914 plans were afoot for creation of an international bureau of criminal identification.

Among the more contentious activities of the police was the regulation of pros-titution. Abolitionist campaigns gathered momentum by drawing public attention to corruption in administration of regulatory regimes and, especially, mistaken arrests. Equally important was growing criticism in the medical community of police control over what was increasingly considered an issue of public health. In Italy and France desire to humanize the treatment of venereal disease (and hopefully make it more effective) led to abolition of prison hospitals and creation of clinics at hospitals where prostitutes would be treated as regular patients. "Neo-regulation" thus saw a reduction in police control of health services in favor of medical authorities, yet police surveillance continued.

Association "Mania"

Expansion of the state made it an increasingly powerful tool for those who controlled it. Establishment of representative government was seen as the leading means by which the state could be made to serve the interests of society as a whole and to some extent progress could be seen in gradual extension of franchises. All the same, participation in parliaments, state executives, and administrations continued to be dominated by small, male elites. More promising was the growth in civil society apparent in an explosion in the number of nongovernmental associations. It is difficult to trace the early stages of growth in associational life with exactitude. In France, for example, state hostility tended to check the spread of voluntary associations prior to 1848; yet it was also the case that officials sometimes preferred to ignore the existence of associations they deemed harmless. Nevertheless, it is clear that the number of associations grew rapidly during the liberal phase of the Second Empire, a trend that continued during the Third Republic. The duration of the latter, and male democracy, had much to do with the enthusiasm with which republicans threw themselves into forming associations ranging from Masonic lodges to educational leagues.

Gradually even the most autocratic regimes began to relinquish their control over this fundamental aspect of civil society. In Austria-Hungary the number of voluntary associations virtually doubled in each decade from 1880 onwards, reaching a total of 100 000 by 1910. After the Revolution of 1906, Russia began a similar transformation with the foundation of some 4800 associations by 1909. Not all such groups were political, either explicitly or implicitly; many of them focused on leisure activities. Partly due to centralization of power and increased nationalization of politics, a large number of associations were, however, designed to influence public policy as associational organization surpassed communal organization.

Comparison of Austria and Hungary helps to identify several factors that influenced the growth of civil society. For reasons discussed in the narrative chapters, the franchise for elections to the Austrian parliament gradually expanded and ultimately reached full manhood suffrage; in Hungary the right to vote remained highly restrictive. Similarly, Austrian and Hungarian governments became less repressive in terms of freedom of expression, association, and assembly, although this trend was much more pronounced in Austria. Perhaps most importantly, in Austria elective bodies at the local and provincial levels of government possessed a good deal of autonomy. In contrast, in Hungary the central government increasingly restricted the influence of local levels of government through the appointment of state officials. In both parts of the Dual Monarchy governments became increasingly active in the provision of public services, but in Austria much of this work was undertaken by local governments, encouraging the formation of political groups that sought to influence, for example, school systems. Thus a web of local associations developed in Austria and, given the extent of the franchise, they provided the grass-roots basis for national mass parties. Austria remained, in essence, autocratic; nevertheless, opportunities for the public to exert influence over the state were growing more rapidly than in Hungary.

Many associations were formed to represent economic interest groups. In terms of numbers, friendly or mutual-aid societies were especially impressive; by the 1870s there were some four million members of friendly societies in Britain and there were over three-quarters of a million members of mutual-aid societies in

France. In essence, such organizations fostered self help as they enabled workers to set aside funds for the calamities that frequently beset them. As they grew the organizations became increasingly bureaucratic, acting essentially as insurance companies. To some extent they can be seen as forerunners of unions in that they provided a means for workers to act collectively. However, they often were patronized by the state and wealthy middle-class elements, and they were frequently drawn into close ties with the state when national insurance programs were established.

Cooperatives also embodied the principle of self-help. By 1897 there were a million members of cooperatives in Britain. Initially a largely urban phenomenon based on the advantages of buying goods in bulk, due to the onset of depression in agriculture in the 1870s farmers' cooperatives spread rapidly. In Italy the number of credit unions and savings banks jumped from 171 to 738 between 1881 and 1890. Cooperatives provided capital to invest in new or more efficient types of production, acquire land, or purchase goods such as chemical fertilizer at reduced prices. They also supplied expertise regarding the quality and proper use of new products.

Less impressive in terms of mass organization, certain middle-class and elite economic interest groups were nevertheless highly effective in influencing state policy. In Germany the Central Association of German Industrialists and the Society of Tax and Tariff Reformers (who mostly represented *Junker* agricultural interests) successfully lobbied for the adoption of protectionist tariff policies. In France the Committee of the Forges (which represented steel manufacturers) and the Society of French Agriculturalists played a similar role. Although by the turn of the century many economic interest groups had formed associations to represent their interests, the extent to which they could extend beyond local origins and build nationally often determined their impact. Moreover, how such groups related to parliamentary party systems also varied considerably. Whereas German parties tended to act as umbrella groups for a wide array of associations, in Spain the tendency was for professional associations to bypass the elite-dominated Conservative and Liberal parties and deal directly with the state, laying the foundation for future corporatist politics.

Size and economic power were not the only criteria for gaining influence. The creation of professional associations among lawyers, doctors, pharmacists, veterinarians, economists, chemists, teachers, architects, engineers, and a host of other groups accelerated dramatically from 1850 onwards. Such associations frequently held national congresses and were not shy about seeking to direct public policy. The relation between the professions and the state was in fact symbiotic. As the state specified qualifications that required long years of preparation and high costs for training, the professions gained legitimacy for remaining exclusive. Meanwhile members of the professions entered state bureaucracies in large numbers and lawyers, in particular, played a disproportionate role in politics. Similarly, as the state increasingly involved itself in public health, the influence of the medical profession steadily rose.

Many associations were organized to provide charity and promote education. The role of women in such organizations was pronounced and frequently such experience proved instrumental in the organization of the women's movement. Philanthropic associations often were organized along religious lines, and women had to assert their right to enter into the public sphere by arguing that such activities were an extension of their domestic responsibilities. Although their efforts were by no means unique, British women were the first to enter into charitable organizations in large numbers and they soon made themselves irreplaceable through their efforts in raising and overseeing the distribution of funds. By the 1850s their example had spread to the continent. As the state increasingly moved into the fields of education, public health, and social welfare, women's groups could draw upon such experience to speak with authority in debates over public policy. Another notable trend was the extent to which male workers formed their own educational societies. There were some 225 such associations formed in Germany between 1860 and 1864. At roughly the same time there were 425 workers' educational societies in Britain, and similar organizations were developing in France, Italy, and Austria-Hungary. Here too, voluntary organizations served as a seedbed for future political activism.

While the influence of older associations such as the freemasons remained strong in France and Italy, the rapid growth of nationalist associations was more striking. The phenomenon was most apparent in Germany, where choral societies gathered for mass singing of patriotic songs, gymnasts marched in unison in military-style parades, and sharpshooters staged contests. By 1864 there were 170 000 members of gymnastic societies in Germany and such associations had already spread to the Czechs in Bohemia. In subsequent decades gymnastic societies would develop among most the nationalities of the Dual Monarchy, a troubling sign for a polyglot Empire. There were 530 000 German gymnasts in the 1890s and 1.4 million by 1914; for the Czechs the figures were 37 000 in the 1890s and 120 000 by 1914. More ominously, German gymnasts took particular interest in the activities of their German counterparts in Austria – a sign of lingering desire for the old *Grossdeutch* solution and growing ethnic nationalism. Such associations were less apparent in the west, but they could be seen in the French League of Patriots and the Irish Republican Brotherhood, which organized partly as a gymnastic society.

Cultural Trends: Positivism and the Cult of Scientific Progress

In the decades following the revolutions of 1848 widening prosperity contributed to optimism about the future. As the philosopher Hubert Spencer put the matter in 1850, "Progress is not an accident but a necessity. ... Surely must the things we call evil and immorality disappear; surely must man become perfect."[119] For contemporaries the great symbol of progress was the rail system – not just the speeding locomotive, but also the track lines, tunneling, viaduct building, and station construction that accompanied it. The obvious impact of scientific discovery and technological application contributed to growing belief that science was the key to progress and the means to discover "truth."

The elevation of science to a quasi-religious status was especially apparent in Auguste Comte's philosophy of positivism. Beginning in the early 1830s Comte had argued that all phenomena could be explained by scientific examination of empirical evidence. By observation and exact description humans could come to understand the laws that governed society, which should be organized along scientific lines. Although there was little in Comte's thought that could not be found in the writings of the *philosophes* or in utopian socialism, in the mid-nineteenth century he could be more overt in his rejection of metaphysics and orthodox religion: "the human spirit, recognizing the impossibility of obtaining absolute ideas, renounces the search for origins and goals of the universe and the effort to know the innermost causes of things, in order to concentrate on discovery, by experiment combined with reason and observation, of the effective laws, that is, their unchanging relations of succession and similarity."[120]

A key component of positivism was its promise to create an overarching synthesis that would enable the explanation of reality in its totality. Along such lines, all disciplines, whether in the natural or social sciences, would ultimately be linked. In the past religion had provided a coherent view of the world, and desire to find a system that could restore a sense of unity was pervasive. Not all thinkers were, however, convinced that science could play such a role. In the early 1830s the German poet Heinrich Heine had expressed regret that the cohesive force of Catholicism had been lost, and closer to mid-century the British poets Alfred Tennyson and Mathew Arnold lamented the demystification or disenchantment of the world that science seemed to bring. Comte too became increasingly concerned by spiritual issues in his later career and he proposed a religion of humanity wherein heroic scientists played a role akin to priests. Nevertheless, his followers tended to discard the spiritual element of Comte's thought, and positivism came to epitomize a scientific rationalism that could be fiercely anti-religious.

The apparent divide between science and religion widened with the publication of the biologist Charles Darwin's *On the Origin of Species* (in 1859) and *The Descent of Man* (in 1871). Darwin's influence derived partly from his ability to combine the theories and observations of various fields into a broad synthesis. There long had been speculation over the idea of evolution and studies in geology and paleontology had demonstrated that the earth was tens of millions of years older than the Bible indicated. Thus evolution could be conceptualized as a long, slow process, and naturalists argued that present plant and animal species had not always existed, at least not in their current form. Moreover, the notion of a struggle for survival could be extrapolated from the works of writers such as Thomas Malthus,

Figure 8.3   Darwin looking at human ancestry. Private Collection/ The Bridgemean Art Library.

a founder of demography, who emphasized that more humans were born than could possibly survive. In this context, Darwin's great contribution was to introduce "natural selection" as the means by which change came about. Given there were more offspring than could survive, all organic beings must struggle for food and habitat and slight variations among species could enhance survival prospects amidst change in environmental conditions. Those that could best adapt would be most likely to reproduce while others declined, and over time such changes could lead to the evolution of new species.

The concept of natural selection was explosive. The idea that humans had descended from apes was, of course, difficult to reconcile with the book of Genesis and belief that God had created Man, a separate species, in his own image. Broader in its intellectual implications was that Darwin had depicted change as an accidental process that revealed no hidden purpose or divine plan. Morality played no part in natural selection and even the human mind was a product of response to the natural environment. Darwin's explanation thus stripped the notion of progress from the process of change, although many contemporaries mistook his point, seeing in evolution a sign of some higher plan.

Darwin's theories triggered a great deal of polemic. Spencer had already gained notoriety for his application of the concept of survival of the fittest to social studies and he soon drew upon Darwin's theory of natural selection. Societies were organisms. They gained strength through competition that allowed the fittest members to distinguish themselves. Improvement could be ensured by the fittest reproducing while the unfit fell by the wayside. Spencer thought largely in terms of economic competition and hence he argued that aiding the weak or poor through charity retarded progress by negating a healthy natural process of selection. Conversely writers such as Thomas Huxley sought to separate Darwin's theories from what came to be known as Social Darwinism. Huxley argued that the development of physical phenomena should not be confused with the progress of human ethics and that cooperation, rather than competition, was also a means toward biological survival.

Spencer was not a racist; all the same, Social Darwinism could be readily adapted to several of the more virulent lines of thought then emerging. Although scholars long had classified humans in terms of race, the French aristocrat Arthur de Gobineau was the first writer to put forward the argument that race was the main determinant of civilization. Far from subscribing to belief in progress, Gobineau emphasized decay and in his *Essay on the Inequality of the Human Races*, first published in 1854, he attributed all the problems of western civilization to the failure of white Aryans to retain racial purity. By mixing with other peoples, Aryans had diluted the qualities of greatness in their blood. Gobineau's work was hardly scientific; yet after Darwin the belief that certain species were better equipped for survival gave theories of racial hierarchy a pseudo-scientific credibility. Later writers such as Austen Chamberlain would argue that previous decline could be reversed through genetics, and in another sign of things to come he shifted blame for racial degeneration to the Jews.

Religious Response

Scientific authority posed a challenge to nonscientists determined to have a say in the elaboration of value systems. By no means did all scientists lose faith in religion and the religious frequently accepted at least part of what science revealed.

Even so, the onslaught on religion was at times direct and shrill. Huxley believed that science and orthodox religion were incompatible, and it was no coincidence that anti-clericals were particularly inclined to endorse Darwin's ideas. Before and after the publication of *On the Origin of Species* writers subjected the Bible to close historical analysis, arguing that it was a collection of myths written to codify certain values by a primitive society rather than a work of divine inspiration.

The Church responded in a variety of ways. The Evangelical movements and religious revival of the first half of the century continued as theologians and preachers shifted from emphasis on punishment of sinners to a "compassionate Christianity" which called on believers to emulate God's love through social action that would benefit one's community. Liberal theologians were, however, sometimes shaken; in the 1850s several leading Anglican churchmen and scholars were charged with heresy because they had argued that the Bible need not be taken literally. In Germany an association formed in 1865 sought to shift Protestantism away from adherence to old dogma in hope of finding an accommodation with contemporary cultural developments, and in France a school of liberal theologians interpreted Christianity as principally an ethical, rather than divine, movement. Meanwhile continental states eased restrictions on association, facilitating the organization and spread of new Protestant sects such as the Salvation Army and Christian Scientists. Intensifying competition was to some extent a sign of vitality, but conflicts among Protestant factions also harmed the Churches' public image and contributed to declining attendance, particularly among urban males.

Division was apparent in Roman Catholicism too. In 1864 Pope Pius IX denounced a wide sweep of contemporary thought, including modern science, in the *Syllabus of Errors*. Ultramontane promotion of devotion to the Virgin Mary and the Sacred Heart of Jesus through the proclamation of miracles and the organization of pilgrimages also constituted a vigorous counter-attack. Equally important was dramatic expansion in the number of religious orders that published journals, provided education, and engaged in missionary work. In France membership rose in religious orders from 37 000 to 162 000 between 1851 and 1901, and growth in Spain would see numbers jump from 15 000 in 1861 to 68 000 in 1920. It would be wrong to think of Catholic revival simply as clerical string pulling; a largely independent resurgence of popular piety was a key component, although direction of the "new Catholicism" fell largely to ultramontanes. When in 1870 Pius summoned an Ecumenical Council to confirm the doctrine of papal infallibility in matters of faith and morals, liberal Catholics began to depart the Church. His message to French pilgrims in 1871 suggests why: "What I fear for you is not that miserable band of Communards (demons escaped from Hell) – but Catholic liberalism … that fatal system that dreams of reconciling two irreconcilables – Church and revolution."[121]

Intellectual challenges to religious authority were more apt to trouble the elite than the common people. At the mass level, keeping up with population movement posed a greater problem. The rapidity of urbanization made it difficult to build enough churches for potential worshipers to attend and meanwhile some rural churches fell into disuse. Increased mobility made the maintenance of contact with the faithful difficult and generations of the urban poor could grow up with virtually no experience of formal religion. Such concerns encouraged Pope Leo XIII to chart a new course when Pius died in 1878. Leo called on Catholics to participate in and cooperate with liberal states and in 1891 his encyclical *Rerum Novarum* condemned socialism while defending private property. Nevertheless, Leo also called on employers to treat their employees justly and to support laws designed to improve working conditions. In many regards he was as conservative and authoritarian as his predecessor; how contemporaries viewed his pontificate, however, derived principally from statements in *Rerum Novarum* such as: "a small number of very rich men have been able to lay upon the teeming masses of the laboring poor a yoke which is very little better than slavery itself."[122]

Thus while the Catholic Church remained hostile to many trends of modern thought, it was moving to address some of the problems created by industrialization. Ultramontanes frequently rejected papal calls for a more accommodating line with secular forces, but Social Catholicism often became a powerful force capable of working in combination with formerly antagonistic liberals. "Compassionate Christianity" constituted a similar movement within Protestantism. Catholics and Protestants frequently formed associations that acted as pressure groups, and they increasingly organized associations that were explicitly international in character.

Growing Doubt

Meanwhile some of the mid-century faith in science was diminishing. In part doubt originated in the scientific community itself. Research at times raised puzzling questions that were difficult to reconcile with Newtonian physics. Identification of X-rays and other forms of radiation led to investigation at subatomic levels, revealing electrons and other particles that refused to act in a regular or predictable fashion. Such discoveries would lead Max Planck and Albert Einstein to put forward, respectively, theories of quantum mechanics and relativity that would revolutionize the study of physics and raise all sorts of new problems. The cultural impact of these developments was, however, limited prior to 1914; disparities between theory and research findings were more apparent in biology. The characteristics of physical heredity were little understood until biologists working in the 1890s developed the new science of genetics by reintroducing the largely ignored studies conducted by Gregor Mendel in the 1860s. In the meantime doubts had emerged over how natural selection could take place from one generation to the next. Moreover, the work of Louis Pasteur in microbiology disproved the theory that life could originate from dead organic matter, once again raising the issue of the ultimate origins of life. Unanswered problems fostered skepticism and created space for alternative explanations.

Developments in the arts frequently challenged belief in progress. In reaction against the idealism of Romanticism, the literary movement known as realism gained prominence in the 1850s. Novelists such as Gustave Flaubert and George Eliot (the pen name of Mary Anne Evans) sought to present a detached, objective depiction of contemporary life based on close observation. Literary artists had of course long positioned themselves as social critics and realism shared certain affinities with positivism; yet the tone of realism was notably pessimistic. Flaubert, in particular, became notorious for the way in which he sought to expose "bourgeois" hypocrisy and critics frequently charged him with being amoral in his handling of taboo subjects such as adultery. The inclination to challenge conventional ideas of morality by exposing misery and degradation became even more pronounced in the school of naturalism, which reached its high water mark in the 1880s and 1890s. In the novels of Emile Zola and Thomas Hardy (frequently unhappy) fate is determined by chance rather than human will, and there is little that is benevolent in the workings of the universe. Especially in the works of Zola, notions of progress gave way to alarm over hereditary degeneration.

Realism's objective of depicting the daily lives of all social classes could also be seen in the visual arts, most notably in the paintings of Gustave Courbet and Edouard Manet. Subsequently, impressionism continued realism's depiction of unposed scenes and portraits of people at work in an attempt to convey the fleeting impressions of modern life. Painters such as Claude Monet and Auguste Renoir, however, pushed beyond realism with their emphasis on the artist's perception. The technique of brush strokes that blurred when viewed from up close, but formed an easily recognizable image when seen from a distance, drew attention away from the object portrayed to the light and color employed in representation. Moreover, by emphasizing a reality below the surface of an object, and with their ability to suggest mood and atmosphere, the impressionists were preparing the ground for more radical departures.

Revolt was especially pronounced in poetry. Like Flaubert, the poet Charles Baudelaire was brought to trial in 1857 after publication of his *Flowers of Evil*. Along with Paul Verlaine and Algernon Swinburne, Baudelaire pursued art for art's sake, propagating a new estheticism based on cultivation of the senses for appreciation of beauty. Much of the poetry was deliberately provocative in its rejection of respectability and celebration of what most contemporaries considered vice. At least as significant as changing content was the inclination of Arthur Rimbaud and Verlaine in the 1860s to separate poetry from prose by eschewing conceptual thought and instead employing images and symbols to stir emotion. By the 1880s symbolism had entered prose, most notably in the works of Oscar Wilde, and was championed by an *avant garde* that wanted to probe the reaches of the mind beyond reason. Romanticism too had sought to recapture what Enlightenment rationalism had ignored, but in the context of the late-nineteenth century symbolist revolt had a decidedly elitist character. Leo Tolstoy, arguably the leading novelist of the era, castigated the symbolists for being intentionally incomprehensible and hence anti-social.

Yet preoccupation with the nonrational remained profound. Some 730 esthetic manifestos were published between 1890 and 1910, suggesting the remarkably fissiparous nature of the revolution known as modernism. In the visual arts expressionism and cubism revealed in differing ways a willingness to depart from convention and experiment with new ways of communicating. They sprang from belief that old forms could no longer represent reality. In breaking from the technique of single-point perspective, cubists Pablo Picasso and George Braque set out to make familiar objects appear odd in order to convey their sense of strangeness in the world. Expressionists such as Edvard Munch sought above all to convey emotions such as anxiety and meanwhile Wassily Kandinsky introduced abstract art as a means to represent the strivings of the soul against a world dominated by materialism.

A similar break from the impress of positivism could be seen in the growing influence of philosophers who questioned whether rationalism could solve the problems of the human condition. While recognizing the utility of reason, Henri Bergson, an inspiring lecturer at the Collège de France, argued that reality is a continuum that cannot be broken into component parts for analysis and is best appreciated by intuition. Our experience of music, for example, transcends the simple aggregation of notes. Logic is insufficient for grasping the full meaning of experience and art, through use of metaphor and imagery, is a better means for communicating reality. Although critics questioned whether Bergson had not gone too far in divorcing conceptual knowledge from the attempt to grasp reality, from the 1890s onwards Bergson's rejection of scientific determinism became highly influential as a vindication of nonrational experience.

By the turn of the century Friedrich Nietzsche's writings, initially published in the 1870s and 1880s, had come into vogue. Nietzsche rejected most the common values of his age and at various points attacked democracy, socialism, Christianity, nationalism, rationalism, and science. In *The Birth of Tragedy* Nietzsche had asserted that irrational impulses were just as valuable as reason and that to try to limit human activity to rational behavior was to impoverish life. In later works such as *Beyond Good and Evil* he questioned whether morality could be based on universal precepts; what was considered good was subjective and a product of circumstance. Values were just the artificial constructs of a given society and hence attempts to establish permanent or universal values were misguided. Nietzsche was no friend of established religion; yet in perhaps his most memorable statement he recognized that something had been lost in the triumph of rationalism: "God is dead. God remains dead. And we have killed him. How shall we, the murderers of all murderers, comfort ourselves?"[123] According to Nietzsche, the basic passions, particularly the will to survive and triumph, were the keys to existence, and over-rationalization had sapped European civilization of its vitality. Fiercely individualist and scornful of mediocrity, Nietzsche's thought resonated deeply with a generation of intellectuals who rebelled against the ascendancy of science and reason.

Although the thought of Sigmund Freud did not become well known until the 1920s, several of his main works were published prior to the Great War and in some regards he can serve as a symbol of late nineteenth-century culture. In developing the field of psychoanalysis Freud was scientific in his approach, but his subject matter lay beyond reason. Freud studied mental trauma and early in his career came to the conclusion that recovery of buried memory was crucial to therapy. He thereafter experimented with ways to bring repressed memory to the patient's consciousness and was struck by the extent to which problems originated in childhood experiences, particularly sexual experiences. Freud also became convinced that dreams were an expression of unconscious desires. While such desires might be repressed during consciousness, they resurfaced in dreams. Subsequently Freud hypothesized a map of the mind wherein three component parts – the id, the ego, and the superego – were in constant struggle. The id consisted of basic instincts and the superego represented the values taken on by an individual within society. The ego acted as the mediator between the two and was essential to achieving the harmony of mental balance.

Many of Freud's ideas were shocking to his contemporaries, although few of them were entirely novel. Previous writers had speculated over the unconscious mind and artists long had used dreams and irrational urges as subject matter. What was different about Freud was that he sought to apply scientific method to such materials and frequently drew upon the arts in deriving his conclusions. Freud increasingly emphasized the importance of the unconscious and instinctual; yet his purpose was to bring them into equilibrium with the conscious and the rational.

Mass Culture

Intellectual and artistic controversies developed within a new context. Over the course of the century the sources of culture became increasingly (though never wholly) institutionalized and secularized. By 1900 most leading urban centers possessed an opera house, concert hall, and museum open to the public. Moreover, increase in the size of the public able to follow new cultural developments gave artists and thinkers new opportunities as prior dependence on aristocratic or religious patrons diminished. Nevertheless, the widespread aspiration to make high culture available to all was limited in practice – not everyone could afford the price of admission or possessed the knowledge required to appreciate what was on display. Far greater numbers instead went to amusement parks, circuses, and variety or dance halls.

Expansion of education produced a much larger literate public which, in turn, provided a vastly expanded market for publishers, particularly those who appealed to popular inclinations or sensibilities. In the novel *New Grub Street*, published in 1891, George Gissing reiterated a point made half a century earlier by Honoré de Balzac: "Literature nowadays is a trade ... your successful man of letters is your skilful tradesman. He thinks first and foremost of markets; when one kind of goods begins to go off slackly, he is ready with something new."[124] Improvements in communications, including railway systems, telegraph lines and (after 1887) the telephone, facilitated information collection and distribution. Technological advances such as mechanical typesetting and the rotary press enabled economies of scale and advertising revenue brought further reduction in prices, greatly increasing the readership of national and local newspapers. When in the 1860s the highly illustrated Parisian *Le Petit Journal* broke from conventional emphasis on politics and shifted to reports on crime, melodramatic human interest stories, literary reviews, and serialized fiction, it set a trend that became widespread, particularly in weekly or monthly journals. The mass public wanted entertainment rather than detailed analysis. In 1880 *Le Petit Journal* had a circulation of 583 000. By the turn of the century it had been surpassed by *Le Petit Parisien*, which captured a circulation of one million in 1902. Meanwhile Alfred Harmsworth's inexpensive and highly imperialist *Daily Mail* possessed a circulation of 1 250 000. Most of the mass media was politically conservative as profit-oriented owners soon discovered that tales illustrating national superiority held wide appeal.

Intellectuals often declaimed against the low quality of writing and taste for sensationalism in the "boulevard" press. In the midst of the Dreyfus Affair, Zola charged that: "we have seen the popular press, the newspapers costing one *sou*, those which target the greatest number and which form mass opinion, we have seen them fan terrible passions, furiously wage sectarian campaigns, killing in our dear people of France all generosity, all concern for truth and justice."[125] It was, however, also the case that publishers began to cater to interests which had previously been ignored or underserved. Family journals and publications devoted to the interests of women were healthy examples of expansion. As reading became a leisure pastime, science fiction, detective mysteries, and Westerns gained mass popularity. Critics dismissed such literature as escapist; yet much more than previously popular culture focused on contemporary life and the wonders of modern science was a frequent theme. By 1914 conservatives could also worry over the impact of the motion picture industry. After the 1860s café concerts, music halls, and variety theaters had begun to replace boulevard theater and gin palaces as centers of entertainment and by the early 1900s café concerts and music halls had begun to show motion pictures. Cinemas mushroomed after 1909 and drew lower-middle-class elements and, to a lesser extent, workers in droves. On the eve of the Great War there were some 4500 cinemas in the United Kingdom, 1500 in Germany, and 1200 in Russia.

The period also saw the rise of sports as a popular pastime. The first golf open championship was held in Scotland in 1860 and the first Wimbledon lawn-tennis championship was held in 1877. International competition for the Davis Cup (in tennis) began in 1900, the first Tour de France bicycle race was held in

Le Petit Journal

Le Petit Journal
CHAQUE JOUR 5 CENTIMES
Le Supplément illustré
CHAQUE SEMAINE 5 CENTIMES

SUPPLÉMENT ILLUSTRÉ
Huit pages : CINQ centimes

ABONNEMENTS

Sixième année   DIMANCHE 13 JANVIER 1895   Numero 217

LE TRAITRE
Dégradation d'Alfred Dreyfus

Figure 8.4   Dreyfus the traitor publicly disgraced. © Leonard de Selva/Corbis.

1903, and in 1904 the international football (soccer in North America) association known as FIFA was formed. By then the "Challenge Cup" of the British football association could draw 110 000 fans, although the sport was just becoming popular in France and Germany. A key to the increasing popularity of sport, in terms of participation, spectatorship, and gambling, was the attention lavished on it by the press. Individuals who believed that the principal role of sport was to improve health and hygiene formed countless hiking, hunting, tennis, bodybuilding, and cycling clubs.

While sport unleashed the passions prized by intellectuals and artists, it also produced clearly identifiable winners and losers, heroes and villains. Like film stars, leading athletes became celebrities and were viewed as role or fashion models. To facilitate the identification of victors, the various national and international leagues set about establishing clearly defined, standardized rules. When he refounded the Olympic games of classical Greece at Athens in 1896, Baron Pierre de Courbertin hoped to combat the emergence of sport as a profit-making enterprise, but he was swimming against the current. The Manchester-based football weekly *Athletic News* was already selling 186 000 copies by 1896, and the cycling and auto industries were busily promoting their interests by offering prize money for competitions.

Standardization was also a defining feature of nascent consumer culture. By the 1860s the Parisian journal *La mode illustrée* could sell 58 000 copies, and thereafter the fashion industry grew rapidly as designers from leading houses sold the rights to their creations to department stores which made less expensive versions available to the public. Here too the press contributed to the development of shopping as a leisure activity principally pursued by women who were encouraged to browse and admire displays, even if they did not (immediately) buy. Like sport (largely a male preoccupation), fashion clearly identified winners and losers by a set of rules. The latter changed frequently in fashion; yet to be "out of fashion" could convey a stigma as debilitating as losing a sporting match. Although what Peter Stearns termed the "steady democratization of costume"[126] was still in its early stages, mass production meant that increasing numbers could have at least some sense of being fashionable (and successful).

The public had far more from which to choose than in the past and desire for novelty became typical of popular culture. Faddism was apparent in the rapid succession of dance "crazes" and the rapidity with which activities such as croquet-playing, roller skating, tennis, bicycling, and car racing became the latest reigning passion. In this regard popular culture seemed to mirror the plethora of artistic "isms" in modernist high culture; volatility in the former was, however, far less angst ridden and the new pastimes seldom required much by way of preparation to appreciate. A generation that could acquire more than past generations expected to gain still more in the future and was not greatly troubled by the thought. For the masses, the mundane "ordinary everyday experience"[127] confirmed belief in progress.

The characteristics of mass culture – emphasis on material acquisition and consumption, standardization, a taste for the moral certitudes of melodrama, and largely indiscriminate pursuit of novelty – were not necessarily or automatically in opposition to the values of high culture, but they were different. The revolt of Nietzsche and *avant-garde* artists against contemporary culture was rhetorically aimed at the bourgeoisie, but it also frequently entailed a loathing of mass culture.

Meanwhile Freud's emphasis on the subconscious fed into the stream of uncertainty among intellectuals about inculcation of rational values as the means to progress.

Fear of mass irrationality and the ways it could be manipulated through modern communications was especially apparent in the field of sociology, most notoriously in Gustave Le Bon's *The Crowd*, published in 1895. The advent of mass democracy meant, according to Max Weber, that acquiring and maintaining power now depended "on the trust of the masses rather than that of parliaments,"[128] creating opportunities for demagogues. Although Weber was in fact less worried by Cesarism than the political folly of the German bourgeoisie, other writers continued to link democracy to political tyranny. Similar concerns over mass influence led Weber and Emile Durkheim to argue that, especially given the apparent decline of traditional religion, society needed something more than materialism and reason to provide individuals with a sense of community and shared endeavor. Underlining such discussion was an uncertainty about the path of European culture that stood in marked contrast with the optimism of mid-century positivism. Meanwhile the parts of mass European society that benefited from increasing prosperity and increased rights happily plunged into new opportunities. For the masses, evidence of progress was not lacking, even if intellectuals and artists questioned its value.

Europe was altering in fundamental ways and change was accelerating. Industrialization and commercial expansion were spreading wealth and, especially in the west, economic growth was altering social relations. In Britain, France, Spain, and Italy the upper-middle classes had joined the nobility as part of the economic and political elite by the end of nineteenth century. Though less developed, this trend was also apparent in central and east Europe, and to many it appeared to be the inevitable path of the future. Elites were evolving and the process generated friction between groups that aspired to enter the corridors of power and those that wished to maintain exclusive control of government. As state power grew, the stakes rose.

Economic change also affected social structure. In many parts of Europe agriculture remained the predominant economic sector and most people lived in rural communities. Nevertheless, urbanization was increasing as industry left the countryside and carried migrants with it. Industrialization, as predicted, swelled the number of working-class families and placed increasing pressure on artisans struggling to compete with mass production. Yet, it also created a rapidly growing service sector of lower-middle-class "white collar" workers. Meanwhile small-scale shopkeepers held on, despite growing alarm over competition from department stores, chain stores, and cooperatives. Society was not polarizing into two warring classes; it was becoming more complex and generating multiple sources of conflict.

States responded to economic and social change by becoming more active as international rivalry and desire for social order sparked a wide range of initiatives.

Expansion of primary education, improvement in communications and transportation infrastructure, increasing regulation of industrial relations, rudimentary provision of social welfare, and growing intervention into public health were just some of the consequences. As a result, the state apparatus grew rapidly.

In combination with growing wealth and technological advance, expansion of education and literacy gave a dramatic boost to civil society. One result was the explosion of the mass press; another was the spread of associations. The net effect was an unprecedented outburst of competing interests expressing opinions and making demands. The age of mass politics had begun and its effects were unsettling. Adjusting political systems to accommodate this basic reality was by no means a simple task, and it was bound to be complicated by resistance, fear, and mistrust. It is, however, difficult to see where the anxieties apparent in high culture had much impact on state policy. The alarm among intellectuals over materialism did not stop governments from pursuing economic expansion, and doubts over the power of human reason did not slow expanding provision of secular education. Meanwhile the flow of professionals claiming some sort of scientific expertise into state bureaucracies showed no sign of abating. For their part, mass elements were far from content with their lot and some could see that while the poor were becoming somewhat less poor, the rich were becoming much richer. All the same, for many the material conditions of day-to-day life were visibly improving and emergent mass culture was far more optimistic about future change than high culture.

9

Toward Destruction?
From the 1890s to the mid-1900s

Consideration of international relations during the period under discussion is inevitably affected by our knowledge of the outcome. Given the importance of the Great War, it makes sense to trace how prior developments led to it. In doing so it is important to keep in mind that there was nothing predetermined about the outbreak of war among the powers. While we can identify trends that point to the origins of the war, we can also uncover developments that pointed toward different outcomes. Similarly, although it seems obvious that volatility in domestic politics played a part in the outbreak of fighting, establishing a direct link between instability and the declarations of war is by no means a simple task.

To varying degrees European states entered an age of democratic politics as the press expanded, voluntary associations mushroomed, and parties devoted more effort to attracting a mass following. On the political Left socialism advanced as parties adopted democratic means. In contrast, anarchism declined due to resort to terrorism. The political Right wooed the masses through appeal to patriotism, but nationalism was not uniform. Identification with the nation as a community of shared values, interests, and responsibilities was commonplace; more troublesome was the growth of an integral nationalism that took on some of the ideas of Social Darwinism and racism by identifying groups who could not be part of the nation and must therefore be excluded or expelled. Given the mobilizing efforts of the Left and Right, other groups needed to follow suit and the organization of Social Catholicism was a striking example of this trend. Meanwhile the women's movement became more complex as associations increasingly reflected their national contexts and differences emerged as to objectives and strategies.

Certain patterns can be discerned in state response to the new context of mass politics. Social legislation, in the form of welfare provision or state regulation of working conditions, gained pace. Particularly in the west, the women's movement registered significant gains in family law, property rights, and educational

Europe's Uncertain Path 1814–1914: State Formation and Civil Society, First Edition. R. S. Alexander.
© 2012 R. S. Alexander. Published 2012 by Blackwell Publishing Ltd.

opportunities. Nevertheless, few advances were made in acquisition of political rights, except in Britain. Clashes between religious groups and advocates of separation of Church and state remained central to politics and while secularism advanced in France and Hungary, elsewhere former divisions between liberals and Catholics diminished due to shared fear of socialism and anarchism.

The extent to which social elites were willing to alter political systems to accommodate mass demand for participation varied considerably. Where males were concerned, France and Britain were largely democratic and politicians and parties became increasingly responsive to mass concerns. Spain and Italy possessed political systems designed to shut the masses out, but there were signs of growing awareness of the need for change in Italy. Despite a flourishing civil society, Germany remained authoritarian. Social legislation failed to prevent growth among opposition parties bent on political reform and often governments could pass important legislation only through appeals to patriotism. Conversely, the growth of nationalism posed the greatest of threats to the Dual Monarchy.

Most regimes were thus undergoing serious challenge; yet few had reached a point where foreign war seemed the only solution. Defeat by Japan led to a revolution that threatened to destroy autocracy in Russia, and thus statesmen were reminded that war might unleash the revolutionary tiger, much as it had done in the Revolutionary-Napoleonic era. Whether they could revive the Concert of Europe as a means to defuse this danger remained to be seen.

Inter-State Relations, 1890–1900: Shifting Alliances

The collapse of the Three Emperors' League and subsequent alliance between France and Russia constituted a major departure. Initially Count von Caprivi, Bismarck's successor, allowed frayed German ties with Russia to unravel and sought instead to strengthen relations with Austria-Hungary, Italy, and Britain. Although his policies paid off in 1891 with renewal of the Triple Alliance (of Germany, Austria-Hungary and Italy) and continued British emphasis on shared interests with Italy in the Mediterranean, they also heightened alarm in Saint Petersburg and Paris. The Dual Alliance between France and Russia, however, progressed at a snail's pace because neither wanted to be drawn into war by the other. Talks begun in 1890 led to nothing concrete, but a visit by a French naval squadron to Kronstadt in August 1891 was followed by an exchange of notes in which the two powers promised to act in concert should either be threatened. By 1892 Russian need of financial aid had induced the Tsar to accede to demands for a more substantial agreement, and in August the two sides signed an accord of mutual defence in the case of aggression by a member of the Triple Alliance. Even so, it was not until Caprivi alluded to the necessity of planning for a two-front war

in the *Reichstag* in the summer of 1893 that Alexander agreed to a military convention negotiated by the French and Russian general staffs.

The escape of the French from isolation led to several diplomatic shifts.
The British Admiralty concluded that the Royal Navy could not alone defend
Constantinople from a combined Franco-Russian assault, and in the spring of 1894
the foreign secretary, Lord Rosebery, informed the Austrians that Britain would
resist a Russian offensive only if Germany were willing to neutralize the French.
By then the Germans had grown disenchanted with the British, partly due to negotiation of a Franco-British agreement over the division of Siam in 1893. Thus when
the Austrian foreign minister Kálnoky contacted Berlin, he found that Caprivi had
returned to a more Bismarckian approach. Austria-Hungary was warned that
Germany would tolerate Russian control of Constantinople and the eastern
Balkans, which led Kálnoky to explore closer ties with Russia in 1894. After the
replacement of Caprivi by Prince Hohenlohe-Schillingsfürst, German policy-makers then adopted a "free hand" strategy. Policy would be based on exploiting imperial rivalries among the other powers whenever opportunity arose, rather than
seeking binding agreements that might compromise Germany's pursuit of a "place
in the sun."

The impact of overseas imperialism on European relations was thereafter demonstrated by response to the actions of a non-European power – Japan. The
Japanese long had harbored designs on Korea, but it was fear of Russian expansion
that triggered war between Japan and China in 1894. Russia had secured permission to build a branch line of the trans-Siberian railway through Manchuria, and
the Japanese suspected the Chinese would allow the Russians to add a warm-water
port in Korea. Rapid victory in 1895 then secured the Treaty of Shimonoseki,
which granted Japan a large indemnity, political control of Korea, and a lease on
Port Arthur.

Due to preoccupation with the Far East, the Russians wanted to avoid diversion
of their forces to the Middle East and the Balkans, opening the door for improved
relations with Austria-Hungary. By 1897 Count Goluchowski, the successor to
Kálnoky, had concluded that the Dual Monarchy no longer could rely on Germany
or Britain for containment of Russia. Terrorist actions by Armenian nationalists
and brutal reprisals by the Turks had again raised questions about the sustainabil-
ity of the Ottoman Empire, and Greek involvement in a rebellion in Crete in 1896
and invasion of Macedonia in 1897 then brought the "Eastern Question" to the
boil once more. While the British took a position sympathetic to the Greeks, the
Russians were willing to back Habsburg desire for preservation of the status quo.
Thus Goluchowski decided to distance Austria-Hungary from the Mediterranean
Agreement and enter directly into an accord with Russia to cooperate in pursuit
of stability.

Unfortunately Goluchowski's actions also had negative repercussions for the
Dual Monarchy. The British subsequently decided that they could defend their
interests from Egypt and that defence of Constantinople was no longer vital.

Moreover, Goluchowski angered the Italians by refusing to include them in discussions with Russia concerning the Balkans. Partly in consequence, in 1898 the Italians dropped their opposition to the French position in Tunis in return for a commercial treaty that ended the tariff war between the two states. By 1900 the two sides had begun a series of agreements in which the Italians effectively recognized that Morocco was within the French sphere of influence, in return for French recognition of Italy's interests in Tripoli.

While the Mediterranean Agreement was thus collapsing, the French and the Germans entered into competition for Russian favor, leading both to back Russia in forcing Japan to disgorge most of her recent gains. By 1896 Germany seemed to be distancing herself from Britain in an attempt to woo the Tsar. Nevertheless, "free hand" maneuvering yielded few rewards as the French negated German attempts to weaken the Dual Alliance by providing most of the funding for a Franco-Russian consortium created to take over the Chinese Imperial Railway. Indeed, Franco-Russian attempts to establish a monopoly over rail building in China forced Germany to work with Britain to secure the Open Door Policy designed to allow all powers to pursue their interests in China. Although for a time it looked as though a "scramble for China" might lead to blows among the powers, fortunately conflict was confined to rivalry among financial interests. When secretary of state Count Bernhard Bülow officially launched German *Weltpolitik* with the seizure of Kiao-Chow from China in 1897, other powers followed suit in a chain reaction that saw Russia secure a lease of Port Arthur, France a lease of Kow-Loon, and Britain a lease of Wei-hei-wei. Thereafter tensions eased as Britain and Russia reached an agreement as to spheres of economic interest in 1899, and the powers (including Japan) united to crush the widespread anti-imperialist Boxer Rebellion in 1900–1.

Such cooperation was a product of circumstance and it implied no inclination to renounce war as a means of pursuing national interests. Concern over the mass slaughter entailed in modern warfare had, however, produced growing calls for international cooperation in pursuit of carnage limitation. The International Red Cross had been founded in 1863 and one year later 12 states had signed the Geneva Convention, thereby agreeing that volunteer relief agencies would be allowed to aid the wounded and medical personnel on the battlefield. Nevertheless, attempts to create accords whereby prisoners of war (POWs) would be placed under the supervision of neutral states or international bodies had foundered. Alarm at the rising costs of armaments then led the Russians to call for a peace conference in 1897 and hope rose that a body of institutions and laws might be developed for the regulation of international affairs. No government wished to be seen as obstructing the Tsar's proposal and hence in 1899 a conference was held at The Hague, where agreement was secured for creation of a Permanent Court of Arbitration. Moreover, The Hague Land and Sea Ordinances banned use of poison gas, prohibited looting, called for humane treatment of POWs, exempted churches, hospitals, museums, and schools from attack, and established regulations for the protection of the civilian population. Yet, as an American participant commented, never before had a body assembled with such "hopeless scepticism as to any good result";[129] individual states would determine what the "necessities of war" entailed and the ordinances would be repeatedly violated when war finally broke out.

By the turn of the century conflict between Britain and France appeared to pose the greatest threat to peace. A British decision to regain the Sudan and the headwaters of the Nile from the Mahdi was taken specifically to deny French attempts to secure a stretch of African territories running from the Atlantic to the Red Sea. Thus after defeating Mahdist forces at Omdurman in September 1898, Lord Kitchener hastened further south to challenge a small French expedition led by Major Jean-Baptiste Marchand. Despite the ravings of jingoistic newspapers, there actually was little chance of armed confrontation at Fashoda, given the overwhelming superiority of Kitchener's forces. Théophile Delcassé, the French foreign minister, wisely concluded that France possessed little leverage and in 1899 accepted an agreement that recognized the Nile valley as a British sphere of influence. In return, the British recognized northwest Africa as a French sphere of influence. That relations remained tense could be seen in modification of the Dual Alliance to include the possibility of war with Britain; nevertheless, a constructive step had been taken.

Inter-State Relations, 1900–1905: Partial Clarification and Continued Flexibility

It was not until the early 1900s that long-term trends started to clarify. In the Far East concern over Russian intentions led the Japanese to search for allies. While the Germans would do nothing to alienate Russia, the British agreed in 1902 to assist Japan should France intervene in a Russo-Japanese war. Whereas at Berlin it appeared that Germany might be able to exploit conflict between Britain and the Dual Alliance, the British were disappointed by German neutrality. By then the British were also becoming concerned by German naval expansion begun in 1898. As propounded by Admiral von Tirpitz, German *Flottenpolitik* (construction of an ocean-going battle fleet) was designed to extract concessions from Britain. Tirpitz had no illusions that Germany could gain parity with the Royal Navy, but he thought that German naval power could reach a point where to counter it the British would have to reduce their presence elsewhere, exposing their Empire to the depredations of other powers. Germany could then bargain from a position of strength.

Until 1902 there was little sign of change in Franco-British relations. Delcassé wanted British support for possible French intervention in Morocco; yet he was initially unprepared to offer much by way of return. He did manage to arrange a deal concerning spheres of influence in Morocco with Spain, but even the latter agreement was contingent on British approval. Shortly thereafter rebellion against the Moroccan Sultan, and the outbreak of war between Russia and Japan in February

1904, forced Delcassé to take a more compromising line. There is little evidence that directly connects the war to formation of the Entente Cordiale; nevertheless it seems probable that desire to avoid involvement in the conflict of their allies led the French and British to seek more harmonious relations. Agreements ranging from exclusion of the French from the Newfoundland fisheries at Dogger Banks to recognition of the French position in Madagascar soon fell into place. The crucial accord was that the French would stop pressing the British to depart from Egypt and cooperate with the British in reforming the International Commission at Cairo in return for British recognition of France's right to "preserve order" in Morocco.

Meanwhile Austria-Hungary and Russia strengthened their entente in the Near East. Bulgarian, Greek, and Serbian nationalist groups in Macedonia gained the opposite of what they intended when they sparked great-power intervention by terrorist actions designed to provoke Ottoman reprisals. In 1903 Austria-Hungary and Russia forced the Sultan to appoint a Turkish Inspector whose mandate was to eliminate abuses in the administration of Macedonia. When the initial measure failed, the two powers then designated reforms to be conducted in the Macedonian *gendarmerie*, judiciary, and financial administration. The reforms would be conducted by the Inspector General, acting upon the advice of Habsburg and Russian officials who, in turn, would be assisted by personnel appointed by the other powers. Relations between Russia and the Dual Monarchy had thus advanced to active cooperation in maintenance of the status quo. Even more striking was that in October 1904 the two states signed a treaty wherein they promised to remain neutral should either become involved in war with another power.

War between Russia and Japan then paved the way for subsequent realignments. Following the Boxer rebellion Russian troops remained in Manchuria allegedly to protect the branch line of the Trans-Siberian Railway. Meanwhile private interests promoted a scheme for timber concessions on the Yalu River, exacerbating fear in Japan that Russia had designs on Korea. When their suggestions of a spheres of influence agreement were not taken seriously, the Japanese resolved to settle the issue by force. In early February 1904 the Russian Pacific squadron was caught off guard in the outer harbor of Port Arthur, beginning a series of disasters for the Russian military. Japanese forces were better prepared and their supply lines were relatively short, whereas the Russians were disorganized, had to send supplies and re-inforcements vast distances, and were rocked by uprisings at home. Gradually the Japanese took Port Arthur and then pushed the Russian army north into Manchuria. When in late May 1905 the Japanese annihilated an archaic Russian fleet that had sailed all the way from the Baltic, Russian ability to sustain the war ended. Similarly, the Japanese had exhausted their finances and there was little prospect that they could eliminate the main Russian Army. Hence an armistice soon led to negotiation of the Treaty of Portsmouth in August 1905. All things considered, the Russians were fortunate: they had to acknowledge paramount Japanese interest in Korea, permanently withdraw from Port Arthur, and cede Japan their lease on Liaotung Peninsula and the southern half of Sakhalin Island.

Russia would not, however, pay an indemnity and both sides agreed to restore Manchuria to China. All the same, damage to Russia's status was full of implication for relations with the other European powers.

Democracy, Mass Politics, and the Women's Movement

Democrats argued that representative government was the best system for ensuring that the needs of society would be served by the state. By the 1890s most males could vote in Britain and France, where parliamentary bodies wielded significant power. Elsewhere the position of representative bodies was less certain, but the decade witnessed the emergence of mass politics as pursuit of power became increasingly tied to ability to mobilize mass support. In this context, the women's movement continued to expand, diversify, and broaden its agenda. International alliances remained characteristic and pro-suffrage activists gained a greater say in congresses; 1902 saw the foundation of the International Woman Suffrage Alliance. Nevertheless, the period was also marked by parallel development of national feminisms that reflected immediate contexts, preoccupations, and opportunities.

While it was in the 1890s that the term feminism came into common usage, there was little consensus as to what it meant and not all women's groups accepted the label "feminist." At base feminism connoted removal of the constraints that limited self realization by making women subordinate to men; yet not all activists accepted egalitarian doctrines that men and women were fundamentally the same and should be governed by the same laws and institutions. Among some feminists early stress on individual rights was tempered by growing emphasis on social control evident in preoccupation with "moral" issues such as working-class alcoholism and willingness to turn to the state for regulation.

Differences were apparent in the response of women's groups to opportunities provided by nationalist preoccupation with fertility rates. On the one hand, women could argue that the state must initiate reforms that enabled them to fulfil their role as mothers. "Familial feminism" did in fact secure advances in France. In 1895 married women gained the right to open savings accounts and make withdrawals without their husband's approval. In 1907 laws gave married women full ownership of the wages they earned, required that husbands consult their wives prior to alienating family property, and made wives the equal of husbands in parental authority over minors. In 1912 mothers gained the right to initiate paternity suits. In Britain, traditional belief that concern for the poor, children, health, and education derived naturally from women's role in the domestic sphere contributed to securing rights for women in local government. On the other hand, the 1890s also gave rise to legislation designed to improve the health of women (and children) by imposing limits on hours of employment, types of employment, and night work. Some women favored such measures, but others saw in them restrictions on a woman's right to make her own decisions. While certain French activists took the latter view, German groups took the former.

The danger of appeals based on motherhood was that they fostered arguments that child rearing was the essential, virtually exclusive, role of women. Contemporary fascination with the "new woman" (generally young, educated, employed, middle-class women who were independent of men) in literature reflected broader debates over whether the "natural" role of women was motherhood or self realization. In 1891 the papal encyclical *Rerum Novarum* championed separate spheres ideology: "a woman is by nature fitted for homework, and it is that which is best adapted at once to preserve her modesty, and to promote the good bringing up of children and the well-being of the family."[130] Catholic women's organizations, while they might fight for a host of reforms in education and employment, stressed that the roles and needs of men and women were different. Familial feminism was not confined to Catholics, and it was not simply a retreat to the past; the British suffragist Garrett Fawcett argued that women should be represented in government because they were different. Nevertheless, opponents such as Gladstone used a similar argument: "A permanent and vast difference of type has been imposed upon women and men respectively by the maker of both."[131]

Implicit, and at times explicit, in the debates over the "new woman" was the issue of whether women had the right to control their own fertility. While the number of advocates of contraception was rising, the French physician Madeleine Pelletier was exceptional in championing the right to abortion. Pelletier gained notoriety for wearing masculine attire, and was highly militant in her publications and organizational work for feminism and socialism. By and large debates over the "new woman" were the concern of middle-class feminists; few working-class women were in a position to cultivate self realization through economic independence.

Meanwhile the class division among women continued. In the German SPD Clara Zetkin, leader of a women's section that included some 175 000 members, pushed her male colleagues to act on their formal endorsement of universal suffrage; yet she also fought against alliance between working-class women and middle-class women's groups. While Keir Hardie backed granting women the vote, other leaders of the British Labour Party were far less supportive. Initially promising attempts to recruit working-class women to the suffrage campaign thus tapered off in the mid 1890s. Unions were similarly slow to mobilize women; only roughly 10% of women workers were unionized. Most male unionists viewed employment of women as a capitalist device to drive down wages and few unions allowed women to assume leadership roles.

Adaptation to Mass Politics in Britain and France

Major challenges were building in Britain. While imperial issues continued to dominate politics, the "social question" regained prominence with the creation of the Labour Party and meanwhile Irish discontent simmered. Still, France appeared far more volatile as the Third Republic lurched from crisis to crisis. By fostering anti-Semitism the ultranationalist New Right sought to build a mass following for its drive to destroy parliamentary government and purge France of allegedly "un-French" elements. The threat posed by integral nationalism then forced the political Center and Left to close ranks, leading to a largely successful defence of the Republic.

In 1892 Gladstone returned to power convinced that he must address the "Irish question." Although a second Home Rule Bill was then passed in the Commons in 1893, it was rejected by the upper house. Gladstone wanted to fight an election on the issue of the Lords' obstruction, but most cabinet members judged that the Lords were more in tune with the electorate than the prime minister. Partly for this reason, Gladstone retired in 1894 and Queen Victoria turned to Lord Rosebery. As a racehorse owner Rosebery had public appeal; unfortunately he also had difficulty working with his cabinet colleagues, and his government had fallen by June 1895. Upon resuming power, Salisbury then consolidated alliance between the Conservatives and Liberal Unionists by appointing several of the latter, including Chamberlain, to his cabinet. He then dissolved parliament and resultant elections revealed Liberal disarray as the Tories and Liberal Unionists won 411 seats. While the Irish Nationalists held on to 82 seats, the Liberals were reduced to 177 MPs.

The driving force in the new cabinet was Chamberlain. A keen advocate of social reform, Chamberlain was also an arch-imperialist and his commitment to strengthening the Empire played a major part in the outbreak of the Boer War. The Boer-dominated states of the Transvaal and the Orange Free State were determined to assert their independence. Their plans, however, collided with the aspirations of Cecil Rhodes, a mining magnate and prime minister of the Cape Colony, who dreamt of establishing a federal south-African state under British rule. Matters were further complicated by the discovery of diamonds in the Orange Free State in 1877 and gold in the southern Transvaal in 1886. Mining drew migrant workers, and the Boers of the Transvaal found themselves a minority among *"Uitlanders"* (foreigners) whom they denied political rights. An initial attempt by Rhodes to overthrow President Kruger and the government of the Transvaal failed in late 1895, but when the Boers refused a petition of some 21 000 British *Uitlanders* for enfranchisement, the British government began to send troop re-inforcements to the Cape Colony and Natal. Fighting commenced in October 1899.

In the absence of intervention by another power, there could be little doubt as to the war's outcome. All the same, the costs of annexation of the Transvaal and the Orange Free State, secured by late 1900, were high. Roughly 5800 British soldiers died in fighting, another 16 000 perished of disease, and close to 23 000 were wounded. After conventional fighting had ended, the Boers adopted guerrilla warfare, leading Kitchener to inter approximately 120 000 women and children in concentration camps. Some 20 000 died of disease and damage to British prestige was great. Moreover, funding expansion of the armed forces forced the government to increase direct taxes, and prevented Chamberlain from acting on plans for welfare reform. In 1897 the government secured passage of a Workmen's Compensation Act that established that employers should pay the costs of work-place accidents, but the projected expense of an old-age pension plan was deemed too high for implementation.

In the short term, the war served Salisbury well. The Left was divided. On the one hand most radicals, including the founders of an Independent Labour Party, believed the war was waged in the interests of finance capitalism and opposed it; on the other hand, some socialists considered imperialism a progressive force and supported the government. Among the Liberals factions such as the "Little Englanders" denounced the war, whereas groups such as the "Liberal Imperialists" supported it. Given high levels of public patriotism, the scene was set for Salisbury to call a "snap" election held in October 1900. The results were similar to those of 1895, save for the election of two Labour MPs.

Salisbury's victory was soon followed by a changing of the guard. Queen Victoria died in 1901 and was succeeded by Edward VII, an ebullient character who symbolized a generational shift away from the staid conventions of the Victorians. Before the coronation could be held in 1902, Salisbury resigned and handed power over to his nephew Arthur Balfour. With previous service as Chief Secretary for Ireland, Leader of the Commons, and Foreign Secretary, Balfour was well qualified, although his critics attributed his career fortunes to nepotism.

Thereafter Chamberlain's advocacy of a preferential tariff system that would favor the Empire and retaliate against states that raised customs barriers to British products caused no end of troubles for Balfour. Some Conservatives saw in protectionism a means to reconcile industrial and agricultural interests, but Chamberlain's proposals sowed division in government ranks and gave Liberals a cause (free trade) around which they could unite. Balfour's attempt to find middle ground by rejecting preference while calling for retaliatory tariffs was then sabotaged when Chamberlain resigned from the cabinet in October 1903 and launched a Tariff Reform League to rally support.

Division also lurked on the Left, but it provided little immediate advantage to the Tories. The early 1900s saw continued growth in TUC membership and in certain areas unions could throw considerable weight behind the fledgling Labour Party. In 1901 the Taff Vale judicial decision gave employers the right to sue unions for costs resultant from industrial conflict. Worker anger fostered political mobilization and enabled Labour to reach advantageous electoral agreements with the Liberals. Elections held in February 1906 saw the election of 53 Labour MPs, 29 of whom were affiliated with the Party and 24 of whom sat as independents. More shocking for Conservatives was that the Liberals shot up to 400 seats, while the Unionists plummeted to 157 MPs. Chamberlain's supporters fared well; however, their leader was paralysed by a stroke in July, permanently removing him from politics. Reunited under the leadership of John Redmond, a Catholic barrister, the Irish Home Rulers won 83 seats. A former follower of Parnell, Redmond was committed to constitutional change by legal means, but given the extent of Liberal victory, the immediate influence of his party would not be great.

In France the development of mass politics contributed to a gravitation of the electorate toward the Left that ultimately stabilized the Republic despite turmoil. As royalism declined in the wake of the Boulanger Affair, Opportunists moved away from cooperation with the Radicals. The Opportunists became known as Moderates and leaders such as Jules Méline, an ardent promoter of protectionism for industry and agriculture, spoke of reconciliation between the Republic and the Church. Such overtures formed the basis for coalition governments of the Moderates and conservative republicans and Pope Leo XIII encouraged the trend when he called on Catholics to defend Church interests by working within the Republic. Most Catholic leaders refused, but several deputies formed a parliamentary group known as the *Ralliés*.

In the early 1890s public attention fixed on social issues due to strikes in which troops were called in and violence ensued. Socialism was the initial beneficiary and in 1893 Jean Jaurès, a philosopher at the University of Toulouse, and some 50 other Socialists were elected. Still, socialism remained highly fragmented: while Jules Guesde provided authoritarian leadership for a Marxist party, there were four other socialist groupings and most deputies remained independent of party affiliation. Meanwhile the labor movement was damaged by anarchists who tossed a bomb into the Chamber of Deputies and assassinated the President. Government response was to tighten press legislation and increase penalties for attacks on property. A more positive consequence was that the Radicals, most Socialists, and social Catholics advocated reforms designed to appease workers. In 1892 an arbitration law was established for industrial disputes, and in 1893 free medical aid was established for the destitute.

Radical fortunes were damaged by scandal in 1892. Ferdinand de Lesseps, famous for having been the driving force in creation of the Suez Canal, had enticed investors into a new canal project in Panama. Unfortunately the Panama Company soon ran into trouble as difficult terrain and rampant disease forced expenditure to skyrocket. To gain more funding, the Company bribed journalists and politicians to provide false reports of progress; some 104 deputies received payments. Yet the Company still went bankrupt, leaving losses for thousands of small investors. An official investigation revealed corruption, but stonewalling by successive governments ensured that unresolved issues provided fodder for attacks on the parliamentary system. Nine of the ten deputies brought to trial were acquitted, and because Jewish financiers had acted as intermediaries between the Company and politicians, the scandal also fostered anti-Semitism. The Radical leader Clemenceau had ties to one of the financiers and hence he was subjected to vitriolic attacks by the Boulangist deputy Déroulède. While fighting a duel with his antagonist may have salved Clemenceau's sense of honor, the voters were not impressed and the "Tiger" subsequently lost his seat.

With the Radicals weakened, the ascendancy of Moderate-conservative coalitions might have long continued had it not been for the Dreyfus Affair.

The latter began in 1894 when Army intelligence officers discovered the existence of a spy. A military tribunal then convicted Captain Alfred Dreyfus, an Alsatian Jew, of providing the German military *attaché* at Paris with secret information. Although Dreyfus was duly dispatched to Devil's Island, the verdict was based partly on documents forged by an officer eager to secure conviction. Due largely to the investigative efforts of the Dreyfus family, troubling information began to leak out in the press, leading military officials to compound their initial errors with further forgeries. The affair became the "Affair" when the novelist Zola intervened with an open letter in Clemenceau's newspaper *L'Aurore* in January 1898. In *"J'Accuse"* Zola attributed miscarriage of justice to the reactionary and religious obsessions of military officials and warned of a conspiracy to subvert the Republic. When Zola was brought to trial and convicted for libel, public attention was focused on the original case and France began to divide over whether the initial verdict should be revised. Thereafter the passions ignited by the Affair could be seen in some thirty duels fought by partisans and fistfights in parliament.

Opposed to revision was an anti-Dreyfusard coalition led by ultranationalists who believed justice for an individual was insignificant compared to the reputation of the Army. Attempts to rehabilitate Dreyfus were interpreted as part of a plot to destroy France and conspiracy theories abounded, usually to the effect that Jews, Protestants, and freemasons were subsidized by Germany. In *La Croix*, a Catholic mass daily run by the Assumptionist order, cartoons depicted Jews gloating over Christ's crucifixion and the Talmud was said to teach Jews to cheat, steal, and commit ritual murder. Appeals to bigotry provoked a wave of violence in the months following publication of *"J'Accuse"* as 60 towns experienced anti-Semitic rioting. Most of the riots were coordinated by the Anti-Semitic League, an offspring of the Boulangist movement that possessed 270 branches in 1898.

Originally rooted in Christian faith and then fortified by association of Jews with usury and capitalism, anti-Semitism increasingly took on racist overtones. In his highly popular *Jewish France*, first published in 1886, the journalist Edouard Drumont had written: "The two races are doomed to come into conflict ... The Semite is mercantile, covetous, scheming, subtle and cunning. ... The Semite is earth-bound with scarcely any concern for the life hereafter; the Aryan is a child of heaven who is constantly preoccupied by higher aspirations."[132] Because it was multi-faceted, Anti-Semitism provided a vehicle to appeal to a wide range of disaffected groups, and hence the extreme Right latched onto it with the argument that no Jew could be truly French.

On the Left there was also an abundance of conjecture concerning plots by ultranationalists, the Army, and the Church to destroy the Republic. Allegations seemed to gain credence when Déroulède again tried to stage a coup in February 1899, although neither the Army nor the Church had any part in what proved to be a farce. Déroulède's actions, and a mob assault on a President who favored a retrial, then jolted republicans into action. The Left was motivated by a mixture of idealism and opportunism. For Zola and Jaurès the essence of the Affair lay in the right of every individual to justice. Others saw opportunity to rekindle republican anti-clericalism.

By revitalizing anti-clericalism the extreme Right had played into a powerful left-wing hand. The Affair soon split the Moderates. A wing led by Méline adopted the title Progressives, emphasized defence of social order, and entered into alliance with *Ralliés* and ultranationalists. But most Moderates adopted the label of Republicans of the Left and allied with the Radicals, who excluded anti-Semites and ultranationalists from their party from December 1898 onwards. Led by René Waldeck-Rousseau, a Catholic barrister known for his deep loyalty to the Republic, they formed a government of "Republican Defence" in June 1899 to liquidate the Affair. Though it was dominated by the Republican Left, Radicals were prominent in the government, and the independent socialist Alexandre Millerand also joined. Unfortunately, Socialists soon divided over the propriety of entry into a "bourgeois" government and the Second International condemned Millerand for class collaboration. Jaurès accepted that no Socialist should enter the government, but he and his followers still backed the cabinet in parliament, ensuring that the government could count on a solid majority. A military retrial in 1899 then led to the implausible verdict of guilty with extenuating circumstances, forcing the government to give Dreyfus a presidential pardon. Dreyfus was not in fact exonerated, by a civil court, until 1906, whereupon he returned to active service. The Captain had by then long been a pawn in a vast power struggle.

Antagonism between republicans and the Church stretched back for over a century, and many republicans were freemasons who viewed themselves as locked in mortal combat with the Church. Such sentiment could be heard in the counsel of Clemenceau's father: "Remember, Georges, there is only one thing worse than a bad priest – and that's a good priest."[133] A lightning rod for discontent was the Napoleonic Concordat of 1802, which stipulated that the state paid the salaries of clergymen. Yet it was also true that the Concordat gave the state significant say in the appointment of Church officials and thus some republicans were reluctant to sever Church-state ties completely.

By acting on a long-ignored law that all associations of over 20 members must have state authorization, the Waldeck-Rousseau government could strike against unauthorized associations. Groups such as the Assumptionists thus were dissolved in 1900. Thereafter Waldeck-Rousseau lost control when a bill to force all religious orders to submit to authorization by the Council of State was altered so that authorization shifted to parliament. Waldeck-Rousseau resigned, leaving the Radical Emile Combes to run the government. Combes was an arch anti-clerical: after studying to become a priest he had instead joined the freemasons. He ensured that the vast majority of the orders were refused authorization, leading to closure of some 3000 Catholic schools. When angry crowds began to protest, Combes hesitated over whether to push matters to their logical conclusion – disestablishment. Meanwhile an attempt to republicanize the Army backfired when the public learned that the minister of war was basing promotion on information gathered, often by freemasons, on the religious affiliation of officers. Discovery brought down the Combes government in 1904.

In fact the Separation bill was steered through the Chamber by Aristide Briand, a Socialist at that point in his wandering career. Passed in July 1905, legislation severed all formal ties between the state and the various Churches in France, although the latter would still have to register for authorization as "associations of religious cults." Church officials would gain pensions, and church property could be placed under the control of religious associations, provided they cooperated with the state. Unfortunately intransigent opposition from Pope Pius X made cooperation difficult and a great deal of property was lost. While emotions ran high, Combes need not have worried. After the elections of May 1906 the Radicals held 247 seats and the Socialists 74 in a Chamber of 588 deputies. Conservative, ultranationalist, and Catholic groups could muster only 175 seats. Power had shifted from the Center-Right to the Center-Left.

Passions unleashed by the Affair accelerated transition to mass politics by stimulating the organization or reorganization of a wide variety of associations ranging from the Dreyfusard "League of the Rights of Man" to the anti-Dreyfusard "League of the French *Patrie*." Simultaneously, among the main parties strides were taken in national organization. The Radicals held a first national congress in 1901, the *Ralliés* organized themselves as the *Action Libéral* in the same year, and the Socialists formed two party organizations in 1901–2, leading to unification in 1905. While divisions among the Socialists continued, a broad consensus emerged as to using democratic means to pursue power. Still, party formation remained incomplete. National organization yielded a more disciplined approach to contesting elections, but creation of party platforms remained beyond the reach of the leading parties.

Mixed Signs in Spain and Italy

Parallels between Spain and Italy were obvious. Both featured political systems designed to maintain elite control, both were racked by civil disorder, and both suffered humiliating defeats abroad. However, while Spanish leaders showed little genuine inclination to accommodate mass politics, Italy seemed to make progress. Despite calls for rejuvenation, little was accomplished after Spain lost most of her remaining empire. Conversely, an embarrassing setback for Italian imperialism was followed initially by the triumph of the Left in a constitutional crisis and then by significant social reform.

The Spanish Restoration sought to ensure stability by arranging for alternation of power exclusively between the Conservative and Liberal parties. While republicans and socialists could overcome the system by organizing mass followings in large urban centers, *cacique* control of rural Spain ensured that the regime was largely impervious to such challenges. Nevertheless, the system had a major flaw in that to maintain loyalty to the regime the Opposition minority was granted extensive powers to block legislation. The constitutional framework thus made reform difficult to enact. Meanwhile a large portion of state revenue was squandered by the military. High numbers of officers meant that too little funding went toward armaments, training, or the rank and file.

The prime example of failure came to be known simply as "the Disaster." The causes of renewed Cuban rebellion in 1895 were familiar. The natural market for Cuba's staples (sugar and tobacco) was the USA, the Spanish economy was inadequate for Cuban exports and imports, and Spain's tariff system exploited Cuba by making trade with other countries prohibitively expensive. Meanwhile mechanization and competition from the sugar-beet industry in Europe intensified competition in the Cuban sugar industry, driving many small farmers out of business. Although Cuba possessed a Spanish loyalist party, failure to offer concessions to a moderate Cuban Autonomist Party swelled the ranks of a separatist Cuban Revolutionary Party. Worse still, the inability of Spain to impose order drew American interest. Difficult terrain, guerrilla warfare, and tropical disease combined to prevent close to 200 000 troops from establishing control, despite use of concentration camps to prevent sympathizers from aiding rebels who burned the cane fields of collaborationist planters. Meanwhile revolt led by a secret society known as the Katupunan also broke out in the Philippine Islands.

By July 1897 Spanish Liberals had broken ranks with Cánovas and Conservatives who insisted that concessions could be offered only after victory. After the (unrelated) assassination of Cánovas by an anarchist in August, Sagasta returned to power and granted autonomy to Cuba, but by then it was too late. While the rebels refused to compromise and the American government pressured Spain to grant full independence, Spanish loyalists rioted, leading President McKinley to send the battleship Maine to protect American interests in Havana. Thereafter the mysterious sinking of the Maine in February 1898 so roused American opinion that McKinley's hand was forced.

From the opening American attack in the Philippines in May 1898 to the destruction of an entire squadron at Santiago de Cuba in July of the same year, the war constituted a comprehensive defeat for Spain. Cuba, Puerto Rico, Guam, and the Philippines were all ceded to the United States in a peace treaty signed in December 1898. Calls for retribution soon followed as Sagasta was forced to resign and a deputy in the *Cortes* asked "Why have these Generals not been shot?"[134] Although the lives of more than 50 000 soldiers and sailors had been lost, the army had in fact been involved in few major engagements; the war had effectively been decided when American naval mastery was established, making it impossible for the Spanish to relieve or supply their colonial armies. While the army thus felt that its honor had not been lost, civilians did not necessarily share the belief that responsibility lay solely with the politicians.

Painful recognition that Spain was not even a middle-ranking power thereafter led to an endless succession of publications calling for "regeneration"; yet little came of prescribed remedies for decline. Groups hostile to the regime received a boost from "the Disaster," but growth in republican, socialist, and anarchist ranks proved ephemeral. Republicanism remained divided between a reformist wing and radicals such as Alejandro Lerroux, a journalist who preached pillage of the elites at Barcelona. Above all a populist who played to the emotions of the people, Lerroux was revolutionary in his discourse, but intentionally vague when it came to elaborating a program. The acquisition of a mass following by Catalan separatism, fueled partly by decline in textile exports to Cuba and increased taxation to service the war debt, was perhaps of greater consequence. However, Catalan nationalism too was divided between conservatives and radicals. When he came of age in May 1902, Alfonso XIII also thought in terms of regeneration. Imagining himself as a soldier-King who represented the national will, Alfonso soon grew contemptuous of civilian politics. Attacks in the press on the abysmal conditions of the common soldier did not sit well with the Generals, and the favoritism of the King encouraged them to take an active role in politics. Thereafter the Canovine system continued its gradual disintegration, as five ineffective cabinets rose and fell between 1902 and 1905.

In Italy elections were largely vitiated by state intervention. Because large urban centers were less easily controlled, parliament possessed an Extreme Left of opposition parties (Radicals, Republicans, and Socialists), but government remained the preserve of the Right and the Left. The latter *blocs* were organized principally toward the pursuit of power and *transformismo* ensured that cabinets were usually drawn from factions of both. The resultant absence of ideological coherence or party discipline meant that short-lived governments seldom put forward meaningful reform.

The regime came under severe strain during the 1890s as revelations of the involvement of politicians in financial scandals contributed to belief that parliamentary government was inherently corrupt. After the fall of Crispi in early 1891, two subsequent prime ministers pondered withdrawal from Africa and reduction of the military as cost-cutting measures. Nevertheless, the conservative Marquis di Rudinì, a Sicilian landowner, and the liberal Giovanni Giolitti, a Piedmontese who had risen rapidly in the ranks of the state financial administration, concluded that such a course would prove too damaging for the regime's prestige. Meanwhile poverty triggered widespread disorder. In Sicily peasant leagues called *fasci* organized strikes of agricultural workers, sought to take control of local government, and demanded land redistribution. Crispi played on fears of social revolution and in December 1893 brought about the fall of Giolitti, who had refused calls for armed intervention; 50 000 troops were soon dispatched, martial law was proclaimed, and some 1000 activists were sent to penal colonies.

Had repression been confined to Sicily, perhaps the sole consequence would have been a massive emigration of Sicilians. Yet Crispi went further as a frightened parliament granted the state exceptional powers, enabling the prime minister to crack down on the opposition press, dissolve the Socialist Party, and cull some 100 000 voters from the electorate. Under such attack, members of the Extreme Left aligned with the Left in opposition to the government, but King Humberto permitted Crispi to suspend parliament for six months. By the time general elections took place in May 1895, Crispi was positioned to use state influence to secure the victory of some 350 supporters.

Crispi then sought a striking achievement to consolidate his position. While he pushed the military to expand Italian empire in Africa, he failed, however, to provide adequate supplies due to fear that parliament would reject increased appropriations. It was badgering by Crispi that led General Oreste Baratieri to advance into Ethiopia, where some 5000 Italian troops were killed and another 2000 captured at Adowa. Shortly thereafter Italian forces withdrew and peace was made with Ethiopia in 1896, although Italy retained Eritrea. Baratieri thereafter added to public discontent by blaming his soldiers for cowardice and the government for inadequate support. He was correct in so much as Adowa was essentially a political failure, and the King forced Crispi to resign.

Wasting resources was all the more irresponsible in that the economy continued to spiral downwards. In early 1898 unemployment and high prices fueled widespread demonstrations and market riots. Worse still, during an insurrection at Milan the army killed at least 80 demonstrators and wounded another 450. Meanwhile a government led by Rudinì fell back on repression as royal edicts enabled the arrest of leaders of the Extreme Left, suspended roughly 100 newspapers, and shut down opposition organizations. Parliamentary criticism then led Rudinì to request dissolution; however, the King instead appointed General Luigi Pelloux, a former minister of war, as prime minister in June 1898. For seven months Pelloux sought calm by refusing to enforce the edicts, but he then sought to gain parliamentary approval of the edicts in February 1899. When the Left blocked passage by the obstructionist tactic of filibuster, Pelloux chose to rule by decree.

In early 1900 the high court of appeal ruled that the decree laws were unconstitutional. Nevertheless, Pelloux managed to force a parliamentary vote on a guillotine law that would cut off endless speech-making. Rather than take part, the Extreme Left and Left walked out and, given the refusal of a large number of deputies to participate, Pelloux decided to hold a general election in June. Although he gained a slender government majority, it was a pyrrhic victory given that both wings of the Left scored major gains and thus Pelloux resigned. One month later the King was assassinated by an anarchist. Ironically, what seemed an escalation of crisis actually marked the beginning of stabilization as all parties condemned the murder. Thereafter it helped a great deal that the new King, Victor-Emmanuel III, understood the importance of not aligning too obviously with any one political group, especially a group that enjoyed little public favor. In the short term he watched as the new cabinet pursued repression. However, when the government's unpopularity revealed the bankruptcy of such policies, the King turned toward the Left.

Subsequent stability could be attributed partly to economic recovery as a commercial treaty negotiated with France in 1898 and low wages placed Italian exporters in a strong position to profit by increased prosperity elsewhere. Improved economic fortunes in turn provided opportunity for Giolitti to champion reform amidst relative calm. Giolitti recognized that the Extreme Left represented a significant section of public opinion and understood that growing lower-class power would have to be accommodated. In 1901 he informed parliament: "If you wish to defend our institutions, you will have to persuade these new classes that they will have more to gain from those institutions than from utopian dreams of violent change."[135]

Not all of the legislation passed in the following years should be attributed to Giolitti. Important steps had already been taken in 1898 when the state made accident insurance, paid by employers, compulsory, and also established a noncompulsory national insurance fund for health and old age. All the same, as minister of the interior from early 1901 to late 1903, and subsequently as prime minister from November 1903 onwards, Giolitti was the primary agent of change. In 1902 laws were passed to regulate child and female labor, and in the same year creation of a Supreme Council of Labour gave workers a say in the preparation of legislation. Social harmony was also pursued by the establishment of provincial bodies of conciliators to arbitrate industrial conflict. To improve public services, a law passed in 1903 enabled municipalities to take over industrial or commercial activities of a public nature.

Giolitti caught everyone by surprise when he sought to reconcile Socialists and Radicals by offering them a place in government in late 1903. Moderate Socialists were tempted; yet they feared that cooperation with bourgeois liberals would deliver the grass-roots of their party into the hands of extremists and hence declined. Meanwhile the party had made progress in the face of repression, restructuring on the basis of individual membership, acquiring a substantial body of support among agricultural workers, gaining 32 deputies in 1900, and organizing new unions. The Radicals had also gained ground; despite lacking much by way of a mass following, they had won 34 seats in 1900. Although their policies differed little from those of Giolitti, for the time being they joined the Socialists in rejecting his blandishments.

Rebuffed by the Left, Giolitti turned instead to the Right during the elections of 1904. Encouraged by Pope Leo XIII, lay Catholics had pursued social reform by forming a broad array of associations, publishing progressive journals, and participating in local government. There was convergence between social Catholicism and Giolitti's desire to prevent revolution by reform and Catholics thus were drawn back into the political system, with several gaining election. The resultant government majority was, however, unstable and Giolitti resigned rather than oversee a contentious nationalization of rail lines. Despite achieving the latter objective, the subsequent government soon fell, enabling Giolitti to return to power in February 1906.

Uncertainty in the Autocracies: Germany and Austria-Hungary

The eastern empires encountered challenges due to growing belief that they were incapable of redressing grievances or adjusting to changing needs. In Germany chancellors experienced difficulty in passing legislation as opposition groups gained increasing representation in the *Reichstag*. All too frequently parliamentary impasses could be broken only by labeling opponents as "unpatriotic." In contrast, in Austria nationalism was the source of, rather than an antidote to, parliamentary stalemate. Attempts to overcome division between Czechs and Germans failed, and in a bid to overcome obstruction the government decided to extend the franchise. Tensions were even more pronounced in Hungary, where Magyar nationalism provoked a showdown with the Imperial government.

Wilhelmine Germany presented a contrast. While little progress was made toward establishing parliamentary government, Germany entered the age of mass politics. Increased politicization resulted partly from the rise of the SPD. In the election of 1890 the SPD doubled its support; in 1912 the party gained better than one-third of the total votes cast. Hundreds of thousands of supporters could be mobilized for May Day demonstrations, and through the press, public meetings, development of local branches, and organization of recreational activities, the SPD made itself a key part of members' identity. In response, other parties made similar efforts. The Center Party coordinated numerous extra-parliamentary organizations, including the People's Association of German Catholics, which could claim a membership of roughly 850 000 in 1914. By coopting an Agrarian League the Conservative Party also broadened its base among the peasantry. Although they were perhaps slower in adapting, by 1914 even the National Liberals could claim a party membership of 300 000. Meanwhile voter turnout grew for every *Reichstag* election, so that it reached 85% of eligible voters in 1912.

By the 1890s nationalism had put down deep roots. Generic love of fatherland was widespread and Catholics and Jews could share in it, but the period also saw the foundation of leagues wherein integral nationalism was on display. To some extent, the state played the role of Frankenstein when Tirpitz fostered the Navy League, a lobby group that demanded that Germany gain "her place in the sun." While organizations such as the Colonial Society advocated overseas imperialism, the preoccupation of the Pan-German League with uniting ethnic Germans in Europe was more typical of extreme nationalism. Still, the two streams could easily merge. The Pan-Germans called for a "rallying of nationally minded citizens, without consideration of party, in the thought that the accomplished unification of the German race is only the foundation of a larger national development of the German people into a cultural and political world power."[136] For such groups, hazy notions of race determined identity, and hence they frequently targeted groups (Poles, Jews, Catholics, and Socialists) whose patriotism was allegedly suspect.

Many of the associations were in fact relatively small; while the Navy League could claim 330 000 members, the Pan-German League possessed a membership of only 28 000. Although governments sought to exploit the Leagues, they were not beholden to them. Conversely, the middle-class character of the Leagues inclined them to challenge elite rule when governments failed to live up to expectations. Hence the Army League argued that public opinion must "compel even the parties and the government to do their duty."[137]

Despite the expectation of Bismarck that his successor would combat socialism, Count von Caprivi, a distinguished army commander and former chief of the navy, distanced the government from association with any particular party and allowed the anti-Socialist laws to lapse. State regulation of the economy increased: laws governing working conditions and hours were tightened, Sunday work and child labor were prohibited, and boards were established to arbitrate industrial disputes. Caprivi thought that lowering import tariffs would also mollify workers; yet his attempt to put Germany on a "new course" was largely unsuccessful. State preference for enormous firms that controlled markets through cartels meant that domestic prices remained high, reducing the lustre of rising real wages. Kaiser William grew so annoyed by Caprivi's failure to stir working-class royalism that he swung in the opposite direction, enabling reactionaries to gain influence at court. Nor did Caprivi gain much gratitude when he secured funding for an increase of 84 000 men in the army. Proposed expansion necessitated compromise: military service would be reduced to two years, and parliament gained the right to review military expenditure every five years. William was angered by the concessions, and Caprivi had to fend off royal approval of proposals for a return to repression. By October 1894 Caprivi had had enough and chose to retire.

The next chancellor, Prince Hohenlohe, had a wealth of experience as a parliamentarian, diplomat, and governor of Alsace. He secured the support of the Conservatives and National Liberals by promising to raise tariffs when Caprivi's commercial treaties expired, but attempts to rally support through attacks on socialism produced stalemate. Proposed anti-subversion and anti-union laws were defeated in the *Reichstag* in (respectively) 1895 and 1899. William fumed: "There remains for us, therefore, only fire-hoses for normal circumstances and cartridges for the ultimate."[138] The sole card that could be played was appeal to patriotism. When a proposal for naval expansion failed in 1897, the Navy League, Colonial Union, and Pan-German League launched aggressive campaigns for increased expenditure. By 1898 Tirpitz had secured approval for raising the number of ships of the line to 19 within seven years, and in 1899 a Supplementary Act increased the number of battleships to 38.

To overcome the impasse that had emerged under the aged Hohenlohe, Count Bülow was appointed chancellor in 1899. Bülow's expertise resided primarily in flattery of the Kaiser and he owed his rapid rise to court patronage. He believed "that the parliamentary system" was "neither desirable nor even possible" in Germany and that his most important task was to preserve "the traditional position of the Crown in Prussia and the *Reich*."[139] Although he did not possess much by way of a program, he did develop a strategy based on reconciling industrial and agricultural interests so that in combination they could provide a counter to socialism. Toward this end agricultural tariffs were restored in December 1902 to their 1892 levels. Exclusion of Russian grain then sent prices soaring and contributed to the SPD gaining 25 seats in the general election of 1903. To achieve a majority thereafter Bülow needed the support of the Center Party, but he could not count on it due to a massive native revolt in German East Africa. In 1905 the Catholic leader Matthias Erzberger denounced the colonial administration for incompetence, corruption, and brutality, and the Center Party combined with the SPD to block approval of funds to cover the costs of repression. Erzberger's claims were sadly accurate; nevertheless, Bülow had little choice but to break with the Center Party. Perhaps some 150 000 Africans were killed before the revolt was quelled in 1906, and in the meantime Bülow had fallen back on tactics that suggested not much had been learned since the days of Bismarck.

Whereas the German regime precluded party leaders from entering government, in the Dual Monarchy the Emperor was willing to appoint party leaders. Responsibility for failure to develop representative government in Austria thus rested partly on politicians. Between 1887 and 1894 ministers president invoked article fourteen of the 1867 Basic Law, initially designed for legislation by decree during an emergency, no fewer than 75 times to secure laws in the face of obstruction in parliament. Count Casimir Badeni, a Polish aristocrat and governor of Galicia, did manage to enact an electoral reform that created a democratic fifth curia that added 72 members to the *Reichsrat*. Inequities remained – whereas roughly 5.5 million voters chose the deputies of the fifth curia, some 5000 landowners selected 85 representatives. All the same, the reform eroded the position of traditional, elite parties. While the Clericals dissolved and the Liberals collapsed, the Young Czechs pushed aside the Old, and the (German) Catholic Party, Christian Socials, and Social Democrats gained ground. Hoping to win Czech support, in April 1897 Badeni issued a decree that required administrators in Bohemia and Moravia to become bilingual within four years. Although most Czechs could communicate in German, the reverse did not hold, and hence the following period was marred by German riots, leading to Badeni's resignation.

Appointed in March 1898, Count Anton Thun, a German Bohemian conservative, sought reconciliation by assembling a cabinet that included German, Czech, and Polish leaders. Nevertheless, German and Czech riots in Bohemia and obstruction in parliament continued. In such circumstances Schönerer could excel; his biological racist doctrines allowed for no compromise and his Pan-German followers saw violence as a revolutionary virtue. Given public disorder and political impasse, by the summer of 1899 Francis Joseph had decided to shift his support base back to the Germans. Thun resigned in October and soon thereafter a short-lived government repealed the Badeni ordinances. In January 1900 Ernest von Koerber, a talented bureaucrat who had ascended to the position of minister of interior in the previous year, formed a new cabinet composed mostly of German civil servants. Koerber dissolved the *Reichsrat* and called on voters to choose representatives who would work to resolve economic problems. Unfortunately the response of the voters in January 1901 only hardened divisions, ensuring continued parliamentary stalemate. Although the government encouraged industrial growth by increasing expenditure on communications, Koerber could make no headway in overcoming nationalist antagonism. He resigned and was replaced by Karl von Gautsch, a former education minister, in late December 1904.

Gautsch had no great plans for reform, but his hand was forced when rumor spread that the Emperor intended to implement franchise reform in Hungary. Worker demonstrations in Austria took on massive proportions, and by early November 1905 Francis Joseph had informed Gautsch that he wanted to introduce general suffrage in both parts of the Dual Monarchy. In preparing legislation Gautsch sought to safeguard against radical change by re-defining constituency boundaries on the basis of tax contribution, which favored the wealthier national groups. Even so, Poles and Germans complained so vociferously that Gautsch resigned, eventually to be replaced by Baron Max Wladimir von Beck, departmental chief of the ministry of agriculture and a personal adviser to Francis Ferdinand. Beck further massaged Gautsch's gerrymandering so that German constituencies had an average population of 40 000, whereas their Czech and Ruthenian counterparts respectively had 55 000 and 102 000. He thereby secured passage in January 1907. Of the 516 seats in the *Reichsrat*, Germans would elect 233, Czechs 107, Poles 82, Ruthenes 33, Slovenes 24, Italians 19, Serbs and Croats 13, and Romanians five. Virtually all males above the age of 24 were now entitled to vote; whether parliament would become an effective institution was another matter.

Economic trends fostered the emergence of new forces, but brought few solutions to old problems. Trade-union membership rose from 46 606 in 1892 to 323 099 in 1905. Working in cooperation with the unions, the Social Democratic Party enjoyed rapid growth while organizing choral groups, hiking expeditions, book clubs, trips to the theater, and adult education. Meanwhile the Christian Socials also built a mass following. By 1897 election of over 20 Christian Socials to the *Reichsrat* had convinced Francis Joseph to drop his opposition to Karl Lueger becoming mayor of Vienna. Although Lueger had initially focused on the discontent of artisans and shopkeepers, his broad objective was to unite the entire middle class. Fears over working-class mobilization and Social Democracy provided opportunity and deployment of anti-Semitism and clericalism enabled Lueger to destroy the anti-clerical Liberal Party in Vienna. Under Lueger the city then took over public utilities and spent heavily on construction of schools, hospitals, parks, roads and bridges. Municipal socialism served to widen support, partly through distribution of patronage. Better yet, by toning down previously radical rhetoric, Lueger was able to reach accommodation with the upper reaches of the bourgeoisie and even the aristocratic elite. Nevertheless, there were limits to what Lueger could contribute at the national level of politics. The Christian Socials were entirely

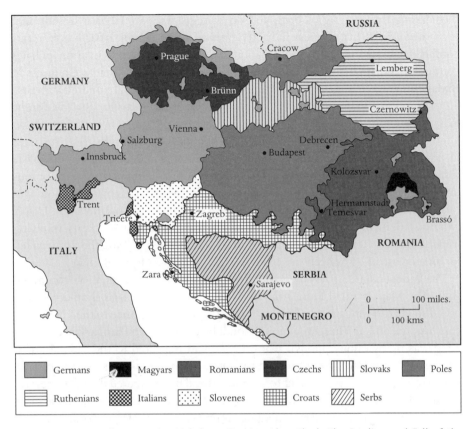

Map 9.1 Nationalities in the Habsburg Empire. Alan Sked, *The Decline and Fall of the Habsburg Empire 1815–1918* (London: Longman, 1989), p. 284.

German and other parties based on social Catholicism were completely separate. Save for his antipathy toward the Magyars, Lueger had little to say about national divisions and matters were not much better at the other end of the ideological spectrum – Czech Socialists would not accept German leadership, and the party was in fact divided into seven national sections.

In Hungary government remained in the hands of the National Liberals. Although the period saw legislation that introduced health and accident insurance, the early years of the 1890s were dominated by religious issues. A law of 1868 had mandated that in mixed marriages children would follow the confession of the parent of the same gender; however, Catholic priests had allegedly baptized children who legally were Protestant. When the state sought in 1890 to enforce compliance through fines of recalcitrant priests, the papacy called for Catholic resistance. On the legislative front, minister president Alexander Wekerle, a former finance minister who had achieved balanced budgets by increasing socially regressive indirect taxes, won the battle by securing mandatory civil marriage and secularizing the keeping of birth and death registers. Nevertheless, resentment promoted growth in a populist and anti-Semitic Catholic People's Party as religious conflict facilitated political mobilization. Meanwhile state assimilation policies continued and when Romanian, Serb, and Slovak politicians held a Congress at Budapest in 1895, the government ordered the arrest of several hundred activists.

Assumption of the leadership of the Independence Party in 1894 by Ferenc Kossuth, son of the hero of 1848, was ominous, and decennial negotiations thereafter provoked crisis. Given growth in the Hungarian economy, the Austrians in 1897 demanded revision of Imperial fiscal quotas. Hungarian nationalists responded with demands for an independent National Bank and an autonomous tariff system. A partial settlement was reached in 1898: the Hungarian quota was raised in return for parity in the Bank. All the same, disputes continued until 1902, when a settlement retained the customs union while renaming it a treaty, implying impermanence. Relations went from bad to worse when in 1902 the army called for an increase of 71 562 recruits from Austria and 53 438 from Hungary.

The Independence Party demanded concessions: the language of command should be Magyar in all Hungarian army units; the officer class should be composed solely of Hungarians who must take an oath of allegiance to the Hungarian constitution, and all Hungarian units should be quartered in Hungary. More troubling was that Count Apponyi, who in 1900 had migrated to the Liberal Party, encouraged dissident Liberals to join the Opposition in making similar demands. Filibustering brought parliament to a standstill and had triggered the fall of several governments by the summer of 1903. In the autumn Francis Joseph made clear that he would accept no infringement of his powers as national warlord. Although negotiation of a compromise position between a Liberal committee and the Imperial government seemed promising and István Tisza (son of the former Liberal leader) formed a new government, Apponyi then broke ranks in 1904. Thereafter Count Andrássy, son of the former Imperial foreign minister, and other prominent Liberals also went into opposition over Tisza's attempts to dictate new parliamentary procedures designed to end obstruction. In January 1905 Tisza decided to put the matter to the public and called elections. The results heralded crisis: while the Liberals slumped to 159 seats, the Independents (whom Apponyi had joined) rose to 166, Andrássy's Constitutional Party gained 27, and the People's Party secured 24. Thereafter the Opposition parties formed a "Coalition of National Parties."

When Andrássy announced that the Coalition would refuse to form a government unless its demands were met, the Emperor appointed General Géza Fejérváry, an Imperial loyalist, as minister president. After negotiations between Fejérváry and Coalition leaders failed, the Emperor summoned the latter and curtly informed them that there would be no concessions and that recently prepared drafts of the Budget and new Army Act must be passed. Francis Joseph was equally firm when Coalition leaders sought to organize resistance; parliament was dissolved by the army, and state officials took control over local government. Meanwhile the government announced plans for an extension of the franchise that would increase the electorate from roughly a million to 2.6 million, while suggesting that it might up the ante to universal manhood suffrage.

Few Coalition leaders wanted complete destruction of the Empire and some envisioned a future wherein a Magyarized Hungary would dominate the Dual Monarchy. Meanwhile massive worker demonstrations gave Magyar leaders cause to rethink as Socialist leaders expressed support for the government's alleged inclination toward universal male suffrage. Nor were messages of support from Croat and Serb leaders appealing. The fact that Slavic groups had formed a coalition based on Serbian support for increased Croatian autonomy and Croatian recognition of Serbian rights was a worrisome portent for Magyar hegemony. Meanwhile the Romanian Nationalist Partly shrewdly decided to push for democracy rather than autonomy. Faced by the prospect of loss of control, the Coalition capitulated. In April 1906 they agreed to accept the Emperor's conditions (in essence to abide by the terms of the Compromise), to join a government that would be led by Wekerle, and to enact the limited franchise reform bill. Given that Tisza thereafter dissolved the fractured Liberal Party, the Coalition parties then swept subsequent elections. Yet their leaders were trapped by their promises.

Revolution in Russia

The problems of the German Empire and Dual Monarchy were overshadowed by chaos in the Russian Empire. Pent-up frustration exploded when news arrived of defeats in the Russo-Japanese War, and for a time it appeared as though the regime would be entirely blown away. Last-minute concessions then divided opposition groups and the state slowly recovered control. The upshot was uncertainty: had Russia become a constitutional monarchy?

When Alexander III died in 1894, Nicholas II was ill prepared for the responsibilities suddenly thrust upon him, and Russians knew little of the young Tsar's intentions. Initially Nicholas worked hard; unfortunately, he spent most of his time on minor issues and vacillated over policy formulation. Later in his reign he became less assiduous in his official duties, retreating into a life of leisure and domestic concerns. In some regards the devotion of the Tsar to his family was admirable, but it also created opportunities for devious characters such as the monk Rasputin, an alleged "holy man" who seemed to alleviate the suffering of Nicholas's son, a hemophiliac. At the time of his coronation Nicholas sought to clarify matters in a response to liberals calling for reform: "Let it be known that I will maintain the principle of autocracy as strongly and as firmly as my late memorable father."[140] Encouraged by his advisers, Nicholas extended the "Temporary Regulations" of Alexander III to constrain the press and control education.

Aggressive Russification continued to stir discontent. In Finland, the appointment of General Nicholas Bobrikov as governor-general in 1898 began a drive toward assimilation. The Finns would no longer be exempt from military service, Russian laws would take precedence over those passed by the Finnish Diet, and Russian would become the language of the state. Passive resistance was met with abrogation of freedom of assembly in 1901, a purge of Finnish officials and judges in 1902, and suspension of the Finnish constitution in 1903. Resistance became revolutionary and Bobrikov was assassinated in 1904. Perhaps the most notorious example of state bigotry was endorsement of anti-Semitism as officials connived in increasingly large pogroms. Several weeks of obscene anti-Semitic stories in a local newspaper prepared the way for two days of attack at Kishinev (in Bessarabia) in April 1903. By the time the army intervened, some 50 were dead, roughly 400 had been wounded, 700 houses had been burned down, and 600 shops had been destroyed.

Despite his regressive political policies, Nicholas allowed finance minister Count Sergei Witte, a former businessman who had specialized in managing private railway companies, to pursue economic modernization. Witte encouraged heavy industry by providing government contracts, cheap credit, and a favorable tariff system. He also focused on extension of the rail network, doubling its mileage between 1895 and 1905, and overseeing virtual completion of the Trans-Siberian line by 1904.

Opposition to the regime had grown steadily since the famine of 1891–2, which had convinced intellectuals and professionals that the state was incapable of improving the lot of the masses. Founded in 1901, the Socialist Revolutionary Party focused on the peasantry and several members participated in uprisings triggered by land hunger and a poor harvest in 1902. Unlike earlier Populists, the Socialist Revolutionaries had imbibed part of Marx's message; they recognized that industrialization was transforming society and that peasants must join with urban workers in promoting revolution. Thus Socialist Revolutionary propaganda was spread not just in the countryside (frequently by village schoolmasters), but also in urban factories. Once again a Populist group had a terrorist wing and the "Battle Organization" gained notoriety through a wave of assassinations.

A more novel development had occurred when Iulii Martov convinced his fellow Marxists to devote less time to doctrinal issues and to involve themselves more in helping workers fight for better wages and working conditions. Marxist participation in strikes held at Saint Petersburg beginning in 1895 led to the arrest and exile of many young socialists, but contributing to strikes established ties with the proletariat.

There was great theoretical diversity among exiled Russian Marxists. It was only during a convention held in Brussels and London in 1903 that the Russian Social Democratic Party truly took shape and even at that stage a scission occurred. The key figure was Vladimir Ilich Ulianov, better known as Lenin, who blended Populism into his version of scientific socialism. Lenin did not believe that workers were capable of understanding their role in destroying capitalist society, and so he advocated that the party must be led by a vanguard of dedicated intellectuals. Nevertheless, the strategies of past revolutionary secret societies such as the Blanquists in France or the People's Will in Russia could not succeed; the fight "must be waged not by conspirators, but by a revolutionary party based on the working-class movement."[141] He also rejected belief that because Russia remained underdeveloped socialists should abet bourgeois liberals in overthrowing the semifeudal Imperial regime and then wait for capitalism to dig its own grave. Lenin argued that the vanguard could bring about bourgeois and proletarian revolution in rapid succession, partly because he (like the Populists) saw revolutionary potential in the peasantry.

Published in 1902, Lenin's *What Is to Be Done?* was distributed in Russia by under-ground agents of *Iskra* (The Spark), the principal organ of the fledgling party, and gained the author a significant following at the 1903 Convention. But not all were convinced and a group led by Martov rejected Lenin's arguments. Because Lenin won a vote to reduce the editorial board of *Iskra* from six to three, his group came to be known as the Bolsheviks (the majority party), whereas Martov and his sup-porters came to be known as the Mensheviks (the minority party). In reality, the Bolsheviks possessed no clear majority, and when Martov convinced Plekhanov, who had introduced Marxism to Russia, to withdraw his support from Lenin, the latter resigned from *Iskra*. As much personal as ideological, the split became permanent.

In addition to swelling the ranks of workers, economic growth promoted the rise of middle-class professionals who frequently were members of the *zemstva*. Moreover, the universities, which expanded from 5000 to 69 000 students between 1860 and 1914, yielded large numbers of radicals. Professional associations such as the unions of doctors and teachers rapidly formed and called for reform. In 1902 radical liberals gathered in Switzerland to form the Union of Liberation, an under-ground political organization whose principal organ *The Liberation* was published abroad by the economist and former Marxist Peter Struve. In his first editorial Struve proclaimed that the journal was not revolutionary; yet he then demanded "a wholesale transformation of Russian life, the replacement of the lawless autoc-racy by the rights of individuals and society."[142] In 1904 the Union came out in public by staging a series of banquets in which speakers demanded a constituent assembly, civil rights, and universal primary education. Such views were largely shared by moderate liberals, who in November 1904 held a national congress of *zemstva* and called for creation of a representative assembly.

It was in this combustive context that news from the Far East arrived, and in early January 1905 the fall of Port Arthur sparked a wave of protest. Mobilization and provision of the armed forces had put strain on the economy, sending prices spiraling. When on January 22, 1905 a peaceful demonstration of workers sought to present a petition to the Tsar at the Winter Palace, police and troops opened fire, killing at least 130 people. A general strike was then staged in the capital and sympathy strikes broke out throughout the Empire. In February Nicholas began to offer concessions, issuing a manifesto that called on his subjects to offer sugges-tions for improvement in the organization of the state and pursuit of the welfare of the people. As revolt spread in the countryside in March, Nicholas announced his intention to convoke a consultative assembly. Meanwhile liberals stepped up their criticisms in the *zemstva*. More troubling in June was a mutiny of sailors on the battleship *Potemkin* that seemed to indicate that the armed forces might no longer be a reliable prop for the dynasty.

During the summer Imperial fortunes continued to plummet. Professional organizations combined to create a Union of Unions in May and shortly thereafter this body joined with the Union of Liberation and various *zemstva* groups to form a Constitutional Democratic Party (the Kadets). The Kadets called for election of a Constituent Assembly, land expropriation to aid the peasantry, universal primary education, and self-determination for the nationalities of the Empire. Equally chilling was the rhetoric deployed by leading liberals such as Paul Miliukov, a former history professor and a keen advocate of parliamentary government. As chairman of the Union of Unions, Miliukov proclaimed: "All means are now legitimate against the frightful menace that is posed by the very fact of the continuing existence of the present government, and all means should be employed."[143]

Proposals for a consultative body were no longer sufficient to appease critics. Workers at St Petersburg formed a Council (Soviet) of Workers' Deputies to coordinate strikes and soon similar bodies were set up in other cities. With the state lapsing into paralysis, the Soviets, advised and to some extent directed by the Menshevik Leon Trotsky, took control of government in several cities. Meanwhile nationalist demonstrations grew to alarming levels in Finland, the Caucasus, and Poland, where the national socialist Jóseph Pilsudski organized paramilitary units that attacked Russian authorities. In Russia a railway strike in October, in combination with troubles among troops recalled from Manchuria, put the regime in jeopardy and so the Tsar issued the October Manifesto. Crafted by Witte, the Manifesto gave acceptance to freedom of speech, conscience, and association, and called for the election of a national assembly (the *Duma*). Russia would thus be transformed into a constitutional monarchy: laws would have to pass through the *Duma*, although the government would remain responsible solely to the Tsar. Many liberals found these provisions inadequate, but, as intended, the Manifesto produced splintering as moderates, who were largely satisfied by the Tsar's concessions, separated from the Kadets and formed the Octobrist Party.

From October onwards Witte ran the government. His priority was the re-establishment of order, and four key factors enabled the state to begin gradual recovery of control. Firstly, the scale of violence began to frighten elements who had initially sought limited reform, leading them to rally to the regime. Secondly, peasant rebellion remained localized. Although an All-Russian Peasant Union was organized in May and gained perhaps 200 000 members, it made no attempt to coordinate revolts. Thirdly, save for one limited exception, mutinous troops did not combine with rebellious workers or peasants. Fourthly, enough of the army remained loyal that it could be used first to crush mutinous elements and then turned against civilian groups. Between January and October the army was used some 2700 times to put down peasant uprisings.

After the proclamation of the October Manifesto workers at St Petersburg lost some of their fervour and many failed to participate when the Soviet called for a general strike in November. Witte was thus able to dissolve the association. When a parallel strike at Moscow turned into close to two weeks of rebellion in late December, the army used artillery to crush the revolt. Ironically, from that point on Witte's influence began to decline as the Tsar regained confidence in the forces of repression. Thereafter the state arrested, executed, and exiled thousands of socialists. Repression in the Baltic and Lithuania was particularly brutal, replete with exemplary executions, robbery, and rape. Latvian peasants who had terror-ized German landlords were the primary target, but atrocities included mass exe-cutions of Jews. For the fanatical, the events of the revolution confirmed allegations of conspiracy and thus Jews were also victims of a police-organized pogrom that left perhaps 800 dead at Odessa in October. Official violence was often abetted by a nationalist organization known as the Union of the Russian People. Patronized by the Tsar, the Union established a paramilitary wing, known as the "Black Hundreds," which specialized in mass counter-revolutionary demonstrations and street fighting. By the end of 1906 the Union had set up close to a thousand branches and could claim 300 000 members.

Reassertion of authority continued in early 1906 as dissident elements were purged from the military and the administration. To balance potential radicalism in the *Duma*, the Council of State was transformed into a conservative upper house composed of members appointed by the Tsar and representatives elected by the towns, Church, guilds, universities, *zemstva*, and nobility. Although laws could be initiated in either house, they would have to pass through both, and Nicholas could veto them. Most importantly, the Fundamental Laws were an assertion that consti-tution making would be the prerogative of the state, not the *Duma*. If a corner had thus been turned, the regime was by no means out of the woods and elections to the *Duma* would provide further opportunity for organization among dissidents.

Thus each of the autocracies was buffeted by the emergence of mass politics. Of the three, Germany appeared most able to cope. Astounding economic growth, a relatively generous welfare system, and a powerful state apparatus seemed to ensure that social grievances would not reach the dangerous levels apparent else-where. Nor did minority groups pose the threat to unity that they did in the other eastern empires. Unlike in Imperial Russia, where nationalism created at least as many problems as it resolved, or in the Dual Monarchy, where nationalism posed the greatest threat to Habsburg rule, in Germany nationalism presented itself as a means by which the elite could maintain mass allegiance. Yet the frequency with which governments manipulated patriotism to ostracize critics also revealed that the strongest of the autocratic states was insecure when confronted by a flourish-ing civil society.

In the west, democratization and parliamentary government seemed to provide means for accommodating mass politics. Britain had established precedents for combining gradual extension of the franchise with relative stability, and male democracy had taken root in France. Each of these states possessed powerful parliaments, and for those who possessed it, the vote was meaningful. These points did not apply to Italy and Spain, although the Italian regime appeared capable of reform.

On their own, democratization and parliamentary government were not sufficient to adjust to mass politics. Broadening freedoms of expression, assembly, and association multiplied the number of voices making demands of the state, requiring mechanisms that could mitigate conflicting interests and foster consensus as to the objectives of government. Mass parties could serve as one such mechanism, provided that leaders did not see them simply as vehicles for gaining power, and that deputies maintained discipline in pursuit of a broadly accepted agenda. Growing sentiment in many continental states that parliamentary government was inherently corrupt sprang partly from disillusionment; early optimism that democratization would cure all ills had been naive. Nevertheless, the growing challenge posed by the extreme Right also resulted from inability to combine representative government with effective government. The latter challenge was crucial to European politics and it was growing more acute.

The temptation to rally support through pursuit of triumph abroad remained in the age of "new imperialism," but there also were plenty of warnings of the dangers of failure. Defeat ruined the careers of leading statesmen in France, Spain, and Italy and it provided the catalyst for a revolution that almost toppled the Romanov dynasty. As the opportunities for overseas conquest diminished, the stakes of international rivalries were apt to rise, but the likelihood of war among the powers was not yet discernibly greater than in the era of Bismarck.

10

Transition Re-routed
From the Mid-1900s to the Great War

The inclination of postwar generations to recall the early 1900s as a "golden age" gives the impression that the Great War constituted a dramatic rupture. Similarly, academic studies of the impact of total war emphasize the transformative character of the wartime experience. Both perspectives have some validity, but adhering to them too closely masks the extent to which Europe was changing prior to August 1914.

The first part of this chapter discusses domestic politics and pays particular attention to the extent to which the decade was one of incomplete transition. To what extent were states adjusting to meet the demands of mass politics? Were the problems encountered intractable or at least perceived as such? Had internal crises reached a point where foreign war seemed to offer the best, or perhaps only, solution to domestic problems?

The second part of the chapter shifts focus to international relations. From 1905 onwards the states system experienced a series of crises wherein war among the powers seemed increasingly likely as alliances were reformulated and tightened. By 1914 two main alliance systems confronted each other – that of the Central Powers (Germany and the Dual Monarchy) and that of the Triple Entente (France, Russia and Britain). Even so, war among the powers was not inevitable and when it did arise, fighting was at least as much a product of miscalculation as intention. The role of diplomatic folly adds a tragic element to the events leading up to the war, although it does not exonerate those who took enormous risks with appalling consequences.

Domestic Politics: The End or Beginning of an Era?

While social issues and cultural battles continued to dominate domestic politics, the women's movement called for changes that would fundamentally alter every

Europe's Uncertain Path 1814–1914: State Formation and Civil Society, First Edition. R. S. Alexander.
© 2012 R. S. Alexander. Published 2012 by Blackwell Publishing Ltd.

walk of European life. It was an utterly unfamiliar world that the movement was seeking to introduce, and although transformation would prove long in the making, enough was achieved that the origins of a new era could be perceived.

Due to their militancy, British suffragettes gained the most attention among women's groups. They were, however, just one among several British pro-suffrage associations, and much spade work had been done before they arrived on the scene. Passage of the Married Women's Property Act in 1882 had undermined arguments for exclusion based on property-ownership requirements, and by 1906 (when the term suffragette was first coined) women already voted at municipal, county, and parish levels. The leading suffragettes were Emmeline Pankhurst and her daughters Christabel and Sylvia. Emmeline was following a family tradition of radicalism that stretched back for several generations; she had become a pro-suffrage activist at a young age and subsequently established contact with many leading socialists.

Initially the Pankhursts promoted suffrage through affiliation with Labour, pressuring ILP branches to commit to the cause, and founding the Women's Social and Political Union (WSPU) at Manchester in 1903. A highpoint of cooperation came in 1905 when Labour leader Keir Hardie put forward a private member's bill, crafted in combination with Emmeline Pankhurst, calling for extension of the current franchise to women. Matters took a more radical turn during the 1906 elections when Christabel Pankhurst and Annie Kenney initiated a practice of disrupting Liberal meetings. Such tactics gained publicity and the WSPU expanded after Emmeline Pankhurst moved the base of operations to London. A demonstration at Hyde Park in June 1908 drew over 250 000, but support for the WSPU increasingly came from middle- and upper-class women and ties to Labour declined.

While some Liberals favored granting women the vote, many feared the Unionists would be the main beneficiaries, and the tactics employed by the WSPU pushed the Liberal leadership into stubborn opposition. Window smashing, assault on MPs, arrest, hunger strikes, and forced feeding riveted public attention and led in 1909 to a Conciliation bill that would have granted perhaps a million women the vote on the basis of an occupation or householder qualification. Proposed by an all-party commission, the bill initially possessed extensive support, but it ran aground against the opposition of the Liberal leadership. Frustrated, Emmeline Pankhurst remained defiant: "We are here not because we are law-breakers; we are here in our efforts to become law-makers."[144]

Accelerating militancy proved divisive. Emmeline Pankhurst expelled hesitant moderates from the WSPU in October 1912 and the remaining suffragettes adopted a slogan of "Deeds not Words" that was reminiscent of anarchism. Thereafter Christabel Pankhurst orchestrated a campaign of arson, telephone line cutting, slashing pictures in public galleries, and throwing bombs. By this stage division had entered the family as Sylvia broke ranks with Emmeline and Christabel. To nullify sympathy for suffragettes, over a thousand of whom had

Figure 10.1 Suffragettes arrested after a demonstration before Buckingham Palace, 1914.
© Hulton-Deutsch Collection/Corbis.

been arrested by 1913, the government passed the Cat and Mouse Act, which enabled the release and then re-arrest of hunger strikers. Actions such as Emily Wilding Davison throwing herself in front of the King's racehorse at the Derby in June 1913 certainly demonstrated conviction. Less helpful was that they also gave credence to arguments based on the alleged irrationality of women when they entered the public sphere. While groups such as the Women's National Anti-Suffrage League revealed that division cut across gender lines, a more telling indictment was the conclusion of Millicent Fawcett, founder of the National Union of Women's Suffrage Societies (NUWSS), that the WSPU was now the primary obstacle to emancipation.

Growing rivalry with the WSPU had stimulated the NUWSS, which adopted a more democratic organizational structure and thereby gained members who, although initially attracted by WSPU, were repelled by violence. Unlike the WSPU, which drew closer to the Unionists as the party most likely to break from gender-based voting restrictions, the NUWSS entered into electoral alliances with Labour as a means to put pressure on the Liberals. By 1914 such strategies held promise. Worried that the Unionists would adopt a limited suffrage reform that would bring upper- and middle-class women into the electorate, the Liberal leadership indicated that it would back reform, provided that it included working-class women.

Negotiations with the WSPU then foundered because Christabel Pankhurst refused to cease militant activity, but the broad scenario boded well for gaining the vote in the near future.

Continental campaigns also made progress. Feminists working in cooperation with the International Woman's Suffrage Alliance founded a French Union for Women's Suffrage in 1909; they eschewed confrontational strategies, preferring to cooperate with republican politicians. At Paris, Marguerite Durand's *La fronde* had established a daily circulation of 50 000 by 1905 and when it ceased publication it was replaced by *La Française*, which gained higher circulation figures. Equally important, the mainstream press became increasingly supportive of feminist arguments. Demand for the vote also gathered pace in Germany and by 1907 anger at state regulation of prostitution had led many activists to conclude that women must have a direct say in government. Thus the relatively conservative Federation of Women's Organizations followed the lead of several smaller groups in calling for the vote. Still, they had to tread softly, given that laws banning women from political association in Prussia and Saxony were relaxed only in 1908. The women's section of the SPD was more assertive and in 1911 it inaugurated Women's Day rallies to mobilize support. The male leadership of the Party was, however, hostile, preferring to prioritize struggles to establish male democracy in state parliaments and fearful that street demonstrations played into the hands of reactionaries. As before, Socialist theoretical commitment gave way to practical considerations among male leaders, and female socialist leaders continued to block collaboration with middle-class feminist organizations.

In Finland women made themselves central to nationalism by promoting Finnish in literature and education in opposition to Russification policies. Finnish feminism was familial in character; in a speech to the Diet in 1897 the author and newspaper publisher Alexandra van Gripenberg described feminism as follows: "Femininity is motherhood in the deepest meaning of the word. That this be given its true value in that greatest of all homes, society, is the primary task of women's rights work."[145] When in October 1905 a general strike compelled the Tsar to restore the constitutional liberties of the Finnish Diet, he also agreed to demands made by the Finnish parties for universal suffrage. In subsequent elections 19 women (including Gripenberg) won seats in the Diet and in 1909 women gained equal rights in a new constitution. By the latter date the Tsarist regime had, however, recommenced Russification through the elimination of Finnish liberties. Thus the import of the vote was largely symbolic until the Russian Revolution of 1917 enabled the Finns to gain independence.

The role of Finnish women as propagators of patriotic values and the "mother tongue" was not untypical, but the outcome of their efforts was. Through cultivation of traditional attire, recipes, folklore, and song, women elsewhere provided symbols of a form of unity that could descend into integral nationalism. As Louise Otto-Peters put it, schools for girls should employ "true German women who find their highest calling in educating German maidens."[146] For their part, Czech women called for female teachers to train future generations of Czech nationalists. In a roughly analogous manner, women had an active role in the "civilizing mission" of imperialism as missionaries, wives of administrators, teachers, and nurses. Unfortunately, nationalism and imperialism both tended to posit a domestic ideal that repeated old stereotypes. Thus despite their role in propagation, women seldom gained political rights once new nations or empires were established; Finland was exceptional.

Evolution in Britain and Stalemate in France, 1906–14

The "social question" and nationalism dominated politics in Britain and France. While concern with the former triggered a major departure in British state formation, France remained slow in adopting social reform. As usual the impact of nationalism varied according to context: while Irish nationalism presented British governments with an increasingly explosive issue, in France patriotism provided unity at a crucial moment.

Over the past decades the British Liberal Party had altered as a group of scholars and journalists pushed for adoption of what they termed "new liberalism." Many academic studies had by then demonstrated that unemployment was a product of economic structure rather than "laxity"; the implication was that there was nothing morally subversive about aiding the impoverished. Moreover, perception of industrial decline had combined with Social Darwinist theories to generate a cult of national efficiency that called on the state to secure more able-bodied men for defence of the Empire. In this context, new liberalism broke from tradition by favoring state intervention to foster universal equality of opportunity and limited wealth redistribution to prevent mass under-consumption from stifling economic growth. Break from the past was not total; Liberal suspicion of the state could still be seen in support for free trade and desire not to undermine self-reliance by creation of a large and invasive bureaucracy. Nevertheless, Liberals had long considered themselves the party of the "people" and as the regime became increasingly democratic, the inclination to use the state for positive objectives grew. Conversely, some conservatives occupied ground previously occupied by liberals by attacking state intervention as an encroachment on individual liberty. Such a position was not, however, easily reconciled with support for protective tariffs, and divisions within the Conservative Party continued to bedevil Balfour.

Of the 401 Liberal MPs in 1906, 205 had not previously sat in the House and many had imbibed the ideas of "new liberalism." The cabinet led by Henry Campbell-Bannerman, who had previously served as Chief Secretary for Ireland and Secretary of the State for War, combined veterans with noteworthy younger members (David Lloyd George and Winston Churchill) and was not lacking in initiative. Control over the House of Lords, however, enabled the Unionists to block measures they deemed too radical. Thus plans to overcome obstruction had been floated by the time that Campbell-Bannerman died and was replaced by Herbert Henry Asquith in early 1908. A middle-class barrister in his early years, Asquith was known primarily for his opposition to Chamberlain's tariff proposals.

The key to the Lords' obstruction was that it blocked Liberal plans for social reform, beginning with provision in the 1908 budget for old age pensions. As chancellor of the exchequer Lloyd George, a Welsh solicitor who had gained prominence due to his opposition to the Boer War, had returned from an investigative trip to Germany in August 1908 convinced of the benefits of German insurance schemes. He informed *The Daily News*: "I never realized before on what a gigantic scale the German pension scheme is conducted. Nor had I any idea how successfully it works."[147] Nevertheless, subsequent rhetoric emphasized differences from bureaucratic German systems and expectations were that only 570 000 lower-income individuals would be covered by old-age pensions. Still, at a time of increased spending on armaments, revenues would have to be raised. Thus the budget of 1909 notably ramped up progressive taxation with a graduated income tax, surtax on the 15 000 highest income earners, increased death duties, and taxation of unearned increment on land values. The Lords took up the gauntlet by rejecting the "People's Budget" in the fall of 1909.

To secure passage, the government tried to convince the King to create a large batch of sympathetic lords. Edward VII was reluctant to do so unless the Liberals won an electoral campaign based on a plan for constitutional revision. Unfortunately elections held in January 1910 provided no obvious path for the future. The campaign was fought over the budget rather than constitutional reform, and the results yielded roughly an equal number of seats for the Liberals and Unionists. Labour held 40 seats, which left the Irish Nationalists holding the balance of power.

The Irish Nationalists prioritized reversing the Lords' previous veto of Home Rule and hence constitutional revision, social reform, and resolution of the "Irish question" all became entangled. The Nationalists backed the Liberals when Asquith introduced a Parliament Bill that would remove the Lords' power to reject or amend a money bill or block any bill if it passed three times in successive sessions of the Commons. The death of the King in early May 1910 brought a temporary ceasefire, but interparty discussions aimed at finding a compromise failed and so Asquith again resorted to dissolution. This time revision was the central campaign issue and the results were similar to those of the previous election. Asquith then formed a government that put forward the Parliament Bill in May 1911. When the Lords amended the bill beyond recognition, the government made public the willingness of George V to name a new batch of lords and enough Unionist lords submitted for the bill to pass in August.

Constitutional revision was a means to other ends. In addition to old-age pensions, labor exchanges and unemployment and health insurance schemes formed the core of Liberal social policy. Strongly advocated by the aristocrat Churchill, a former army officer, war correspondent, and writer who had broken with the Unionists over protectionism, labor exchanges provided sites where employers could advertise and workers could look for work. Organized by the Board of Trade, the exchanges began in 1910 and roughly two million had registered at them by 1914. Lloyd George was the leading champion of the two insurance schemes. Unemployment proved the less contentious; although it was limited to the trades most subject to cyclical depression, some 2 250 000 workers were covered by 1913. Health insurance required hard bargaining with friendly societies, private insurance companies, and the British Medical Association. Ultimately a state insurance scheme wherein employers, employees, and the state contributed was established in 1912; some 14 million Britons were thus provided with basic medical care.

The Liberals had thus put down the foundations of a welfare state; yet social conflict grew as economic growth, price inflation, and declining unemployment encouraged militancy among workers determined to make up for previous stagnation in wages. Union membership jumped from roughly two and a half million to over four million between 1910 and 1914 and industrial relations were rocked by strikes. Certain gains were achieved: strikes by dock workers, seamen, and railway workers forced employers to accept unionization, and striking miners convinced the government to legislate an enforceable minimum wage. The extent of strike activity pushed the state to become increasingly involved in arbitration and, on the whole, the Liberals took a conciliatory line toward labor.

An aura of crisis that hovered over the period was due largely to the "Irish problem." When the Liberals again initiated a Home Rule bill in April 1912, the issue was highly volatile. Opposition from the Conservatives was to be expected. More potentially lethal was the anger of Irish Protestants concentrated in Ulster. Whereas Edward Carson, a Dublin lawyer and leader of an Irish Unionist parliamentary group, was prepared to support a settlement that excluded Ulster, Redmond and the Nationalists wanted inclusion of all of Ireland. Shortly after passage of the Parliament Law, Ulster Unionists took steps to set up a provisional government in the event that Home Rule passed and, following a demonstration in September 1912, some 471 000 men and women pledged to resist the authority of a Home Rule Parliament. Equally ominous, in January 1913 Orange Lodges and Unionist clubs combined to form a paramilitary Ulster Volunteer force of 100 000 men. Churchill's description of such actions as a "treasonable conspiracy" and ruminations that there were "worse things than bloodshed even on an extended scale" further envenomed relations.[148] Knowledge that the Ulster Volunteers were importing arms then triggered formation of a counterforce in the south, the Irish Volunteers, who were soon infiltrated by the Irish Republican brotherhood.

The threat of violence led to strenuous efforts to find a compromise, but no solution was found. The Home Rule bill proposed in 1912 constituted only a limited devolution of powers; the Irish would continue to elect MPs to Westminster, and the British parliament would retain control over defence, foreign policy, and revenue. The bill was, however, seen by both sides as a step toward full independence.

Introduction of the bill produced tumult as the opposition screamed "rat" at Churchill. Thereafter Asquith forced Redmond to accept that Ulster would have extensive autonomy within an all-Irish parliament, that Ulster would be excluded from Home Rule for six years, and that the Ulster counties could vote on whether they wished to be part of such exclusion. Yet Redmond agreed only because he expected Carson to reject the proposal. In March 1913 Carson did so and the Lords took a similar line in June when they amended the bill to enable the nine Ulster counties to choose exclusion in perpetuity. Interparty discussions and a conference held at Buckingham Palace in July 1914 yielded no agreement and shortly thereafter Irish Volunteers exchanged gunfire with British troops at Dublin. Given developments on the continent, Asquith decided to postpone second reading of the bill. But when on September 15 he had it put on the statute book, with its operation suspended for the duration of the war, the Ulster Unionists walked out of parliament in a portent of the intransigence to come.

In France Socialists had long claimed that the Radicals used anti-clericalism as a smokescreen to hide their indifference to social reform; now that Church and State had been separated, it was time for Radicals to prove their alleged support for "the little man." Under the Clemenceau Ministry, beginning in 1906, the Radicals seemed to make a good start with bills calling for introduction of progressive income tax, a ten-hour workday maximum, and old age pensions. Yet contradictions within the Radical Party made passage difficult. Although there was a left-wing bloc of Radical-Socialists whose supporters resided mostly in urban centers, the main Radical base was in small towns and villages where peasants, artisans, and shopkeepers did not want increased taxation and feared labor militancy. Thus to secure legislation the Radicals needed Socialist support, but relations between the two parties soured due to the way Clemenceau dealt with escalating labor protest.

Worker militancy reflected the influence of revolutionary syndicalism spread by the Federation of Labor Exchanges. Begun in 1887, the Exchanges had become trade union centers that focused on social, educational, and propaganda activities. By 1905 all of the Exchanges were coordinating their activities in a Federation and by 1908 there were 157 of them. The key figure in the movement, Ferdinand Pelloutier, had concluded that anarchism should turn away from "individualistic use of the bomb";[149] the wave of terrorist assassinations in the 1890s had done little to attract the masses. Revolutionary syndicalists believed that class consciousness should instead be promoted through strikes, until all workers combined in a General Strike that would paralyse the capitalist state and commence revolution. Each strike would increase militancy and the securing of concrete goals, such as higher wages, would sustain loyalty until revolution finally occurred. The growth of revolutionary syndicalism initially produced a split in the union movement as Marxists formed a rival General Confederation of Labor (CGT); yet when the CGT absorbed the Federation of Labor Exchanges in 1902 anarchism triumphed. Hammered out at a CGT conference in 1906, the Charter of Amiens proclaimed the General Strike as the ultimate revolutionary weapon, declared that the CGT was independent of all parties, and prohibited CGT officials from running for parliament.

Although there were some 1309 strikes in 1906, it was not easy to intimidate "France's number one cop."[150] The way Clemenceau reacted to challenges had already been demonstrated by his actions as minister of the interior in a previous government. When in March 1906 a pit disaster in the north killed some 1100 miners and sparked a strike wave in neighboring coalfields, Clemenceau had sent in 20 000 troops to impose order. Thereafter the CGT called for a General Strike and Clemenceau ordered the arrest of CGT leaders on charges of conspiracy. Clemenceau was particularly determined to prevent disruption of public services; in 1907 teachers were ordered not to join the CGT and in 1909 striking postal workers were dismissed. Under such circumstances, Clemenceau could not count on Socialist support and instead had to rely on former Progressives who now styled themselves the Democratic Republican Alliance (ARD). The ARD opposed strikes and wanted fiscal restraint. Thus little had been accomplished by the fall of the government in 1909. Old age pensions were subsequently secured in 1910, but it was not until 1914 that the Senate finally approved an income tax.

The absence of left-wing cooperation was all the more significant in that socialism, guided by Jaurès, was growing. Following the unification of the main socialist groups in the SFIO (the French Section of the Worker's International) in 1905, progress was impressive. In 1906 the SFIO collected 877 000 votes and 54 seats; by 1914 the figures stood at 1 400 000 votes and 103 seats, making the Socialists the second largest party in the lower house. To secure unification, Jaurès had agreed with Guesde that the SFIO would eschew class collaboration. All the same, the SFIO sought to widen its base by appealing to peasants, artisans, and shopkeepers with election manifestos that called for proportional representation while making no mention of nationalization of industry.

By 1909 international affairs had begun to reshape domestic politics. When Joseph Caillaux, leader of the left-wing Radical bloc, ceded part of the French Congo to Germany in 1911, many French leaders concluded that war with Germany was inevitable. This line of thinking began to guide policy when ARD co-founder Raymond Poincaré became prime minister in January 1912. Previously known for his expertise in finance and education, Poincaré would make his mark in foreign relations. He was not a warmonger, but the unwillingness of Russia to back France militarily over Morocco gave him nightmares. Thus in 1912 he traveled to St Petersburg to ensure the Russians of French loyalty and he pursued the same policy in February 1913 when he became an untypically activist French President. Poincaré had also concluded that the French were insufficiently patriotic for the forthcoming challenge he expected. A possible remedy was to focus attention on the Army. There were strategic arguments for passage in 1913 of the Three Year Law, which increased service to a three-year minimum, but during debates war minister Millerand went out of his way to praise military virtues. Given that in the aftermath of the Dreyfus Affair the state had banned public military parades, the policies of Poincaré and Millerand constituted a major reversal.

Important as it was, the nationalist revival should not be exaggerated. In early 1914 Caillaux and Jaurès built an electoral alliance between Radical-Socialists and the Socialists based on plans for introduction of proportional income tax and repeal of the Three Year Law. In the elections of April–May 1914 the alliance won half of the seats in the Chamber and might have been placed to form the government had Caillaux not been engulfed in a scandal. Whether Poincaré's attempt to focus attention on international affairs had succeeded could be questioned, given public fixation on the trial of Madame Caillaux. What mattered in early August, however, was that the vast majority had decided that war could not be avoided.

What Poincaré termed the "Sacred Union" came as a surprise. Socialists had put their faith in the collaboration of workers from all countries to pressure for arbitration of international disputes. Meanwhile from 1910 onwards CGT leaders had retreated from revolutionary syndicalism, a somewhat ironic fulfilment of prophesies that concrete gains won in strikes might lead to reformism rather than revolution. In the years immediately prior to World War One the SFIO and CGT had combined to stage demonstrations against any future imperialist war. Nevertheless, when war finally arrived, both the CGT and SFIO rallied to the government. Efforts to unite with the German SPD had foundered and few French workers showed much disposition to follow strike orders. In the eyes of most workers France was not the aggressor. Thus national allegiance trumped loyalty to class, even after Jaurès had been gunned down by a nationalist fanatic on July 31, 1914. Then again, in his speech to the International Socialist meeting in Brussels on July 29 Jaurès had stated: "We [French Socialists] do not have to impose a policy of peace on our government. It is carrying one out."[151] At the funeral on August 4, leaders of the SFIO and the CGT called on workers to obey mobilization orders. There were no celebrations and foreigners commented on the silence of Paris as troops streamed toward the front. Save for ultranationalists who were far removed from power, the French were not eager for war, but they were resolved to fight.

Failure in Spain and Italy

After a period of significant social reform, Italy seemed to progress further through dramatic expansion of the franchise. Yet Italian elites were no better than their Spanish counterparts when it came to drawing the masses into their political parties, which would have required extensive grass-roots organization. Thus there was plenty of opportunity in both states for the extreme Left and Right to woo mass support.

Between 1905 and 1907 Spanish Liberals directed most of their efforts toward a futile attempt to implement increased state control over the Catholic Church.

Worse still, they took no steps to discipline army officers who in November 1905 ransacked the offices of a Catalan nationalist journal that specialized in satirizing the military. Confronted by threats of a coup, the government allowed declaration of a state of war, which enabled the military to terrorize Catalan organizations. What amounted to capitulation was highly divisive and by 1907 cabinet instability had led the King to turn to the Conservative Antonio Maura, who would launch the first of two concerted attempts to modernize the regime.

A former Liberal who had departed when the party failed to act on his calls to grant autonomy to Cuba, Maura put forward a program that in theory was designed to draw the nation into citizenship. *Cacique* control of elections would be broken, municipal government authority would be strengthened, and the educational system would be expanded. Maura's government did in fact have notable achievements: indirect taxes were reduced, old-age pensions and a voluntary state insurance system were introduced, the rights to strike and to lock out were recognized, juries were established to arbitrate industrial disputes, and steps were taken to settle landless laborers on uncultivated lands. Nevertheless, Maura's government also had a reactionary side. Bomb throwing provided a plausible pretext for banning the anarchist movement and strengthening security forces. Yet state endorsement of intensive anti-pornography campaigns and increasing censorship of the arts reflected basic mistrust of, and desire to control, the masses. Moreover, Maura's sympathy for the Church was bound to antagonize the Left: "all my life I have believed that the State commits a gross error ... when it uses its power ... to contradict religious sentiment, which in Spain is equivalent to Catholicism."[152]

It was a combination of Catalan nationalism, left-wing radicalism, and imperialism that provoked the "Tragic Week" that brought Mora down. In Spanish Morocco official desire to occupy the hinterland of coastal ports necessitated a call up of reservists in July 1909. At a time when tensions were running high in Barcelona due to recession in the textile industry and the army's crusade against Catalan nationalism, news of a military reversal convinced anarchists to call for a General Strike on 25 July. With most of the local garrison dispatched to Morocco, workers were able to take over the city. Unfortunately republican, socialist, and anarchist militants soon lost control of the rebellion and the strike descended into attacks on Catholic establishments, particularly convents that provided primary education and Catholic workers' circles. Some fifty buildings were set ablaze and four clergymen killed. Within a week the army had regained control, after fighting had claimed the lives of eight soldiers and 150 civilians. Repression was predictably harsh and, with the city placed under martial law, Francisco Ferrer, a well-known anarchist advocate of secular education, was arrested and executed by firing squad without trial, triggering international condemnation.

Maura's grip on the Conservative Party had already been loosened by concerns over his attempts to overhaul the electoral system and fear that decentralization of government would encourage Catalan nationalism. Oblivious to public opinion, Maura then reconvened the *Cortes* just two days after the execution of Ferrer and was greeted with opposition demand that he resign before "this storm produces the lightning bolt which strikes the topmost peak."[153] When the Liberals threatened to align with the Left unless Maura departed, King Alfonso concluded that the monarchy was indeed in danger and hence he accepted Maura's (insincere) resignation in October 1909. In the end, Maura's "revolution from above" had fizzled out. His bill to reform local government was lost with his departure and the electoral reform he had secured in 1907 had sufficient loopholes that the *caciques* were left untroubled.

After the departure of Maura, Alfonso turned again to the Liberals and in December 1909 appointed José Canalejas as prime minister. Unlike the haughty Maura, Canalejas possessed some of the attributes of a modern democratic politician: he was keen to cultivate a popular image with the press, and he understood the value of grass-roots campaigning. Upon gaining office, Canalejas launched a package of reform that included removal of corruption from the electoral system. Like Maura, he achieved certain limited objectives; local-government finance would be raised by urban property taxes rather than consumption taxes, maximum working hours were fixed for miners, and night work was banned for women and children. The position of Canalejas was, however, similar to that of Clemenceau in that he could not count on support from the Left due to the way he handled labor unrest. While Canalejas accepted the right to strike for economic gain, he drew a line at revolutionary syndicalism and over-reacted when challenged. When resumption of fighting in Morocco triggered agitation, in September 1911 anarchist leaders again called for a General Strike. Canalejas responded by suspending constitutional guarantees and declaring a state of war on anarchists, socialists, and republicans alike. With support from the Left, including left-wing Liberals, evaporating, Canalejas found he had to appeal to the Conservatives for backing. By the time that he was assassinated in November 1912 by an anarchist, Canalejas had been no more able to reform the Canovine system than Maura.

Subsequent leaders were unwilling to take the risk of genuine democratization. Maura's anger that the King had not brought him back into power led him to found a proto-fascist movement that featured ultra-patriotism, mass demonstrations, and attacks on parliament. Meanwhile failure to reform contributed to the rapid growth of anarchism and socialism. The war in Morocco remained a festering sore with dangerous implications in terms both of an army inclined to defy civilian authority, and growing working-class anti-militarism. That the Canovine system was crumbling could be seen in the elections of 1914; despite holding power, the Conservatives actually failed to secure a majority for government candidates!

Prospects for successful accommodation of mass politics looked better in Italy. After his return to power in 1906, Giolitti secured legislation that regulated employment conditions and service contracts, and made a rest-day compulsory each week. Given volatility in the labor movement, it was not surprising that he did not again invite the Extreme Left to join a Ministry that was confined to the Center-Left. Assessing the character of the Extreme Left was in fact no easy matter.

Promotion of agricultural strikes by revolutionary syndicalists failed when landowners formed defensive leagues and organized armed forces that assisted the police when street fighting broke out in Parma. Moderates then took over leadership of a newly formed General Confederation of Labor in 1908, and moderate Socialists expelled revolutionary syndicalists from the Party in the same year. Yet while moderate leaders would preach democratic means for the next four years, a younger generation of radicals, including the journalist Benito Mussolini, pushed for a more revolutionary approach.

After a brief period out of office, in early 1911 Giolitti returned to power by advocating franchise extension. All the main political groups could see advantage in the parliamentary act of 1911–12 that raised the electorate from three to eight million men. Conservatives and Catholics thought the addition of southern peasants would counter increasing worker militancy in the north. The Socialist Party moderate leadership was committed to democracy. Having brought about reform, Giolitti expected to harvest gratitude. Few politicians recognized that they had opened the doors for mass parties that would break the political system, and in the short term Giolitti could continue pushing for reform. Measures such as a maternity fund for women industrial workers, and for the state to take over provision of life insurance, were in line with his previous social policy.

Unfortunately Giolitti also wanted to court a growing movement that had led to the foundation of a Nationalist Party in 1910. The latter possessed many of the beliefs apparent among proto-fascist groups elsewhere. Nations were engaged in a struggle in which only the strongest could survive. Devotion to the nation must supersede liberal advocacy of individual rights and socialist belief in class struggle. By 1914 Alfrédo Rocco, a former Marxist professor of commercial law, had convinced a Nationalist Congress to adopt a corporatist program. Unions and employer associations should be placed under the direction of the state, which would supervise economic production and negotiate industrial relations. While the Nationalists thus established a domestic program, their chief concern lay in foreign policy. Designs upon Trieste remained from the days of the *Risorgimento*, and ultranationalists fantasized that North Africa could provide a first step toward rebuilding the Roman Empire.

The Libyan War of 1911–12 was primarily a bid for prestige, although it was also fostered by false accounts of economic potential. Had the campaign been more successful, or the economic rewards equal to the costs, perhaps Giolitti would have achieved his purpose of attracting nationalists to the political center. But Arab resistance proved stiffer than expected and economic gains were meager. Moreover the war simply wet the appetite of ultranationalists who spread their cult of "heroic" action by attacking critics of the war. Arrested for trying to organize a General Strike to prevent mobilization, Mussolini was nevertheless impressed by nationalist emphasis on passion and aversion for representative government. When he and his faction gained control of the Socialist Party in July 1912, the trend toward democratic socialism was reversed. As the future dictator put it, socialism was "ever more class and ever less democracy."[154]

It would take time before the mass parties were positioned to challenge the regime. Like many observers, Giolitti thought that franchise extension would favor the Right and in preparation for elections he agreed to a voting pact with the Catholic Union. As a result of the elections of February 1914 the Nationalists first entered parliament with four deputies. More striking was that Socialist representation rose from 41 to 78 seats, with 52 of the deputies pledged to work toward the destruction of parliament. To the right of the constitutional parties, the number of militant Catholics also rose, from 20 to 29. Giolitti still had a majority, but he knew that expenditure on the Libyan War was about to put the state in financial difficulty and hence he resigned.

Not long thereafter the government was confronted by a revolt that began in early June at Ancona when the police killed three anti-militarist demonstrators. Republicans and anarchists protested furiously and the Socialist Directorate called for a General Strike as insurrection spread throughout Emilia and the Romagna during the "Red Week." Government offices and churches were sacked, gun shops were plundered, and trains were burned. It took over 100 000 troops aided by nationalist vigilante groups to repress peasants, workers, and activists busily proclaiming a republic. The regime was thus far from secure when it confronted the issue of whether to participate in the Great War. The dominant sentiment was opportunism, an inclination to wait until there was clear advantage in joining one side or the other. Such thoughts were all too prevalent among the deputies of the mainstream parties.

Parliamentary Conflict and the Limits to Opposition in Germany

Mass politics presented the autocracies with growing problems, but they were not on the verge of collapse in July–August 1914. In Germany, little response was made to growing demand for change and the consequence was the difficulty governments experienced in passing legislation. Even so, there were few signs that opposition groups were willing, let alone able, to contest state authority.

Bülow had decided by the end of 1906 to build a new coalition that combined conservative parties, the National Liberals, and several left-wing liberal groups. In the election campaign of early 1907 the government press stigmatized the Center and Socialist parties as disloyal while Bülow defended the colonial administration. While the Center Party registered small gains, the SPD fell from 79 to 43 seats, enabling Bülow to ignore the Center Party while looking for parliamentary majorities. Largely due to expanding naval expenses, Bülow needed fiscal reform. Yet while the Liberals lobbied for increased land taxes, in September 1908 Conservative leaders stated their opposition to any increase in income, property, or inheritance taxes. The Center Party deftly exploited such rifts by announcing their opposition to extension of inheritance taxes until more effort had been made to tax mobile capital. They thus drove a wedge between Conservatives, who represented agrarian interests, and urban middle-class Liberals.

Bülow then compromised his standing with the Kaiser by mishandling the *Daily Telegraph* Affair in November 1908. Prior to publication in October, William had submitted an interview for reading by the government, but Bülow had failed to examine it carefully. William's comments angered the public by suggesting that thoughtful Germans did not share in mass Anglophobia, and outcry was so intense that all the parties briefly combined to demand that restrictions be placed on the Kaiser's political activities. Far from admitting his own negligence, Bülow suggested that the Kaiser would have to be more circumspect in the future. When in early 1909 Bülow proposed a tax bill designed to appease the Liberals, the Conservatives joined the Center Party in opposition, signaling an end to Bülow's coalition. A new tax on stocks and increased taxes on consumer goods were gained, but the point was that Bülow had not secured them. The chancellor asked William to dismiss him and was duly obliged.

Bülow's successor Bethmann Hollweg, a former Prussian minister of the interior and *Reich* state secretary for the interior, was determined to prevent what he saw as a "disturbing descent" into parliamentary government.[155] Nevertheless, he too was frequently stymied by the combination of conservative influence at court and resultant parliamentary difficulties. The iniquities of the Prussian three-tier electoral system for the lower chamber had again been exposed in 1908 when the Conservatives won 152 seats with 14% of the total vote. In stark contrast, the Socialists had gained only one seat with 24% of the total vote. Despite strong demand in the *Reichstag*, Conservative protest in the Prussian *Landtag* led Bethmann to abandon a reform bill in 1910. He did manage in 1911 to overcome *Junker* opposition to granting Alsace a new constitution that included a parliament with a lower house elected on the basis of universal male suffrage. The measure gained the approval of the political Left and Center; yet such advantage was soon lost due to the Saverne (Zabern in German) Affair (see below). Moreover, to appease conservatives Bethmann implemented an Expropriation Law that enabled sequestration of Polish estates for the benefit of German peasants. The latter step led the political Left and Center to vote a parliamentary censure of the government in 1913.

Given the fractured nature of the *Reichstag*, Bethmann preferred to avoid fiscal reform despite spiraling state debt and matters deteriorated further when during the 1912 elections the Socialists exploited resentment at rising food prices by attacking state tariff and taxation policies. While the SPD gained 67 new seats, for a total of 110 (making them the largest party in the *Reichstag*), all the other major parties registered losses. The party leadership had become increasingly reformist and the SPD drew heavily upon middle-class support during elections. Even so, the Socialists could not risk losing support among workers by dropping revolutionary rhetoric and entering into collaboration with bourgeois liberals. Nor, given the conservative tendencies of the court, military, and administration, was it feasible for Bethmann to consider drawing the Socialists into a coalition.

It was only the worsening international climate that enabled Bethmann to pass fiscal legislation as alarm over the "menace of Slavdom" spread by the nationalist leagues generated support for expansion of the army. Thus an increase in the Army Bill of 1912 added some 29 000 soldiers and was soon followed in 1913 by a second that added another 117 000. Better yet for the chancellor, the government gained a capital gains tax despite Conservative resistance. Perhaps the most strik- ing feature of the legislative process was the backing given to the government by the SPD despite a long-standing tradition of anti-militarism. There were several reasons for this reversal. Support for military expansion did secure direct property taxation, and Socialist leaders had to take into account the extent to which nationalism had spread among workers. Moreover, Socialist and union leaders saw their country as a bastion of progress that must be protected from reactionary Russia. All the same, after the finance bill of 1913 Bethmann did not present another major piece of legislation until the outbreak of war in 1914.

An integral prop of German autocracy was the independence of the military, a point that was amply demonstrated by the Saverne Affair. In November 1913 a Prussian lieutenant insulted the people of Alsace in a speech to new recruits gathered in the town of Saverne. The speech touched off disorders that led the garrison commander to supersede civilian authorities by declaring a state of siege and incarcerating demonstrators in the regimental barracks. Fearing the impact on the public, the civilian head of the Imperial government in Alsace sought a disciplining of the officers involved. The Kaiser then intervened and asserted that the issue was a purely military one that fell solely within his power of command. He would brook no interference, despite questions raised in the *Reichstag*. For his part, Bethmann was reluctant to act in any way that might seem to discredit the army or recognize parliamentary authority in the matter. Thus while he convinced William to send an officer to investigate the incident, he fol- lowed the Kaiser's order not to announce the investigation to parliament. Bethmann did speak to the *Reichstag* in December, but he could not address the concerns of the deputies and he would not answer questions. In consequence the deputies, save for the Conservatives, passed a vote of nonconfidence in the gov- ernment. Most deputies were, however, unwilling to force the issue. In truth, relatively few political leaders thought that parliamentary democracy along the lines of Britain or France was suitable for Germany and it was only the Socialists who called for Bethmann to resign.

The vast majority of Germans entered the war united in belief that they were fighting a war of defence. Notions of world struggle, frustration at the limits of imperial expansion, and assumption that the French were bent on revenge were so engrained that few stopped to consider whether hostility was a product of inept Imperial foreign policy. Anti-war demonstrations held as late as 25 July by the SPD soon gave way to cooperation with the government and the unions called off all labor strikes on August 2. In a speech to the *Reichstag* on August 4, William proclaimed that he no longer knew parties, he knew only Germans. In fact all along the government had given little recognition to the parties; none of them had been consulted throughout the crisis.

Nationalist Divisions in the Dual Monarchy

Problems within the Dual Monarchy were many and they were growing more acute. Neither the Austrian nor the Hungarian parliament provided a forum wherein divergent aspirations could be mediated and meanwhile the Imperial autocracy lumbered along under an aged leader determined not to yield power. Nevertheless, most opposition groups wanted reform, rather than destruction, of the Imperial regime and conflict with Magyar nationalism was, if anything, diminishing.

Upon first glance, accounts of Austrian politics make for dreary reading. The significance of franchise reform in early 1907 was limited because the *Reichsrat* remained dysfunctional. After the fall of the Beck government in 1908, ministers president gave up trying to form coalition governments that could produce parliamentary majorities. Instead they adjourned parliament and ruled by decree. Closer analysis reveals a more complex situation. Parliaments are not necessarily the best place for compromise as speakers seek above all to secure the loyalty of their followers. Given nationalist rivalries, this tendency was especially pronounced in the *Reichsrat*, where obstruction was the norm. However, the emergency decrees issued by the government while parliament was adjourned still had to be passed when parliament reconvened and often they were. In the interim, government ministers frequently entered into negotiations with party leaders and at times this process proved successful. Moreover, agreements were reached regarding national representation in the provincial diets and administrations of Moravia (in 1905), Bukovina (1910), and Galicia (1914). Such measures perhaps suggested a new departure based on recognition of group rights, and they indicated that politics had not come to a complete halt due to nationalist rivalry. All the same, it is difficult to see where the regime was any closer to compromising autocracy amidst increasing demand for genuine representative government.

Franchise extension inevitably affected the parties. Although the Social Democratic Party grew from ten deputies in 1907 to 82 in 1911, it was weakened by fissiparous nationalism as the Czech section broke away. In general elite parties such as the Young Czechs saw their representation decline while mass-based parties surged forward. Most Czech leaders hoped for constitutional reorganization along federalist lines rather than independence. Even so, when Young Czech leaders toyed with the idea of entering the government, they had to back off for fear of losing their followers to the Czech Agrarians. Conversely, extreme nationalism declined among the Austro-Germans. The German National Association went into steep decline from 1900 onwards. After fusing with the Catholic People's Party in 1907, the Christian Socials became essentially a conservative Catholic party that appealed mostly to Alpine peasants, although they retained their base in Vienna. They progressed significantly in elections, rising from 22 seats in 1907 to 76 in 1911, but the death of Lueger in 1910 commenced a period of factionalism, uncertainty, and decline. While they backed measures such as social insurance, the Christian Socials found that social or economic remedies could not overcome nationalist divisions, and their hopes that Catholicism might convert the working classes to their cause went largely unfulfilled.

In Hungary reduction in friction between the Imperial regime and Magyar nationalism exacerbated other antagonisms. The Coalition government formed in 1906 was unable to deliver promised franchise reform. Although a faction of the Independence Party favored democratization, most Magyar leaders were convinced that extensive enfranchisement would destroy Magyar domination and thus the Coalition government had broken down by April 1909. After a period of impasse, in January 1910 Francis Joseph appointed Count Károly Khuen-Héderváry, an old personal advisor to the Emperor, as minister president. Héderváry brought the Liberals back into the administration, dissolved parliament, and held elections in May. In preparation for the elections Tisza reconstituted the Liberals as the Party of Work and "worked" control of the administration to full advantage, staging an electoral "triumph" that gave his party a clear majority. As speaker of the lower house in 1912, Tisza secured a new electoral law that restricted the franchise to about 10% of the nation. More importantly, Tisza overcame obstruction by forcing revision of parliamentary procedure and thus delivered passage of the long-delayed Army bill. It did not matter that Tisza's methods sparked riots orchestrated by socialists and revolutionary syndicalists at Budapest in May 1912; the Emperor dropped his insistence on democratization and Tisza became minister president in June 1913.

Tisza was prepared to live within the confines of the Compromise of 1867. Otherwise, however, his policies did not differ greatly from those of the nationalist parties. In 1905 a Serb-Croat coalition had offered support to the Magyar nationalist parties in their struggle with the Imperial government; yet in 1907 Apponyi had introduced laws making state subsidies to private schools conditional on non-Magyar pupils learning to speak and write Magyar by the end of their fourth year. Also in 1907 the Coalition government had introduced a law that made knowledge of Magyar compulsory for all employees of the State railway system, including those who worked on the lines in Croatia. By then the Serb-Croat coalition had swept to victory in elections for the Croat Diet, and the *Sabor* declared the bill a violation of the Hungarian-Croatian Compromise of 1868. Because the Serb-Croat coalition opposed annexation of Bosnia-Herzegovina, 53 Serbs and Croats were thereafter brought to trial for treason at Zagreb in 1909. Although the defendants were subsequently exonerated, obstruction in the *Sabor* led to suspension of the constitution until Tisza brokered a compromise wherein he removed the linguistic requirements on the railways in late 1913. Relations with the Croats then simmered down; yet none of this suggested enduring reconciliation.

Relations between the Hungarian state and other national groups were no better. Members of the Romanian Nationalist Party and the Slovak People's Party were repeatedly subjected to imprisonment and in one notorious incident in 1906 a crowd of Slovaks was attacked by the *gendarmerie*, leaving fifteen people dead. Hopes that Francis Ferdinand, heir apparent to the throne, might favor autonomy turned to disillusion and, in the Romanian case, belief that the solution to oppression lay outside the Empire. Tisza did try to reach an accommodation with the Romanian National Party; however, in response to a list of demands he commented "A Magyar stomach can't digest that"[156] and thus the Party remained officially banned. Instead Tisza turned to repression: use of juries to try legal cases was reduced, libel and press laws were strengthened, and local authorities gained increased powers to restrict public meetings and associations.

Ultimately the chief threat to the Empire lay in failure to deal constructively with the "South Slav Question." On their own, the South Slavs did not in fact pose an immediate danger to the Imperial regime. The key was that the "Question" was linked to international rivalry and, in the absence of compromise, could only grow worse in the future. There were three main groups – Croats, Serbs, and Slovenes. Close to 3 000 000 lived in Hungary, more than 2 000 000 resided in Austria, and somewhat less than 2 000 000 lived in Bosnia-Herzegovina.

Although German and Magyar domination fostered it, one should not exaggerate the extent of nationalism, or unity, among South Slav groups. Most peasants, the vast majority of the population, were unaffected by nationalism. Moreover, fear that the alternative to Habsburg rule might be inclusion in a greater Germany, Russia, or Italy led most South Slav groups to promote solutions based on gaining equal rights within the Empire. An example of the latter was a proposed "trialist" reform in which areas where the South Slavs were numerically predominant would become a third Monarchy. Because for a time Francis Ferdinand advocated "trialism" he gained a reputation as someone who might reconcile South Slavs to Habsburg rule. Other groups thought of a separate Yugoslavian state which might or might not include Serbia and Montenegro. A third element consisted of Serbs looking for inclusion in a specifically Serb state. Agents from Serbia were highly active in Bosnia-Herzegovina, organizing nationalist societies.

Yet geostrategic and pragmatic considerations, in combination with traditional rivalries and religious differences, posed major obstacles to South Slav unity. Slovenes worried that the Serbs and Croats might compromise Slovene interests as part of a deal with Italy. Catholic Croats had doubts about Orthodox Serbs. While the Serb-Croat Coalition could unite against Magyarization, the two groups did not necessarily agree as to whether the ultimate objective was to secure the rights of Croatia-Slavonia within the Empire or to form some new state. Several (noncoalition) Croatian parties were hostile to the Serbs, and in Bosnia-Herzegovina the two groups competed for the support of Moslems. The Serb-Croat Coalition had no part in the formation of a new Slovene-Croat Party in 1912, and the latter soon splintered over whether to work with the Serbs.

The cautious pragmatism of most South Slav leaders frustrated a younger generation of intellectuals and students who formed the backbone of several revolutionary societies. The latter were not connected to the South Slav parties, and they were not directed by the Serbian government; yet Imperial authorities made few distinctions, seeing all such groups as subversive. By overestimating the threat posed and refusing to address grievances, officials made matters worse, a trend that accelerated with the beginning of World War One. Most South Slav leaders denounced the assassination of Francis Ferdinand, but all Slavs would soon be subjected to heightened suspicion and at times brutal repression.

Imperial Russia: One Step Back from the Brink of Revolution?

By the Fundamental Laws of 1905–6 Tsar Nicholas had formally transformed Russia into a constitutional monarchy. Both parliamentary houses had the right to initiate, amend, or veto legislation. While the Tsar could issue emergency decrees when parliament was in recess, the decrees would have to be retroactively approved by both houses. Parliament could not block a government budget, but it could refuse to increase taxes. Whether Nicholas truly understood that he had placed limits on royal power seems doubtful, however, given that he insisted that the new political system still be termed an autocracy.

Desire to appease the public had in December 1905 led prime minister Witte to formulate an electoral law that was remarkably liberal. Most adult males could vote, although voters were grouped in a curial system according to social status. Among the roughly 500 deputies of the first *Duma*, 231 were peasants, 180 were nobles, and the remainder were drawn from the middle and working classes. Whereas the Right won only 15 seats and Center-Right Octobrists 17, the Center-Left Kadets gained 179. The Socialist Revolutionaries boycotted the elections, but their peasant sympathizers won 94 seats and formed the *Trudoviki* (Labor) Party. Social Democrats ran only in the Caucasus, where mostly Mensheviks collected 18 seats. Although many peasant deputies claimed no party affiliation, sizeable groups represented various nationalities and generally allied with the Kadets. Among the western nationalities, only the Poles formed a separate bloc as 51 deputies established an Autonomist group. When it convened in May 1906 the *Duma* was soon at loggerheads with a new government led by Ivan Goremykin. Nicholas blamed Witte for past concessions and hence had replaced him in January with a man whose chief attribute, according to Witte, was his whiskers.

The Kadets appeared to be in the driver's seat, but they made critical errors of judgement. By denying the *Duma* constitution-making powers, the Tsar had put them in a fighting mood and, like the Left, the Kadets refused to join a government staffed largely by reactionaries. Moreover, their demands were high: a Constitutional Assembly, political amnesty for all who had taken part in revolt, and land redistribution to benefit the peasantry. Nicholas refused any alienation of private lands and in a speech to the *Duma* Goremykin linked the inviolability of property rights to social progress and the legitimacy of the state. Within three months Nicholas had dissolved the *Duma*. Thereafter most Kadet deputies joined with the *Trudoviki* in signing a manifesto that called on the public to refuse taxation and conscription. Few responded and the government sentenced individuals who had signed the manifesto to three months of imprisonment while banning them from participation in elections for the Second *Duma*.

This time the state applied pressure during the electoral campaign, and the result was polarization when the Second *Duma* convened in March 1907. While the Center-Left Kadets declined to 92 deputies, they were now joined by 101 *Trudoviki*, 65 Social Democrats, and 34 Socialist Revolutionaries. Right-wing representation also increased as the number of unaffiliated deputies dropped; the Center-Right Octobrists rose to 32, and the Right gained 63 seats. Partly because Goremykin had given way to the more assertive Peter Stolypin, a former provincial governor and minister of the interior, and partly because the Court was horrified by criticism of the army, there was little chance that the Second *Duma* could find any agreement with the government. Stolypin perhaps believed evidence of Social Democratic sedition manufactured by the police; at any event insistence in the *Duma* that charges be thoroughly investigated prior to lifting the parliamentary immunity of the Social Democratic deputies provided a pretext for dissolving the Second *Duma* slightly more than three months after its commencement.

Given that voters had failed to provide a pliant body, on June 3, 1907 Nicholas and Stolypin arbitrarily altered the electoral system. Representation of peasants, workers, and non-Russian nationalities was cut dramatically, enabling members of the gentry and urban rich to choose a majority of the deputies, thus ensuring a more conservative body. The following parliaments were in fact more cooperative with the government; hence the Third *Duma* served its full term from 1907 to 1912, and the Fourth lasted until revolution erupted in 1917. Nevertheless, the *Dumas* were not lap poodles for the state and government could not be based solely on right-wing support. While the Kadets fell in 1907 to 52 seats and the Left declined even more precipitously, the Octobrists gained 120 deputies. The Right rose to 145 deputies affiliated with various parties, but support from the Octobrists was required to secure legislation.

The Octobrists were committed to constitutional monarchy. For his part, Stolypin wished to demonstrate that he could gain the support of the *Duma*, and even Nicholas came to accept the necessity of compromising with a body that largely represented the elite. Thus government ministers submitted to parliamentary interpellation and deputies used budgetary discussions to investigate all sorts of matters. Parliamentary committees successfully pushed for re-establishment of justices of the peace, and health and accident insurance programs were created for factory workers. Nicholas viewed the armed forces as his private domain; nevertheless, to secure expansion he needed parliamentary approval and the *Duma* was able to insist on reform of the naval ministry.

The *Duma* had become a forum wherein grievances could be expressed, and political consciousness spread. In 1913 there were roughly a thousand small circulation newspapers in the Empire (not including Poland and Finland) and at St Petersburg the mass-production *Gazetta-kopeika* (the Kopeck Newspaper) could sell a quarter of a million copies daily. While the state still used fines, suspension, and closure to censor the press, the volume of information provided, and the diversity of opinion expressed, broadened. Given that the press could report anything said in the *Duma*, opportunities for questioning state policy were not lacking.

Alteration of the composition of the *Duma* facilitated Stolypin's attempts to stabilize the regime. The state waged war on revolutionary organizations in the summer of 1906 by introducing summary courts-martial that executed over a thousand individuals within a couple of months. As revolutionaries fled abroad, relative calm returned and peasant unrest diminished as the state halved redemption payments in 1906 and terminated them entirely in 1907. Also constructive was that Stolypin launched laws designed to create a loyal block of prosperous peasants by enabling them to gain legal ownership of communal lands. To reduce subsequent division of landholdings, household ownership was replaced by a system wherein the eldest member of the household became the sole owner of household land.

Stolypin had a vision of how to address Russia's problems; unfortunately he alienated most groups at one point or another and his legislative initiatives had mixed success. Stolypin's cultivation of a Bismarckian image did not please rivals at court, and proposals to expand the state primary education system and ease discrimination against religious minorities were blocked by reactionaries in the Church, state administration, and the court. Conservatives were angered by Stolypin's willingness to work with the Octobrists and their strength in the Council of State enabled them to block proposed abolition of the land captains. The Octobrists, in turn, were exasperated by the prime minister's high-handed methods. In one instance Stolypin found his plans to extend the *zemstva* system into the western borderlands blocked. In a maneuver of dubious legality, he prorogued parliament for three days and implemented the measure by decree, but he thereby damaged his relationship with the Octobrists. Use of courts martial in 1906 ensured that many shared Lenin's view of Stolypin as the "hangman-in-chief"[157], and thereafter the Left was dissatisfied by his refusal to expropriate land from the gentry. Equally vexatious was the state's toleration of ultranationalist organizations that copied the extreme Left's proclivity for assassination.

When Stolypin was himself assassinated in September 1911, Russia lost a firm but controversial hand on the tiller. *Duma* elections in 1912 continued the drift to the Right and the Nationalist Party, by advocating Russification, anti-Semitism, and financial support for the peasantry, gained 91 seats. Well organized and inclined to take an independent line from the government, the Nationalist Party could not, however, dominate the Right given that other conservative parties had gained 63 deputies and the Octobrists had maintained 95 seats. A new Center Party had won 31 seats and the Center-Left Kadets now numbered 53 deputies. Meanwhile the Left had been reduced to 15 Social Democrats and 10 *Trudoviki*. Thus two largely ineffectual successors of Stolypin faced a highly divided *Duma* as the Empire drifted toward World War One.

Given the collapse of the regime three years later, the question of whether Russia was on the brink of revolution in 1914 arises. Few historians now think so. Given the depth of poverty, rapid growth of civil society, and dislocating impact of economic modernization, it was hardly likely that Russia would suddenly become tranquil. Nevertheless, most indicators pointed toward increased stability.

From 1906 onwards Russian industry grew at a pace of roughly 6% annually, and to some extent workers benefited as wages rose. Better yet, in 1912 the state built on previous social legislation with a labor insurance act that covered accidents and illness among factory workers. A less favorable trend could, however, be seen in growing worker militancy in response to state harassment of unions; in the half year prior to World War One some 1 250 000 workers went on strike. In July 1914 the St Petersburg Bolsheviks instituted a strike against police repression that led to barricade building. Times had, however, changed since 1905; the strikers gained little sympathy from other social elements, and order was soon restored.

Living conditions for the peasantry also began to ameliorate after 1905 as bumper harvests and the spread of credit and consumer cooperatives contributed to increased profits and rising per capita income. The Peasant Land Bank became more active in providing finance, enabling peasants to purchase roughly 11.5 million acres of land between 1906 and 1915. Agricultural productivity was also improving; yet in the long run it was Stolypin's land reform that seemed most likely to transform rural conditions. Such vast change was bound to create problems; most peasants remained attached to communal ways and resented those who opted out. Peasants who chose to sell their lands and went to the cities in search of better prospects did not necessarily find them. Nevertheless, it would seem that by 1916 roughly 24% of households had legally withdrawn from the commune.

Political discontent remained. After Stolypin's departure, reformist elements grew disillusioned as governments ignored past concessions by arresting the leaders of legal organizations and confiscating legal publications. Divisions emerged within the Octobrist and Kadet parties over whether to continue working within the system or to seek to break it, and a new pro-business Progressist Party actually made overtures to the Bolsheviks. With the influence of the likes of the Siberian peasant "holy man" Rasputin rising at Court, exasperation with the sheer backwardness of the regime mounted among professionals and middle-class elements. Even so, the decision to go to war in 1914 reflected confidence in Russia's relative stability. As elsewhere, declaration of war brought a surge of patriotism and a period of unity that suggested the Tsar still possessed reserves of support. It was only after total war fully exposed the incompetence of the regime that the Romanov dynasty finally fell.

Toward the Abyss: Inter-State Relations, 1905–14

The First Moroccan Crisis initiated a process wherein the states system became increasingly rigid. As flexibility declined, so too did ability to reach agreement. The rigidity of the alliance systems in place in 1914 sprang largely from the provocative conduct of German diplomacy and the willingness of the Central Powers to resolve conflict through resort to force, or at least the threat of it. These points do not confirm earlier interpretations that Germany was bent on achieving hegemony on the continent, or that the Central Powers necessarily wanted a war among the powers in 1914. But the Central Powers were increasingly disposed to risk such a conflagration. Their actions provoked suspicion, and there were limits as to the number of times the Entente Powers would concede when confronted by the threat of war.

From the First Moroccan Crisis to the Annexation of Bosnia-Herzegovina, 1904–9

Led by foreign minister Delcassé, the French had laid the foundations for seizing control of Morocco through prior negotiations with the Italians, Spanish, and British. Local agitation against the regime of Sultan Abdul Aziz then provided a pretext for intervention and by January 1905 the French had begun discussions with the Sultan for establishment of what amounted to a protectorate. In response Kaiser William visited Tangier in late March and proclaimed that he would deal with the Sultan as an independent sovereign and warned the French that he intended to defend German interests. In legal terms, William was on solid ground; French actions violated an international convention that guaranteed Moroccan independence.

German motivation had little to do with concern for Morocco. Defeat by Japan had decimated Russian influence and given Germany an opportunity to assert her will. Despite the urging of some military officials, Chancellor Bülow planned only to use the threat of war to demonstrate that France was weak and an unworthy ally. By demanding an international conference, Germany could seek to sow doubt between the French and British as to how much they could rely on each other, and perhaps extract concessions. To enhance their bargaining position, the Germans took a hard-line approach, refusing French offers of bilateral negotiations. The French government was sufficiently alarmed that his ministerial colleagues forced Delcassé to resign in June 1905, but it was not only the French who reacted to German sabre rattling. For the British, the key concern was that German domination might reduce the French to the level of a satellite. When it was finally held in January 1906, the Algeciras Conference turned into a disaster for German diplomacy. France and Spain were given effective control of the Moroccan police and France gained predominant influence over a Moroccan state bank. Save for Austria-Hungary, Germany received little support on major issues as the other 11 participating states were alienated by abrasive German conduct. Indeed it was tacitly understood that Spain and France would gradually implement full protectorates over their respective spheres. For the French, the one fly in the ointment was that Russia had made clear that the Dual Alliance did not extend to war over an imperial conflict.

The Crisis had crucial impact on the states system. Although the Entente Cordiale had begun as simply an imperial spheres of influence agreement, the British foreign minister Sir Edward Grey had drawn the conclusion that Germany was bent on altering the continental balance of power. In consequence the French and British began discussion of joint military operations in the event of war with Germany. Moreover in April 1906 Britain and Russia began talks that led to an accord in August 1907. Like the Entente Cordiale, the Anglo-Russian Entente started as a series of agreements designed to reduce imperial friction. Germany's "free hand" strategy was, however, based on assumption that conflicts with France and Russia would render the British vulnerable to pressure for concessions. Such an assumption no longer held water and in certain German circles the Ententes were taken as signs of intent to encircle and destroy Germany. Grey's strategy was essentially defensive; yet he was well aware that the Ententes could evolve into alliance: "An *entente* between Russia, France and ourselves would be absolutely secure. If it is necessary to check Germany it could then be done."[158]

It would be hard to overstate the importance of a parallel collapse of cooperation between the Dual Monarchy and Russia. In June 1903 Serbian nationalist army officers had staged a coup at Belgrade by assassinating King Alexander and replacing him with a puppet monarch. Wishing to break from dependence on Austria-Hungary, the new government entered into a customs union with Bulgaria in 1905, and began placing armaments contracts with French, rather than Bohemian, manufacturers. To bring the Serbs back into line, in 1906 the Habsburg government placed an embargo on import of Serbian livestock. The Serbs then found other markets (including Germany), and meanwhile antagonism toward Austria-Hungary spread among the masses.

Conflict between the Dual Monarchy and Serbia thereafter corroded cooperation between Austria-Hungary and Russia. Trouble began when Habsburg foreign minister Baron Aehrenthal backed plans to build a line linking the Bosnian and Turkish rail networks through the Sanjak of Novibazar. When he announced the project in January 1908 Aehrenthal justified it in terms of economic development. Yet his intentions were transparently political – to maintain a wedge between Serbia and Montenegro, and to prevent the Serbs from acquiring Albanian terri- tory and a port on the Adriatic coast. Russia protested; nevertheless, neither for- eign minister Alexander Izvolsky nor Stolypin was prepared for direct confrontation. Instead the Russians increased their cooperation with the British in Macedonia by pushing for judicial reforms opposed by the Ottomans and, hence, by the Dual Monarchy (to secure Turkish support for the rail line). The prospect of further foreign intervention then contributed to the outbreak of the Young Turk Revolution in July as army officers forced the Ottoman Sultan Abdul Hamid to accept a constitution and a government that was liberal and nationalist in character.

Despite his alarm at growing Anglo-Russian cooperation, Aehrenthal was encouraged when in July Izvolsky offered a deal. In return for Austro-Hungarian support of Russia gaining the right to send warships through the Turkish Straits, Russia would back Habsburg annexation of Bosnia, Herzegovina, and the Sanjak of Novibazar. Aehrenthal was initially skeptical, but his position altered as reports arrived from Constantinople of demands that Bosnia, Herzegovina, and the Sanjak be represented in a Turkish parliament. In August the Imperial government decided to annex Bosnia and Herzegovina while withdrawing from the Sanjak. Annexation would convince the Serbs that their designs on Bosnia were futile and withdrawal from the Sanjak would indicate that the Empire had no plans for further expansion. Nevertheless, annexation violated the Treaty of Berlin and hence Aehrenthal sought to smooth the way in October by giving an informal acceptance to Izvolsky's proposal. The two powers also agreed to pursue full independence for Bulgaria.

Izvolsky's conduct thereafter was either duplicitous or foolish. When Austria- Hungary went ahead with the annexations and Bulgaria declared independence in early October, the Russian government opposed the annexations and demanded an international conference to sort matters out. Although Izvolsky claimed that he had been misled by Aehrenthal, there is little evidence to support this contention. Thus it would appear that he had either acted deviously from the onset or, more probably, underestimated the strength of Pan-Slav sentiment in Russia – while the press raged against the annexations, Izvolsky's cabinet colleagues rounded on him for failing to secure Serb interests. Thereafter Russian opposition to the annexations triggered a crisis that foreshadowed the events of 1914.

Whereas France and Britain supported Russia's demands, Germany gave unequivocal backing to their Habsburg ally's refusal to agree to a conference. At Vienna the Imperial Chief of Staff Conrad von Hötzendorf argued for immediately launching war against Serbia, a view shared by General von Moltke (the younger),

Conrad's counterpart at Berlin. Fortunately cooler heads prevailed. By the time that Austria-Hungary smoothed matters by agreeing to pay compensation to the Turks in January 1909, the outcome of the crisis was already a foregone conclusion. Russia was still too weak to risk war and neither of her western Allies was willing to fight over the issue. When in desperation Izvolsky turned to the acting German foreign minister Alfred von Kiderlen-Waechter for mediation, the response was effectively an ultimatum – Russia must immediately accept the annexation. Russia had little choice and complied. Thus in the Bosnian Crisis the two Alliance systems had come face to face. Given the military preponderance of the Central Powers, the Triple Entente had blinked.

Temporary Stabilization and the Return of Crisis, 1909–12

Thereafter resumption of bilateral discussions that cut across alliance lines suggested that the states system still retained some flexibility. Izvolsky was in 1910 replaced as foreign minister by Sergei Sazonov, who sought to steer a middle course with Germany. Meetings between the Kaiser and the Tsar in July 1909 and November 1910 contributed to an agreement that Germany would support Russia in northern Persia in return for Russian support of Germany in the construction of the Baghdad Railway. Unfortunately there was no parallel thaw in relations between Russia and Austria-Hungary as Sazonov continued Izvolsky's attempts to form an alliance among the Balkan states and Turkey to prevent further Habsburg expansion. Such efforts were unlikely to succeed, but they did encourage the Balkan states to concert their forces, a development that was as dangerous for Turkey as it was for the Dual Monarchy. In contrast, Aehrenthal became a champion of the status quo in the Balkans. Assurances that the Dual Monarchy had no territorial ambitions on the Adriatic Coast improved relations with the Italians and, better yet, the British grew skeptical of Russian claims of Habsburg expansionist designs.

If there were clouds gathering, they were to be found hovering over Anglo-German relations. By associating the naval program with patriotism, German governments had placed themselves in a position where reducing naval expenditure was apt to be unpopular. Yet expenditure steadily increased, especially after the British introduced the Dreadnought, a costly state-of-the art battleship. When a German naval bill in 1908 provided for construction of four Dreadnought-type vessels per year, the British parliament responded in 1909 by granting funds for construction of eight Dreadnoughts. Moreover, by 1910 chancellor Bethmann was confronted not just by pressure from Tirpitz, but also by demands from Moltke for increased army funding. Thus, beginning in 1910, Bethmann presented the British with proposals for mutual reduction in naval programs. Unfortunately British insistence on a fixed ratio that would ensure the superiority of the Royal Navy and

German determination that any agreement must include British neutrality in the event of a continental war rendered discussion futile.

German attempts to undermine Entente collaboration backfired once more during the Second Moroccan Crisis. In the spring of 1911 French officials decided to exploit demonstrations against foreigners by occupying Fez. In so doing they violated the Act of Algeciras, providing Germany with another opportunity to intervene. Kiderlen stirred up German public opinion with a press campaign that drew attention to economic interests, but his real objective was to force France to hand over the French Congo. The threat of war was again deployed when the gunboat *Panther* was dispatched to the Moroccan port of Agadir, and as before the British were drawn in by their desire to preserve the Entente Cordiale. British buttressing of the French led Kiderlen to seek more realistic objectives and negotiations produced an agreement in February 1912. France ceded Germany strips of the French Congo and Cameroons that connected the German Cameroons with the Congo and Ubanghi Rivers.

In France exasperation contributed to the victory of the moderate Right in elections in January 1912. A government led by Caillaux, who favored *rapprochement* with Germany, thus gave way to one led by Poincaré. Disenchantment was also pronounced in Germany, where public discussion of war became widespread. During the crisis von Moltke had written "If we slink out of this affair again with our tail between our legs … then I despair of the future of the German Reich."[159] In the bellicose atmosphere that followed the Second Moroccan Crisis a supplementary naval bill easily passed in the Reichstag. Yet the tide was running against Tirpitz as doubts about the efficacy of *Flottenpolitik* led to increasing emphasis on the army. Meanwhile France and Britain in the summer of 1912 coordinated the positioning of their battle fleets so as to prepare for the possibility of war with Germany.

The Final Destruction of the European States System, 1911–14

French expansion in North Africa encouraged the Italians to follow suit in September 1911 when the Giolitti government demanded that the Ottomans accept occupation of Tripolitania-Cyrenaica so that "order" could be restored. A conciliatory response was then ignored and war declared.

With much of the Ottoman army engaged in North Africa, the Balkan states saw an opportunity and, encouraged by Sazonov, formulated military pacts among themselves. Of all the powers, Austria-Hungary saw most clearly the danger in fighting that might end the role of the Ottoman Empire as a buffer state. Thus when in August 1912 Bulgaria issued an ultimatum demanding that Turkey grant autonomy to Macedonia, the Habsburg government appealed to the other powers

Map 10.1 The Balkan Wars, 1912–1913. John Lowe, *The Great Powers, Imperialism and the German Problem 1865–1925* (London: Routledge, 1994), p. 194.

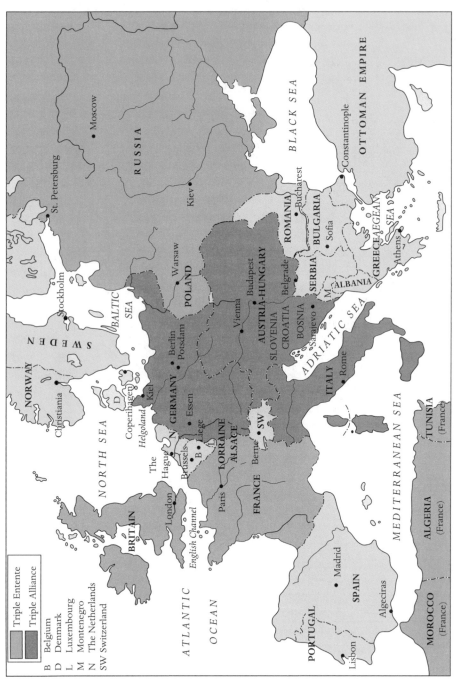

Map 10.2 Europe, 1914 (with alliances). Richard G. Hamilton and Holger H. Herwig, *Decisions for War, 1914–1917* (Cambridge: Cambridge University Press, 2004), p. xiii.

to set up a commission that would introduce reforms in Macedonia and remove any pretext for aggression. By then the Russians had realized the potential for a general conflagration, and they joined in the call for a return to Concert diplomacy. Heedless of the concerns of the powers, the Balkan states nevertheless launched their attack in October. Italy immediately benefited as the Turks made peace and withdrew from Tripolitania-Cyrenaica. The latter step did not help, however, in the Balkans as the Greek navy hindered the transfer of re-inforcements, leaving some 320 000 Ottoman troops to contend with roughly 700 000 combined Balkan forces. Bulgarian victories in Thrace put Constantinople in jeopardy; the Serbs advanced to the Adriatic, and the Greeks took Thessaly and much of Macedonia.

The sudden expiration of the "sick man" of Europe created a host of problems for the powers. Russian alarm that the Bulgarians might seize Constantinople led them to begin preparations for war. For the Dual Monarchy, Serbian and Montenegrin occupation of the Sanjak of Novibazar and Greek, Serb, and Montenegrin occupation of the region between the Albanian Mountains and the Adriatic were similarly threatening. Neither the French nor the British relished the prospect of Russia seizing Constantinople, and hence Poincaré proposed that the powers mediate between Bulgaria and Turkey to ensure that Constantinople remain within the Ottoman Empire. All the same, Poincaré advised the Russians that they must back Serbia. Meanwhile Grey warned the Germans that Britain could not remain neutral in the event of a conflict among the powers.

In a meeting in December with his military commanders the Kaiser apparently concurred with Moltke that Germany should immediately declare war on France and Russia; yet nothing came of this somewhat obscure conference. Similar eruptions were to be expected of Conrad at Vienna. Francis Joseph, backed by Count von Berchthold, foreign minister since the death of Aehrenthal in February 1912, decided instead to pursue Habsburg interests by diplomacy. While the Emperor was prepared to be flexible regarding the Sanjak, he was determined to prevent the Serbs from gaining a port on the Adriatic. He could expect backing from the Italians and Serbian massacre of Albanians increased international support for creation of an independent Albanian state. Nevertheless Sazonov talked of war in support of Serbia. While the Tsar pondered partial mobilization, Austria-Hungary strengthened its forces against both Serbia in the south and Russia in Galicia.

A revival of Concert diplomacy initiated by Britain and Germany in December then failed to re-establish stability. Although the Treaty of London of May 1913 forced the Turks to give up their European possessions, save for a narrow strip around Constantinople, it proved impossible to divide the spoils of war in a way that would satisfy the victors. Believing they had been denied their fair share, and hoping that Russia would help negotiate a more favorable settlement of claims, the Bulgarians launched an attack on Serbian and Greek forces in Macedonia in late June. Yet the Russians remained preoccupied with the threat Bulgaria posed to Constantinople and they actually facilitated Romania joining in coalition with

Greece and Serbia. Worse still for the Bulgarians, Turkey also re-entered the fray. The Second Balkan War led rapidly to defeat for the Bulgarians, who lost territory to Romania, had to accept the claims of Serbia and Greece in Macedonia, and yielded Adrianople to the Turks. All the same, little had been resolved. Bulgaria remained intent on revision and meanwhile pan-Slav ambitions had not been satiated by the near doubling in size of Serbia. During negotiation of the Treaty of Bucharest in August 1913 Serbian prime minister Nicholas Pasic spoke openly of desire to expel the Habsburgs from the Balkans.

The issue of Albanian independence continued to fester and tensions again rose when in late September Serbian troops invaded. Assured of German backing, in mid-October Austria-Hungary sent Serbia an ultimatum demanding withdrawal within eight days. Given that the powers had agreed to Albanian independence, the Serbs could only comply. Nevertheless, the imperious terms of the ultimatum caused resentment in Serbia, among the Balkan states, and in Russia, and Habsburg officials drew the conclusion that such a minor victory was far from sufficient.

Instability in the Balkans frayed the nerves of statesmen and minor conflicts took on heightened significance. When ultranationalists gained control over the Turkish government, they set about recruiting foreign advisors. While they turned to the French for westernization of the civil administration, they recruited Britons for naval reform and Germans to modernize the army. The German government, however, insisted that General Liman von Sanders take direct command of the First Turkish Army stationed at Constantinople. Not surprisingly, the Russians protested. Although they were partially appeased by the transfer of Sanders to Adrianople, Sazonov concluded that Germany was intent on establishing hegemony in the Balkans and making a satellite of Turkey. In the spring of 1914 the Russians sought to form another Balkan League aimed at the Central Powers. These maneuvers, concern over Italian ambitions, and frustration at German policies, then led the foreign ministry at Vienna to draw up a memorandum outlining the vulnerability of the Dual Monarchy. Designed to secure German sympathy, the memorandum was still under consideration by Berchtold when news came of one of the more fateful events in history.

The assassination of Archduke Francis Ferdinand and his wife Sophie at Sarajevo on June 28, 1914 was conducted by Gavrilo Princip, a South Slav nationalist associated with a Serbian revolutionary group that styled itself Union or Death, but became better known as the Black Hand. Francis Ferdinand had been targeted because he was thought to be an advocate of constitutional reforms that might reconcile South Slavs to Habsburg rule. The Serbian government did not direct the Black Hand; yet it effectively condoned its operations by allowing it to set up a terrorist training school. Moreover, the founder of the Black Hand was a leading Serbian military intelligence official. Although the extent of state complicity in the assassination remains murky to this day, Austrian advocates of using force against Serbia had been given plenty of ammunition.

To exploit international sympathy, the Dual Monarchy needed to act swiftly. In its original form, the memorandum under consideration by Berchthold pointed toward a diplomatic offensive; after the assassinations Berchthold added a postscript that implied that diplomacy was insufficient. He also drafted a personal letter from Francis Joseph to the Kaiser in which the assassinations were attributed to Russian and pan-Slav desire to destroy the Empire. Serbia must be isolated through creation of a Balkan League favorable to the Central Powers and such an objective could be achieved only by eliminating Serbian power. Taken in combination, the memorandum and the letter thus suggested a combination of diplomacy and force, without specifying what the latter might entail. The Kaiser's response on July 5 was the notorious "blank check." William did not even consult with his leading officials before replying that the Emperor could count on Germany's full support. He did not, however, think that the Russians were in a position to intervene militarily.

Unconditional German support enabled the Habsburg government to act somewhat more decisively. Almost all the ministers assembled at a conference on July 7 agreed with Berchthold that diplomatic measures would produce no change in Serbian conduct. Voicing Magyar opposition to the addition of more Slavs to the Empire, Tisza withheld his approval until the ministerial council agreed that there would be no substantial annexation of Serbian territory. It was not until July 19 that the council completed an ultimatum designed to provoke war – within forty-eight hours of reception the Serbian government must agree to suppress all propaganda and revolutionary activity hostile to the Dual Monarchy and accept the collaboration of Austro-Hungarian officials in pursuit of these objectives. Given the extent to which the latter demand infringed on Serbian independence, Imperial officials could reasonably expect the Serbs would reject the ultimatum. Thereafter the Imperial government decided to delay delivery of the ultimatum until Poincaré had departed from a visit to Russia and therefore would not be on the scene to fortify Russian resolve. Thus the ultimatum was not delivered until the evening of July 23, long after the initial impact of the assassinations had dissipated.

In fact the Russians had broken the Austro-Hungarian diplomatic code and knew the main points of the ultimatum by the time the French arrived on July 20. By July 21 Sazonov had already warned the German and Habsburg ambassadors against military measures and Poincaré had informed the Dual Monarchy that Russia possessed a loyal ally in France. Despite these warnings, Austria-Hungary went ahead with the ultimatum and the militarization of diplomacy began when Sazonov directed the chief of the Russian army general staff to prepare for partial mobilization. In theory, the latter entailed mobilization of the military districts opposite the Dual Monarchy, but not those opposite Germany, and was thus designed to avoid German entry in the event of conflict. On July 24 the Russians decided in a ministerial council that any concessions to the Central Powers would simply encourage more unreasonable demands. Austria-Hungary must extend the time limit to their ultimatum and the Serbs should respond in a conciliatory manner that did not compromise their independence. Further warnings to the Imperial and German ambassadors were blunt; even so, Russian suggestions that suppression of revolutionary groups in Serbia be supervised by an international body were construed by the Germans as a sign that Russia did not intend intervention.

The Serbian response to the ultimatum was tactful enough to stir international sympathy; yet it rejected crucial demands. The Serb government would suppress anti-Habsburg propaganda and organizations, provided the Imperial government supplied evidence of guilt. It would also open an investigation into the assassinations, although it would not accept the participation of Austro-Hungarian officials. Should the Dual Monarchy not be satisfied, Serbia was ready to accept mediation by an international body. The Imperial government was, however, bent on military action and hence the reply was insufficient to prevent war. Within three hours of reception of the reply, on July 25 Francis Joseph ordered mobilization, but solely against Serbia.

Despite German advice, the Imperial government continued to proceed at a leisurely pace. In discussions with Berchthold on July 26 Conrad revealed that completion of mobilization would require two weeks and that war should not be declared until that point. Moreover, prior to declaration of war Austria-Hungary should determine whether Russia intended to intervene. Should Russia intend to do so, Austro-Hungarian forces must be concentrated against her; otherwise they could be focused on Serbia. Conrad had a point in that in the event of war with Russia German forces would concentrate on attacking France and could offer relatively little aid to Austria-Hungary. Given German requests for swift action, Berchthold nevertheless opted for declaration of war on Serbia on July 28.

Just as the Habsburg government finally precipitated matters, the Germans had second thoughts. The Kaiser thought the Serbian reply had given Austria-Hungary most of what it wanted and that remaining points of dispute could be negotiated. Austria-Hungary would require a pledge and, toward that end, Imperial troops should occupy Belgrade and remain there until Serbian promises had been fulfilled. When on July 29 the British proposed mediation with a similar pledge plan, the Germans were encouraged, although Grey's warning that Britain would not stand aside should the conflict spread finally raised alarm bells in Berlin. Bethmann repeatedly advised the Habsburg government to clarify that it had no desire for territorial acquisition and to enter into negotiations at least with Russia, if not with Serbia. Sadly, such advice fell on deaf ears at Vienna, where the Emperor had concluded that international mediation would inevitably favor Serbia.

Whether these last-minute attempts to stem the tide had a chance of success is doubtful. Moreover, given the chaos that reigned in German high circles where decisions were made, it is difficult to assess the sincerity of Germany's response to British peace initiatives. When Imperial forces began bombarding Belgrade on July 28, the Russians ordered partial mobilization. The inadequacies of the transport system meant that Russian mobilization was slow and hence orders needed to be given as soon as possible. Worse still, Russian disorganization was such that partial mobilization was effectively impossible. Although General Yankushevich, chief of the general staff, knew of the latter problem, it was not until July 30 that he explained it to Sazonov. Thereafter Sazonov had to inform Nicholas that he had only two alternatives – full mobilization or none. Determination to retain great power status counted as much for Nicholas as it did for Francis Joseph and the Tsar approved full mobilization on July 30.

Among the falling dominoes, the Tsar's decision was perhaps the crucial one in that it ensured there could be no localization of the conflict. Russian full mobilization put Germany under threat, and the two-front war strategy known as the Schlieffen Plan ensured that German conflict with Russia necessarily entailed war with France and violation of Belgian neutrality. Attack would have to be launched rapidly so as to exploit the slowness of Russian mobilization, leaving little opportunity for German diplomats to find some other solution. And in a development that paralleled events at St Petersburg, the Kaiser was surprised to learn that an attempt at partial mobilization aimed solely at Russia would throw the entire mobilization procedure into confusion. Thus both the Kaiser and Tsar found their hands tied by military planning.

The French played their cards cautiously. During his visit to Russia Poincaré had assured Sazonov and the Tsar that France would honor the Dual Alliance, but he had not offered unconditional support. After Poincaré's departure, chaotic communications prevented French warnings against mobilization from arriving in a time to affect the Tsar's decision. In truth, Poincaré had little room for maneuver: he could not abandon Sazonov for fear of advancing German interests at the Russian court, and he could not allow Russia to be defeated. Hence Poincaré's priority was to maintain unity domestically and with France's allies. Toward these ends, he sought to avoid giving any impression of aggression. Although they began partial mobilization on July 30, the French also announced that all troops would withdraw to 10 kilometers away from the German border so as to prevent any sort of incident that might spark fighting. Meanwhile Poincaré continued to assure the Russians of French support. No such guarantees were offered by the British; nevertheless, on July 26 the government ordered the navy to its battle station at Scapa Flow (off the northeastern tip of Scotland).

One day after the Tsar ordered full mobilization the German government issued an ultimatum demanding Russia suspend all military measures against Austria-Hungary within 12 hours, and a second demanding that within 18 hours the French declare whether they would remain neutral in the event of a Russo-German war. Not having received a satisfactory reply from either, on August 1 Germany ordered full mobilization and declared war on Russia. On the following day Germany sent Belgium an ultimatum demanding entry of German troops to "prevent" an alleged French invasion that would establish a launching base for attacks on Germany. On August 3 Germany declared war on France. By the end of August 4 German invasion of Belgium had brought Britain into the war. The Concert System born of the Napoleonic Wars finally died as the great powers set about destroying each other.

The Causes of World War One

Because the Great War was so consequential, there is a vast volume of writing on its origins. Much of the writing has been highly polemical, in part due to the imposition of the war guilt clause upon Germany in the Treaty of Versailles. Although this is not the place for a detailed account of a highly complex and ongoing debate, we can at least discuss some of the principal causes by way of concluding the above narrative.

Assessing the role of nationalism is highly complex because it varied dramatically in character. Nationalist movements that sought territorial expansion differed profoundly from those that sought to defend a country from aggression. Images of rejoicing crowds of men throwing their hats in the air at news of the declarations of war can be misleading; most Europeans were shocked and alarmed. Those who thought that war would prove morally cathartic were a distinct minority. Beneath the bravado, millions rallied in support of what they considered a war to defend the nation. Similarly, fascination with the roots of interwar fascism should not mislead us as to the influence of nationalist organizations on policy formulation prior to World War One. Leaders of the ultranationalist leagues in Germany, France, and Italy were not part of the governments of their respective countries, and they played no direct role in decision-making.

None of this demonstrates that nationalism was not a factor. Nationalism made the Eastern Question more difficult to manage by creating Balkan states that paid little heed to the international implications of their actions, and by weakening an Ottoman regime that had played the role of buffer state. Although their response to the ultimatum of Austria-Hungary was pragmatically "diplomatic," the Serbs were consistently bellicose. Moreover, nationalism could influence statesmen in both a positive or negative sense: Giolitti wished to attract nationalists, whereas Francis Joseph wanted to destroy them. Finally, we can also note that nationalism was nothing new in 1914. Was nationalism any greater after the Sarajevo assassinations than it had been during, say, the Moroccan or Bosnian Crises? If not, how then do we explain why war occurred in August 1914 rather than earlier?

Citing the existence of alliance systems as a cause of war is also unhelpful unless the proposition is carefully qualified. The Italians were formally aligned with Germany and Austria-Hungary; yet they declared their neutrality on August 3. In truth the key variable was strategic calculation that entry into the war was less dangerous than non-entry. In prior crises one or more of the powers had concluded that war was not justified by the issues involved and hence concessions had been made. Alliances could be put to the purpose of revising the status quo, but they also could be used to restrain allies to maintain peace. The Concert of Europe had been based on the latter premise until the Crimean War, and Bismarck had sought to revive alliance as a means of restraint after having achieved his objective of Prussian-dominated German unification.

Thus much rested on the character of alliances and here we can note two critical shifts that undermined the states system prior to 1914. Especially in the aftermath of the Russo-Japanese War, the Central Powers increasingly used their alliance for the purpose of confrontation. In the short term the threat of war succeeded in extracting limited concessions from the French over Morocco and from the Serbs concerning Bosnia-Herzegovina and Albania. These gains came, however, at a heavy price as they drove the Entente Powers into closer alliance, making the states system increasingly polarized and heightening the possibility that a local conflict might turn into a general conflagration. The arms race in which all the powers engaged was in essence a complementary development. It did not inevitably lead to war, but it did increase tension and bred mistrust, making resort to force all the more dangerous.

The old contention that the war resulted directly from German plans to achieve mastery over the continent is unconvincing. Almost to the very end, the Kaiser hoped that the July crisis would lead to a diplomatic victory and thereby rupture the Entente. All the same, it certainly was the case that leading German political and military officials feared that Russian military and industrial expansion, funded partly by French loans, was altering an imbalance of power that long had favored Germany on the continent. In so much as the Entente alliances were aimed at Germany, they were largely a product of German aggression; nevertheless fear of encirclement was genuine and it strengthened arguments in favor of a preventive war.

Alarm bordering on paranoia stalked the court at Vienna. On their own, neither Serbian aggression nor South-Slav movements within the Empire posed a dire threat to the Dual Monarchy; the key was perception that Russia was abetting Pan-Slavism in a bid to destroy Habsburg rule. Given that French intervention on behalf of Piedmont-Sardinia had driven the Austrians out of Italy, and that war with Prussia had excluded the Habsburgs from Germany, one can understand why a dangerous combination of fatalism and defiance entered into Imperial decision-making. By fracturing the Austro-Russian Entente and provoking the Bosnian Crisis, Russia exacerbated such fears; subsequently, ill-conceived Russian encouragement of the Balkan Leagues made matters worse.

The decision to strengthen the Dual Monarchy's position in the Balkans by force rather than mediation was nevertheless reckless in the extreme. Refusal to negotiate had succeeded when Austria-Hungary annexed Bosnia-Herzegovina, but the Emperor well knew that circumstances had changed since 1908. As Francis Joseph noted, Russia would not be able to "swallow" the ultimatum sent to Serbia, and there was every reason to believe that France would not jeopardize her alliance with Russia. In back of the Dual Monarchy's gamble was, of course, Germany's "blank check." While the latter did not necessarily indicate desire for war among the powers, it did demonstrate willingness to take such a risk and was based on

THE BOILING POINT.

Figure 10.2   The boiling point. © Bettmann/Corbis.

misconception of how far the Entente Powers could be pushed. The Kaiser had long been prone to rash decisions, and his response to Serbia's reply to the Habsburg ultimatum suggests strongly that he had not fully grasped the consequences of his actions. Sadly, by then it was too late as military considerations closed off diplomatic options.

Culmination?

Was the Great War the culmination of the long nineteenth century? It was in the sense that Europe was radically altered by the destruction that began in August 1914. The war was not, however, a logical or inevitable outcome of the many conflicts that characterized European domestic politics. It was a product of corrosion of the states system and was not entered into as a solution for otherwise intractable domestic problems.

Because the Eastern Empires collapsed during World War One, it is tempting to assume that they must have been vulnerable prior to 1914 and that the war simply accelerated the final outcome. The essential problem with such an assumption is that it underestimates the enormous burden that wartime sacrifice placed on the loyalty of the subjects of the three monarchs. Europe was in transition and the challenges of mass politics would not have disappeared, or even diminished, had the war not occurred. Even so, we simply cannot say what would have happened had the Great War not re-routed the course of European politics.

We can, however, identify unresolved conflicts. Germany remained an autocracy. Governments did not rule on the basis of a parliamentary majority and, given growth in the ranks of the SPD, the prospects for such an evolution were diminishing. Moreover, there was little likelihood that conservative forces, from the Kaiser downwards, would willingly accept parliamentary government and an end to elite domination. Nor would the military readily bow to the sovereignty of a representative institution. To overcome parliamentary impasse governments repeatedly appealed to nationalism. The stratagem was dangerous in foreign relations, and it encouraged ultranationalists to become increasingly critical when the state failed to live up to the bellicose image projected by the Kaiser. All the same, even in combination these points do not demonstrate that the Empire was in great danger in 1914. The SPD was willing to take a gradualist approach, few deputies of the Left or union leaders wanted direct confrontation with the state, and the majority of the electorate probably did not want a showdown over parliamentary government. State fiscal problems were not yet intractable, and social policies were largely a source of satisfaction. If there were few signs that the regime was capable of accommodating the increasing demands of civil society, neither were there many indications that opposition forces were sufficient, or even willing, to risk a direct assault on the regime.

The scenario of failure to adjust was more pronounced in the Dual Monarchy. Despite a broad franchise, there was no representative government in Austria because nationalist rivalry rendered the *Reichsrat* dysfunctional, allowing "neutral" governments of administrators to rule largely in the interests of the Germans. Use of emergency decrees, even if politicians subsequently agreed to pass some of them as legislation, was at best a temporary makeshift; it did not secure government by elected representatives. Whereas in Hungary the electoral system secured the domination of elite Magyar interests, excluded groups were becoming increasingly organized. Civil society remained relatively underdeveloped in Hungary, but growth in the labor movement and the emergence of peasant parties demanding land redistribution were threatening portents. State "Magyarization" policies could not rectify social inequities, and they triggered growing South Slav movements throughout the Dual Monarchy.

That there were many problems did not necessarily indicate that the regime was in terminal decline, that it was incapable of reform, or that opposition groups were poised to destroy it. Socialism and the labor movement were weakened by the same nationalist movements that challenged governments. Given the predatory instincts of neighboring states, most Czech, Polish, Magyar, Croat, Slovenian, and Serb leaders surmised that their best option lay in increased autonomy within an Empire capable of defending itself. Hence they proposed reform along federalist lines. Revolutionary organizations bent on complete independence, mostly among Serbs and Romanians, were dangerous only because of the sympathy they elicited outside the Empire. Although the record of the Imperial regime in coping with mass politics was not good, the Compromise of 1867 had set a precedent for dramatic reconstitution, and the aged Emperor had a long history of seeking to adjust to changing circumstance. Whether a Habsburg monarch could yield on the fundamental issue of autocratic government seems questionable; yet it is evident that the regime had not exhausted its resources by 1914.

Imperial Russia was, for the moment, edging toward stability. Most workers lived in deplorable conditions and rural poverty was so entrenched that it could not possibly be overcome for decades to come, but conditions were improving and these problems were not new. What had changed was that creation of a constitutional regime perhaps offered an alternative to autocratic imposition of "order." The emergence of a relatively free press was a potentially positive development, and key figures such as the Kadet leader Struve had come to the conclusion that revolution was a poor choice when reform was possible. Stability required, however, that the *Duma* could provide more than just a forum for dissent; parliament had to be a place where grievances could be redressed. Whether Tsar Nicholas could truly grasp this point seems unlikely.

In the west accommodation of mass politics progressed to varying degrees according to where one looks. Britain and France both possessed flourishing civil societies. Britain was not fully democratic even where adult males were concerned, but was moving in that direction. Better yet, there was cause for optimism concerning women's suffrage, and the state was increasingly active in promoting social harmony through provision of, admittedly limited, social welfare. This is not, of course, to suggest that the British did not face serious problems. Labor militancy required an increasingly nuanced approach to industrial relations, and Britain faced a potential civil war in Ireland. In some regards the prewar situation resembled that of the 1830s with widespread expression of discontent, political polarization, and fragmentation within the Liberal and Unionist parties. At an ideological level, "new liberalism" constituted a remarkable progression; yet whether it was sufficient to enable the Liberal Party to adapt to growing demand that working men represent themselves in parliament was another matter. All the same, the foundation of the regime, parliamentary government, was not under serious threat.

France presented a different scenario. Preoccupation with securing the Third Republic meant that finding a balance between representative and effective government remained a problem. Hence the Third Republic was relatively slow to enact social or gender legislation as politics lapsed into a stalemate that would become dangerously pronounced in the interwar years. Nevertheless, the regime had emerged from the challenges of the Boulangist Movement, the Panama Scandal, and the Dreyfus Affair stronger and more resilient. Royalism was in steep decline and it was increasingly unlikely that either the Army or the Catholic Church would provide the basis for a successful attack on republicanism. Better yet, mainstream French political parties had followed the examples of the British Tories and Liberals in two crucial regards. Firstly, they sought to gain power by democratic means; in this regard the emergence of democratic socialism was a major step forwards. Secondly, they set about organizing mass support in earnest, and parties such as the Radicals and the Socialists advanced significantly in grass-roots networking and mobilization. The importance of this point becomes clear if we turn our attention to the two other west European states covered closely in this volume.

Italy and Spain were becoming increasingly volatile. Given postwar developments, it is not surprising that Giolitti was initially scorned by Italian writers who charged that his opportunism had destroyed idealism and prepared the ground for fascism. Certainly his attempt to woo nationalists was ill-judged and he well knew that the Italian assault on the Ottoman Empire might produce a dangerous chain reaction in the states system. In these regards, Giolitti made the same mistake as the Spanish leaders Maura and Canalejas. Spain and Italy could pursue prosperity that would provide a stable environment for change to unfold, or they could pursue imperial glory. They could not do both. Giolitti had not made much progress in reforming the tax system or in reducing glaring disparities between the north and south. Nor was he overly scrupulous about how he pursued power, although it would be difficult to argue that he differed greatly from his predecessors, including former leaders of the *Risorgimento*, in his manipulation of the political system.

Subsequent analysts have taken a more balanced view of Giolitti, recognizing his positive contributions as well as his flaws. Such a perspective is all the more convincing if one considers Italy in combination with Spain. In both states elitist systems were failing to adapt to mass politics. Unlike Spanish leaders, Giolitti did initiate extensive social reform and his pragmatic liberalism also fostered dramatic expansion of the franchise. He thus was on the right track in two regards, but a third essential step remained to be taken. The problem thereafter lay in the inability of the leaders (including Giolitti) of the political Left and Right to adopt modes of behavior, organization, and programs that could draw the masses into the political mainstream. As in Spain, the political elite left such strategies to the parties of the extremes and the consequences would become sadly apparent in the interwar years.

Conclusion

The principal political project of the nineteenth century was to design and implement systems that could cope with emergent mass society. Although the full character of mass society was not apparent until the later decades of the century, its broad outlines were already discernible in 1814 and it created both hope and fear. Thereafter regime reconstruction occurred incessantly, and it was still underway when World War One radically altered the context in which politics developed.

After two decades of war and revolution, in 1814 the statesmen of the leading powers sought to reorder Europe at the Congress of Vienna. They fostered peace in the states system by creating a rough equilibrium of power, and pursued stability in domestic politics by establishing regimes that combined elements of the old order with some of the values and institutions that had arisen since 1789. Thereafter the Concert of Europe succeeded in avoiding war among the powers until 1854. Conversely, armed intervention was already required to block regime change in Spain and Italy by the early 1820s. Successful revolution in Greece was an exception that could be attributed to highly particular circumstance as desire to rescue the "cradle of western civilization" from the clutches of Ottoman rule over-rode Metternich's insistence on maintenance of the status quo.

Several elements were required for revolution to succeed. Part of the elite and part of the masses had to combine forces to overthrow an unwanted regime. Economic hardship, attributable to population growth and economic dislocation, could contribute, but what was crucial was shared perception of bad government. Geostrategic considerations also constituted an important variable; British acceptance of the revolutions of 1830 in France and Belgium was vital to blocking foreign intervention. The position of the army could also prove decisive. Where the army remained loyal, conservatives were largely secure; where the army backed revolution, monarchs were in trouble. When officers engaged in politics, it

Europe's Uncertain Path 1814–1914: State Formation and Civil Society, First Edition. R. S. Alexander.
© 2012 R. S. Alexander. Published 2012 by Blackwell Publishing Ltd.

was, however, seldom the case that the army remained a cohesive force. The example of Spain repeatedly demonstrated that politicization could divide the army into competing factions, while exacerbating political instability. In France, many officers drew the conclusion that the army must remain politically neutral, allowing the Liberal Opposition to overturn the Bourbon Monarchy.

As the Great Reform Act of 1832 revealed, revolution was not the only way to secure fundamental change. Amidst growing popular disorder, the landowning British elite decided to buttress the regime by including middle-class elements in the political system. Especially noteworthy in the British scenario was the relatively advanced state of key components of civil society – the free press and freedom of association. These attributes were also apparent in France, but they were less developed, and the British were also precocious in the organization of a party system wherein power could alternate without recourse to revolt. In the aftermath of the 1830 revolutions, governments in the autocracies and the smaller German and Italian states sought to repress the institutions of civil society. While they were largely successful in the short term, there were limits as to what they could achieve, especially as nationalism and liberalism began to intersect. Not every meeting of allegedly cultural associations could be monitored by a police spy, and not every political allusion could be censored from the press, especially given elite participation in clubs and desire for information and editorial.

There are three main ways to assess the revolutions of 1848. The first is to note that much of what was initially accomplished was subsequently lost. Conservatives gradually recovered from initial disarray, successfully exploited divisions between moderates and radicals over the "social question," and played divide and rule among competing nationalist groups. The second is to recognize that although most change proved ephemeral, significant advances were made. Constitutional monarchy progressed in Piedmont-Sardinia and gained a toehold in Prussia. While representative government was curtailed by Louis-Napoleon's emasculation of parliament, male democracy remained in France. Serfdom was abolished in the Habsburg Empire, and the society of orders was dealt a lethal blow by the termination of the old system of estates.

The third form of assessment involves consideration of long-term impact. By loosening the constraints imposed by conservative regimes, the revolutions enabled large numbers to gain initial experience of political activity. Expansion of the political press, participation in associations, and voting all enhanced political consciousness and left deeply embedded memories. The experience was profoundly unsettling. The "social question" had long been discussed publicly; nevertheless, it was experience of the "springtime of the peoples" that pushed political elites toward giving the state a more robust role in dealing with social problems, particularly those resultant from the industrial revolution and urbanization. State response might take the form of beefing up the forces of order, expanding efforts to promote material welfare, or increasing efforts to inculcate the masses with "desirable" values; in each case it was stimulated by the eruption of the masses into the political arena. 1848 also briefly enabled women to engage in political activism. Most activities were not gender specific and the response of governments to demands for recognition of women's rights was almost uniformly negative; all the same, the "woman question" had been launched and future feminist leaders had gained valuable experience.

One of the turning points of 1848 was conservative recognition that steps had to be taken to secure mass allegiance to elite-dominated regimes. Appeal to patriotism was one such measure. In seeking to gain prestige in the Ottoman Empire, Louis-Napoleon probably did not intend to provoke war with Russia; however, he certainly intended to enhance his domestic credentials at the expense of the Tsar. One way or another the Crimean War unleashed a series of events that would alter the states system in a way that the 1848 revolutions had not done. Russia was the short-term "loser" and the damage to her status as a great power led to a period of concentration on domestic reform and retreat from the role of *gendarme* of Europe.

The main victim of the Crimean War was the Habsburg Monarchy. Alienation of the Russians made Austria vulnerable to the revisionist inclinations of Louis-Napoleon and the aspirations of Prussia to achieve ascendancy in Germany. Despite Cavour's clever preparations and rising nationalism within part of the elite, Italian unification could not have occurred without French connivance. Thereafter equally shrewd Bismarckian diplomacy and a superior army enabled Prussia to inflict a second massive defeat upon Austria. The man who had triggered the entire sequence of events, then also fell victim to superior cunning and power. By the end of the Franco-Prussian war Germany had been united under Prussian leadership and France had been displaced as the leading potential continental hegemon. Especially corrosive for the states system was the way in which Italian and German unification had been achieved. Rugged pursuit of realpolitik, entailing deception, manipulation of nationalism, and ruthless disregard for the interests of other regimes, severely damaged the Concert of Europe.

After 1871 Europe entered another period of sustained peace as Bismarck sought to preserve a status quo that suited Prussian interests. The result was an increasingly armed peace, based on a series of alliances that presumed France must be bent on revenge. For a time, the advent of the "new imperialism" enabled the powers to conduct their rivalries overseas, where conflict was less likely to produce war in Europe. The safety-valve effect of the "new imperialism" could not, however, last forever and meanwhile the "Eastern Question" remained unresolved. Pushed out of Italy and Germany, Habsburg aspirations were redirected toward the Balkans and meanwhile Pan-Slavism and expansion of the grain trade made the region all the more vital to Russia. By the time that Bismarck was pushed into retirement in 1890, his, at times duplicitous, attempts to bind the three autocracies had fallen apart. A major shift in the states system would soon follow; unfortunately suspicion and presumption of aggression remained.

The close relation between foreign and domestic politics could be seen in the impact of war. Success enabled Piedmont-Sardinia and Prussia to impose constitutions that favored their own interests on the rest of (respectively) Italy and Germany. Defeat led Tsarist Russia to undertake the abolition of serfdom and a host of related reforms, forced the Habsburgs to accept compromise in the form of the Dual Monarchy, and brought the fall of the French Second Empire. Nationalism, and by extension imperialism, thus became a very delicate issue for governments and regimes. It could be used to bestir support; it could prove lethal given defeat, and it raised the stakes of inter-state rivalry.

For polyglot Empires such as Austria-Hungary and Russia, nationalism posed more problems than it provided solutions, and it was also troublesome in Britain and Spain. Conversely, in many states nationalism held appeal for politicians as a means to promote unity and cohesion. Frequently it was linked to efforts to combat socialist and anarchist promotion of class conflict; in certain scenarios nationalism could also be employed to subordinate the Church to state authority. In the three decades prior to the turn of the century, when states were asserting increased direction over education, public health, and provision of charity or welfare, conflicts between (generally liberal) proponents of secularism and religious authorities often were at the core of domestic politics. Such battles can be termed "culture wars," but they were intricately tied to social and political struggles and played out according to specific national contexts. A particular faith might, or might not, be considered an integral element of national identity, and the impact of such perception could be determined by which groups happened to hold power. A particular faith might be seen as an enemy of progress at one point, and subsequently appear as a potential ally against the greater threat of socialism at another. One way or another, national context was complex and crucial.

If state expansion at times triggered conflict with religious authorities, it was primarily a response to the "social question." Beyond appeals to patriotism through commemoration of alleged tradition and past accomplishment, states could seek to promote civil order, if not loyalty, by a variety of means. The urban renewal programs initiated by Louis-Napoleon in the 1850s were designed to showcase concern for material welfare and they were soon emulated throughout Europe. Contemporaneous state initiatives to spur economic growth through development of communications and transportation infrastructure, or to facilitate provision of credit for entrepreneurs, served similar ends. Expanded provision of primary education also constituted an attempt to address the "social question." In all of these regards motivation sprang from a mix of desire for control, humanitarian concern, and determination to enhance state power.

None of these measures prevented socialism and the labor movement from growing after the repression of the 1850s and the setback that followed the Paris Commune. The development of socialist parties and trade unions was, however, part of a much broader phenomenon – mass politics. Economic growth, increased literacy, improved communications, technological innovation, and the desire of competing elite groups to recruit a mass following all contributed to the advent of the mass press, nationally (and sometimes internationally) organized political parties and movements, and a myriad of associations The management of an increasingly complex civil society made government more difficult as an expanding public spoke in a multitude of often contradictory and sometimes intolerant voices.

The emergence of mass politics meant that a number of fundamental political principles had to be established, or re-established, in a new context. Politics consists, at base, of competition. For competition to yield something more than chaos or tyranny there must be broadly accepted rules of engagement. In a developed civil society, there must also be pluralism – toleration of the right of other individuals or groups to pursue their interests within generally accepted bounds, willingness to compromise, and an understanding that compromise entails recognition that no group ever gains all of what it might want. In combination, rules of engagement and pluralism constitute a good start; yet they are insufficient. For a modern political system to function, the many competing interests within society must somehow be linked and bound in a coherent instrument. Mass parties serve this function. To be effective they must be able to mediate among a wide range of groups, and they must be able to channel the aspirations of the various groups into a coherent program for government. There are various means for doing so. The party leadership can, for example, identify a common enemy or, more constructively, prioritize an urgent need. Strategy depends very much on current context, but the key is that large numbers be brought to concur on the objectives of government.

Individual states responded to the challenges of mass politics in varied ways. None of them, of course, was fully successful in adjusting its political system to the new context, but some made greater headway than others. Male democracy advanced gradually in Britain, where parliamentary government was well established. In France manhood suffrage was combined with parliamentary government under the Third Republic. While the vote was meaningful for those who held it in both these states, elsewhere the principle of representative government was weakened by political systems in which representative bodies held relatively little power or elections were a sham.

The establishment of democracy within a parliamentary system was not a panacea; as the Third Republic demonstrated, good government also required achieving an effective relationship between the executive and the legislature, and a coherent party system. Gladstone's famous Midlothian campaign is frequently cited as a landmark in democratic politics because he outlined his program directly to the mass of voters. At least as important were his efforts to unite the wide-ranging groups within the Liberal Party in support of a limited set of reform proposals. Gladstone used the strategy of turning specific issues into a moral crusade, and it has become a familiar part of modern politics. The key was not just that Gladstone held the Liberals together; it was that his strategy could make them an effective force of government. While the French Radicals could bring together a diverse range of groups, they were far less able to construct a coherent legislative program and then steer it through the National Assembly. Clemenceau was skilled at defending the republican status quo from attack; he was less successful in addressing the changing needs of French society.

Gladstone's advantage was not that he operated in what effectively was a two-party system. The Canovine system in Spain demonstrated that political parties must be actuated by more than simple pursuit of power. Italy illustrated the same point until Giolitti dramatically altered the political system. Thereafter, destruction of the regime would show that, on its own, democratization was also insufficient. Neither of the traditional mainstream Italian parties proved adept at grass-roots organization and mobilization of the masses. The French were more fortunate in that after the Boulanger Affair the Radicals and Socialists became mass parties. Moreover, by distancing themselves from their insurrectionary tradition and seeking change through democratic means, French Socialists accepted the rules of engagement of the political system.

By the turn of the century, mass politics had been further complicated by the growth of the two new forces. Especially after 1900 women's groups grew increasingly vocal in demanding the vote. Overcoming separate spheres ideology would prove a long, hard struggle. While progress could be seen in legal reform and increased educational provision, among the leading states it was only in Britain and perhaps France that gaining the right to vote at the national level seemed anything more than a distant possibility. The cause of women rights had to be promoted on many fronts, and there were many divisions within the women's movement. More immediately threatening to the status quo was the emergence of the proto-fascist New Right. Aggressively nationalist, xenophobic, anti-socialist, and illiberal, the New Right was a bewildering mix of the political Left and Right that rebuked older traditions. While the New Right attacked parliamentary government as inherently corrupt, in championing the people it also threw down the gauntlet to royal sovereignty. Prior to 1914 ultranationalists remained far from the centers of power, but they were positioned to exploit the perception of regime failure that World War and its aftermath brought.

Governments were particularly preoccupied by socialist parties and trade unions because of their capacities for economic disruption and sheer force of numbers. Nevertheless, the evolution of socialism toward democratic means, the decline of anarchism, and the tendency of unions toward pragmatic reformism gave grounds for continued belief that reform might prevent social revolution. State regulation or mediation of industrial relations increased steadily, albeit slowly, in the decades preceding the Great War. Elements of Bismarck's, admittedly partial, social welfare program were adopted in most European states, most notably in Britain, where the Liberal Party also introduced the innovation of using fiscal policy for, again highly limited, redistribution of wealth. State intervention in the realm of public health also accelerated, suggesting that the emergence of civil society was by no means an inherently liberal phenomenon that would inevitably check growth in state power.

Control of the state thus became increasingly consequential. It is hard to escape the impression that politics was growing more volatile prior to the Great War, although even the autocracies had demonstrated some capacity to evolve. Whether decisions to go to war actually were a product of domestic strife is, however, another question.

The autocracies were not on the verge of collapse in 1914. Despite serious flaws in the political system, Germany was relatively stable and few groups were willing to challenge the regime aggressively. The Habsburg decision to attack Serbia was partly a product of overblown concern over the "South-Slav" question, but the South-Slavs within the Empire were little threat to the regime and most opposition groups sought reform, rather than destruction, of the Empire. The key to Habsburg policies was fear of Russian intentions in the Balkans. In Russia material conditions were improving and while immense challenges remained, the regime was slowly stabilizing. For the Tsar foreign policy formulation must be guided by issues of prestige, and the latter were connected to domestic politics. Even so, recent experience was anything but an argument for attempting to resolve domestic problems through foreign war; defeat by Japan had let the revolutionary genie out of the bottle in 1905 and might do so again.

War arose because long-term corrosion of the states system hindered statesmen from resolving a critical diplomatic crisis. There was no straight line from the formation of the Franco-Russian alliance in the early 1890s to the clash between the Triple Entente and the Central Powers in 1914. In forming the Dual Alliance, neither France nor Russia was looking to provoke war with Germany; indeed they were far more likely to clash with Britain in their empire building. It was the resort of German governments to a combination of threat and bluster that drove the British into increasingly close cooperation with France and Russia. Agreements of imperial spheres of influence were not a threat to Germany, but military agreements following the two Moroccan Crises were testimony to the consequence of repeated attempts to intimidate the other powers.

Because nationalist aspirations made the Balkans unstable and difficult for the great powers to manage, it was the "Eastern Question" that posed the greatest danger to peace. Russian preoccupation with the Far East encouraged cooperation with Austria-Hungary, until Izvolsky bungled Russian interests during the Habsburg annexation of Bosnia-Herzegovina. In the Bosnian Crisis of 1908 the two alliance systems came into direct conflict and firm German backing enabled Austria-Hungary to force acceptance rather than compromise. An unhappy precedent had thereby been set. Russia was forced to back down by the threat of war, just as France was forced to cede part of French Congo during the Second Moroccan Crisis in 1911. Thereafter Russian encouragement of Balkan leagues that rapidly spun out of control was equally misguided.

Despite various agreements between states on either side of the alliance systems, the states system became increasingly rigid. Confrontations with the Central

Powers deepened suspicion that Germany was bent on a war that would alter the balance of power, tightened the Triple Entente, and reduced the chances of France and Russia backing down again in the future. Meanwhile alarm in Germany over the possibility of a two-front war was stoked by French investment in Russian industry and military expansion – the balance of power appeared to be tilting against the Central Powers. After Italy initiated the final collapse of the Ottoman Empire, the Balkans Wars triggered even higher levels of alarm at Vienna. Thereafter the key was that the governments of Germany and Austria were willing to run the risk of war in seeking to force their resolution to the problem posed by Serbia. The Concert of Europe had been built on the premise that the powers, while pursuing their interests, must not be completely blind to the interests of the other powers and push them into a corner where they felt obliged to fight. Sadly for all involved, the Central Powers ignored this cardinal rule.

It is tempting and perhaps esthetically pleasing to view World War One as somehow a logical culmination of all that had gone before it. Attempts to link all the sources of domestic conflict and intellectual uncertainty at the turn of the century to the Great War are, however, unconvincing; not all roads led to Sarajevo. Similarly, viewing the Belle Époque as a moment frozen in time obscures the extent to which Europe was in transition, with a host of problems yet to be resolved, but with at least some progress apparent. Material life was better than in 1814 and if states had not yet succeeded in grappling with mass politics, neither had they necessarily failed. Pessimism about the future was largely confined to a small group of academics and artists who were far from representative of mass culture. World War One would make matters far worse and alter Europe's path dramatically, but it was a product of diplomatic failure rather than perception of social or cultural decline.

Notes

1 Quoted in Robin Okey, *Eastern Europe 1740–1980: Feudalism to Communism* (London, 1982), p. 62.

2 Quoted in Tim Chapman, *The Congress of Vienna: Origins, Process and Results* (London, 1998), p. 18.

3 Quoted in Enno E. Kraehe, *Metternich's German Policy*, II (Princeton, NJ, 1983), p. 209.

4 See Paul W. Schroeder, *The Transformation of European Politics 1763–1848* (Oxford, 1994), pp. 477–582. Older use of the term "balance" can be found in works such as Harold Nicolson, *The Congress of Vienna* (London, 1946), Charles Webster, *The Congress of Vienna* (London, 1963), and Henry A. Kissinger, *A World Restored* (New York, 1964).

5 For a brief summary of principal developments in France, see Malcolm Crook, "The French Revolution and Napoleon, 1788–1814," in Malcolm Crook, ed., *Revolutionary France* (Oxford, 2002), pp. 8–35.

6 Quoted in Norman McCord, *British History 1815–1906* (Oxford, 1991), p. 54.

7 See Robert Tombs, *France 1814–1914* (London, 1996), p. 332.

8 Quoted in Charles Esdaile, "Enlightened Absolutism versus Theocracy in the Spanish Restoration, 1814–1850," in David Laven and Lucy Riall, eds, *Napoleon's Legacy* (Oxford, 2000), p. 70.

9 Quoted in William J. Callahan, *Church, Politics, and Society in Spain, 1750–1874* (London, 1984), p. 112.

10 See Michael Rowe, *From Reich to State: the Rhineland in the Revolutionary Age, 1780–1830* (Cambridge, 2003), pp. 244–5.

11 As Holy Roman Emperor, he was Francis II. In anticipation of the 1806 abolition of the Holy Roman Empire, he had taken the title of Emperor of Austria and thus become Francis I in 1804.

12 Quoted in Richard Pipes, *Russia under the Old Regime* (London, 1974), p. 241.

13 Quoted in Janet M. Hartley, *Russia, 1762–1825: Military Power, the State, and the People* (London, 2008), p. 205.

14 Quoted in Robert Bideleux and Ian Jeffries, *A History of Eastern Europe: Crisis and Change* (London, 1998), p. 169.

Europe's Uncertain Path 1814–1914: State Formation and Civil Society, First Edition. R. S. Alexander.
© 2012 R. S. Alexander. Published 2012 by Blackwell Publishing Ltd.

15   See Michael Broers, *Europe after Napoleon: Revolution, Reaction and Romanticism, 1814–1848* (Manchester, 1996).

16   For an account that defines conservatism somewhat differently as a "philosophy of imperfection" directed toward a "limited style of politics," see Noel O'Sullivan, *Conservatism* (London, 1976), pp. 9–31.

17   Quoted in Dieter Langewiesche, *Liberalism in Germany* (Princeton, NJ, 2000), p. 12.

18   See Benedict Anderson, *Imagined Communities: Reflections on the Origin and Spread of Nationalism*, revised edition (London, 2006).

19   See Charles J. Esdaile, *Spain in the Liberal Age: From Constitution to Civil War, 1808–1939* (Oxford, 2000), p. 46.

20   Quoted in J.M. Roberts, *The Mythology of the Secret Societies* (London, 1972), p. 301.

21   Quoted in Philip Harling, *The Modern British State: An Historical Introduction* (Cambridge, 2001), p. 77.

22   Quoted in Isabel Burdiel, "The Liberal Revolution, 1808–1843," in José Alvarez Junco and Adrian Shubert, eds., *Spanish History since 1808* (London, 2000), p. 24.

23   Quoted in A.L. Macfie, *The Eastern Question 1774–1923* (London, 1989), p. 91.

24   Quoted in Daniel H. Thomas, *The Guarantee of Belgian Independence and Neutrality in European Diplomacy, 1830s–1930s* (Kingston, RI, 1983), p. 15.

25   See Vernon Mallinson, *Belgium* (London, 1969), p. 55.

26   See Roland Quinault, "The French Revolution of 1830 and Parliamentary Reform," *History*, 79 n. 257 (Oct. 1994), pp. 377–93.

27   Quoted in Norman Gash, *Aristocracy and People: Britain, 1815–1865* (Cambridge, MA, 1979), p. 147.

28   Quoted in Thomas Nipperdey, *Germany from Napoleon to Bismarck 1800–1866*, trans. Daniel Nolan (Princeton, NJ., 1996), p. 324.

29   Quoted in David Blackbourn, *Germany 1780–1918: The Long Nineteenth Century* (London, 1997), p. 127.

30   On civil society generally, see Stefan-Ludwig Hoffmann, *Civil Society, 1750–1914* (Basingstoke, 2006) and Nancy Bermeo and Philip Nord, eds, *Civil Society before Democracy: Lessons from Nineteenth-Century Europe* (Lanham, MD, 2000).

31   Quoted in Brendan Simms, *The Struggle for Mastery in Germany, 1779–1850* (New York, 1998), p. 116.

32   For the quote, see Norman Rich, *Great Power Diplomacy 1814–1914* (New York, 1992), p. 65.

33   Quoted in James L. Richardson, *Crisis Diplomacy: the Great Powers since the mid-nineteenth century* (Cambridge, 1994), p. 56.

34   Quoted in Colin Heywood, "Society," in T.C.W. Blanning, ed., *The Short Oxford History of the Nineteenth Century* (Oxford, 2000), p. 65.

35   Quoted in Alan Kidd, *State, Society and the Poor in Nineteenth-Century England* (Basingstoke, 1999), p. 19.

36   Quoted in Michael Bentley, *Politics without Democracy. Great Britain, 1815–1914* (Oxford, 1984), pp. 83–4.

37   Quoted in Lucy Riall, *Risorgimento: The History of Italy from Napoleon to Nation-State* (London, 2009), p. 135.

38   Quoted in Clara M. Lovett, *The Democratic Movement in Italy 1830–1876* (Cambridge, MA, 1982), p. 99.

39   Quoted in David E. Barclay, *Frederick William IV and the Prussian Monarchy 1840–1861* (Oxford, 1995), p. 122.

40   As translated by Sarah Hanbury-Tenison in Hagen Schulze, *The Course of German Nationalism* (Cambridge, 1991), p. 65.

41   Quoted in A.J.P. Taylor, *The Habsburg Monarchy 1809–1918* (London, 1948), p. 47.

42   For the analogy to colonialism, see Bideleux and Jeffries, *Eastern Europe*, p. 302.

43   For the quote, see Stanley Payne, *Politics and the Military in Modern Spain* (Stanford, 1967), p. 24.

44   Quoted in Theodore S. Hamerow, *The Birth of a New Europe: State and Society in the Nineteenth Century* (Chapel Hill, NC, 1983), p. 19.

45   See Pamela M. Pilbeam, *The Middle Classes in Europe 1789–1914: France, Germany, Italy and Russia* (London, 1990), p. 302.

46   Quoted in Geoffrey Crossick and Heinz-Gerhard Haupt, *The Petite Bourgeoisie in Europe 1780–1914* (London, 1995), p. 3.

47   Quoted in Jonathan Sperber, *Revolutionary Europe 1780–1850* (Harlow, 2000), p. 236.

48   See Merry E. Wiesner, Julius R. Ruff, and William Bruce Wheeler, *Discovering the Western Past: Volume II: Since 1500*, 6th edition (New York, 2008), pp. 149–50.

49   Quoted in Gordon Wright, *Between the Guillotine and Liberty: Two Centuries of the Crime Problem in France* (Oxford, 1983), p. 54.

50   Quoted in Mary Gibson, *Prostitution and the State in Italy* (Columbus, 1986), p. 15.

51   Quoted in Darrin M. McMahon, *Enemies of the Enlightenment: The French Counter-Enlightenment and the Making of Modernity* (Oxford, 2001), p. 156.

52   Quoted in Ivan T. Berend, *History Derailed: Central and Eastern Europe in the Long Nineteenth Century* (Berkeley, CA, 2003), pp. 49–50.

53   Quoted in Warren Breckman, *European Romanticism: A Brief History with Documents* (Boston and New York, 2008), p. 12.

54   See Lilian R. Furst, *Romanticism in Perspective*, 2nd edition (London, 1979), p. 113.

55   Quoted in Axel Körner, "The European Dimension in the Ideas of 1848 and the Nationalization of Its Memories," in Körner, ed., *1848 – A European Revolution?* 2nd edition (London, 2004), p. 15.

56   Quoted in Barclay, *Frederick William IV*, p. 134.

57   Quoted in Heinz-Gerhard Haupt and Dieter Langewiesche, "The European Revolution of 1848," in Dieter Dowe *et al.*, eds, *Europe in 1848: Revolution and Reform* (Oxford, 2001), p. 4.

58   Quoted in Rachel G. Fuchs and Victoria E. Thompson, *Women in Nineteenth-Century Europe* (Basingstoke, 2005), p. 163.

59   Quoted in Lynn Abrams, *The Making of Modern Woman* (London, 2002), p. 226.

60   For the quote of Ulysse Trélat, see Roger Price, *The French Second Republic: A Social History* (London, 1972), p. 156.

61   For the quote, see Roger Price, *The Revolutions of 1848* (Atlantic Highlands, NJ, 1988), p. 50.

62   For the quote, see Dieter Langewiesche, "Germany and the National Question in 1848," in John Breuilly, ed., *The State of Germany* (London, 1992), p. 63.

63   Quoted in Jonathan Sperber, *The European Revolutions, 1848–1851* (Cambridge, 1994), p. 130.

64   Quoted in Peter N. Stearns, *1848: The Revolutionary Tide in Europe* (New York, 1974), p. 137.

65   Quoted in William Carr, *A History of Germany 1815–1945* (London, 1972), p. 60.

66   Quoted in Eric J. Hobsbawm, "Marx, Engels and Politics," in Hobsbawm, ed., *The History of Marxism: Volume 1: Marxism in Marx's Day* (Bloomington, IN, 1982), p. 244.

67   Quoted in James Joll, *The Anarchists* (London, 1964), p. 62.

68   As quoted in Gerald Brenan, *The Spanish Labyrinth* (Cambridge, 1978), p. 133.

69   Quoted in James F. McMillan, *Napoleon III* (London, 1991), p. 74.

70   For the quotes, see C.J. Bartlett, *Peace, War and the European Powers, 1814–1914* (New York, 1996), p. 54.

71   For the quote of Nicholas, see F.R. Bridge and Roger Bullen, *The Great Powers and the European States System 1814–1914*, 2nd edition (London, 2005), p. 119.

72   Quoted in Paul Kennedy, *The Rise and Fall of the Great Powers: Economic Change and Military Conflict from 1500 to 2000* (London, 1988), pp. 227–8.

73   Quoted in Trevor Royle, *Crimea: The Great Crimean War 1854–1856* (Basingstoke, 2000), p. 503.

74   Quoted in W.D. Rubenstein, *Britain's Century: A Political and Social History 1815–1905* (London, 1998), p. 132.

75   Quoted in Raymond Carr, *Spain 1808–1975*, 2nd edition (Oxford, 1982), p. 255.

76   Quoted in Lucy Riall, "Garibaldi and the South," in John A. Davis, ed., *Italy in the Nineteenth Century: 1796–1900* (Oxford, 2000), p. 138.

77   For the quote of Francis Joseph, see Alan Sked, *The Decline and Fall of the Habsburg Empire 1815–1918* (London, 1989), p. 173.

78   Quoted in Hajo Holborn, *A History of Modern Germany 1840–1945* (Princeton, NJ, 1982), p. 162.

79   See Geoffrey Wawro, *The Austro-Prussian War: Austria's War with Prussia and Italy in 1866* (Cambridge, 1996), p. 5.

80   Quoted in Carr, *Germany*, p. 122.

81   Quoted in Miklós Molnár, *A Concise History of Hungary* (Cambridge, 2001), p. 207.

82   Quoted in Jonathan Parry, *The Rise and Fall of Liberal Government in Victorian Britain* (New Haven, CT, 1993), p. 11.

83   Quoted in Asa Briggs, *The Age of Improvement* (London, 1959), p. 513.

84   Quoted in Spencer Di Scala, *Italy: From Revolution to Republic, 1700 to the Present* (Oxford, 1995), p. 121.

85   Quoted in Nicholas Doumanis, *Inventing the Nation: Italy* (London, 2001), p. 87.

86   Quoted in Martin Clark, *The Italian Risorgimento* (London, 1998), p. 92.

87   Quoted in Carr, *Spain*, pp. 314–15.

88   Quoted in Alain Plessis, *The Rise and Fall of the Second Empire 1852–1871* (Cambridge, 1985), p. 168.

89   Quoted in Roger Price, *The French Second Empire: An Anatomy of Political Power* (Cambridge, 2001), p. 446.

90   See Sudhir Hazareesingh, *From Subject to Citizen: The Second Empire and the Emergence of Modern French Democracy* (Princeton, NJ, 1998), p. 314.

91   Quoted in Geoffrey Wawro, *The Franco-Prussian War: the German Conquest of France in 1870–1871* (Cambridge, 2003), p. 305.

92   Quoted in John Lowe, *The Great Powers, Imperialism, and the German Problem, 1865–1925* (London, 1994), p. 50.

93   Quoted in Bonnie S. Anderson and Judith P. Zinsser, *A History of Their Own: Women in Europe from Prehistory to the Present* (New York, 1989), II, p. 362.

94   See Susan Groag Bell and Karen M. Offen, *Women, the Family, and Freedom: The Debate in Documents* (Stanford, 1983), I, p. 513.

95   Quoted in E. J. Feuchtwanger, *Democracy and Empire: Britain 1865–1914* (London, 1985), p. 70.

96   Quoted in Bernard Porter, *The Lion's Share: A Short History of British Imperialism 1850–1970* (London, 1975), p. 82.

97   Quoted in Earl R. Beck, *A Time of Triumph and of Sorrow: Spanish Politics during the Reign of Alfonso XII 1874–1885* (Carbondale and Edwardsville, IL, 1979), p. 34.

98   Quoted in Robert W. Kern, *Liberals, Reformers and Caciques in Restoration Spain 1875–1909* (Albuquerque, NM, 1974), p. 32.

99   Quoted in John A. Davis, *Conflict and Control: Law and Order in Nineteenth-Century Italy* (Basingstoke, 1988), p. 317.

100   Quoted in Katharine Anne Lerman, *Bismarck* (Harlow, 2004), p. 265.

101   Quoted in Abigail Green, *Fatherlands: State-Building and Nationhood in Nineteenth-Century Germany* (Cambridge, 2001), p. 299.

102   Quoted in Robin Okey, *The Habsburg Monarchy c. 1765–1918: From Enlightenment to Eclipse* (Basingstoke, 2001), pp. 215–16.

103   Quoted in Paul Dukes, *A History of Russia c. 882–1996*, 3rd edition (Basingstoke, 1997), p. 153.

104   Quoted in H.L. Wesserling, *The European Colonial Empires 1815–1919* (London, 2004), p. 127.

105   See W.O. Henderson, *The German Colonial Empire 1884–1919* (London, 1993), p. 74.

106   Quoted in Bridge and Bullen, *Great Powers*, p. 241.

107   See Paul Heywood, *Marxism and the Failure of Organised Socialism in Spain, 1879–1936* (Cambridge, 1990), p. 1.

108   Quoted in Christopher Duggan, *Francesco Crispi,1818–1901: From Nations to Nationalism* (Oxford, 2002), p. 5.

109   Quoted in Dennis Mack Smith, *Modern Italy: A Political History* (Ann Arbor, 1997), p. 134.

110   Quoted in Martin Clark, *Modern Italy 1871–1982* (London, 1984), p. 99.

111   Quoted in Carl E. Schorske, *Fin-de-Siècle Vienna: Politics and Culture* (New York, 1980), p. 131.

112   Quoted in Andrew C. Janos, *The Politics of Backwardness in Hungary 1825–1945* (Princeton, NJ, 1982), p. 117.

113   Quoted in Geoffrey Hosking, *Russia: People and Empire 1552–1917* (Cambridge, MA, 1997), p. 338.

114   Quoted in Hans Rogger, *Russia in the Age of Modernisation and Revolution 1881–1917* (London, 1983), p. 182.

115   Definition of the tertiary sector is notoriously difficult, but there is little doubt that it was rapidly growing. For our purposes, it is probably best to think of the service sector as comprised of individuals who were employed, but not in industry or agriculture. See R.M. Hartwell, "The Service Revolution: The Growth of Services in

Modern Economy," in Carlo M. Cipolla, ed., *The Fontana Economic History of Europe: The Industrial Revolution* (London, 1973), p. 361.

116 Quoted in Peter Baldwin, *Contagion and the State in Europe, 1830–1930* (Cambridge, 1999), p. 533.

117 Quoted in Clive Emsley, *Crime, Police, and Penal Policy: European Experiences 1750–1940* (Oxford, 2007), p. 181.

118 Quoted in Ruth Harris, *Murders and Madness: Medicine, Law, and Society in the fin de siècle* (Oxford, 1989), pp. 152–3.

119 Quoted in Michael Biddiss, "Progress, Prosperity, and Positivism: Cultural Trends in Mid-century," in Bruce Waller, ed., Themes in Modern European History, 1830–1890 (London, 1990), p. 190.

120 Quoted in Roland N. Stromberg, *European Intellectual History Since 1789*, 6th edition (Englewood Cliffs, NJ, 1994), p. 86.

121 Quoted in Hugh McLeod, *Religion and the People of Western Europe 1789–1970* (Oxford, 1981), p. 52.

122 Quoted in Eamon Duffy, *Saints and Sinners: A History of the Popes*, 3rd edition (New Haven, CT, 2006), p. 311.

123 Quoted in James J. Sheehan, "Culture," in T.C.W. Blanning, ed., *The Nineteenth Century: Europe 1789–1914* (Oxford, 2000), p. 133.

124 Quoted in T.C.W. Blanning, "The Commercialization and Sacralization of European Culture in the Nineteenth Century," in Blanning, ed., *The Oxford History of Modern Europe*, p. 138.

125 See William Fortescue, *The Third Republic in France 1870–1940: Conflicts and Continuities* (London, 2000), p. 63.

126 See Peter N. Stearns, *European Society in Upheaval: Social History since 1750*, 2nd edition (New York, 1975), p. 191.

127 See Michael D. Biddiss, *The Age of the Masses: Ideas and Society in Europe since 1870* (Harmondsworth, 1977), p. 45.

128 Quoted in Peter Baehr, "Max Weber and the Avatars of Caesarism," in Peter Baehr and Melvin Richter, eds, *Dictatorship in History and Theory: Bonapartism, Caesarism, and Totalitarianism* (Cambridge, 2004), p. 165.

129 Quoted in Bartlett, *Peace*, p. 136.

130 Quoted in Karen Offen, *European Feminisms* (Stanford, California, 2000), pp. 196–7.

131 Quoted in Martin Pugh, "The Limits of Liberalism: Liberals and Women's Suffrage, 1867–1914," in Eugenio F. Biagini, ed., *Citizenship and Community: Liberals, Radicals and Collective Identities in the British Isles, 1865–1931* (Cambridge, 1996), p. 51.

132 Quoted in Peter Davies, *The Extreme Right in France, 1789 to the Present* (London, 2002), p. 74.

133 Quoted in Gordon Wright, *France in Modern Times*, 4th edition (London, 1987), p. 233.

134 Quoted in Joseph Smith, *The Spanish-American War: Conflict in the Caribbean and the Pacific 1895–1902* (London, 1994), p. 209.

135 Quoted in Mack Smith, *Modern Italy*, pp. 193–4.

136   Quoted in Geoff Eley, "Some Thoughts on Nationalist Pressure Groups in Imperial Germany," in Paul Kennedy and Anthony Nicholls, eds, *Nationalist and Racialist Movements in Britain and Germany Before 1914* (London, 1981), p. 44.

137   Quoted in Roger Chickering, "Militarism and Radical Nationalism," in James Retallack, ed., *Imperial Germany 1871–1918* (Oxford, 2008), p. 213.

138   Quoted in Gordon A. Craig, *Germany 1866–1945* (Oxford, 1978), p. 264.

139   Quoted in Katherine Anne Lerman, *The Chancellor as Courtier: Bernhard von Bülow and the Governance of Germany 1900–1909* (Cambridge, 1990), p. 255.

140   Quoted in J.N. Westwood, *Endurance and Endeavour: Russian History 1812–2001*, 5th edition, (Oxford, 2002), p. 150.

141   Quoted in John Gooding, *Socialism in Russia: Lenin and his Legacy* (Basingstoke, 2002), p. 38.

142   Quoted in Adam B. Ulam, *Russia's Failed Revolutions: From the Decembrists to the Dissidents* (New York, 1981), p. 142.

143   Quoted in Abraham Ascher, *The Revolution of 1905: A Short History* (Stanford, CA, 2004), p. 44.

144   See Groag Bell and Offen, eds, *Women*, II, p. 239.

145   Quoted in Offen, *European Feminisms*, p. 216.

146   Quoted in Abrams, *Making*, p. 235.

147   Quoted in E.P. Hennock, "The Origins of British National Insurance and the German Precedent 1880–1914," in W.J. Mommsen, ed., *The Emergence of the Welfare State in Britain and Germany, 1870–1930* (London, 1981), p. 87.

148   Quoted in Feuchtwanger, *Democracy*, p. 343.

149   Quoted in Ulrich Linse, "Propaganda by Deed and Direct Action: Two Concepts of Anarchist Violence," in Wolfgang J. Mommsen and Gerhard Hirschfeld, eds, *Social Protest, Violence and Terror in Nineteenth- and Twentieth-Century Europe* (London, 1982), p. 215.

150   Clemenceau's self description is quoted in R.D. Anderson, *France 1870–1914: Politics and Society* (London, 1984), p. 27.

151   Quoted in John F. V. Keiger, "France," in Keith Wilson, ed., *Decisions for War 1914* (New York, 1995), p. 124.

152   Quoted in William J. Callahan, *The Catholic Church in Spain, 1875–1998* (Washington, DC, 2000), p. 66.

153   Quoted in José Alvarez-Junco, *The Emergence of Mass Politics in Spain: Populist Demagoguery and Republican Culture, 1890–1910* (Brighton, 2002), p. 147.

154   Quoted in Di Scala, *Italy*, p. 172.

155   Quoted in Wolfgang J. Mommsen, "The latent crisis," in his *Imperial Germany 1867–1918* (London, 1995), p. 153.

156   Quoted in C.A. Macartney, *The Habsburg Empire 1790–1918* (London, 1971), p. 770.

157   Quoted in Abraham Ascher, *P.A. Stolypin: The Search for Stability in Late Imperial Russia* (Stanford, CA, 2001), p. 3.

158   Quoted in James Joll, *The Origins of the First World War* (London, 1984), p. 45.

159   Quoted in Richard F. Hamilton and Holger H. Herwig, *Decisions for War, 1914–1917* (Cambridge, 2004), p. 72.

Bibliography

Abrams, Lynn, *The Making of Modern Woman, Europe 1789–1918* (London, 2002).

Adler, Franklin Hugh, *Italian Industrialists from Liberalism to Fascism: The Political Development of the Industrial Bourgeoisie, 1906–1934* (Cambridge, 1995).

Agulhon, Maurice, *The Republican Experiment, 1848–1852* (Cambridge, 1983).

Aldrich, Robert, *Greater France: A History of French Overseas Expansion* (Basingstoke, 1996).

Alexander, R.S., *Napoleon* (London, 2001).

Alexander, R.S., *Re-Writing the French Revolutionary Tradition: Liberal Opposition and the Fall of the Bourbon Monarchy* (Cambridge, 2003).

Alvarez-Junco, José, *The Emergence of Mass Politics in Spain: Populist Demagoguery and Republican Culture, 1890–1910* (Brighton, 2002).

Alvarez-Junco, José, and Adrian Shubert, eds, *Spanish History since 1808* (London, 2002).

Anderson, Benedict, *Imagined Communities: Reflections on the Origin and Spread of Nationalism*, revised edition (London, 2006).

Anderson, Bonnie S., and Judith Zinsser, *A History of Their Own: Women in Europe from Prehistory to the Present*, II (New York, 1989).

Anderson, Margaret L., *Practicing Democracy: Elections and Political Culture in Imperial Germany* (Princeton, NJ, 2000).

Anderson, M.S., *The Ascendancy of Europe 1815–1914*, 2nd edition (London, 1985).

Anderson, R.D., *France 1870–1914: Politics and Society* (London, 1977).

Armour, Ian D., *A History of Eastern Europe 1740–1918* (London, 2006).

Ascher, Abraham, *P.A. Stolypin: The Search for Stability in Late Imperial Russia* (Stanford, CA, 2001).

Ascher, Abraham, *The Revolution of 1905: A Short History* (Stanford, CA, 2004).

Ashley, Susan A., *Making Liberalism Work: The Italian Experience, 1860–1914* (Westport, CT, 2003).

Aston, Nigel, *Christianity and Revolutionary Europe c. 1750–1830* (Cambridge, 2002).

Avrich, Paul, *Anarchist Portraits* (Princeton, NJ, 1988).

Baehr, Peter, and Melvin Richter, eds, *Dictatorship in History and Theory: Bonapartism, Caesarism, and Totalitarianism* (Cambridge, 2004).

Bairoch, P., International industrialization levels from 1750 to 1980, *Journal of European Economic History* (1982), 11, 296.

Baker, Alan R.H., *Fraternity Among the French Peasantry: Sociability and Voluntary Associations in the Loire Valley, 1815–1914* (Cambridge, 1999).

Baldwin, Peter, *Contagion and the State in Europe, 1830–1930* (Cambridge, 1999).

Balfour, Sebastian, *The End of the Spanish Empire, 1898–1923* (Oxford, 1997).

Barclay, David E., *Frederick William IV and the Prussian Monarchy 1840–1861* (Oxford, 1995).

Barraclough, Geoffrey, *From Agadir to Armageddon: Anatomy of a Crisis* (London, 1982).

Barry, Jonathan, and Colin Jones, eds, *Medicine and Charity Before the Welfare State* (London, 1991).

Bartlett, C.J., *Peace, War and the European Powers, 1814–1914* (New York, 1996).

Bartlett, Roger, *A History of Russia* (Basingstoke, 2005).

Baudelaire, Charles, *The Flowers of Evil*, edited by Marthiel and Jackson Mathews (New York, 1989).

Beales, Derek, *The Risorgimento and the Unification of Italy* (London, 1971).

Beck, Earl R., *A Time of Triumph and of Sorrow: Spanish Politics during the Reign of Alfonso XII 1874–1885* (Carbondale and Edwardsville, IL, 1979).

Bentley, Michael, *Politics without Democracy. Great Britain, 1815–1914: Perception and Preoccupation in British Government* (Oxford, 1984).

Berdahl, Robert M., *The Politics of the Prussian Nobility: The Development of a Conservative Ideology, 1770–1848* (Princeton, NJ, 1988).

Berend, Ivan, *History Derailed: Central and Eastern Europe in the Long Nineteenth Century* (Berkeley, CA, 2003).

Berenson, Edward, *The Trial of Madame Caillaux* (Berkeley, CA, 1992).

Berger, Stefan, *A Companion to Nineteenth-Century Europe 1789–1914* (Oxford, 2009).

Berghahn, V.R., *Imperial Germany, 1871–1914: Economy, Society, Culture, and Politics* (Oxford, 1994).

Bermeo, Nancy, and Philip Nord, eds, *Civil Society before Democracy: Lessons from Nineteenth-Century Europe* (Lanham, MD, 2000).

Bertier de Sauvigny, Guillaume de, *The Bourbon Restoration* (Philadelphia, PA, 1966).

Best, Geoffrey, *War and Society in Revolutionary Europe 1770–1870* (Montreal, 1998).

Biagini, Eugenio F., *Liberty, Retrenchment and Reform: Popular Liberalism in the Age of Gladstone, 1860–1880* (Cambridge, 1992).

Biagini, Eugenio F., ed., *Citizenship and Community: Liberals, Radicals and Collective Identities in the British Isles, 1865–1931* (Cambridge, 2002).

Biddiss, Michael D., *The Age of the Masses: Ideas and Society in Europe since 1870* (Harmondsworth, 1977).

Bideleux, Robert, and Ian Jeffries, *A History of Eastern Europe: Crisis and Change* (London: Routledge, 1998).

Billinger, Robert D., *Metternich and the German Question: State Rights and Federal Duties 1820–1834* (London, 1991).

Blackbourn, David, *Germany 1780–1918: The Long Nineteenth Century* (London, 1997).

Blanning, T.C.W., ed., *The Oxford History of Modern Europe* (Oxford, 2000).

Blanning, T.C.W., ed., *The Short Oxford History of Europe: The Nineteenth Century* (Oxford, 2000).

Boyer, John, *Political Radicalism in Late Imperial Vienna: Origins of the Christian Social Movement* (Chicago, 1981).

Boyer, John, *Culture and Political Crisis in Vienna: Christian Socialism in Power, 1897–1918* (Chicago, 1995).

Breckman, Warren, *European Romanticism: A Brief History with Documents* (Boston, 2008).

Brenan, Gerald, *The Spanish Labyrinth* (Cambridge, 1943).

Breuilly, John, *Nationalism and the State* (London, 1982).

Breuilly, John, *Labour and Liberalism in Nineteenth-Century Europe* (Manchester, 1992).

Breuilly, John, ed., *The State of Germany: The National Idea and the Making, Unmaking and Re-making of a Modern Nation State* (London, 1992).

Breuilly, John, ed., *Nineteenth-Century Germany: Politics, Culture and Society 1780–1918* (London, 2001).

Breuilly, John, *Austria, Prussia and Germany 1806–1871* (London, 2002).

Breunig, Charles, and Matthew Levinger, *The Age of Revolution and Reaction, 1789–1850*, 3rd edition (London, 2002).

Bridge, F.R., and Roger Bullen, *The Great Powers and the European States System 1814–1914*, 2nd edition (London, 2005).

Briggs, Asa, *The Age of Improvement* (London, 1959).

Broers, Michael, *Europe after Napoleon: Revolution, Reaction and Romanticism, 1814–1848* (Manchester, 1996).

Brubaker, Rogers, *Citizenship and Nationhood in France and Germany* (Cambridge, MA, 1992).

Brundage, Anthony, *The Making of the New Poor Law: The Politics of Inquiry, Enactment, and Implementation, 1832–1839* (New Brunswick, NJ, 1978).

Callahan, William J., *Church, Politics, and Society in Spain, 1750–1874* (Cambridge, MA, 1984).

Callahan, William J., *The Catholic Church in Spain, 1875–1998* (Washington, DC, 2000).

Cannon, John, *Parliamentary Reform 1640–1832* (Cambridge, 1973).

Carr, Raymond, *Spain, 1808–1975* (Oxford, 1982).

Carr, William, *A History of Germany 1815–1945* (1972).

Chamberlain, Muriel, *The Scramble for Africa*, 2nd edition (London, 1999).

Chapman, Tim, *The Congress of Vienna: Origins, Process and Results* (London, 1998).

Chevalier, Louis, *Labouring Classes and Dangerous Classes in Paris during the First Half of the Nineteenth Century* (New York, 1973).

Chickering, Roger, *We Men Who Feel Most German: A Cultural Study of the Pan-German League, 1886–1914* (Boston, 1984).

Christiansen, E., *The Origins of Military Power in Spain 1800–1854* (Oxford, 1967).

Church, Clive H., *Europe in 1830: Revolution and Political Change* (London, 1983).

Cipolla, Carlo, *The Economic History of World Population* (Harmondsworth, 1962).

Cipolla, Carlo, ed., *The Fontana Economic History of Europe: The Emergence of Industrial Societies*, 2 vols (London, 1973).

Cipolla, Carlo, ed., *The Fontana Economic History of Europe: The Industrial Revolution* (London, 1973).

Claeys, Gregory, *Machinery, Money and the Millennium: From Moral Economy to Socialism, 1815–1860* (Cambridge, 1987).

Clark, Christopher, and Wolfram Kaiser, eds, *Culture Wars: Secular-Catholic Conflict in Nineteenth-Century Europe* (Cambridge, 2003).

Clark, J.C.D., *English Society 1688–1832* (Cambridge, 1985).

Clark, Martin, *Modern Italy 1871–1982* (London, 1984).

Clark, Martin, *The Italian Risorgimento* (London, 1998).

Cohen, Gary, "Nationalist Politics and the Dynamics of State and Civil Society in the Habsburg Monarchy, 1867–1914," *Central European History*, 40 (2007), pp. 241–78.

Collingham, H.A.C., *The July Monarchy* (London, 1988).

Coppa, Frank J., ed., *Studies in Modern Italian History: From the Risorgimento to the Republic* (New York, 1986).

Corbin, Alain, *Women for Hire: Prostitution and Sexuality in France after 1850* (Cambridge, MA, 1990).

Cornwall, Mark, ed. *The Last Years of Austria-Hungary: A Multi-national Experiment in Early Twentieth-Century Europe* (Exeter, 2002).

Craig, Gordon, *Germany 1860–1945* (Oxford, 1978).

Craig, Lee A., and Douglas Fisher, *The Integration of the European Economy 1850–1913* (Basingstoke, 1997).

Craitu, Aurelian, *Liberalism under Siege: The Political Thought of the French Doctrinaires* (Lanham, MD, 2003).

Cranston, Maurice, *The Romantic Movement* (Oxford, 1994).

Crook, Malcolm, ed., *Revolutionary France 1788–1880* (Oxford, 2002).

Crossick, Geoffrey, and Heinz Gerhard Haupt, eds, *Shopkeepers and Master Artisans in Nineteenth-Century Europe* (London, 1984).

Crossick, Geoffrey, and Heinz Gerhard Haupt, *The Petite Bourgeoisie in Europe 1780–1914* (London, 1995).

Darwin, Charles, *On the Origin of Species,* edited by David Quammen (London, 2008).

Davies, Peter, *The Extreme Right in France, 1789 to the Present* (London, 2002).

Davis, John A., *Conflict and Control: Law and Order in Nineteenth-Century Italy* (Basingstoke, 1988).

Davis, John A., ed., *Italy in the Nineteenth Century: 1796–1900* (Oxford, 2000).

Davis, John A., and Paul Ginsborg, eds, *Society and Politics in the Age of the Risorgimento* (Cambridge, 1991).

De Grand, Alexander, *The Hunchback's Tailor: Giovanni Giolitti and Liberal Italy* (Westport, CT, 2001).

Di Scala, Spencer, *Italy: From Revolution to Republic* (Boulder, CO, 1995).

Doumanis, Nicholas, *Inventing the Nation: Italy* (London, 2001).

Dowe, Dieter, *et al.*, eds, *Europe in 1848: Revolution and Reform* (Oxford, 2001).

Drescher, Seymour, *From Slavery to Freedom: Comparative Studies in the Rise and Fall of Atlantic Slavery* (New York, 1999).

Drescher, Seymour, *Abolition: A History of Slavery and Anti-Slavery* (New York, 2009).

Duffy, Eamon, *Saints and Sinners: A History of the Popes*, 3rd edition (New Haven, CT, 2006).

Duggan, Christopher, *Francesco Crispi, 1818–1901: From Nations to Nationalism* (Oxford, 2002).

Dukes, Paul, *A History of Russia: Medieval, Modern, Contemporary, c. 882–1996*, 3rd edition (Durham, NC, 1997).

Dwyer, Philip G., ed., *The Rise of Prussia: 1700–1830* (Harlow, 2000).

Echard, William, *Napoleon III and the Concert of Europe* (Baton Rouge, LA, 1983).

Eley, Geoff, *Forging Democracy: The History of the Left in Europe, 1850–2000* (Oxford, 2002).

Eley, Geoff, and James Retallack, eds, *Wilhelminism and Its Legacies: German Modernities, Imperialism, and the Meanings of Reform, 1890–1930* (Oxford, 2003).

Emmons, Terence, *The Formation of Political Parties and the First National Elections in Russia* (Cambridge, MA, 1983).

Emsley, Clive, *Crime, Police, and Penal Policy: European Experiences, 1750–1940* (Oxford, 2007).

Esdaile, Charles J., *Spain in the Liberal Age: From Constitution to Civil War, 1808–1939* (Oxford, 2000).

Evans, Richard, *The Feminists: Women's Emancipation Movements in Europe, America and Australasia 1840–1920* (London, 1977).

Evans, Richard, *Comrades and Sisters: Feminism, Socialism and Pacifism in Europe, 1870–1945* (Brighton, 1987).

Farr, James R., *Artisans in Europe, 1300–1914* (Cambridge, 2000).

Fasel, George, *Europe in Upheaval: The Revolutions of 1848* (Chicago, 1970).

Ferguson, Niall, *The Pity of War: Explaining World War I* (New York, 1999).

Feuchtwanger, Edgar J., *Democracy and Empire* (London, 1985).

Fieldhouse, D.K., *Colonial Empires* (New York, 1965).

Figes, Orlando, *A People's Tragedy: The Russian Revolution, 1891–1924* (London, 1996).

Finn, Margot C., *After Chartism: Class and Nation in English Radical Politics, 1848–1874* (Cambridge, 1993).

Fischer, Conan, *Europe between Democracy and Dictatorship 1900–1945* (Oxford, 2011).

Fitzpatrick, Brian, *Catholic Royalism in the Department of the Gard, 1814–1852* (Cambridge, 1983).

Fitzsimmons, Michael P., *From Artisan to Worker: Guilds, the French State, and the Organization of Labor, 1776–1821* (Cambridge, 2010).

Floud, Roderick, and Paul Johnson, eds, *The Cambridge Economic History of Modern Britain: Volume I: Industrialisation, 1700–1860* (Cambridge, 2004).

Fortescue, William, *Revolution and Counter-Revolution in France, 1815–1852* (Oxford, 1988).

Fortescue, William, *The Third Republic in France, 1870–1940: Conflicts and Continuities* (London, 2000).

Fortescue, William, *France and 1848: The End of Monarchy* (London, 2005).

Foucault, Michel, *Discipline and Punish: The Birth of the Prison* (New York, 1976).

Freifeld, Alice, *Nationalism and the Crowd in Liberal Hungary, 1848–1914* (Washington, DC, 2000).

Fuchs, Rachel G., and Victoria E. Thompson, *Women in Nineteenth-Century Europe* (Basingstoke, 2005).

Furet, Francois, *Revolutionary France 1770–1880* (Oxford, 1995).

Furst, Lilian R., *Romanticism in Perspective*, 2nd edition (London, 1979).

Gash, Norman, *Aristocracy and People: Britain, 1815–1865* (London, 1979).

Geary, Dick, ed., *Labour and Social Movements in Europe Before 1914* (Oxford, 1989).

Geary, Dick, *European Labour Politics from 1900 to the Depression* (Atlantic Highlands, NJ, 1991).

Gibson, Mary, *Prostitution and the State in Italy, 1860–1915* (Columbus, OH, 1986).

Gilbert, Felix, with David Clay Large, *The End of the European Era, 1890 to the Present*, 4th edition (London, 1991).

Gildea, Robert N., *The Third Republic from 1871 to 1914* (London, 1988).

Gildea, Robert N., *The Past in French History* (New Haven, CT, 1994).

Gildea, Robert N., *Barricades and Borders: Europe 1800–1914*, 2nd edition (Oxford, 1996).

Gissing, George, *New Grub Street*, edited by Bernard Bergonzi (London, 1985).

Gobineau, Arthur, *The Inequality of Human Races*, translated by Adrian Collins (New York, 1967).

Goldberg Moses, Claire, and Leslie Wahl Rabine, *Feminism, Socialism, and French Romanticism* (Bloomington, IN, 1993).

Gollwitzer, Heinz, *Europe in the Age of Imperialism 1880–1914* (New York, 1979).

Gooding, John, *Socialism in Russia: Lenin and his Legacy* (Basingstoke, 2002).

Goring, Charles, *The English Convict: A Statistical Study* (Montclair, NJ, 1972).

Green, Abigail, *Fatherlands: State-Building and Nationhood in Nineteenth-Century Germany* (Cambridge, 2001).

Green, E.H.H., *The Crisis of Conservatism: The Politics, Economics and Ideology of the British Conservative Party, 1880–1914* (London, 1995).

Groag Bell, Susan, and Karen Offen, *Women, the Family, and Freedom: The Debate in Documents*, 2 vols (Stanford, CA, 1983).

Gunn, J.A.W., *When the French Tried to Be British: Party, Opposition, and the Quest for Civil Disagreement, 1814–1848* (Montreal, 2009).

Hales, E.E.Y., *Revolution and Papacy 1769–1846* (London, 1960).

Hall, Richard C., *The Balkan Wars 1912–1913: Prelude to the First World War* (London, 2000).

Hamerow, Theodore, *The Birth of a New Europe: State and Society in the Nineteenth Century* (Chapel Hill, NC, 1983).

Hamilton, Richard F., and Holger H. Herwig, *Decisions for War, 1914–1917* (Cambridge, 2004).

Harling, Philip, *The Waning of "Old Corruption": The Politics of Economical Reform in Britain, 1779–1846* (Oxford, 1996).

Harling, Philip, *The Modern British State: An Historical Introduction* (Cambridge, 2001).

Harris, Ruth, *Murders and Madness: Medicine, Law, and Society in the fin de siècle* (Oxford, 1989).

Harrison, J.F.C., ed., *Society and Politics in England, 1780–1960: A Selection of Readings and Comments* (New York, 1965).

Harsin, Jill, *Policing Prostitution in Nineteenth-Century Paris* (Princeton, NJ, 1985).

Harsin, Jill, *Barricades: The War of the Streets in Revolutionary Paris, 1830–1848* (Basingstoke, 2002).

Hartley, Janet M., *Russia, 1762–1825: Military Power, the State, and the People* (London, 2008).

Hause, Steven C., and Ann Kenney, *Women's Suffrage and Social Politics in the French Third Republic* (Princeton, NJ, 1984).

Hayes, Paul, ed., *Themes in Modern European History 1830–1890* (London, 1992).

Hazareesingh, Sudhir, *From Subject to Citizen: The Second Empire and the Emergence of Modern French Democracy* (Princeton, NJ, 1998).

Hazareesingh, Sudhir, *The Saint-Napoleon: Celebrations of Sovereignty in Nineteenth-Century France* (Cambridge, MA, 2004).

Hearder, Harry, *Italy in the Age of the Risorgimento 1790–1870* (London, 1983).

Henderson, W.O., *The Industrial Revolution on the Continent: Germany, France, Russia 1800–1914*, 2nd edition (London, 1967).

Henderson, W.O., *The Industrialization of Europe 1780–1914* (London, 1969).

Henderson, W.O., *The German Colonial Empire 1884–1919* (London, 1993).

Henig, Ruth, *The Origins of the First World War*, 3rd edition (London, 2002).

Hennessy, C.A.M., *The Federal Republic in Spain: Pi y Margall and the Federal Republican Movement, 1868–1874* (Oxford, 1962).

Herrmann, David G., *The Arming of Europe and the Making of the First World War* (Princeton, NJ, 1996).

Heywood, Paul, *Marxism and the Failure of Organised Socialism in Spain, 1879–1936* (Cambridge, 1990).

Higgs, David, *Ultraroyalism in Toulouse* (Baltimore, 1973).

Higgs, David, *Nobles in Nineteenth-Century France: The Practice of Inegalitarianism* (Baltimore, 1987).

Hobsbawm, Eric J., ed., *The History of Marxism: Volume 1: Marxism in Marx's Day* (Bloomington, IN, 1982).

Hobsbawm, Eric J., *Nations and Nationalism since 1780: Programme, Myth, and Reality* (London, 1992).

Hoffmann, Stefan-Ludwig, *Civil Society, 1750–1914* (Basingstoke, 2006).

Holborn, Hayo, *A History of Modern Germany 1648–1840* (Princeton, NJ, 1982).

Holborn, Hayo, *A History of Modern Germany 1840–1945* (Princeton, NJ, 1982).

Holt, Edgar, *The Carlist Wars in Spain* (London, 1967).

Hoppen, K. Theodore, *Ireland since 1800: Conflict and Conformity* (London, 1989).

Hoppen, K. Theodore, *The Mid-Victorian Generation 1846–1886* (Oxford, 1998).

Hosking, Geoffrey, *Russia: People and Empire 1552–1917* (Cambridge, MA, 1997).

Hughes, Steven C., *Crime, Disorder and the Risorgimento: The Politics of Policing in Bologna* (Cambridge, 1994).

Hutchinson, John F., *Late Imperial Russia 1890–1917* (London, 1999).

Janos, Andrew C., *The Politics of Backwardness in Hungary* (Princeton, NJ, 1982).

Jardin, André, and André-Jean Tudesq, *Restoration and Reaction 1815–1848* (Cambridge, 1983).

Jelavich, Barbara, *The Habsburg Empire in European Affairs, 1814–1918* (Chicago, 1969).

Jelavich, Barbara, *Modern Austria: Empire and Republic 1800–1980* (Cambridge, 1987).

Jelavich, Barbara, *Russia's Balkan Entanglements, 1806–1914* (Cambridge, 1991).

Jelavich, Charles and Barbara, *The Establishment of the Balkan National States, 1804–1920* (Seattle, 1977).

Jenkins, T.A., *The Liberal Ascendancy, 1830–1886* (London, 1994).

Jennings, Lawrence C., *French Anti-Slavery: The Movement for the Abolition of Slavery in France, 1802–1848* (Cambridge, 2000).

Johnson, Lonnie, *Central Europe: Enemies, Neighbours, Friends* (Oxford, 2002).

Johnson, Martin P., *The Dreyfus Affair: Honour and Politics in the Belle Epoque* (New York, 1999).

Joll, James, *The Anarchists* (London, 1964).

Joll, James, *The Origins of the First World War* (London, 1984).

Jones, Larry Eugene and James Retallack, eds, *Between Reform, Reaction, and Resistance: Studies in the History of German Conservatism from 1789 to 1945* (Oxford, 1993).

Jones, P.M., *Politics and Rural Society: The Southern Massif Central c. 1750–1880* (Cambridge, 1985).

Jordan, David P., *Transforming Paris: The Life and Labors of Baron Haussmann* (Chicago, 1995).

Judson, Pieter M., *Exclusive Revolutionaries: Liberal Politics, Social Experience, and National Identity in the Austrian Empire, 1848–1914* (Ann Arbor, MI, 1996).

Kahan, Alan S., *Liberalism in Nineteenth-Century Europe: The Political Culture of Limited Suffrage* (London, 2003).

Kann, Robert A., *A History of the Habsburg Empire 1526–1918* (New York, 1974).

Kaplan, Temma, *Anarchists of Andalusia 1868–1903* (Princeton, NJ, 1977).

Keiger, J.F.V., *Raymond Poincaré* (Cambridge, 1997).

Kemp, Tom, *Industrialization in Nineteenth-century Europe* (London, 1969).

Kennedy, Paul, *The Rise and Fall of the Great Powers: Economic Change and Military Conflict from 1500 to 2000* (London, 1988).

Kennedy, Paul, and Anthony Nicholls, eds, *Nationalist and Racialist Movements in Britain and Germany before 1914* (London, 1981).

Kern, Robert W., *Liberals, Reformers and Caciques in Restoration Spain 1875–1909* (Albuquerque, NM, 1974).

Kidd, Alan *State, Society and the Poor in Nineteenth-Century England* (Basingstoke, 1999).

Kiernan, V.G., *The Revolution of 1854 in Spanish History* (Oxford, 1966).

Kiernan, V.G., *The Lords of Human Kind: European Attitudes towards the Outside World in the Imperial Age*, 2nd edition (London, 1972).

King, David, *Vienna, 1814* (New York, 2008).

Kissinger, Henry *A World Restored* (New York, 1964).

Kocka, Jürgen, and Alan Mitchell, eds, *Bourgeois Society in Nineteenth-Century Europe* (Oxford, 1993).

Körner, Axel, ed., *1848 – A European Revolution?* 2nd edition (London, 2004).

Kraehe, Enno E., *Metternich's German Policy, Volume 2: The Congress of Vienna* (Princeton, NJ, 1983).

Kroen, Sheryl, *Politics and Theater: The Crisis of Legitimacy in Restoration France, 1815–1830* (Berkeley, CA, 2000).

Kudlick, Catherine J., *Cholera in Post-Revolutionary Paris: A Cultural History* (Berkeley, CA, 1996).

La Berge, Ann F., *Mission and Method: The Early Nineteenth-Century French Public Health Movement* (Cambridge, 1992).

Ladd, Brian, *Urban Planning and Civic Order in Germany, 1860–1914* (Cambridge, MA, 1990).

Landes, David, *The Unbound Prometheus: Technological Change and Industrial Development in Western Europe from 1750 to the Present*, 2nd edition (Cambridge, 2003).

Langewiesche, Dieter, *Liberalism in Germany* (Princeton, NJ, 1999).

Langhorne, Richard, *The Collapse of the Concert of Europe: International Politics, 1890–1914* (London, 1981).

Laven, David, and Lucy Riall, eds, *Napoleon's Legacy* (Oxford, 2000).

Le Bon, Gustave, *The Crowd: A Study of the Popular Mind* (New York, 1960).

Lee, Loyd E., *The Politics of Harmony: Civil Service, Liberalism and Social Reform in Baden, 1800–1850* (Newark, NJ, 1980).

Lenin, Vladimir Il'ich, *What Is to Be Done?*, translated by S.V. and Patricia Utechin (Oxford, 1963).

Lerman, Katherine Anne, *The Chancellor as Courtier: Bernhard von Bülow and the Governance of Germany* (Cambridge, 1990).

Lerman, Katherine Anne, *Bismarck* (Harlow, 2004).

Lichtheim, George, *A Short History of Socialism* (New York, 1970).

Lieven, Dominic, *The Aristocracy in Europe, 1815–1914* (New York, 1992).

Lieven, Dominic, *Empire: The Russian Empire and Its Rivals* (London, 2000).

Lieven, Dominic, ed., *The Cambridge History of Russia: Volume II Imperial Russia, 1689–1917* (Cambridge, 2006).

Lincoln, W. Bruce, *The Great Reforms: Autocracy, Bureaucracy, and the Politics of Change in Imperial Russia* (DeKalb, IL, 1990).

Lovett, Clara M., *The Democratic Movement in Italy 1830–1876* (Cambridge, MA, 1982).

Lowe, John *The Great Powers, Imperialism, and the German Problem, 1865–1925* (London, 1994).

Macartney, C.A., *The Habsburg Empire 1790–1918* (London, 1971).

McCord, Norman, *British History* (Oxford, 1991).

McDougall, Mary Lynn, ed., *The Working Class in Modern Europe* (London, 1975).

Macfie, A.L., *The Eastern Question 1774–1923* (London, 1989).

Mack Smith, Dennis, *Cavour and Garibaldi: A Study in Political Conflict* (Cambridge, 1954).

Mack Smith, Dennis, *Modern Italy: A Political History* (Ann Arbor, MI, 1997).

MacKenzie, John M., *Propaganda and Empire: The Manipulation of British Public Opinion 1880–1960* (Manchester, 1984).

McLeod, Hugh, *Religion and the People of Western Europe 1789–1970* (Oxford, 1981).

McMahon, Darrin M., *Enemies of the Enlightenment: The French Counter-Enlightenment and the Making of Modernity* (Oxford, 2001).

McMillan, James F., *Napoleon III* (London, 1991).

McMillan, James F., *Twentieth-Century France: Politics and Society in France 1898–1991* (London, 1992).

McMillan, James F., *France and Women, 1789–1914* (London, 1999).

McMillan, James F., *Modern France 1880–2002* (Oxford, 2003).

Magraw, Roger, *France 1815–1914: The Bourgeois Century* (Oxford, 1983).

Mallinson, Vernon, *Belgium* (London, 1969).

Mann, Michael, *The Sources of Social Power: Volume II: The Rise of Classes and Nation-States, 1760–1914* (Cambridge, 1993).

Marichal, Carlos, *Spain (1833–1844): A New Society* (London, 1977).

Martel, Gordon, *Origins of the First World War*, 3rd edition (Harlow, 2008).

Matthew, Colin, *The Nineteenth Century: The British Isles 1815–1901* (Oxford, 2000).

Mayer, Arno J., *The Persistence of the Old Regime: Europe to the Great War* (New York, 1981).

Mayeur, Jean-Marie, and Madeleine Rebérioux, *The First Republic From Its Origins To the Great War 1871–1914* (Cambridge, 1984).

Mazour, Anatole, *The First Russian Revolution, 1825: The Decembrist Movement, Its Origins, Development, and Significance* (Stanford, CA, 1961).

Merriman, John, *The Agony of the Republic: The Repression of the Left in Revolutionary France 1848–1851* (New Haven, CT, 1978).

Merriman, John, ed., *Consciousness and Class Experience in Nineteenth-Century Europe* (London, 1980).

Merriman, John, *A History of Modern Europe: From the Renaissance to the Present*, 3rd edition (London, 2010).

Mill, John Stuart, *The Subjection of Women*, edited by Stanton Coit (London, 1909).

Miller, James Edward, *From Elite to Mass Politics: Italian Socialism in the Giolittian Era, 1900–1914* (Kent, OH, 1990).

Milward, Alan S., and S.B. Saul, *The Economic Development of Continental Europe 1780–1870*, 2nd edition (London, 1979).

Molnár, Miklós, *A Concise History of Hungary* (Cambridge, 2001).

Mommsen, Wolfgang J., *Imperial Germany 1867–1918: Politics, Culture and Society in an Authoritarian State* (London, 1995).

Mommsen, Wolfgang J., ed., *The Emergence of the Welfare State in Britain and Germany, 1870–1930* (London, 1981).

Mommsen, Wolfgang J., and Gerhard Hirschfeld, eds, *Social Protest, Violence and Terror in Nineteenth- and Twentieth-Century Europe* (London, 1982).

Morazé, Charles, *The Triumph of the Middle Classes: A Political and Social History of Europe in the Nineteenth Century* (Garden City, NY, 1968).

Moulin, Annie, *Peasantry and Society in France since 1789* (Cambridge, 1991).

Müller, Detlef K., Fritz Ringer, and Brian Simon, eds, *The Rise of the Modern Educational System: Structural Change and Social Reproduction 1870–1920* (Cambridge, 1987).

Naarden, Bruno, *Socialist Europe and Revolutionary Russia: Perception and Prejudice 1848–1923* (Cambridge, 1992).

Nicolson, Harold, *The Congress of Vienna: A Study in Allied Unity* (London, 1946).

Nietzsche, Friedrich Wilhelm, *The Birth of Tragedy, or Hellenism and Pessimism*, 3rd edition, translated by William A. Haussmann (London, 1923).

Nietzsche, Friedrich Wilhelm, *Beyond Good and Evil: Prelude to a Philosophy of the Future*, edited by Rolf-Peter Horstmann and Judith Norman (Cambridge, 2002).

Nipperdey, Thomas, *Germany from Napoleon to Bismarck, 1800–1866*, trans. Daniel Nolan (Princeton, NJ, 1989)

Nord, Philip, *The Republican Moment: Struggles for Democracy in Nineteenth-Century France* (Cambridge, MA, 1995).

O'Day, Alan, *Irish Home Rule 1867–1921* (Manchester, 1998).

Offen, Karen, *European Feminisms* (Stanford, CA, 2000).

Okey, Robin, *Eastern Europe 1740–1980: Feudalism to Communism* (London, 1982).

Okey, Robin, *The Habsburg Monarchy c. 1765–1918: From Enlightenment to Eclipse* (Basingstoke, 2001).

Osiander, Andreas, *The States System of Europe: Peacemaking and the Conditions of International Stability* (Oxford, 1994).

O'Sullivan, Noel, *Conservatism* (London, 1976).

Packer, Ian, *Liberal Government and Politics, 1905–15* (Basingstoke, 2006).

Palmer, Alan, *The Banner of Battle: The Story of the Crimean War* (London, 1987).

Parker, David, ed., *Revolutions and the Revolutionary Tradition* (London, 2000).

Parry, D.L.L., and Pierre Girard, *France since 1800: Squaring the Hexagon* (Oxford, 2002).

Parry, Jonathan, *The Rise and Fall of Liberal Government in Victorian Britain* (New Haven, CT, 1993).

Payne, Stanley G., *Politics and the Military in Modern Spain* (Stanford, CA, 1967).

Payne, Stanley G., *A History of Spain and Portugal* (Madison, WI, 1973).

Pearson, Raymond, *European Nationalism, 1789–1920* (New York, 1994).

Pilbeam, Pamela, *The Middle Classes in Europe 1789–1914: France, Germany, Italy and Russia* (London, 1990).

Pilbeam, Pamela, ed., *Themes in Modern European History 1780–1830* (London, 1995).

Pilbeam, Pamela, *Republicanism in Nineteenth-Century France* (New York, 1995).

Pilbeam, Pamela, *French Socialists before Marx: Workers, Women, and the Social Question in France* (Montreal, 2000).

Pilbeam, Pamela, *The Constitutional Monarchy in France* (Harlow, 2000).

Pipes, Richard, *Russia under the Old Regime* (New York, 1974).

Pipes, Richard, *Russian Conservatism and Its Critics* (New Haven, CT, 2005).

Pitts, Jennifer, *A Turn to Empire: The Rise of Imperial Liberalism in Britain and France,* (Princeton, NJ, 2005).

Plessis, Alain, *The Rise and Fall of the Second Empire* (Cambridge, 1985).

Pollard, Sidney, *The Integration of the European Economy since 1815* (London, 1981).

Pollard, Sidney, *Peaceful Conquest: The Industrialization of Europe 1760–1970* (Oxford, 1981).

Porter, Andrew, *European Imperialism 1860–1914* (London, 1994).

Porter, Bernard, *The Lion's Share: A Short History of British Imperialism 1850–1995,* 3rd edition (London, 1996).

Porter, Roy, and Mikulas Teich, *Romanticism in National Context* (Cambridge, 1988).

Powell, David, *The Edwardian Crisis: Britain 1901–14* (Basingstoke, 1996).

Price, Roger, *The French Second Republic: A Social History* (London, 1972).

Price, Roger, *The Revolutions of 1848* (Atlantic Highlands, NJ, 1988).

Price, Roger, *The French Second Empire: An Anatomy of Political Power* (Cambridge, 2001).

Pugh, Martin, *The Making of Modern British Politics 1867–1939* (Oxford, 1982).

Pulzer, Peter G., *The Rise of Political Anti-Semitism in Germany and Austria* (London, 1964).

Quataert, Donald, *The Ottoman Empire 1700–1922* (Cambridge, 2005).

Quinault, Roland, "The French Revolution of 1830 and Parliamentary Reform," *History,* 79, n. 257 (Oct. 1994), pp. 377–93.

Ránki, György, ed., *Hungary and European Civilisation* (Budapest, 1989).

Reinerman, Alan J., *Austria and the Papacy in the Age of Metternich: Between Conflict and Cooperation, 1809–1830* (Washington, DC, 1979).

Reinerman, Alan J., *Austria and the Papacy in the Age of Metternich: Revolution and Reaction, 1830–1838* (Washington, DC, 1989).

Rémond, René, *The Right Wing in France from 1815 to De Gaulle* (Philadelphia, PA, 1966).

Retallack, James, ed., *Imperial Germany 1871–1918* (Oxford, 2008).

Riall, Lucy, *Risorgimento: The History of Italy from Napoleon to Nation-State* (London, 2009).

Riasanovsky, Nicholas, *A History of Russia* (Oxford, 1984).

Rich, Norman, *The Age of Nationalism and Reform, 1850–1890* (London, 1977).

Rich, Norman, *Why the Crimean War? A Cautionary Tale* (New York, 1991).

Rich, Norman, *Great Power Diplomacy 1814–1914* (New York, 1992).

Richardson, James L., *Crisis Diplomacy: the Great Powers since the mid-nineteenth century* (Cambridge, 1994).

Ripa, Yannick, *Women and Madness: The Incarceration of Women in Nineteenth-Century France* (Cambridge, 1990).

Ritter, Gerhard *The Sword and the Scepter: the problem of militarism in Germany,* 2 volumes (Coral Gables, FL, 1970).

Roberts, J.M., *The Mythology of the Secret Societies* (London, 1972).

Rogger, Hans, *Russia in the Age of Modernisation and Revolution 1881–1917* (London, 1983).

Rosenblatt, Helena, *Liberal Values: Benjamin Constant and the Politics of Religion* (Cambridge, 2008).

Rosenblatt, Helena, ed., *The Cambridge Companion to Constant* (Cambridge, 2009).

Ross, Ronald J., *The Failure of Bismarck's Kulturkampf: Catholicism and State Power in Imperial Germany, 1871–1887* (Washington, DC, 1998).

Rowe, Michael, *From Reich to State: the Rhineland in the Revolutionary Age, 1780–1830* (Cambridge, 2003).

Royle, Trevor, *Crimea: The Great Crimean War 1854–1856* (Basingstoke, 2000).

Rubenstein, W.D., *Britain's Century: A Political and Social History 1815–1905* (London, 1998).

Saunders, David, *Russia in the Age of Reaction and Reform, 1801–1881* (London, 1992).

Saville, John, *1848: The British State and the Chartist Movement* (Cambridge, 1987).

Schorske, Carl E., *Fin-de-Siècle Vienna: Politics and Culture* (New York, 1980).

Schroeder, Paul, *The Transformation of European Politics 1763–1848* (Oxford, 1994).

Schulze, Hagen, *Germany: A New History* (Cambridge, MA, 1998).

Schulze, Hagen, ed., *Nation-Building in Central Europe* (Leamington Spa, 1987).

Schulze, Hagen, *The Course of German Nationalism, 1763–1867* (Cambridge, 1991).

Sheehan, James, *German History, 1770–1866* (Oxford, 1989).

Simms, Brendan, *The Struggle for Mastery in Germany, 1779–1850* (New York, 1998).

Sked, Alan, *The Decline and Fall of the Habsburg Empire, 1815–1918* (London, 2001).

Sked, Alan, ed., *Europe's Balance of Power 1815–1848* (London, 1979).

Smith, Harold L., *The British Women's Suffrage Campaign, 1866–1928*, 2nd edition (London, 2007).

Smith, Joseph, *The Spanish-American War: Conflict in the Caribbean and the Pacific 1895–1902* (London, 1994).

Sperber, Jonathan, *Rhineland Radicals: The Democratic Movement and the Revolution of 1848–1849* (Princeton, NJ, 1991).

Sperber, Jonathan, *The European Revolutions, 1848–1851*, 2nd edition (Cambridge, 1994).

Sperber, Jonathan, *Revolutionary Europe, 1780–1850* (London, 2000).

Sperber, Jonathan, *Europe 1850–1914: Progress, Participation and Apprehension* (London, 2009).

Spring, David, ed., *European Landed Elites in the Nineteenth Century* (Baltimore, 1977).

Stearns, Peter N., *1848: The Revolutionary Tide in Europe* (New York, 1974).

Stearns, Peter N., *European Society in Upheaval: Social History since 1750*, 2nd edition (London, 1975).

Sternhell, Zeev, with Mario Sznajder and Maia Asheri, *The Birth of Fascist Ideology: from Cultural Rebellion to Political Revolution* (Princeton, NJ, 1994).

Stites, Richard *The Women's Liberation Movement in Russia: Feminism, Nihilism, and Bolshevism 1860–1930* (Princeton, NJ, 1978).

Stone, Judith, *The Search for Social Peace: Reform Legislation in France, 1890–1914* (New York, 1985).

Stromberg, Roland N., *European Intellectual History Since 1789*, 6th edition (Englewood Cliffs, 1994)

Stuart, Robert, *Marxism at Work: Ideology, Class and French Socialism during the Third Republic* (Cambridge, 1992).

Sugar, Peter F., Hanák, Péter, and Tibor Frank, eds, *A History of Hungary* (Bloomington, IN, 1994).

Talmon, J.L., *Romanticism and Revolt* (New York, 1967).

Taylor, A.J.P., *The Habsburg Monarchy 1809–1918* (London, 1948).

Taylor, A.J.P., *Revolutions and Revolutionaries* (Oxford, 1981).

Taylor, Miles, *The Decline of British Radicalism, 1847–1860* (Oxford, 1995).

Teich, Mikuláš, and Roy Porter, eds, *The National Question in Europe in Historical Context* (Cambridge, 1993).

Thomas, Daniel H., *The Guarantee of Belgian Independence and Neutrality in European Diplomacy, 1830s–1930s* (Kingston, RI, 1983).

Thomas, Hugh, *The Slave Trade: The History of the Atlantic Slave Trade 1440–1870* (New York, 1997).

Thompson, Alistair P., *Left Liberals, the State, and Popular Politics in Wilhelmine Germany* (Oxford, 2000).

Tilly, Charles, Louise, and Richard, *The Rebellious Century 1830–1930* (London, 1975).

Tombs, Robert, *The War against Paris 1871* (Cambridge, 1981).

Tombs, Robert, *France 1814–1914* (London, 1996).

Tombs, Robert, *The Paris Commune, 1871* (Harlow, 1999).

Ulam, Adam B., *Russia's Failed Revolutions: from the Decembrists to the Dissidents* (New York, 1981).

Ulam, Adam B., *Prophets and Conspirators in Revolutionary Russia* (New Brunswick, NJ, 1998).

Ullman, Joan Connelly, *The Tragic Week. A Study of Anticlericalism in Spain, 1875–1912* (Cambridge, MA, 1968).

Vidler, Alec R., *The Church in an Age of Revolution* (Harmondsworth, 1971).

Vincent, David, *The Rise of Mass Literacy: Reading and Writing in Modern Europe* (Oxford, 2002).

Waller, Bruce, ed., *Themes in Modern European History 1830–1890* (London, 1990).

Wawro, Geoffrey, *The Austro-Prussian War: Austria's War with Prussia and Italy in 1866* (Cambridge, 1996).

Wawro, Geoffrey, *The Franco-Prussian War: The German Conquest of France in 1870–1871* (Cambridge, 2003).

Weber, Eugen, *Peasants into Frenchmen: The Modernization of Rural France, 1870–1914* (Stanford, CA, 1979).

Weber, Eugen, *France fin de siècle* (Cambridge, Mass., 1986).

Webster, Charles, *The Congress of Vienna 1814–1815* (London, 1963).

Weiss, John, *Conservatism in Europe 1770–1945: Traditionalism, Reaction and Counter-Revolution* (London, 1977).

Wesserling, H.L., *The European Colonial Empires 1815–1919* (London, 2004).

Westwood, J.N., *Endurance and Endeavour: Russian History 1812–2001* (Oxford, 2002).

Whelan, Heide, *Alexander III and the State Council: Bureaucracy and Counter-Reform in Late Imperial Russia* (New Brunswick, NJ, 1982).

Whiteside, Andrew, *The Socialism of Fools: Georg von Schönerer and Austrian Pan-Germanism* (Berkeley, CA, 1975).

Wiesner, Merry E., Julius R. Ruff, and William Bruce Wheeler, *Discovering the Western Past Volume II: Since 1500*, 6th edition (Boston, 2008).

Wilson, Keith, ed., *Decisions for War 1914* (New York, 1995).

Wilson, Peter H., ed., *1848: The Year of Revolutions* (Aldershot, 2006).

Winks, Robin W., and Joan Neuberger, *Europe and the Making of Modernity 1815–1914* (Oxford, 2005).

Winock, Michel, *Nationalism, Anti-Semitism, and Fascism in France* (Stanford, CA, 1998).

Wright, Gordon, *Between the Guillotine and Liberty: Two Centuries of the Crime Problem in France* (Oxford, 1983).

Wright, Gordon, *France in Modern Times: From the Enlightenment to the Present*, 4th edition (New York, 1987).

Wright, Quincy, *A Study of War*, 2nd edition (Chicago, 1965).

Index

Note: Page numbers in italics represents table and figures.

Europe's Uncertain Path 1814–1914: State Formation and Civil Society, First Edition. R. S. Alexander.
© 2012 R. S. Alexander. Published 2012 by Blackwell Publishing Ltd.